"*Saving God's Face* is a sophisticated and thoughtful monograph written at the intersection of Chinese culture, contextualization theory, and debates about the New Perspective on Paul. Wu leverages a dialogical theory of contextualization in order to show how honor-shame concepts in Chinese culture can help Christians understand the 'glory' and 'honor' images found in the Bible. By reading the Bible with Chinese eyes, a Christian can understand these images in ways that are underemphasized in traditional western theologies. Along the way, Wu manages to draw upon a diverse array of thinkers including Enoch Wan, John Piper, and N. T. Wright. Even if you find yourself in disagreement with Wu, you won't regret the journey upon which he takes you."

Bruce Riley Ashford
Provost and Dean of Faculty
Associate Professor of Theology and Culture
Fellow for the Bush Center for Faith and Culture
Southeastern Baptist Theological Seminary

"Jackson Wu's work pulls together several fields that go naturally together—exegetical and theological insights drawing upon the 'New Perspective on Paul' integrated with theological discussions of contextualization. This integration ought to be seen to be quite obvious, especially since the Apostle Paul is not a professional theologian writing in a dusty office situated in a de-contextualized ivory tower. He is, rather, a missionary practitioner himself, wrestling theologically with the contextual challenges of proclaiming Israel's good news to a non-Jewish world. While this integrative work is a natural and obvious extension of several scholarly conversations in diverse fields, few have the missiological expertise and exegetical skill to pull it off. The publication of Wu's work will be a significant contribution to the study of Paul and to scholarly discussions of contextualization."

Timothy Gombis
Associate Professor of New Testament
Grand Rapids Theological Seminary

"Contextualization is arguably the most important issue in contemporary missiology, as well as one of the most difficult tasks to do well. It requires both an in depth knowledge of a culture and in depth knowledge of the Bible and theology, plus skill in bringing the two together. Author Jackson Wu's work, *Saving God's Face*, reflects all these and thus gives us an excellent example of contextualization done well. He brings an exceptional understanding of the Chinese concept of honor and shame into a helpful dialogue with an insightful theological analysis of the doctrine of atonement in a way that brings out aspects of the doctrine that have been there in Scripture all along but have gone unnoticed or underemphasized by Western theologians. Some may quibble with Wu's use of the New Perspective on Paul but all should be challenged to rethink how they understand and proclaim the atonement, especially those who do so in a Chinese context. This is an important book, well worth the effort necessary to grapple with its argument."

John S. Hammett
Professor of Theology
Associate Dean for Theological Studies
Southeastern Baptist Theological Seminary

Saving God's Face

A Chinese Contextualization of Salvation
through Honor and Shame

Jackson Wu

This book is dedicated to

my wife,

who continually encourages me
to seek God's face.

Published by WCIU Press
EMS Dissertation Series

1539 E. Howard Street
Pasadena, CA 91104
wciupress@wciu.edu

ISBN: 9780865850477
Library of Congress Control Number: 2013937441

This work was originally submitted to the faculty of Southeastern Baptist Seminary in partial fulfillment of the requirements for the degree Doctor of Philosophy.

Editor's Preface

In order to encourage and make known Evangelical missiological scholarship the Evangelical Missiological Society (EMS) launched a dissertation series in 2010. In collaboration with William Carey International University Press, the Society is publishing up to four dissertations per year that its reviewers have judged as scholarly, relevant, and timely for advancing the global cause of Christ. We pray you will find this dissertation informative and stimulating.

Thomas J. Sappington, Editor

EMS Dissertation Series

ACKNOWLEDGEMENTS

God, the Creator King, is worthy of all honor for whatever contribution this book may have for readers. He has manifested his righteousness in Christ who bore our shame.

He has borne the fruit of the Spirit in my wife. To my bride, I am grateful for your graciousness, encouragement, perseverance, and vision to help me see this through. I pray that you would always rejoice in the Lord, "knowing that in the Lord your labor is not in vain" (1 Cor 15:58).

He has provided dear friends who have challenged, corrected, and cultivated the ideas expressed in this book. I am especially thankful to Brad M. and Ian L., who were primary dialogue partners in this process. In addition, the Spirit has used so many others, including DaYu, Gerald L., Tim H., Patrick L., Jerrell A., Nick and Stephanie S., Scott B., Eric M., Barrett F., Zane P., Kevin P., Kevin F., Kyle F., Enya, Seb, Caleb, Kayla, Amanda and our weekly prayer team.

He has granted me extraordinary leaders and teachers. There are three theologians and pastors who have greatly influenced this project. John Piper has taught me the centrality of God's glory. N. T. Wright continues to stretch my mind and heart to wonder at the expanse of that glory. Finally, I will always be indebted to Scott Hafemann for demonstrating and passing along a love for biblical exegesis. Within my current ministry, I am constantly thankful for Ian B., whose love, boldness, foresight, and determination spur me forward and have enabled many Chinese Christians to know God's word.

He has wisely used Bruce Ashford to advise me through the Ph.D and the dissertaton from which this book came. Bruce, I have appreciated your humility, zeal, candor, and Christ-like love for missions.

I am likewise grateful for my dissertation committee members, John Hammett and Timothy Gombis, who offered valuable suggestions and encouragement.

Praise God who sends his Church to bless all nations. This is evident through countless others whose influence is evidenced in these pages. Thank you, Peter and Susan, for your ongoing support. I also wish to honor those who have trained me among the faculties of SEBTS and GCTS. Finally, to our Chinese brothers and sisters: 我感谢天父. 他让我们一起成为他的名下. 我们本身不是中国人或西方人, 而是人类大家庭.

TABLE OF CONTENTS

ABBREVIATIONS

ABD	*The Anchor Bible Dictionary*
Altern. Global Local Polit.	*Alternatives: Global, Local, Political*
AM ANTHROPO	*American Anthropologist*
AM J SOCIOL	*American Journal of Sociology*
AJSP	*Asian Journal of Social Psychology*
AJT	*Asia Journal of Theology*
ASIAN PERSPEC	*Asian Perspective*
AUST J CHINESE AFF	*Australian Journal of Chinese Affairs*
BBR	*Bulletin for Biblical Research*
BCAS	*Critical Asian Studies*
BDAG	*Greek-English Lexicon of the New Testament and Other Early Christian Literature*
BTB	*Biblical Theology Bulletin*
BTDB	*Baker Theological Dictionary of the Bible*
BYU J. Pub. L.	*BYU Journal of Public Law*
CBQ	*Catholic Biblical Quarterly*
CBR	*The China Business Review*
Cogn Emot	*Cognition & Emotion*
Colloq	*Colloquium*
CTJ	*Calvin Theological Journal*
CTR	*Chinese Theological Review*
CurTM	*Currents in Theology and Mission*
CULT PSYCHOL	*Culture & Psychology*
DAO	*Dao: A Journal of Comparative Philosophy*
DBI	*Dictionary of Biblical Imagery*
DBT	*Dictionary of Biblical Theology*
DCH	*Dictionary of Chinese History*
DOTHB	*Dictionary of the Old Testament: Historical Books*
DOTP	*Dictionary of the Old Testament: Pentateuch*
DOTWPW	*Dictionary of the Old Testament: Wisdom, Poetry and Writings*
DTWT	*Dictionary of Third World Theologies*
EAJET	*East Africa Journal of Evangelical Theology*
EDNT	*Exegetical Dictionary of the New Testament.*
EDWM	*Evangelical Dictionary of World Missions.*
EJEAS	*European Journal of East Asian Studies*
EMQ	*Evangelical Missions Quarterly*
Enc	*Encounter*

ERT	*Evangelical Review of Theology*
ExAud	*Ex Auditu*
GDT	*Global Dictionary of Theology*
HTS	*Harvard Theological Review*
IBMR	*International Bulletin of Missionary Research*
IDB	*The Interpreter's Dictionary of the Bible*
IJERE	*International Journal of Evaluation and Research in Education*
IJFM	*International Journal of Frontier Missions*
IJLE	*International Journal of Leadership in Education*
IJP	*International Journal of Psychology*
IJST	*International Journal of Systematic Theology*
IS	*Issues & Studies*
JapChrQ	*Japan Christian Quarterly*
JAPSS	*Journal of Alternative Perspectives in the Social Sciences*
JBL	*Journal of Biblical Literature*
JCP	*Journal of Chinese Philosophy*
JETS	*Journal of the Evangelical Theological Society*
JME	*Journal of Moral Education*
JOCP	*Journal of Chinese Philosophy*
JOSP	*Journal of Social Philosophy*
JP	*The Journal of Psychology*
JPh	*The Journal of Philosophy*
JR	*The Journal of Religion*
JSNT	*Journal for the Study of the New Testament*
JSOT	*Journal for the Study of the Old Testament*
JTP	*Journal of Theory and Practice*
JTSB	*Journal for the Theory of Social Behaviour*
L&N	*Greek-English Lexicon of the New Testament Based on Semantic*
MDB	*Mercer Dictionary of the Bible*
NDBT	*New Dictionary of Biblical Theology*
NIB	*The New Interpreter's Bible*
NovT	*Novum Testamentum*
PEGLMBS	*Proceedings–Eastern Great Lakes and Midwest Biblical Societies*
PSB	*Princeton Seminary Bulletin*
PTR	*Princeton Theological Review*
QR	*Quarterly Review*
SEAJT	*South East Asia Journal of Theology*
SJT	*Scottish Journal of Theology*
Soc Sci Med	*Social Science and Medicine*
SSC	*Social Sciences in China*
SWC	*Studies in World Christianity*
TDNT	*Theological Dictionary of the New Testament*
ThTo	*Theology Today*

TJTh	*Taiwan Journal of Theology*
TNDT	*The New Dictionary of Theology*
TynBul	*Tyndale Bulletin*
VeE	*Verbum et Ecclesia*
VT	*Vetus Testamentum*
WBC	*Word Biblical Commentary*
WTJ	*Westminster Theological Journal*
WW	*Word & World*

BEFORE YOU READ THIS BOOK

It's alright to question assumptions

Years ago, I had a startling realization. Theologians and pastors have long taught on the glory of God and its central importance in the Bible. However, because I was living in East Asia, it also dawned on me that this sort of talk about God's glory, praising him, and magnifying his name was simply another way of talking about honor and shame. When I looked at most theology and missions-related books, I found that honor and shame seemed to be treated differently. Anthropologists talked about honor-shame, but theologians largely focused more on legal metaphors. I could see both themes in Scripture but couldn't find help as to how to bring them together.

The problem became more serious for me as I thought about Chinese culture. In Mandarin, the word for "sin" is translated literally as "crime." Therefore, when people hear the gospel, they were being told, "You are criminals!!" Naturally, people do not understand what they are hearing. In China, as in other countries, people think primarily in terms of "face" and relationships. "Law" is less a prominent theme in daily life.

This raised a number of questions.

Theologically, why have Christians favored law-language when so much of the Bible emphasizes God's glory and his people not being put to shame? How could I reconcile the gap between these two metaphors, not choosing one over the other? Why did people get nervous whenever I would talk about honor-shame, as if I were denying what the Bible said about law and absolute truth?

Missiologically, how do we share the gospel in honor-shame cultures in a way that both reflects what the Bible really says and does not come across as superficial? How are we supposed to reconcile the conviction that God's word is absolutely true but that our perspectives are limited? Why has so much been written about contextualization yet there is little agreement about how to actually do it?

Beware of two temptations

Many readers will face one of two temptations when reading this book.

First, some will jump right into the discussion about contextualization and culture but be discouraged by the slower pace required in the last major chapter, where the book deals with weighty issues like the atonement and justification. At times, the argument will get a bit technical, especially in the footnotes. Be patient and remember this—the entire book was written ultimately in order to better understand what the Bible says about salvation. This is a central concern for every Christian, whether a missionary, theologian, pastor, or layperson.

Second, others will be more eager to do the detailed work of exegesis and assess my conclusions about salvation. I understand it is important to keep the end in mind when reading longer books. However, I want to remind those people that perspective is critical for seeing truth. We all have assumptions that influence the way we read Scripture. Our perspectives are always limited by our culture and experience. The early chapters play a critical role. They attempt to help the reader see the world through a distinct pair of "cultural" glasses. Reading Scripture with a new cultural lens can be humbling, confirming, and correcting.

Keep in mind the big picture

So many of the problems we face are systemic. They require a broad perspective and integrative solutions. Yet, contemporary scholarship tends towards greater specialization. It is easy to lose track of the big picture and the practical importance of what is being said. Life and ministry are too complex to easily compartmentalize.

Accordingly, I have intentionally taken an interdisciplinary approach in this study. The advantage is that more voices are brought into dialogue. Therefore, we gain a more comprehensive understanding of the various topics. However, one disadvantage is that readers face a more difficult challenge. Those who tend to read missiology and anthropology may not be aware of many currents debates within other fields, like theology or New Testament studies. The converse could also be true. Consequently, the lack of interaction across academic fields makes it increasingly difficult to solve some of our most pressing problems.

CHAPTER 1: INTRODUCTION

This book argues that a dialogically contextualized Chinese soteriology, which draws heavily upon honor-shame concepts prevalent in Chinese culture, issues forth in a biblical understanding of atonement and justification. It proposes an interdisciplinary method of theological contextualization that intentionally utilizes a cultural worldview for the sake of exegesis. This approach demonstrates how the integration of cultural, historical, and biblical contexts is critical for developing a theology that both draws from Chinese culture and builds upon traditional theological debates. As a result, this study illustrates the point that "[t]here is no such thing as 'theology'; there is only *contextualized theology*."[1]

"Dialogical contextualization"[2] tempers some of the bias and limitation inherent in any culture, paradigm, or scholarly research. After all, theological contextualization involves a number of contexts, including those of Scripture, the interpreter, the missionary/messenger, and the recipient of the message. Those who contextualize theology can bring these contexts into dialogue. Biblical truth transcends any single context. Unfortunately, efforts to produce contextualized theology tend either to minimize the original meaning of the text or else import theological categories foreign to

---

[1] Stephen Bevans, *Models of Contextual Theology* (rev. and expanded ed.; Maryknoll, N.Y.: Orbis Books, 2002), 3. Similarly, see David Bosch, *Transforming Mission: Paradigm Shifts in Theology of Mission* (Maryknoll, N.Y.: Orbis Books, 1991), 423. Emphasis in original.
[2] David K. Clark, *To Know and Love God: Method for Theology* (Wheaton, Ill.: Crossway, 2003).

1

a given culture.[3] These problems are evident in past attempts to contextualize the Christian message in Chinese culture in particular and in honor-shame (HS) cultures in general. Rather than first interpreting the Bible and then applying the findings to a cultural context, this book shows that by taking a Chinese HS lens, there emerge a number of critical theological issues that have otherwise been overshadowed by other motifs, such as law. If one takes seriously a Chinese collectivist orientation, what happens when that perspective is applied to biblical interpretation? To be clear, this book prioritizes exegesis, not eisegesis, so that the interpretations reflect the original meaning of the biblical text itself. Without forging false dichotomies, one finds that HS comprehensively accounts for the diversity of biblical texts related to soteriology, all the while challenging the primacy of traditional Western theological categories.[4] As a result, one gains helpful insight into how to share the gospel of salvation in a Chinese context. The proposed soteriology, contextualized in Chinese culture, can contribute to common views of theology and missiological method—and correct misleading ones.

This book assumes a conservative, evangelical perspective. Therefore, the Bible is regarded as ultimately authoritative in theological and missiological questions. Truth

---

[3] For a sample of contextualization attempts, see K. K. Yeo, *Musing with Confucius and Paul: Toward a Chinese Christian Theology* (Eugene, Ore.: Cascade, 2008). Also, K. K. Yeo, *What Has Jerusalem to do with Beijing: Biblical Interpretation from a Chinese Perspective* (Harrisburg, Pa.: Trinity Press, 1998). Also, C. S. Song, *Third-Eye Theology: Theology in Formation in Asian Settings* (Eugene, Ore.: Wipf & Stock, 2002). From Hong Kong and mainland Chinese theologians, see Pan-chiu Lai and Jason Lam, eds., *Sino-Christian Theology* (New York, N.Y.: Peter Lang, 2010); Yang Huilin and Daniel H. N. Yeung, eds., *Sino-Christian Studies in China* (Newcastle: Cambridge Scholars Publishing, 2006).

[4] For instance, soteriology has traditionally been framed in forensic or judicial language. This forensic emphasis is mitigated by a more "covenantal" view found in Michael Bird, "Justification as Forensic Declaration and Covenant Membership: A Via Media between Reformed and Revisionist Readings of Paul," *TynBul* 57, no. 1 (2006): 109–30. A classical articulation of the traditional Protestant formulation of the gospel can be found in Greg Gilbert, *What Is the Gospel?* (Wheaton, Ill.: Crossway, 2010). For implications of a guilt-based perspective on theology, see Krister Stendahl's famous essay "The Apostle Paul and the Introspective Conscience of the West," in his work *Paul Among Jews and Gentiles, and Other Essays* (Philadelphia, Pa.: Fortress Press, 1976).

exists apart from any particular culture. In that sense, it is "supracultural." However, biblical theology must never be reduced to an abstraction. The human act of theologizing is always expressed within a cultural context. In that respect, theological formulations may be incomplete or flawed. Given human limitations, theologies can improve as they become more intercultural. The ensuing chapters interact with scholars of various theological persuasions across academic disciplines. However, at critical points, concentrated attention is generally given to evangelical thinkers.

Chapter 2 ("Theological Contextualization in Practice") argues that a practical model for theological contextualization is most basically a work of biblical interpretation. In short, contextualizers read Scripture through the lens of those in a local culture. Missionaries stunt this process when they prioritize a particular formulation of the gospel before having answered the question, "What is contextualization?" In so doing, they effectively "beg the question" since their assumptions predetermine the framework, emphases, and motifs that must be used to contextualize theology in a given culture. As a result, Western missiological thinking has largely reduced contextualization merely to application and communication.

All human cultures express limited points of view, including Western cultures that have produced the preponderance of traditional Christian theology. Because Western theologies overwhelmingly emphasize the legal motif and the individual, other themes, like HS and collectivism, can be muted. This is despite the fact that one finds these latter ideas in Scripture and the ancient biblical world. Although biblical truth transcends any one culture, it is always contextualized in some cultural form. All people bring to Scripture a worldview, which at points intersects with and diverges from the perspective

3

of a biblical author. Missionaries and theologians compensate for their subjective limitations by using an interdisciplinary approach to contextualization. The chapter proposes a method to help people intentionally broaden their own worldview lens.

Chapter 3 ("Theologizing for a Chinese Culture") identifies a number of prominent themes and concerns within Chinese culture that will shape a contextualized theology in China. Scholars from various fields agree that Chinese people have consistently valued honor (i.e. "face"), harmony, and hierarchy.[5] They are more group-oriented (versus individualistic) and focus on the practical aspects of life and religion. People think most basically in terms of relationships (or *guanxi*) not law. In history, the Chinese worldview divides the world into those who are insiders and those who are outside the "Middle Kingdom." The increased presence and power of foreigners has fostered differing degrees of ethnocentrism and nationalism.

Many people have addressed the question of Chinese theology, largely agreeing on what constitutes a Chinese worldview.[6] Nevertheless, they sometimes differ with

---

[5] A sample of relevant works include Enoch Wan, "Practical Contextualization: A Case Study of Evangelizing Contemporary Chinese," *Global Missiology* 1, no. 1 (Oct 2003), n.p. [cited 27 Dec 2011]. Online: http://ojs.global missiology.org/index.php/english/issue/view/27; Enoch Wan, "Christianity in the Eye of Traditional Chinese," *Global Missiology* 1, no. 1 (Oct 2003), n.p. [cited 21 Nov 2011]. Online: http://ojs.global missiology.org/index.php/english/ issue/view/27; Enoch Wan, "Critiquing the Method of Traditional Western Theology and Calling for Sino-Theology," *Global Missiology* 1, no. 1 (Oct 2003), n.p. [cited 21 Nov 2011]. Online: http://ojs.globalmissiology.org/index.php/english/ issue/view/27; Andrew Kipnis, *Producing Guanxi: Sentiment, Self, and Subculture in a North China Village* (Durham, N.C.: Duke University Press, 1997); Richard R. Cook and David W. Pao, eds., *After Imperialism: Christian Identity in China and the Global Evangelical Movement* (Eugene, Ore.: Pickwick, 2011); Chan Kei Thong and Charlene L. Fu, *Finding God in Ancient China: How the Ancient Chinese Worshiped the God of the Bible* (Grand Rapids, Mich.: Zondervan, 2009); Haihua Zhang and Geoffrey Baker, *Think Like Chinese* (Annandale, N.S.W.: Federation Press, 2008); Margaret N. Ng, "Internal Shame as a Moral Sanction," *JCP* 8 (Mar 1981): 75–86.

[6] Many works address the issue like Ralph Covell, *Confucius, the Buddha, and Christ: A History of the Gospel in Chinese* (Maryknoll, N.Y.: Orbis Books, 1986); Bruce J. Nicholls, "Contextualisation in Chinese Culture," *ERT* 19, no. 4 (Oct 1995): 368–80; James Pan, "Contextualization: A Methodological Enquiry with Examples from the History of Theology," *SEAJT* 21, no. 2–1 (1981): 47–64; Chengmian Wang, *Contextualization of Christianity in China: An Evaluation in Modern Perspective* (Collectanea serica; Sankt Augustin; Nettetal: Institut Monumenta Serica; Steyler Verlag, 2007); Benoît Vermander,

respect to how this applies to contextualization. The chapter identifies six general approaches, each with its own distinctive emphasis. A "situational" methodology accentuates the Chinese context, even sounding hostile to the West. "Sino" theologians give greatest weight to ethnic identity. A "synchronistic" approach uses cultural concepts to convey theological meaning. Others more heavily interact with "scriptural" questions and categories. A number of "systematic" writers focus on the theoretical concerns of Chinese contextualization. Finally, missionary practitioners are "soterian" in that they typically stress soteriology and evangelism. Although the chapter offers a number of insights about Chinese culture, these issues seem to have little or no effect on the tools used by this group. This chasm between missionary practice and scholarly consensus is noteworthy.

Chapter 4 ("Honor and Shame in Context") compares HS in Chinese culture, the Ancient Near East (ANE), and Scripture in order to understand its relevance for Chinese theology. Humans universally have a concern for HS. Although the desire for "face" expresses itself in variegated ways, a few principles are evident.[7] "Honor" refers to the value placed upon people within their social context. It may either be ascribed or

---

"Jesus-Christ and the Chinese Religious World," *Studia Missionalia* 50 (2001): 391–405; Edmond Tang, "The Cosmic Christ: The Search for a Chinese Theology," *Studies in World Christianity* 1, no. 2 (1995): 131–42; Pan-chiu Lai, "Chinese Culture and the Development of Chinese Christian Theology," *Studies in World Christianity* 7, no. 2 (2001): 219–40.

[7] One of the most famous anthropological treatments is J. G. Peristiany and Julian Pitt-Rivers, *Honor and Grace in Anthropology* (Cambridge, UK: Cambridge University Press, 2005). See also Jin Li, Lianqin Wang, and Kurt W. Fischer, "The Organisation of Chinese Shame Concepts?," *Cogn Emot* 18, no. 6 (Oct 2004): 767–97; Whitley Kaufman, "Understanding Honor: Beyond the Shame/Guilt Dichotomy," *STP* 37, no. 4 (Oct 2011): 557–73; Olwen Bedford and Kwang-Kuo Hwang, "Guilt and Shame in Chinese Culture: A Cross-Cultural Framework from the Perspective of Morality and Identity," *JTSB* 33, no. 2 (1 June 2003): 127–44; Chester Chun-Seng Kam and Michael Harris Bond, "Emotional Reactions of Anger and Shame to the Norm Violation Characterizing Episodes of Interpersonal Harm," *British Journal of Social Psychology* 48, no. 2 (Jun 2009): 203–19; David Yau-Fai Ho, Wai Fu, and S. M. Ng, "Guilt, Shame and Embarrassment: Revelations of Face and Self," *Culture & Psychology* 10, no. 1 (Mar 2004): 64–84; Stella Ting-Toomey, ed., *The Challenge of Facework: Cross-Cultural and Interpersonal Issues* (Suny Series in Human Communication Processes; Albany, N.Y.: State University of New York Press, 1994).

achieved. A person's public identity consists in his or her relationships. Thus, those who live in cultures that emphasize HS are especially sensitive to the importance of gaining, losing, or lacking honor. "Shame" is the ill repute brought upon a person for some perceived deficiency or failure to meet the standards issued by his or her community. Every culture has manifold ways of conveying, assessing, and regulating HS. Laws are simply one way society expresses its HS standards.[8]

Not only does HS encompass the whole of human life, it is especially pervasive in Chinese culture. The Chinese language is rich with idioms and terms related to HS. "Face," typically translated *mianzi* or *lian*, is a kind of "currency" with which social transactions take place. "Face" is a practical and daily consideration in China. When it comes to moral issues, Chinese people tend to speak in terms of what is honorable and shameful. They are cognizant of the fact that different standards of right and wrong are used in different relationships and situations. HS can be shared collectively, reinforcing a divide between insiders and outsiders (e.g., "Chinese" versus "foreigners").

Not surprisingly, the Bible consistently demonstrates an HS perspective. Anthropologists have written extensively to show how HS-related issues influenced ancient biblical cultures and thus Scripture. Theologians have long recognized the importance of God's glory through the Bible. Yet, on the whole, people have given little notice to how this theme is but the tip of the iceberg when it comes to HS's influence on

---

[8] A few articles that employ too narrow a view of HS relative to theology include Paul W. Pruyser, "Anxiety, Guilt, and Shame in the Atonement," *ThTo* 21, no. 1 (Apr 1964): 15–33; Jackie D. Leigh, "Honor, Shame, Resurrection," *Proceedings-Eastern Great Lakes and Midwest Biblical Societies* 23 (2003): 101–8; Brad A. Binau, "When Shame is The Question, How Does The Atonement Answer?," *Journal for Pastoral Theology* 12, no. 1 (Jan 2002): 89–113; Wayne L. Alloway Jr., John G. Lacey, and Robert Jewett, eds., *The Shame Factor: How Shame Shapes Society* (Eugene, Ore.: Cascade, 2010); Laurel Arthur Burton, "Original Sin or Original Shame," *QR* 8, no. 4 (Winter 1988): 31–41; R. Atkins, "Pauline Theology and Shame Affect: Reading a Social Location," *Listening* 31, no. 2 (1996): 137–51.

Scripture. HS is foundational to the entire biblical narrative. A number of writers have formulated theologies of HS.[9] Jonathan Edwards famously argues that God does all things for the sake of his glory/honor.[10] Humans are made in God's image and so should publically reflect his worth. All people "have sinned and fall short of the glory of God" (Rom 3:23). As will be seen, writers are frequently concerned about how to use HS to explain "sin" and thus what Jesus accomplished. However, their attempts are introductory and not comprehensive. At times, they treat HS primarily as a social-science issue, not as a "theological" problem on the same level of law.

Using the mosaic of insights gained thus far, Chapter 5 ("A Soteriology of Honor and Shame") demonstrates how HS frames and gives color to the biblical doctrine of salvation. Texts related to soteriology are diffused throughout the Bible. The gospel of salvation is more comprehensive and complex than some might suggest. Rather than restricting one's interpretive lens to a few select texts that highlight the legal-motif, this chapter notes the diversity of ways that Scripture applies HS language to salvation.[11] In

---

[9] Some efforts include: Grant DeVries, "Explaining the Atonement to the Arabic Muslim in terms of Honour and Shame: Potentials and Pitfalls," *St. Francis Magazine* 2, no. 4 (Mar 2007): 1–68; Bruce J. Nicholls, "The Servant Songs of Isaiah in Dialogue with Muslims," *ERT* 20 (1996): 168–77; Ruth Lienhard, "Restoring Relationships: Theological Reflections on Shame and Honor Among the Daba and Ban of Cameroon" (PhD diss.; Pasadena, Calif.: Fuller Theological Seminary, 2000); Christopher L. Flanders, "About Face: Reorienting Thai Face For Soteriology and Mission" (PhD diss.; Pasadena, Calif.: Fuller Theological Seminary, 2005); Bruce J. Nicholls, "The Role of Shame and Guilt in a Theology of Cross-Cultural Mission," *ERT* 25, no. 3 (Jul 2001): 231–41; Timothy D. Boyle, "Communicating the Gospel in Terms of Shame," *JapChrQ* 50, no. 1 (Winter 1984): 41–46; Rafael Zaracho, "Communicating the Gospel in a Shame Society," *Direction* 39, no. 2 (Fall 2010): 271–81.

[10] Jonathan Edwards, "The End for Which God Created the World," in *God's Passion for His Glory* (ed. John Piper; Wheaton, Ill.: 1998), 117–252.

[11] The relationship between the gospel and salvation has become an increasingly debated topic in recent years. See Scot McKnight, *The King Jesus Gospel: The Original Good News Revisited* (Grand Rapids, Mich.: Zondervan, 2011); Michael W. Goheen, *A Light to the Nations: The Missional Church and the Biblical Story* (Grand Rapids, Mich.: Baker Academic, 2011); Kevin DeYoung and Greg Gilbert, *What Is the Mission of the Church?: Making Sense of Social Justice, Shalom, and the Great Commission* (Wheaton, Ill.: Crossway, 2011); Gilbert, *What Is the Gospel?*. For a wonderful survey of the use of the word "gospel" in ancient literature, see John Dickson, "Gospel as News: ευαγγελ- from Aristophanes to the Apostle Paul," *NTS* 51 (2005): 212–30.

the atonement, Christ "saves God's face" and objectively pays the honor-debt all humans owe to God.[12] Subjectively, Christ's death inaugurated the new covenant. God gives his people new hearts and the Holy Spirit, thus enabling them to obediently honor God in community. Naturally, one sees in Scripture a constant theme—group identity. On the one hand, sinful people prefer the approval of others to the praise that comes from God. On the other hand, Jesus and Paul challenge the boasting of the Jews who honored themselves as Abraham's offspring. In Romans, Paul expounds upon the doctrine of justification in part to undermine the notion that salvation is tied to ethnic identity. The gospel challenges every sense of cultural superiority. Those who boast in Christ are ascribed as righteous. Because God upholds his own honor, all who trust in Christ are reckoned as Abraham's offspring and will not be put to shame.[13]

Finally, Chapter 6 concludes the study by posing a series of questions and possible applications. This book seeks to lay a foundation for theological contextualization in China. It is impossible to address the variety of implications for

---

[12] A spectrum of views can be found in Mark D. Baker and Joel B. Green, *Recovering the Scandal of the Cross: Atonement in New Testament and Contemporary Contexts* (Downers Grove, Ill.: IVP Academic, 2000); C. Norman Kraus, "The Cross of Christ: Dealing with Shame and Guilt," *JapChrQ50* 53, no. 4 (Fall 1987): 221–27; Scot McKnight, *A Community Called Atonement: Living Theology* (Nashville, Tenn.: Abingdon, 2007); Robert Jewett, "Shame and Atonement in Romans: A Potential Resource for Theology in Korea" (Yonsei University, Seoul, Korea, 1 Nov 2007), Online: http://cafe321.daum.net/_c21_ /bbs_search_read?grpid=DzmC&fldid=TMZ2&contentval=00001zzzzzzzzzzzzzzzzzzzzzzzzz&nenc=&fen c=&from=&q=%B0%A5%B6%F3%B5%F0%BE%C6%BC%AD%BF%E4%BE%E0&nil_profile=cafetop &nil_menu=sch_updw&listnum=; Thomas Schreiner et al., *The Nature of the Atonement: Four Views* (ed. James Beilby and Paul R. Eddy; Downers Grove, Ill.: IVP Academic, 2006); Charles E. Hill and Frank A. James III, eds., *The Glory of the Atonement: Biblical, Theological & Practical Perspectives* (Downers Grove, Ill.: IVP Academic, 2004).

[13] See Halvor Moxnes, "Honour and Righteousness in Romans," *JSNT* 32 (1988): 61–77; Leland J. White, "Grid and Group in Matthew's Community-The Righteousness/Honor Code in the Sermon on the Mount," *Semeia* 35 (1986): 61–90; Robert Jewett, *Romans: A Commentary* (ed. Eldon Jay Epp; Minneapolis, Minn.: Fortress Press, 2006); N. T. Wright, *The Letter to the Romans* (NIB 10; Nashville, Tenn.: Abingdon, 2002); Robert Jewett, *Saint Paul Returns to the Movies: Triumph over Shame* (Grand Rapids, Mich.: Eerdmans, 1998); Mark A. Garcia, "Imputation as Attribution: Union with Christ, Reification and Justification as Declarative Word," *IJST* 11, no. 4 (Oct 2009): 415–27.

missiological theory and practice as well as biblical and theological studies.[14] Methodologically, the book may open doors for more fruitful dialogue and integration between missiology and theology. For instance, this study shows what dialogical contextualization looks like when applied to a specific cultural context, namely, a Chinese context. It demonstrates that contextualization and theology cannot be so neatly separated; in fact, they essentially refer to the same process as described from different perspectives. Examining how others have utilized the HS motif can assist prospective attempts to theologize in HS cultures, train church leaders and missionaries, and more broadly foster unity within the global church. One benefit gained in the process is that Christians from both East and West alike can become increasingly cognizant of all the Bible teaches so as not to fall prey to theological or cultural provincialism. Naturally, since the Bible conveys a message for the world, it is hoped that people in the West would likewise benefit from these insights from Asian culture. Many who are more accustomed to a law-based presentation of salvation could benefit from hearing a message about the restoration of God's glory and the removal of human shame.

---

[14] An example of how honor-shame may influence ecclesiology can be found in Jackson Wu, "Authority in a Collectivist Church: Identifying Crucial Concerns for a Chinese Ecclesiology," *Global Missiology* 1, no. 9 (Oct 2011), n.p. [cited 21 Dec 2011]. Online: www.globalmissiology.org.

CHAPTER 2: THEOLOGICAL CONTEXTUALIZATION IN PRACTICE

This chapter lays out a methodology for theological contextualization. First, it reveals a flaw in many traditional views of contextualization. This flawed view assumes that contextualization is primarily an act of communication or application when in fact it is primarily an act of interpretation that emerges from a particular cultural perspective. Second, it explains why culture provides a framework on which to build a contextualized theology. Finally, it proposes a model for mapping the contextualization process.

Assuming the Gospel: A Logical Fallacy in Theological Contextualization

If we assume the gospel in contextualization, we commit a logical fallacy by begging the question. Accordingly, assuming the gospel largely predetermines the results of contextualization. Thus, begging the question renders faithful contextualization all but impossible. The problem is systemic since all Christian theology centers on the question, "What is the gospel?" This goes beyond saying that theological background inevitably influences contextualization. Missiologically, if the gospel is presupposed, what is the value in doing theological contextualization? By examining this tendency to make premature assumptions, contextualization methods can be corrected and improved.

One who writes about theology and contextualization can tacitly assume a particular formulation of the gospel and even open a door to syncretism.[1] While many

---

[1] Even if there is one gospel, people may disagree about the scope or expression of the "gospel."

10

affirm the centrality of Jesus' life, death, and resurrection, there is too little explicit focus on *what* exactly should be contextualized.[2] Consequently, syncretism goes unnoticed since the contextualized theology does little more than restate a doctrine in traditional theological categories. Many scholars may not see the problem since their definition of "syncretism" is limited to only that which deviates from the gospel.[3] Yet, theological syncretism also results when culturally bound conceptions of the gospel become the assumed framework of contextualization. It is easier to identify syncretism with a foreign culture than the sort of syncretism that grows from a traditional theological system.

A presupposed gospel assumes *a priori* that the task and nature of contextualized theology is that of communication and application. Yet, theology most basically concerns interpretation not simply communication. This is no less true of *contextualized* theology. If so, contextualization, as a concept, needs to be reconceived. Accordingly, this chapter reviews the diverse ways the Bible articulates the "gospel." Further, it examines the themes and scope of the gospel within Western theology. Next, readers will observe the problems and lack of consensus plaguing various methods of contextualization. Then, the chapter explains how presupposing a gospel *a priori* thwarts and potentially sabotages theology from the start. It concludes by arguing that contextualization is an act of biblical interpretation, not simply the application or communication of biblical truth.

---

[2] For instance, Justice Anderson and Don Jones, eds., *Contextualizing the Gospel* (Richmond, VA: International Centre for Excellence in Leadership, International Mission Board, 2000).
[3] A good discussion on the topic can be found in Gailyn Van Rheenen, ed., *Contextualization and Syncretism* (Pasadena, Calif.: William Carey Library, 2006).

The Diversity of "Gospel" Articulations in Scripture

Scripture explicitly frames the "gospel" in terms of the grand biblical narrative. The "gospel of God" (Mark 1:14) was promised "beforehand through his prophets in the holy Scriptures," climaxing in the life, death, and resurrection of Jesus the Christ (Rom 1:2; cf. Acts 13:32–40; 1 Cor 15:3–4).[4] Thus, it is noteworthy that Paul's condensed summary in Gal 3:8 does *not* mention Christ; rather, it explicitly equates the gospel with the promise given to Abraham, "In you shall all the nations be blessed."[5] In the gospel, God makes known the ancient mystery "that the Gentiles are fellow heirs, members of the same body, and partakers of the promise in Christ Jesus" (Eph 3:6; cf. Eph 6:19).

The OT illustrates that the word "gospel" carries significant royal connotations. Isaiah 52:7 (cited in Rom 10:15) proclaims, "How beautiful upon the mountains are the feet of him who brings good news, who publishes peace, who brings good news of happiness, who publishes salvation, who says to Zion, 'Your God reigns.'" In Luke 4:18–19, Jesus inaugurates his ministry by quoting Isa 61:1, "The Spirit of the Lord GOD is upon me, because the LORD has anointed me to bring good news to the poor; he has sent me to bind up the brokenhearted, to proclaim liberty to the captives, and the opening of the prison to those who are bound." In secular usage, a "gospel" typically announces a king's victory or ascension (cf. 1 Sam 31:8–9; 2 Sam 18:19–31; Ps 68:10–11).[6]

The NT continues this royal motif in view of the resurrection. Jesus and his followers preach the "gospel of the kingdom" (Matt 4:23, et al; cf. Acts 8:12). The gospel

---

[4] All Scripture citations come from the English Standard Version (ESV) unless otherwise noted.

[5] Of course, Christ is mentioned in the context. The point is that Paul's concise summary is strikingly unusual, as if to say the gospel *includes* the narrative context behind Christ's life and work.

[6] For an extensive study of the term in ancient history, see Dickson, "Gospel as News," 212–30.

concerns "his Son, who was descended from David according to the flesh and was declared to be the Son of God in power according to the Spirit of holiness by his resurrection from the dead, Jesus Christ our Lord" (Rom 1:3–4). The gospel of the risen King/Christ means, "Death is swallowed up in victory" (1 Cor 15:54, citing Isa 25:8). Thus, "he delivers the kingdom to God the Father after destroying every rule and every authority and power. For he must reign until he has put all his enemies under his feet" (1 Cor 15:24–25). The "gospel of Christ" (Phil 1:27) is called "the gospel of your salvation" since his death is "for our sins" (Eph 1:13).

A plethora of images explain the effects of the gospel. In Colossians alone, Christ's death brings about ". . . redemption of those in slavery (1:14); forgiveness of sins (1:4; 2:13); reconciliation of enemies and of the whole world (1:20–22); making peace through the cross (1:20); liberation from assorted rulers (1:13; 2:15); transfer into a new realm (1:13); an inward spiritual circumcision (2:11); participation in Jesus' death (2:12–13; 3:3); granting of new life (2:12–13; 3:3–4); and the canceling of debt (2:14)."[7]

The various gospel themes are intertwined and mutually explanatory. Paul says "the gospel of the blessed God" is ". . . the power of God for salvation to everyone who believes, to the Jew first and also to the Greek. For in it the righteousness of God is revealed from faith for faith, as it is written, 'The righteous shall live by faith'" (1 Tim 1:11; Rom 1:16–17). John adds that the "eternal gospel" will be "proclaim[ed] to those who dwell on earth, to every nation and tribe and language and people" (Rev 14:6). Second Corinthians 3–4 uses creation and covenant as motifs to explain "the light of the

---

[7] Dean Flemming, "Paul the Contextualizer," in *Local Theology for the Global Church: Principles for an Evangelical Approach to Contextualization* (ed. Matthew Cook et al.; Pasadena, Calif.: William Carey Library, 2010), 8–9.

gospel of the glory of Christ, who is the image of God" (2 Cor 4:4). While calling himself Christ's "ambassador" (2 Cor 5:20; Eph 6:20), Paul also calls gospel labor a "priestly service" (Rom 15:16; cf. Phil 2:17, 22).

The biblical writers emphasize different aspects of this good news without contradiction. Authors may have any number of situational, pastoral, or canonical reasons to use a metaphor in one instance but not another. A few ideas are especially pronounced. The gospel centers on Jesus Christ as foretold in Israel's story since Abraham and carries definitive royal overtones. However it is articulated, the gospel deals with sin and evil, bringing salvation through the life, death, and resurrection of Jesus the Christ.

The Gospel in Western Theology

A few features generally typify Western theology. First, typical Western constructions of the gospel are oriented on law, guilt, justification, and judgment. Second, gospel content tends to focus narrowly on the life, death, and resurrection of Jesus wherein people find forgiveness from sin and eternal life. This book does not use the term "Western" in a derogatory manner. Using this word does not imply that Western Christianity has been mistaken in its primary forms of theologizing. Instead, this label is used because certain patterns and emphases are especially prominent in Western theology.

A sample of representative authors demonstrates a strong emphasis on the law motif within Western theology. Famously, Martin Luther articulated a gospel that justifies humans contra the law of condemnation.[8] Packer depicts Christ as "Lawgiver" and "Judge."[9] God's wrath is pacified. Thus, the gospel magnifies "the righteousness of

---

[8] Martin Luther, *Table Talk* (ed. William Hazlitt; Gainesville, Fla.: Bridge-Logos, 2004), 175–91.
[9] J. I. Packer, *Evangelism and the Sovereignty of God* (Downers Grove, Ill.: IVP, 2008), 55.

God the Judge."[10] Roger Nicole echoes these sentiments, saying, "the gospel, the good news, which must be proclaimed to every man, woman or child whom we can reach by the ministry of the Word" is that Jesus takes "on himself the guilt and punishment due for all their sins and provides them with his own immaculate righteousness before the divine tribunal."[11] John Murray adds, "That we are justified by faith advertises the grand article of the gospel of grace that we are not justified by works of the law."[12] In justification, he says that a judge "simply declares that in his judgment the person is not guilty of the accusation but is upright in terms of the law relevant to the case."[13]

Hence, the gospel centers upon "a verdict regarding our judicial status."[14] Millard Erickson asserts, "The true gospel, argues Paul, categorically maintains that one is justified by faith in the gracious work of Jesus Christ in his death and resurrection."[15] When one surveys his chapter on justification, his meaning is unambiguously "forensic."[16] Sinclair Ferguson depicts the gospel as a message about people's objective, forensic justification where human guilt is imputed to Christ.[17] In The Cambridge Declaration, the Alliance of Confessing Evangelicals confirms, "There is no gospel except that of Christ's substitution in our place whereby God imputed to him our sin and

---

[10] J. I. Packer, *Knowing God* (20th Anniversary ed.; Downers Grove, Ill.: IVP, 1993), 188.

[11] Roger Nicole, "Postscript on Penal Substitution," in *The Glory of the Atonement: Biblical, Theological & Practical Perspectives* (ed. Charles E. Hill and Frank A. James III; Downers Grove, Ill.: IVP Academic, 2004), 452.

[12] John Murray, *Redemption: Accomplished and Applied* (Grand Rapids, Mich.: Eerdmans, 1980), 130.

[13] Ibid., 119.

[14] Ibid., 121.

[15] Millard Erickson, *Christian Theology* (2nd ed.; Grand Rapids, Mich.: Baker Book House, 2002), 1073.

[16] Ibid., 968–73.

[17] Sinclair Ferguson, "Preaching the Atonement," in *The Glory of the Atonement: Biblical, Theological & Practical Perspectives* (ed. Charles E. Hill and Frank A. James III; Downers Grove, Ill.: IVP Academic, 2004), 431–36.

imputed to us his righteousness,"[18] although no mention is made of the resurrection.[19]

Mark Dever summarizes the gospel, "It's the news that the Judge will become the Father, if only we repent and believe."[20] This is because, he says, Jesus "lived a perfect life, and died on the cross, thus fulfilling the law himself and taking on himself the punishment for the sin of all those who would ever turn and trust in him [such that] God's wrath against us has been exhausted."[21] Finally, John Piper remarks, "The good news is that God himself has decreed a way to satisfy the demands of his justice."[22]

The use of these themes is intentional. Murray asserts the gospel of reconciliation has a "forensic character."[23] Since Jesus' death satisfies a "retributive justice," Packer laments that many reject "the categories of wrath, guilt, condemnation, and the enmity of God."[24] He makes a clear contrast when he says of Christ, "As Judge, he is the law, but as Savior he is gospel."[25] Only brief comments about the Atonement are possible here. Suffice it to say, the bulk of Protestant theology would agree with Thomas Schreiner when he writes, "The theory of *penal* substitution is the heart and soul of an evangelical view of the atonement."[26]

---

[18] *The Cambridge Declaration of the Alliance of Confessing Evangelicals*, 20 Apr 1996, n.p. [cited 25 Oct 2011]. Online: http://www.reformed.org/documents/index.html?mainframe=http://www.reformed.org/documents/cambridge.html.

[19] This observation was noted by Tim Gombis, Blog Comment, *The Gospel and Double Imputation*, 25 Oct 2011, n.p. [cited on 25 Oct 2011]. Online: http://www.patheos.com/community/jesuscreed/2011/10/25/the-gospel-and-double-imputation/?utm_source=feedburner&utm_medium=feed&utm_campaign=Feed%3A+PatheosJesusCreed+%28Blog+-+Jesus+Creed%29.

[20] Mark Dever, *What is a Healthy Church?* (Wheaton, Ill.: Crossway, 2007), 76.

[21] Mark Dever, *The Gospel and Personal Evangelism* (Wheaton, Ill.: Crossway, 2007), 43.

[22] John Piper, *Desiring God: Meditations of a Christian Hedonist* (Sisters, Ore.: Multnomah Books, 1996), 59.

[23] Murray, *Redemption*, 41.

[24] Packer, *Knowing God*, 189, 196.

[25] Ibid., 147.

[26] Tom Schreiner, "Penal Substitution View," in *The Nature of the Atonement: Four Views* (ed. James Beilby and Paul R. Eddy; Downers Grove, Ill.: IVP Academic, 2006), 67. Emphasis mine.

A narrow concentration on the legal motif tends to constrict the scope of gospel presentations to a limited range of biblical texts and events. Greg Gilbert's *What is the Gospel?* explicitly limits what constitutes the gospel when he argues, "'Jesus is Lord' is not good news unless there is a way to be forgiven of your rebellion against him."[27] By this, he restricts the idea of Jesus' Lordship to that of his "right to judge."[28] Gilbert's contracted view of messianic lordship leads him to conclude that for sinners, "the declaration that 'Jesus is Lord' is nothing but a death sentence."[29] Although he calls the gospel "the Bible's main story line," he nevertheless claims the biblical plot of "creation-fall-redemption-consummation . . . is not the gospel."[30] He says the problem lies in wrongly placing "the emphasis of the gospel on God's promise to renew the world, rather than on the cross."[31] Yet, he seems to make a straw man argument since he does not cite anyone who actually makes this dichotomy. He claims that some texts talk about the "gospel" without ever using the word itself (cf. Acts 2). Therefore, he says, "Let me suggest that, for now, we approach the task of defining the main contours of the Christian gospel not by doing a word study, but by looking at what the earliest Christians said about Jesus and the significance of his life, death, and resurrection."[32] He immediately appeals to Rom 1–4 as representative of the NT gospel. He concludes that the gospel

---

[27] Gilbert, *What Is the Gospel?*, 106.

[28] Ibid., 105.

[29] Ibid. Contra Rom 10:9.

[30] Ibid., 106.

[31] Ibid.

[32] Ibid., 27. This move is inexplicable. First, are not the "earliest Christians" also those whom one would listen to when doing such a word study? Second, why the arbitrary use of Romans 1–4 as opposed to a word study or other texts? Is this another instance of narrowing the scope of the gospel to Romans?

always addresses our accountability before God the judge.[33] For Gilbert, then, the gospel of 1 Cor 15 can be summarized in four words, "God. Man. Christ. Response."[34]

Gilbert and Piper treat 1 Cor 15:1–5 in exactly the same way. Referencing 1 Cor 15:3–4, Gilbert writes, "But salvation comes in this: 'Christ died for our sins . . . was buried . . . was raised.'"[35] Likewise, Piper quotes 1 Cor 15:3–4 two times on a single page, using ellipsis in the exact same places as Gilbert. He says, "The heart of the gospel is that 'Christ died for our sins . . . was buried . . . was raised . . . and appeared to more than five hundred people.'"[36] The significance lies in what they omit. Both men jump over the phrase, "in accordance with the Scriptures," repeated twice by Paul in 1 Cor 15:3–4. This is particularly noteworthy because, as was seen above, the NT elsewhere makes much of the OT's foretelling of the gospel (cf. Acts 13:32–33; Rom 1:1–3). The propensity to limit the scope of gospel content leads to a selective reading of Scripture, overlooking other very clear emphases. Not surprisingly, reducing the gospel to the doctrine of justification apart from law means that many traditional gospel presentations will draw predominantly from just two books—Romans and Galatians.

The Gospel Coalition's book *The Gospel as Center* echoes mainstream evangelical thought on the gospel.[37] Its sixteen contributors do not focus on biblical passages that directly use "gospel" language.[38] Paul's summaries in Gal 3:8 and 2 Tim

---

[33] Ibid., 32.

[34] Ibid.

[35] Ibid., 33.

[36] John Piper, *The Passion of Jesus Christ: Fifty Reasons Why He Came to Die* (Wheaton, Ill.: Crossway, 2004), 104–5.

[37] D. A. Carson and Timothy J. Keller, eds., *The Gospel as Center: Renewing our Faith and Reforming our Ministry Practices* (Wheaton, Ill.: Crossway, 2012).

[38] "Gospel" language refers to the standard terminology that translates words like "gospel" or "to preach the gospel." In the NT, the typical noun is εὐαγγέλιον; the verb is εὐαγγελίζω. The most common

2:8, Luke's account of Paul in Acts 13:32, 14:15, and OT texts like Isa 40:9, 52:7 are

never discussed. Also, 1 Cor 15:1–8 is mentioned quite briefly in only two places.[39]

Romans 1:1–4 is cited once.[40] Neither Rom 1:1–4 nor 1 Cor 15:1–8 are used in the

chapter "What is the Gospel?"[41] By contrast, words about "justification" and

"righteous(ness)" are used approximately 385 times.[42]

A few popular methods of evangelism illustrate how traditional Western

emphases limit the scope of the gospel and drift toward individualism.[43] By confining the

gospel to legal language, the broader scriptural narrative and its possible corporate

implications are often lost. For instance, CRU (formerly known as Campus Crusade for

Christ) has popularized *The Four Spiritual Laws* the world over. Although these "laws"

are likened to natural laws rather than legal laws,[44] they simplify the good news to

illustrate how God works according to laws to make himself available to individuals. The

---

OT term is בשׂר. I do not suggest that one's understanding of the gospel should be restricted to such passages; yet, one would expect them to carry great weight in how one formulates or frames the gospel.

[39] Ibid., 243, 276. Page 243 uses 1 Cor 15:3 simply to explain the Lord's Supper.

[40] Ibid., 141.

[41] Bryan Chapell, "What is the Gospel?," in *The Gospel as Center: Renewing our Faith and Reforming our Ministry Practices* (ed. D. A. Carson and Timothy J. Keller; Wheaton, Ill.: Crossway, 2012), 115–34.

[42] Attempting not to count source citations, a search of the book estimates at least 186 instances of the words "justify," "justified," and "justification." "Righteous(ness)" is used approximately 200 times. Also, observe "impute(d)" and "imputation" appear about 27 times. Romans 3 alone is cited 25 times.

[43] The term "individualism" here refers to a perspective primarily oriented around the individual. It is often contrasted with "collectivism," which regards the group as the basic unit of human society. For a famous essay connecting Western theology, law, and individualism, see Stendahl, *Paul Among Jews and Gentiles,* 78–96. In an interview, Dever agrees that the word "gospel," lexically and biblically, conveys more than individual salvation. Despite this, he says the church has "a long tradition of reflection" that allows people to focus primary on personal salvation. He fears that "kingdom" language tends to minimize the focus on the individual conversion. He seems to associate a "kingdom" gospel with doing good deeds in society. He adds, "I understand God is going to restore the whole world but that is no good news for me in particular." See Mark Dever, "The Whiteboard Sessions—Mark Dever" (Interview with Ed Stetzer at The Whiteboard Conference, Reston, Va., 23 May 2008), [cited 29 Aug 2012]. Online: http://www.ustream.tv/recorded/431730.

[44] CRU, "Four Spiritual Laws," n.p. [cited 26 Jul 2011]. Online: http://www.campuscrusade.com/fourlawseng.htm.

presentation is tapered to address every person: "[B]ecause of his own stubborn self-will, he chose to go his own independent way." Key phrases include, "God loves you and offers a wonderful plan for your life," "We Receive Christ Through Personal Invitation," and the tract poses "two kinds of lives": "Self-Directed Life" versus the "Christ-Directed Life."[45] Also, *The Roman Road* is a well-known presentation intending to summarize the way of salvation. It uses Rom 3:23, 5:8, 6:23, 10:9–10, 13.[46] Most of these verses are also utilized by Evangelism Explosion's *Steps to Life*[47] and in the Training for Trainers (T4T) methodology.[48] *The Story* appeals to a broader biblical narrative. Yet, it still reiterates the human problem in traditional, Western legal terms, "Everyone is guilty before God."[49]

The aforementioned observations are not an implicit condemnation of Western theology. Rather, it is essential that those seeking to contextualize the gospel plainly recognize the long theological current that moves much Western missiological thinking. If particular Western conceptions of the gospel are assumed and *then* contextualized for another cultural context, serious questions arise about the viability of a genuinely non-Western articulation of the gospel. This is not to say other contextual theologies must contradict historically Western theologies. Susan Baker highlights a danger of contextualization, namely "reductionism."[50] She warns against constricting theology to

---

[45] Ibid.

[46] Cf. "The Roman Road," n.p. [cited 26 Jul 2011]. Online: http://theromanroad.org/.

[47] See Evangelism Explosion, "Steps to Life," n.p. [cited 26 Jul 2011]. Online: http://www.ccinternational.org/pages/page.asp?page_id=31469.

[48] David Garrison and Richard Beckham, "Lesson 1–God's Plan of Salvation," *T4T Online Trainer's Manual* (Feb 2011): 55. Cited 31 Aug 2012. Online: http://t4tonline.org/wp-content/uploads/2011/02/T4TOnline-Trainers-Manual.pdf.

[49] SpreadTruth, "View the Story," n.p. [cited 26 Jul 2011]. Online: http://viewthestory.com/.

[50] Susan S. Baker, "The Social Sciences for Urban Ministry," in *The Urban Face of Mission: Ministering the Gospel in a Diverse and Changing World* (ed. Manuel Ortiz and Susan S. Baker; Phillipsburg, N.J.: P & R Publishing, 2002), 77.

any one set of themes and texts, cautioning, "In this [reductionism] we find that we have reduced Scripture to only one part of what the Lord has to say to us, and we lose sight of the overall redemptive-historical unfolding of God's complete plan for us."[51] In short, uncritically assuming the gospel can undermine the credibility of contextualization.

A comparison can be made with biblical theology, where scholars have debated at length how best to conceive the gospel.[52] Stendahl's conclusion deserves consideration, "We should venture to suggest that the West for centuries has wrongly surmised that the biblical writers were grappling with problems which no doubt are ours, but which never entered their consciousness."[53] If subjectivity affects biblical interpretation, certainly it is also true of theological contextualization. Accordingly, the globalization of theological discourse is necessary to free it from merely being a Western academic exercise.

Common Methods of Contextualization

Missiologists may implicitly assume a particular form of the gospel when they define "contextualization" and develop methodology. For example, David Hesselgrave and Edward Rommen write,

> Christian contextualization can be thought of as the attempt to communicate the message of the person, works, Word, and will of God in a way that is faithful to God's revelation, especially as it is put forth in the teachings of Holy Scripture, and that is meaningful to respondents in their respective cultural and existential contexts.[54]

---

[51] Ibid., 77.
[52] A provocative but helpful treatment of this is found in McKnight, *The King Jesus Gospel.*
[53] Stendahl, *Paul Among Jews and Gentiles*, 94–95.
[54] David J. Hesselgrave and Edward Rommen, *Contextualization: Meanings, Methods, and Models* (Grand Rapids, Mich.: Baker, 1989), 200.

They survey possible definitions of the term, such as "making concepts of ideals relevant in a given situation,"[55] "the translation of the unchanging content of the Gospel of the kingdom into verbal form meaningful to the peoples in their separate culture . . . ,"[56] and "to discover the *legitimate implications* of the gospel in a given situation."[57] Baker also cites Louis Luzbetak's description that says, "We understand contextualization as the various processes by which a local church integrates the Gospel message (the 'text') with its local culture (the 'context')."[58] Scott Moreau, agreeing with Bevans, suggests the most common idea of contextualization held by evangelicals is the "translation" model where ". . . there is a core message of universal truth which must be translated into each new cultural setting in a way that remains faithful to the core. Because the content of that message is absolute and authoritative, the contextualizer's task is to change the *form* of the message."[59] Kevin Greeson says it is "[a]ttempting to adapt the style, form and language of the Christian faith and message to the culture of the people one is seeking to reach."[60] Paul Hiebert's "critical contextualization" takes seriously the role of culture in forming a contextual theology, yet he applies it more piecemeal, evaluating particular

---

[55] Byang H. Kato, "The Gospel, Cultural Context, and Religious Syncretism," in *Let the Earth Hear His Voice* (ed. J. D. Douglas; Minneapolis, Minn.: World Wide, 1975), 1217. Cited in Hesselgrave and Rommen, *Contextualization*, 33.

[56] Bruce J. Nicholls, "Theological Education and Evangelization," in *Let the Earth Hear His Voice* (ed. J. D. Douglas; Minneapolis, Minn.: World Wide, 1975), 647. Cited in Hesselgrave and Rommen, *Contextualization*, 33.

[57] George W. Peters, "Issues Confronting Evangelical Missions," in *Evangelical Missions Tomorrow* (ed. E. L. Frizen and Wade Coggins; Pasadena, Calif.: William Carey Library, 1977), 169. Cited in Hesselgrave and Rommen, *Contextualization*, 34.

[58] Louis J. Luzbetak, *The Church and Cultures: New Perspectives in Missiological Anthropology* (Maryknoll, N.Y.: Orbis Books, 1988), 69. Cited in Baker, "Social Sciences," 75.

[59] Scott Moreau, "Evangelical Models of Contextualization," in *Local Theology for the Global Church: Principles for an Evangelical Approach to Contextualization* (ed. Matthew Cook et al.; Pasadena, Calif.: William Carey Library, 2010), 169. He cites Bevans, *Models of Contextual Theology*, 37.

[60] Kevin Greeson, *The Camel: How Muslims Are Coming to Faith in Christ!* (rev. ed.; Monument, Colo: WIGTake Resources, 2010), 199–200.

issues and customs rather than drawing out the gospel itself.[61] For Hiebert, it seems that

contextualization is foremost an issue of communication, not interpretation.[62] Sills

concurs, "[C]ontextualization is simply the process of making the gospel understood."[63]

From the many examples given, it is evident that many view contextualization as

a process that comes *after* one has already settled on the meaning of the gospel, that is,

what constitutes its content. Vanhoozer, critical of this approach, says,

> Contextual theology, according to this view, is a matter of extracting the
> doctrinal kernel from its original cultural husk and then reinserting it in, or
> adapting it to, a new cultural husk. The key presupposition of this model is
> that the essential message is supracultural, able to be abstracted from its
> concrete mode of expression. Contextualization, according to this view, is
> primarily a matter of communication: decoding and encoding. How does it
> work? Typically, a missionary or theologian decodes the message of the
> Bible and extracts the revealed, supracultural proposition, then encodes
> the proposition into the local idiom and culture.[64]

Few scholars would deny that people enter a culture with an entire collage of assumptions;

yet, it is difficult for contextualizers to suspend their own understanding of the gospel

while taking on the worldview of local people. Certainly many applaud Kraft when he

says, "Biblically, the contextualization of Christianity is not simply to be

---

[61] Paul Hiebert, *Anthropological Insights for Missionaries* (Grand Rapids, Mich.: Baker, 1985), 186–90. Also, see Moreau, "Evangelical Models," 174.

[62] Paul Hiebert, "Cultural Difference and the Communication of the Gospel," in *Perspectives on the World Christian Movement: A Reader* (ed. Ralph Winter et al.; 3rd ed.; Pasadena, Calif.: William Carey Library, 1999), 373–83. Sills agrees that Heibert's proposal mainly concerns appropriate *applications* of Scripture. See M. David Sills, *Reaching and Teaching: A Call to Great Commission Obedience* (Chicago, Ill.: Moody Publishers, 2010), 205–7.

[63] Sills, *Reaching*, 195.

[64] Kevin Vanhoozer, "'One Rule to Rule Them All?' Theological Method in an Era of World Christianity," in *Globalizing Theology: Belief and Practice in an Era of World Christianity* (ed. Craig Ott and Harold Netland; Grand Rapids, Mich.: Baker Academic & Brazos Press, 2006), 100.

passing on of a *product* that has been developed once for all in Europe or America. It is, rather, the imitating of the *process* that the early apostles went through."[65] What is less clear is how "[t]he gospel is to be *planted as a seed* that will sprout within and be nourished by the rain and nutrients in the cultural soil of the receiving peoples" yet without a lot of foreign presuppositions as to what seed to plant.[66] Therefore, one must heed Sills' warning and reexamine the concept itself. He asserts, "[I]f one does not contextualize, he is doing just that—changing the gospel. He becomes a modern-day Judaizer. He is in effect telling his hearers that they must become like him to be saved."[67]

If people absolutize their cultural articulation of the gospel, then contextualization will naturally be reduced to simply building bridges. For example, Greeson's Camel method aims "to bridge to the Bible for an explanation of Christ and give the person of peace an opportunity to respond."[68] Don Richardson's *Peace Child* is a famous "redemptive analogy" intending to link biblical and cultural concepts.[69] It is quite possible that evangelistic bridges lead listeners to cross the cultural divide in the wrong direction. Converts first come to accept the missionary's own cultural thought forms; after which, they reenter their own context not just as "sojourners and exiles in the world," but as "Judaized" Christians (as Sills warns above). If contextualizers limit the relationship between Scripture and culture to a few select points, their "bridges" may in

---

[65] Charles H. Kraft, "Culture, Worldview, and Contextualization," in *Perspectives on the World Christian Movement: A Reader* (ed. Ralph Winter et al.; 3rd ed.; Pasadena, Calif.: William Carey Library, 1999), 389.

[66] Ibid., 389.

[67] Sills, *Reaching*, 198.

[68] Moreau, "Evangelical Models," 177.

[69] Don Richardson, "Redemptive Analogy," in *Perspectives on the World Christian Movement: A Reader* (ed. Ralph Winter et al.; 3rd ed.; Pasadena, Calif.: William Carey Library, 1999), 397–403. His more developed thought is found at Don Richardson, *Peace Child* (Glendale, Calif.: Regal Books, 1974).

fact act as a wedge between the gospel and the local culture.

Contextualization must humbly utilize a different methodology. Thus one admits, "We don't simply read cultural texts but we read *through* them. In short: the cultural texts we love best come to serve as the lens through which we view everything else and as the compass that orients us toward the good life."[70] Similarly, Clark's words are certainly true of one's interpretation of the gospel: "All interpretation begins with the assumptions, values, beliefs, and experiences that a reader brings to the text."[71] If so, how does this contest conventional thinking on contextualization? Dean Flemming is right that contextualization as communication is "too narrow," so "the message should be in some way shaped by the context of the people to whom it is being expressed."[72] Baker is more to the point, "Contextualization is not confined to the message alone. It touches on *how we do theology*."[73]

The Problem of Begging the Question

When missiologists assume the gospel, they may beg the question and thereby undermine contextualization. People "beg the question" when they assume their conclusion within a premise of an argument. For instance, an atheist may argue that Christianity is irrational based on the belief that God's resurrecting Jesus is impossible. First, he claims as a premise that "rational" people disavow supernaturalism, including miracles. Second, he claims that religions are irrational because they believe God works miracles. As a result,

---

[70] Kevin Vanhoozer, ed., *Everyday Theology: How to Read Cultural Texts and Interpret Trends* (Grand Rapids, Mich.: Baker Academic, 2007), 36. Such "texts" may include movies, events, music, etc.
[71] Clark, *To Know and Love God*, 107.
[72] Dean Flemming, *Contextualization in the New Testament: Patterns for Theology and Mission* (Downers Grove, Ill.: IVP Academic, 2005), 20.
[73] Baker, "Social Sciences," 75. Emphasis mine.

25

Christianity (a theistic religion) is irrational since divine miracles like resurrections are assumed to be supernatural, thus not rational. The atheist objector assumes God does not exist, a supernatural worldview is irrational, and so Jesus' resurrection is impossible. More subtly, missiologists commit a similar error when they assume the gospel yet without having decided what counts as a genuine contextualization. Contextualization inevitably turns into a task of communication, application, and bridge building. One then measures biblical faithfulness by the degree to which the "contextualized" theology conveys the narrower guilt/law based message prevalent in Western theology.

Various authors have proposed alternative themes and emphases around which to develop contextualized theologies. Philip Jenkins surveys a diversity of ways the Bible is being interpreted (not simply communicated) by non-Western Christians.[74] Tim Tennent poses a number of non-Western ways of seeing the gospel. For example, Africans may exalt Jesus as "Healer and Life-Giver."[75] He sketches a biblical argument for understanding the atonement in terms of HS.[76] Thus, he argues, "[T]he Christian faith is not only *culturally* translatable, it is also *theologically* translatable. I am defining theological translatability as *the ability of the kerygmatic essentials of the Christian faith to be discovered and restated within an infinite number of new global contexts*"].[77] The word "discovered" is key. Wan speaks about evangelization among the Chinese, "The Christian vocabulary (e.g., incarnation, sin, justification, etc.) may be foreign to many

---

[74] Philip Jenkins, *The New Faces of Christianity: Believing the Bible in the Global South* (Oxford: Oxford University Press, 2006).

[75] Timothy C. Tennent, *Theology in the Context of World Christianity: How the Global Church is Influencing the Way We Think about and Discuss Theology* (Grand Rapids, Mich.: Zondervan, 2007), 105–34.

[76] Ibid., 77–104.

[77] Ibid., 16. Emphasis in original

traditional Chinese (who instead know well of reincarnation and human error). Terms

such as 'heaven,' 'saved,' etc. might mean something entirely else to them culturally,

totally at variance with the biblical usage."[78] Therefore, he concludes,

> The message of the Gospel within the Chinese cultural context should be characterized by the emphasis on honor, relationship, and harmony, which are at the core of traditional Chinese cultural values. It should be different from [traditional Western theology]'s overemphasis on the forensic nature of the Gospel, the legal dimension of Christ's penal substitution and divine justification.[79]

Wan calls for a reoriented gospel that concerns "Jesus Christ for the Chinese" rather than

"Jesus Christ from the West," one that breaks from a rigid "either-or" approach to

theology and employs a "relational interpretation" highlighting HS.[80] Not surprisingly, he

defines contextualization as "the efforts of formulating . . . the Christian faith."[81]

Others have noted how guilt-oriented theologies insufficiently convey the gospel

message, particularly in HS oriented contexts. Hannes Wiher[82] and Christopher

Flanders[83] have written dissertations examining the problems that result from the neglect

of the latter. In a Thai context, the presumption that humans universally struggle with a

guilty conscience and seek "pardon" can create a "disconnect" between the missionary's

---

[78] Wan, "Practical Contextualization."

[79] Ibid.

[80] Wan, "Jesus Christ for the Chinese." See also his "Theological Contributions of Sino-Theology to the Global Christian Community (Part 1)," *Chinese Around the World* (Jul 2000), n.p. [cited 27 Dec 2011]. Online: http://www.missiology.org/new/wp-content/uploads/2011/ 01/Theo_contributions_of_sino _theo_to_the_global_chistian_comm_part_1_July_20001.pdf and "Critiquing."

[81] Wan, "Practical Contextualization," 18–19.

[82] Hannes Wiher, "Understanding Shame and Guilt as a Key to Cross-Cultural Ministry: An Elenctical Study" (PhD diss., Potchefstroom, South Africa: Potchefstroom University for Christian Higher Education, 2002).

[83] Christopher L. Flanders, "About Face: Reorienting Thai Face For Soteriology and Mission" (PhD diss., Pasadena, Calif.: Fuller Theological Seminary, 2005).

message and "face" oriented Thai.[84] Some see a similar need for a Muslim context.[85]

These proposals and critiques go far past a shift in verbal categories. They demand a very

different sort of biblical hermeneutic lens. There is no room here to review the various

articles on "de-westernizing" the gospel and the "releasing of the gospel from western

bondage."[86] Mark Harling suggests, "[T]heologies are bridges between the Bible and our

own cultures."[87] This perspective properly distinguishes theology and the Bible but

without using contextualization as a bridge between culture and a particular theology.

These observations yield a few conclusions. First, if missionaries initially assume

a "Western" gospel, they will tend to minimize other major biblical and human categories.

For instance, HS will be downplayed as mere anthropology or psychology, secondary to

the "real" problem of law and guilt.[88] Second, missionaries may draw upon these "other"

categories to build their theologies and gospel presentations. Scores of books, articles,

---

[84] Ibid., 39–66.

[85] Also, Grant DeVries, "Explaining the Atonement to the Arabic Muslim in terms of Honour and Shame: Potentials and Pitfalls," *St. Francis Magazine* 2, no. 4 (Mar 2007); Bruce Thomas, "The Gospel for Shame Cultures: A Paradigm Shift," *EMQ* (Jun 1994): 284–90; Boyle, "Communicating the Gospel in Terms of Shame"; Andrew M. Mbuvi, "African Theology from the Perspective of Honor and Shame," in *The Urban Face of Mission: Ministering the Gospel in a Diverse and Changing World* (ed. Manuel Ortiz and Susan S. Baker; Phillipsburg, N.J.: P & R Publishing, 2002), 279–95.

[86] Hans M. Weerstra, "De-Westernizing the Gospel The Recovery of a Biblical Worldview," *IJFM* 16, no. 3 (Fall 1999): 129–34; Jonathan Campbell, "Releasing the Gospel from Western Bondage," *IJFM* 16, no. 4 (Winter 2000): 167–71; Mark Harling, "De-westerning Doctrine and Developing Appropriate Theology in Missions," *IJFM* 22, no. 4 (Winter 2005): 159–66.

[87] Harling, "De-westernizing Doctrine," 163.

[88] Hesselgrave shows the complexity and disagreement surrounding the meaning and importance of guilt and shame. In the end, it still seems he sees shame and fear as mere entry points to arrive at the more fundamental issue of guilt. See his work, "Missionary Elenctics and Guilt and Shame," *Missiology* 11, no. 4 (Oct 1983): 461 83. Brad A. Binau's article compares the atonement with psychotherapy, so treating shame as a mere psychological issue. See Binau, "When Shame is The Question, How Does The Atonement Answer?"; Nancy R. Bowen treats honor and shame through the lenses of psychology, abuse, and healing from victimization. See her work, "Damage and Healing: Shame and Honor in the Old Testament," *Koinonia* 3, no. 1 (Spring 1991): 29–36. It appears that Alex Toorman, drawing upon anthropology, assumes that rendering the gospel in HS terms will inevitably amount to cultural relativism (which is in no way a necessary corollary). See his work, "Selfless Love: The Missing Middle in Honor/Shame Cultures," *EMQ* 47, no. 2 (Apr 2011): 160–67.

and essays establish the major *theological* role of honor, glory, and shame in Scripture.[89] The range of this literature sufficiently exemplifies a "contextualization that is comprehensive," per the multidimensional criteria set forth by Moreau.[90] Third, such HS contextualizations appear possible if law is not the precondition or foundation on which all else begins.

The HS theme is no mere husk for the kernel of guilt. *That one feels guilty but not ashamed for sin is no credit to a theological tradition.* It is insufficient for sinners simply to know their guilt. They must also sense the weight of shame proper to sin. The awareness of shame is not in itself atoning; rather it should spur repentance. If a person knows his or her shame before the King and Father, who is worthy of all honor, then repentance and conversion are anything but a mechanical decision to conform to a legal standard. Therefore, He Guanghu calls for openness: "We should not focus on a certain need at the expense of other needs. Neither should we meet the needs of a particular group of people at the expense of other groups."[91] He points out, "Setting aside the fact that [philosophical theology, moral theology, and cultural theology] are the legitimate

---

[89] Some helpful works include an excellent introductory essay from Jayson Georges, "From Shame to Honor: A Theological Reading of Romans for Honor-Shame Contexts," *Missiology* 38, no. 3 (Jun 2010): 295–307. Other prominent writers include David A. DeSilva, who demonstrates how these themes influence hermeneutics. See his work, *The Hope of Glory: Honor Discourse and New Testament Interpretation* (Collegeville, Minn.: Liturgical Press, 1999). Also, see his work, *An Introduction to the New Testament: Contexts, Methods, and Ministry* (Downers Grove, Ill.: IVP, 2004). He applies these insights in *Despising Shame: Honor Discourse and Community Maintenance in the Epistle to the Hebrews* (Revised ed.; Atlanta, Ga.: Society of Biblical Literature, 2008). Another well-regarded sample comes from Jerome H. Neyrey, *Honor and Shame in the Gospel of Matthew* (Louisville, Ky.: Westminster John Knox Press, 1998). Bruce Malina has produced many relevant works, including Bruce Malina, *The New Testament World: Insights from Cultural Anthropology* (3rd ed.; Atlanta, Ga.: John Knox, 2001).

[90] Scott Moreau, "Contextualization That Is Comprehensive," *Missiology* 34, no. 3 (Jun 2006): 325–35.

[91] Guanghu He, "A Methodology of and Approaches to Sino-Christian Theology," in *Sino-Christian Studies in China* (ed. Yang Huilin and Daniel H. N. Yeung; Newcastle, UK: Cambridge Scholars Publishing, 2006), 109. We should note that arguments for openness work both ways. Just as Chinese have much to learn from historical, Western theology, so westerners should avoid the "narrow-mindedness" that can make foreign missionaries resistant to what he calls an "inside-out" approach, in contrast to an "outside-in" translation (p. 114).

components of theology, the issues they deal with are actually those that capture the utmost concerns of the largest ethnic group in this world."[92] The latter observation compels one to wonder whether traditional, historical theologies largely reflect the "utmost concerns of the [most disproportionately powerful minority] ethnic group in this world." What does the gospel look like if the Bible is read with Chinese eyes?

Two problems persist in connecting contextualization and hermeneutics.[93] First, Christians have not sufficiently reckoned with the detrimental consequences of succumbing to the temptation of "assuming" the very gospel one is contextualizing. Second, there is a struggle to develop a contextually aware methodology that takes seriously biblical hermeneutics and theology while intentionally and explicitly accounting for the foreigner's own culture. While numerous authors rightly assess "the role of context in shaping theology,"[94] the conversation persists in dichotomizing Scripture and culture to the point that progress is nearly impossible. Perhaps, this dichotomy stems from the conflation of Scripture and theology, collapsing these two things into one. Instead, one best conceives of theology as Scriptural truth *in* culture, in much the same way we cannot separate the incarnation, parting the divine from human nature. Contextualization then is Scripture *in* (not "and") culture. This is Lesslie Newbigin's meaning when he declares, "We must start with the basic fact that there is no

---

[92] Ibid., 117.

[93] For survey on this connection, see Raymond Hundley, "Towards An Evangelical Theology of Contextualization" (PhD diss., Deerfield, Ill.: Trinity Evangelical Divinity School, 1993), 7–70. On p. 19, he points to Grant Osborne's comment: "In one sense contextualization could virtually be identified with hermeneutics, since the exposition of a text's meaning is also a 'contextualization' of its message." The quotation is from Grant Osborne, *The Hermeneutical Spiral: A Comprehensive Introduction to Biblical Interpretation* (2nd ed.; Downers Grove, Ill.: IVP, 2006), 544.

[94] An excellent survey on this point comes from Steve Strauss, "The Role of Context in Shaping Theology," in *Contextualization and Syncretism: Navigating Cultural Currents* (ed. Gailyn Van Rheenen; Pasadena, Calif.: William Carey Library, 2006), 99–128.

such thing as a pure gospel if by that is meant something which is not embodied in a culture."[95] Regarding "the matter of relating gospel and culture," he says the typical way of "dichotomizing [the two] reveals the dualism in our thinking . . . "; hence, "[w]e must recognize the falsity of this dualism and acknowledge the fact that there is not and cannot be a gospel which is not culturally embodied."[96] If this is true, initially assuming the gospel limits its relevance from the perspective of the local culture. A comprehensive contextualization comes out of one's interpretive lens, that is, a *worldview*, not simply by adapting forms to clothe a truth.

Other dangers emerge by constricting the gospel to a narrow set of texts, themes, or a single historical event. A "canon within a canon" can develop to the point that one's version of the gospel arbitrarily excludes Gal 3:8.[97] D. A. Carson is right that to properly contextualize is "to formulate a comprehensive theology . . . based on the whole Bible itself."[98] Pastorally, the gospel quickly gets reduced to news that individuals can be forgiven because of a past event, which makes the gospel seem only distantly relevant for the Christian life (i.e. post-conversion). The Christian life is lived out of a gratitude, or a "debtor's ethic," rather than by faith.[99] Theologically, the gospel slowly ceases to be the announcement that Jesus is the king who fulfills OT promises. A subtle and false division

---

[95] Lesslie Newbigin, *The Gospel in a Pluralist Society* (Grand Rapids, Mich.: Eerdmans, 1989), 144. Though not citing Newbigin, David Bosch concurs in *Transforming Mission*, 297.
[96] Newbigin, *The Gospel in a Pluralist Society*, 189.
[97] Galatians 3:8 says, "And the Scripture, foreseeing that God would justify the Gentiles by faith, preached the gospel beforehand to Abraham, saying, 'In you shall all the nations be blessed.'" Paul is quite explicit in calling the Abrahamic promise "gospel," yet despite this fact, this verse is regularly excluded from many, if not most, summaries and discussions of the gospel.
[98] D. A. Carson, "Reflections on Contextualization: A Critical Appraisal of Daniel Von Allmen's 'Birth of Theology'," *EAJET* 4, no. 1 (1984): 51. Cited by Hundley, "Towards," 68–69.
[99] See John Piper, *Future Grace* (Sisters, Ore.: Multnomah Press, 1995). By "debtor's ethic," he refers to the inclination or tendency of people to "obey Christ *out of gratitude*" as if "paying back" what God has done and thus "to nullify grace." The contrast is to glorify God by having "faith in future grace." See especially pp. 31–49.

between Jesus as Savior and Lord perpetuates a dualism between the so-called spiritual and material. Salvation becomes escapist if not individualistic. Contextually, the preconceived scope of the gospel determines the subject matter to be contextualized. Implicitly, one can talk about the legal transaction of a past event but make other issues, according to this logic, mere implications, application, or scriptural context for what is judged to be the core gospel. A cultural preference for a past forensic transaction can actually inhibit talk about themes that are important to non-Western hearers and are central, not peripheral, to the gospel. Such themes include the whole salvation narrative, covenant fulfillment (Gal 3:8; Acts 13:32–33) and the kingly reign of God in Christ (Isa 52:7; Rom 1:2–4; "gospel of the kingdom" language; 1 Cor 15:24–25, 54 expanding on vv. 1–8), the glory of God in Christ (2 Cor 4:4–6), the union of Jews and Gentiles in Christ (Eph 2:11–3:12), as well as the freedom to obey "from the heart" in all areas of life (Rom 6:17; cf. Ezek 36:26–27). Therefore, presuming the gospel may inherently undermine contextualization by restricting its immanence, relevance, demands, and intentions for groups and communities.

To discern the original meaning of a biblical author, interpreters must be careful not to set one culture-laden motif against another. Using HS as a central theme does not at all deny that the Bible makes legal, guilt-oriented claims. However, theologizing is shaped by "the problem of preunderstanding," the increased or decreased "awareness of aspects of the text," and the contextually influenced questions brought to a text.[100]

---

[100] Strauss, "Role of Context," 107–14.

32

Working cross-culturally complicates the process. Yet, Yeo rightly adds, "[A] cross-cultural reading is more objective than a monocultural reading of the biblical text."[101]

Foundational Principles and Perspectives on Contextualization

A person's view of contextualization follows from his or her doctrine of Scripture. If the gospel is an organizing principle within one's doctrine of Scripture, one will expect all texts to eventually lead to the gospel, even if it is articulated in untraditional ways.[102] A person, "for the sake of argument," sets aside preconceived notions to find where another perspective might lead. The limitations of any perspective create risk. Traditional conceptions of the gospel are no exception since these formulations may import unwarranted assumptions and emphases. Reading Scripture with Asian eyes may reveal some problems endemic to Western culture.

Second, a proper view of contextualization hinges upon one's principles of biblical interpretation. A basic goal of biblical interpretation is to find what a text says *without* assuming theological implications. Biblical interpreters attempt to maintain some measure of objectivity (even if imperfectly) in order to guard against importing errant notions into a text. Likewise, cross-cultural contextualizers can seek to interpret a text without prioritizing their own native cultural categories.

Third, one's perspective on theology shapes his or her approach to contextualization. This chapter concurs with Bevans, who says, "There is no such thing

---

[101] Yeo, *What Has Jerusalem?*, 5.

[102] Spurgeon's analogy is fitting: Just as all English roads lead to London, so one could preach Christ from any text. See Dennis E. Johnson, *Him We Proclaim: Preaching Christ From All the Scriptures* (Phillipsburg, N.J.: P & R Publishing, 2007), 15–16. He likens biblical interpretation to his grandmother's playing Chinese checkers. She always moved pieces directly from one end of the board to the other but without showing every jump. This is because "She had seen the pattern so clearly that she didn't need to set the marble down at every jump; but we needed to be shown step by step, jump by jump" (p. 134).

as 'theology'; there is only *contextualized* theology."[103] Bruce Nicholls says it differently: "It is now widely accepted that all theology, including biblical theology, is culturally conditioned and therefore in some sense relative. Theologizing is understood as a human fallible process, so that no theology is perfect or absolute."[104] Yet, if this is the case, one would expect more clamor among evangelicals about the value of the grammatical-historical method of exegesis, in fear that this might lead to syncretism *with Western culture*.[105] Bosch warns against

> . . . the danger of absolutism of contextualization . . . where theology, contextualized in the West, was in essence elevated to gospel status and exported to other continents as a package deal. Contextualization thus means universalizing one's own theological positions, making it applicable to everybody and demanding that others submit to it.[106]

Many who seek a contextualized gospel undermine it by implicitly holding strongly to a certain articulation of it.[107]

Contextualization methodology can temper *both* Western and non-Western influences by recognizing two principles. First, there is a difference between biblical truth and theological interpretation. Second, Scripture is relevant to all cultures and not restricted to any one pattern of thinking. If these two propositions are true, then it is

---

[103] Bevans, *Models of Contextual Theology*, 3. Similarly, see Bosch, *Transforming Mission*, 423.

[104] Bruce J. Nicholls, *Contextualization: A Theology of Gospel and Culture* (Vancouver, BC, Canada: Regent College, 2003), 25.

[105] The remark does *not* reject the grammatical-historical method of exegesis. Johnson's discussion is quite helpful in *Him We Proclaim*, 126–66. He remarks that the grammatical-historical method ". . . could also pose the danger of ignoring or devaluing essential contexts for the valid and complete interpretation of biblical passages. Specifically, we need to be critical enough to entertain the possibility that our discomfort with apostolic hermeneutics is a signal that grammatical-historical exegesis falls short if it leads us to exclude or ignore the redemptive historical setting of the fulfillment of God's covenantal relation to his people in Jesus the Messiah, as that setting appears in the documents of the New Testament, which completed the canon of the written Word of God" (p. 150).

[106] Bosch, *Transforming Mission*, 428.

[107] Flemming raise the question, "But could it be that *refusing* to contextualize the gospel poses an even *greater* risk of syncretism?" Dean Flemming, "Paul the Contextualizer," 18.

reasonable for people to exercise a degree of suspicion towards their own traditions. Accordingly, writers will question their assumptions and actively seek to intuit others' cultural sensibilities.[108] Tite Tienou writes, "Biblical writings do not teach us concepts of God; they show us how people encountered God, learned to know him and walked with him"; Vanhoozer adds, "In sum, the task of systematic theology is to train actors with good improvisatory judgment, actors who know what to say and do to perform and advance the gospel of Jesus Christ *in terms of their own cultural contexts*."[109] Since assumptions are unconscious, contextualization is less about a method than a mentality, empathizing with a local context and then finding affinity with the Scripture.

Contextualization as Interpretation

Contextualization is more interpretation than application. It is foremost to interpret Scripture in one context rather than another.[110] All interpretations use contextual vantage points. No one perspective can be absolutized so as to void other interpretations that use different worldview lenses. One's methodology should assist him to see the world *as the Scripture interprets the world*. When a Christian reads the Bible in other people's cultural language (i.e. their categories of thought), he gains a new capacity to hear the meaning of Scripture, no longer being content to settle on a single translation filtered by one's own

---

[108] Vanhoozer, "'One Rule'," 113. He compares contextualization to improvisation: "Good improvisers are trained to resist the temptation of preplanning, that is, of deciding what one will says and do before the scene begins." Also, "Memory is actually more foundational for improvisation than originality. An improviser seeks not to innovate but respond to the past . . . for the future is formed out of the past" (p. 114).

[109] Tite Tienou, "Biblical Foundations for African Theology," *Missiology* 10, no. 4 (Oct 1982): 441. Tienou's quotation and Vanhoozer's summary come from Vanhoozer, "'One Rule'," 121.

[110] Mikel Neumann is succinct on this point, "Contextualization begins with the interpreter understanding his or her culture." See his work, "Contextualization: Application or Interpretation" (Evangelical Theological Society papers; ETS-5017; Presented at the 50th National Conference of the Evangelical Theological Society, Orlando, Fla, 19–21 Nov 1998).

cultural grammar and character. *Perhaps, aspects of their culture more closely reflect the biblical context.* Will Western scholars intentionally facilitate global conversation with majority-world Christians, even expending energy to help the latter publish their own scholarly works? Vanhoozer warns, "Western theologians must be aware of the cultural beams in their own eyes before attempting to remove specks from non-Western eyes. It is ultimately for the sake of better biblical interpretation that Western theologians need to attend to how the Bible is being read and practiced in the non-Western world."[111]

Strauss, following Clifford Geertz and E. D. Hirsch, suggests that context and background shape the way people interpret both Scripture and culture; in effect, just as someone today is an outsider to the Scripture's culture yet ventures to understand and communicate its meaning, so also a foreigner in another country.[112] This raises the question as to who is the best person to initialize contextualization. Is it the missionary who has theological training or might it be local believers, who know their culture best but lack theological education? In either case, it is possible to "beg the question" by assuming a particular view of the gospel. While local Christians may read their culture's prominent religious beliefs into Scripture, the missionary may bring traditional gospel categories derived in part from his or her *historical* and cultural context.

It appears that dialogical contextualization initially requires a certain type of missionary. These missionaries best facilitate contextualization by personally seeking to internalize and appreciate the culture's thought forms, existential concerns, and social

---

[111] Vanhoozer, "'One Rule'," 116.
[112] Strauss, "Role of Context," 105–24. He cites Clifford Geertz, *Local Knowledge* (New York, N.Y.: Harper Collins, 1983); E. D. Hirsch, *Validity in Interpretation* (New Haven, Conn.: Yale, 1967). Strauss notes Acts 15 where the circumstances concerning the Gentiles enabled James to become "aware of the implications of Amos 9" (p. 114–15).

practices.[113] Local believers often lack the educational background to consider the historical contexts involved. Yet, the cross-cultural missionary who truly identifies with other people learns to question a myriad of assumptions. The quality of one's proposed contextualization depends on whether he or she *personally* identifies with that context.[114] This is more than superficial familiarity. Scholarly books catalyze integration and inquiry but do not replace thinking, feeling, and sensing as locals do. Being an outsider provides an invaluable measure of objectivity, which adds friction to resist the slide into syncretism. Therefore, the contextualization process is not merely about language learning, clothing, and strategy plans; rather, it stems from the very way a missionary embraces the culture and handles cultural shock and the conflicts that come with crossing cultures. It begins with a thousand small habits upon entering the new culture.

If missionaries are to contextualize theology in the way proposed in this chapter, it will be difficult to distinguish missiology from theology. An emphasis on theological method would entail studies in philosophy, worldview analysis, history, and the like. In this way, more missionaries would imitate the Apostle Paul, who wrote Romans in part for missiological reasons (cf. 1:14–15; 15:19–29). Yet, Romans is highly theological. As

---

[113] Zane Pratt identifies some common obstacles to contextualization, such as missionaries communicating too frequently with family and friends from their home country and focusing more on their team than nationals. See his unpublished paper "Biblical Foundations and Guidelines for Contextualization." We could well add the overuse of the Internet (Facebook, etc.), excessive time spent with family, and rarely eating local foods.

[114] Vanhoozer explores the potential of a post-Western theological method. He writes, "Theology in an era of world Christianity is still hermeneutical, but hermeneutics now means not 'rules for interpretation' but 'reading from one's lived experience.'" See his essay, "'One Rule'," 94.

a missionary, Paul wrote letters of theology. On the other hand, people should study theology to become missionaries.[115]

A contextualization that is comprehensive speaks from a worldview, entailing a metanarrative that frequently resists rigid systematization.[116] Worldviews have countless assumptions that are confronted by the realities of daily life. Therefore, if the gospel is to reshape people's worldviews forever, a "comprehensive" approach will rely more on biblical theology[117] than formulaic bridges and single-issue contextualizations.[118] The biblical narrative, like any story, contests assumptions in surprising yet systemic ways. Therefore, the evangelistic method Creation-to-Christ (C2C) was formed on a good premise; however, it falters in its one-size-fits-all understanding of sacrifice, as if biblical systems of sacrifice match those types of sacrifice found in countless people groups. Another weakness is its being taught via rote memory. Also, C2C rests on a particular theme that arguably does not well integrate with the rest of normal life. Consequently, the C2C methodology lacks contextual flexibility, both cultural and biblical.

---

[115] John Piper, "The Revelation of God's Righteousness Where There Is No Church," *Desiring God*, 7 Nov 1999, [cited 29 Jun 2012]. Online: http://www.desiringgod.org/resource-library/sermons/the-revelation-of-gods-righteousness-where-there-is-no-church.

[116] On the importance of the gospel's transforming worldviews, see Paul Hiebert, *Transforming Worldviews: An Anthropological Understanding of How People Change* (Grand Rapids, Mich.: Baker, 2008). He rightly notes, "[I]f the worldview is not transformed, in the long run the gospel is subverted and the result is a syncretistic Christo-paganism, which has the form of Christianity but not its essence" (p. 11). Concerning a lack of contextualization, Flemming warns, "Ironically, a gospel that neglects such worldview issues may unwittingly end up promoting syncretism instead of preventing it." See his work, "Paul the Contextualizer," 19.

[117] Harley Talman, "Islam, Once a Hopeless Frontier, Now? Comprehensive Contextualization," *IJFM* 21, no. 1 (Spring 2004): 11.

[118] Yang Huilin suggests that Chinese Buddhism flourished in China whereas Christianity did not because Christians employed "adaptation" while Buddhism used "inculturation." In the terms used in this essay, "adaption" may be likened with communication, and "inculturation" with "contextualization." The distinctives between Buddhism and Christianity mean the comparison has limits, yet his observation deserves further reflection in order for Christians to discern any possible lessons to be learned. See his work, "Inculturation or Contextualization: Interpretation of Christianity in the Context of Chinese Christianity," in *Sino-Christian Studies in China* (ed. Yang Huilin and Daniel H. N. Yeung; Newcastle, UK: Cambridge Scholars Publishing, 2006), 152. His distinction between "inculturation" and "contextualization" (p. 159) is subtle and unimportant for the present point.

Summary

The gospel suggests a worldview that critiques traditional theological assumptions that undermine contextualization efforts and constrict the biblical witness. Humility demands that one listen to Christians outside one's own culture. These Christians offer fresh theological perspective. Missionaries must become proficient theologians, since contextualization is basically a work of interpretation and incarnation rather than mere application, communication, or translation. Flemming captures a key idea of this chapter:

> There is still a risk that attempts at doing contextual theology will result in something other than a genuine representation of the gospel. Indeed, it might be "safer" to resist diversity altogether—to simply memorize and recycle specific formulations of Christian doctrine that were developed for another time and place. We might even be tempted to think that our tried and true ways of telling the story are timeless expressions of the "pure" gospel. But we would only be fooling ourselves. *All* theology is *contextual* theology, from the creeds of the early church to the modern "Four Spiritual Laws."[119]

Numerous roadblocks to contextualized theologies are easily removed if one guards against prematurely assuming the gospel and so begging the question.

A Method of Contextualization: Using Culture to Interpret Scripture

A contextualized theology assumes both a worldview and a biblical theology. Contextualization interprets both a text and a context. A faithful treatment of Scripture requires missiologists to respect the author's meaning in its original context. Contextualization is a creative interaction, a dialogue[120] demanding labor and compromise. A contextualized theology struggles to reconcile the tensions that exist

---

[119] Flemming, *Contextualization*, 298. Emphasis in original.
[120] Clark, *To Know and Love God*, 113–22.

between theology and the social sciences, such as anthropology, psychology, or philosophy. In the process, missiologists cannot assume their own worldview is entirely biblical. One's experiences inevitably influence his or her interpretations. Thus, this section puts forth a method to guide our *theological* contextualization efforts.[121] Specifically, it demonstrates how one can use culture to formulate a biblical theology that speaks to the worldview of a context while still remaining faithful to biblical truth.

Contextualization attempts could easily be ruined by superficiality. They can be too weighted towards traditional (Western) theologies or the contemporary culture. Using local terminology may mask the fact that there is nothing particular to the local culture in the prescribed theology. On the other hand, missionaries may use local literature and customs to highlight important religious concepts yet hardly compare local assumptions and values with the Bible.[122]

Vanhoozer concisely defines culture as "everything that humans do voluntarily as opposed to involuntarily (e.g., by nature, reflex, or instinct)."[123] Paul Hiebert explains it as "the more or less integrated system of ideas, feelings, and values and their associated patterns of behavior and product shared by a group of people who organize and regulate what they think, feel, and do."[124] Individuals may come from a number of subcultures, be it our ethnicity, our country, a family, or even a church culture. One's culture(s) shape(s)

---

[121] I am distinguishing this from applied contextualization, which focuses on practice (what we *do* as opposed to what we teach or believe). Although it is impossible to ultimately separate the two, it is feasible to articulate truths propositionally or narratively, irrespective of particular methods and practices.

[122] Famously, Matteo Ricci and other Jesuits permitted sacrifice to ancestors. See Hwa Yung, *Mangoes or Bananas: The Quest for an Authentic Asian Christian Theology* (2nd ed.; Eugene, Ore.: Wipf & Stock, 2008), 126–28.

[123] Vanhoozer, *Everyday Theology*, 21.

[124] Hiebert, *Anthropological Insights*, 30.

the worldview lens through which he or she interprets the world.[125] A worldview generates meaning and is embodied in "cultural texts" (such as art, movies, books, and architecture), thus giving a "sense of direction."[126] Cultures and worldviews are complex. Vanhoozer explains, "Cultural texts offer us either narrative or bits of narrative that provide us with various 'schemas'—storied frameworks—with which to make sense of everyday life."[127]

Towards a Method: Exegeting the Word and the World

Why does contextual theology assume a biblical theology?[128] Every theologian, missiologist, reader, and listener has a worldview that makes certain theological claims. They may not be explicit, but they nevertheless exist. As Tillich puts it, every culture has a great anxiety and a great hope.[129] Worldviews (thus theologies) are not reductionistic; they tell stories, answer basic questions about existence, use symbols, and suggest praxis.[130] They are integrated wholes, mysterious even to those who hold them. Lifetimes are spent searching out the implications of our systems, practices, values, and assumptions. Someone might disagree by saying that contextualized theologies can be narrowly focused tools and that forming entire biblical theologies is superfluous. Yet,

---

[125] Hesselgrave and Rommen, *Contextualization*, 212.

[126] Vanhoozer, *Everyday Theology*, 26–36.

[127] Ibid., 51.

[128] "Biblical theology" refers to the discipline wherein one interprets Scripture as a unified whole, in keeping with the authors' original meaning according to the categories and themes most prominent in the Bible. For a helpful discussion on Biblical theology in the life of the church, see Michael Lawrence, *Biblical Theology in the Life of the Church: A Guide for Ministry* (Wheaton, Ill.: Crossway, 2010).

[129] Cited in Vanhoozer, *Everyday Theology*, 19. Paul Tillich discusses this more fully in his *Dynamics of Faith* (New York, N.Y.: Harper and Row: 1957); See also his work *Courage to Be* (New Haven, Conn.: Yale, 1952).

[130] N. T. Wright, *The New Testament and the People of God* (Atlanta, Ga.: Augsburg Fortress, 1992), 123–24. Connecting worldview and theology, especially see chapters 2, 3, 5, 12–14.

consider what happens when the missionary asserts some view on the nature of evangelism, eschatology, or the church, yet refrains from speaking about other things, like the role of a pastor, Christian parenting, studying the Bible, the atonement, obedience, and missions. Silence then becomes the Trojan horse where culture imports meaning, values, and practice. Human beings demand answers to life questions. A myriad of life experiences push a person towards one conclusion over another, whether consciously or unconsciously. Inevitably, if not informed by a holistic biblical theology, many will simply default to the prevailing cultural norms. As Vanhoozer aptly writes, "We don't simply read cultural texts but we read through them. In short: the cultural texts we love best come to serve as the lens through which we view everything else and as the compass that orients us towards the goal."[131]

Contextualizations are inadequate if they limit themselves to using analogies.[132] For example, if one preached to people on a small ocean island, it would be biblical to speak of Jesus as the one who walks on water or the God who parts water; however, it only addresses one aspect of their thinking, not the whole of their worldview, i.e. their values, family, view of time, metaphysics, ethics.[133] If contextualization is constantly done by mere analogy, one can implicitly communicate two things: (1) the only thing that matters in the Bible is the information it takes to "get saved," thus short-circuiting genuine conversion and Christian growth, (2) the entire Bible is neither very important

---

[131] Ibid., 36.

[132] I am referring to things like Don Richardson's *Peace Child* or the *Four Spiritual Laws*. Although these can be helpful tools for evangelism, they are limited in their ability to transform one's entire worldview. They are too narrow in scope to be considered full contextualizations.

[133] For a flawed attempt at contextualization. See Yeo, *Musing*. He ignores the fact that Confucius and Paul come from far different views of God and *tian* (heaven). He even admits this difference leads to very different understandings on morality and human nature.

nor essential, thus implying that the revelation of God's glory is not infinitely valuable. When we reduce the gospel to less than a coherent story of God's work in human history, Flemming warns, "[I]t is hard to avoid remaking the gospel in line with our own cultural and doctrinal biases."[134] By contrast, the desired goal is *worldview conversion*—how people see the world, what they value, their thought categories and ways of living. All people participate in one of two cultures—either a gospel culture or the culture of a fallen world. Christian conversion entails one's transformation and entrance into a gospel culture and worldview.

Contextualization emerges from the interaction of diverse worldviews. Missiologists exegete the multiple cultural worlds found in Scripture. In addition, they strive to see the world from the perspective of neighbors. In short, "Christians must learn to read the Bible and cultures alike."[135] This inevitably forces people to examine their own cultural influences. They always bring a theological worldview to the task of contextualization, interpreting both the contemporary context and the diverse historical settings of Scripture. One's personal point of view influences his or her hermeneutics, communication, and theology. Contextualization is not a monologue.

To illustrate the complexity of contextualization, consider what constitutes the most basic unit of human identity. Is it the individual or the family? Even this choice of answers presumes a standard—size—answering the question of what is the smallest social unit of identification. However, what if by "basic," one means most important or essential? Then, a person might say their ethnicity or nationality is most basic. Others

---

[134] Flemming, *Contextualization*, 301.
[135] Ibid., 35.

might locate identity in an ideology or in what they do. Thus, for them, most fundamental to the human identity is their vocation or what they believe. How one categorizes human society and identity influence his or her *theological* categories. These starting points and guiding principles lead the interpreter to notice some details in Scripture while dismissing others. Consider a very common way of discussing biblical theology, via creation, fall, redemption, consummation. Arguably, this division uses soteriology and puts greatest emphasis on humanity's role. That is, being "man-oriented" tells the biblical story from mankind's perspective—being created, sinning, being redeemed, and being with God forever.[136] What if the story were told from the perspective of what God does? Though there is overlap, there may well be distinguishing emphases. Perhaps, the story could be retold as: God created. God entered into covenant. God incarnated in Christ. God commissions his Church to glorify him among the nations.

Personal backgrounds influence how people contextualize the gospel. In *Contextualization*, Hesselgrave and Rommen offer examples of contextualization from around the world.[137] Certain patterns emerge. Euro-American approaches spawn from contemporary issues, such as economics or politics, whereas the more ancient civilizations, like Asia, Africa, and the Middle East, base their theologies on their own historical philosophies and culture. The same thing happens in theology. In *Created in God's Image*, Anthony Hoekema reviews numerous interpretations of the phrase "image

---

[136] To be clear, the phrase "man-oriented" is in no way pejorative. Certainly, rendering the biblical narrative in terms of "creation, fall, redemption, consummation" is biblical. However, the perspective one uses to tell the story tends to highlight different things. One tells a story differently in order to make different emphasis. Many who use the markers "creation, fall, redemption, consummation" are indeed God-centered. The term here makes a *narrative* point. By analogy, a sentence directs attention to its subject. Yet, passive sentences have the implied subjects, which minimizes or ignores the actor in the sentence. Thus, the sentence "Humans were created" is accurate but does not highlight the fact that *God* created.

[137] Hesselgrave and Rommen, *Contextualization*, 197–257.

of God." One notices how Greek philosophy influenced the early church fathers and

Aquinas; existentialism shaped Barth, and modern rationalism directed Emil Brunner's

analysis.[138] Each man's historical setting influenced his reading of Scripture and the

world. This raises a question, "What do *we* bring to the text?" Readers come with

questions arising from and related to the world as they see it. These questions by

definition are limited by our own social context. Worldviews shape theology. This

dynamic has been noticed by Asian Christians, who accuse Western theology of

embracing the Enlightenment's "anthropocentric rationalism and narrow empiricism."[139]

A multidisciplinary approach keeps in check the competing voices that influence

contextualization. Vanhoozer concurs, "Everyday theology is faith seeking nonreductive

understanding. Understanding is not served by simplistic theories that account for

everything in culture in terms of one factor only, whether the factor be sin, technology, or

economics."[140] One question often has many answers. A multidisciplinary approach deals

with a contemporary, collective worldview (culture) *and* a biblical-historical set of

worldviews (Scripture). Politics, religion, economics, medicine, art, and psychology all

influence and produce "cultural texts." To understand both the Bible and the present

context, other disciplines need to be heard, even if one rejects their theories. An array of

views serves as initial hypotheses for selected missiological and theological problems.

Theology is distinct from Scripture itself. Theology implies an interpreter or a

storyteller. It is impossible to escape from theology into unmitigated truth. Theology and

absolute biblical truth are not identical. Theology "is not itself proclamation of the

---

[138] Anthony Hoekema, *Created in God's Image* (Grand Rapids, Mich.: Eerdmans, 1986), 33–58.
[139] Yung, *Mangoes or Bananas*, 4.
[140] Vanhoozer, *Everyday Theology*, 45.

message, but reflection on that message and on its proclamation."[141] Clark adds that theology is a "second-order discipline," which discusses beliefs coming out of our experience in the form of interpretations and applications. As a result, we have to clarify "the difference between direct expressions of the Bible and our interpretations of those expressions."[142] Hwa Yung asserts that many missionaries have assumed Western theology is ". . . absolutely true. Since other religions and cultures were at best partial reflections of the truth, the task of missionaries was merely to implant the same theology unchanged in the mission fields."[143] Western theology does not exhaust biblical truth. Differences in theology are often differences in emphasis. It is plausible that contrasting emphases derive more from culture than from Scripture. Newbigin shares a similar concern, "We must always be ready to recognize that we have misrepresented the intention of Jesus because of our own self interests."[144] Jenkins comments, "Many of the contrasts [between religious faiths] reflect the cultures in which the two religions exist, rather than intrinsic qualities of the faiths themselves."[145] A dose of critical realism is needed so as to make "a distinction between reality and our knowledge of it."[146] There are always traces of culture in one's theology.

How Culture Leads the Conversation

How does one stay faithful to the Bible while still respecting the unique contemporary context to which it speaks? Hiebert's "critical contextualization" tries to bring together

---

[141] Bosch, *Transforming Mission*, 298.
[142] Clark, *To Know and Love God*, 88–89.
[143] Yung, *Mangoes or Bananas*, 63–64.
[144] Newbigin, *The Gospel in a Pluralist Society*, 152.
[145] Jenkins, *The New Faces of Christianity*, 182.
[146] Paul Hiebert, *Anthropological Reflections on Missiological Issues* (Grand Rapids, Mich.: Baker, 1994), 25.

culture and Scripture. In step one, the missionary learns the local culture, discovering its values, practices, and ways of thinking. Second, he exegetes the Bible, hoping to grasp its meaning and relate it to the culture's most prominent features. Finally, local people evaluate their customs and beliefs in light of Scripture. The community decides what to change and what remains the same. An outside missionary often leads this process.[147] His proposal improves upon other methods. It balances and integrates both text and context, giving Scripture an authoritative place. Yet, it masks a commonly overlooked problem. It does not distinguish between biblical truth and theology. There is no humble critique of the missionary's own theology. Yung warns, "[W]e need to guard against 'the danger of absolutism of contextualism' . . . This was the problem of Western theology in the past wherein Western theological formulations were elevated to the status of absolute divine truth before which all other peoples and cultures must bow."[148] In Hiebert's method, all improvements move from Scripture to culture. This is not true dialogue. Clark commends a "dialogical model," whereby the Bible spurs a *mutual* dialogue between theology and culture. He says, "Not only does the Scripture correct the culture's questions, but a new contextualized theology may correct blind spots in the theology that theologians initially produce."[149] Practically, what does this look like?

If contextualization is really going to be a dialogue between culture and Scripture, a few intentional steps are required. Implementing these steps requires humility, courage, and curiosity. A person will at times risk sounding unorthodox. The first step is simply asking where do culture and theology agree. Second, on what do they disagree? What

---

[147] Ibid., 88–91. For a more extensive treatment, see his work, *Anthropological Insights*, 171–92.
[148] Yung, *Mangoes or Bananas*, 63. He cites Bosch, *Transforming Mission*, 428.
[149] Clark, *To Know and Love God*, 119.

does each contribute? For many, this stage may be uncomfortable. Finally, these findings are synthesized into a contextualized theology.

The first step to doing theology cross-culturally is finding common ground. This step has two parts. Charles Anderson and Michael Sleasman give useful suggestions.[150] In the first part, one dissects culture, seeking to understand its values, customs, and patterns of thinking. A person looks for the significance of various cultural texts, refraining from quick judgments or reductionism. Next, one turns to "look at how the text or trend interacts with our world," trying to find the influences that lie behind the cultural text or characteristic.[151] It is helpful at this point to utilize the research of social sciences. Articles, interviews, books, site visits, and the Internet contribute to forming a broader, more holistic view of the culture. Anthropological work sheds light on one's worldviews and assumptions, typically suggesting categories and concepts never before considered.[152] Although social sciences can "distort our vision by defining the categories, the logic and the theories we use to analyze human realities,"[153] nevertheless, "[c]orrectly categorizing a cultural work may point to the right biblical points of contact."[154]

Secondly, finding common ground requires simply knowing the Bible well. Contextualization requires a robust theology. Good missiologists will be good

---

[150] Charles A. Anderson and Michael J. Sleasman, "Putting into Practice: Weddings for Everyday Theologians," in *Everyday Theology: How to Read Cultural Texts and Interpret Trends* (ed. Kevin Vanhoozer; Grand Rapids, Mich.: Baker Academic, 2007), 229–44.

[151] Ibid., 236.

[152] One such example for Americans is Edward C. Stewart, *American Cultural Patterns: A Cross-Cultural Perspective* (Yarmouth, Maine: Intercultural Press, 1972). For Chinese culture, a few summary works include *An Introduction to the Mainland Chinese Soul* (Raleigh, N.C.: LEAD Consulting, 2001). Also, Wenzhong Hu and Cornelius Lee Grove, *Encountering the Chinese: A Guide for Americans* (Yarmouth, Maine: Intercultural Press, 1991).

[153] Paul Hiebert, "The Social Sciences and Missions: Applying the Message," in *Missiology and the Social Sciences: Contributions, Cautions, and Conclusions* (ed. Gary Corwin and Edward Rommen; Pasadena, Calif.: William Carey Library, 1996), 204.

[154] Anderson and Sleasman, "Putting into Practice," 238.

theologians. At a minimum, this demands constant, thorough reading and reflection of the full canon of Scripture. This includes reading theological works outside of one's faith tradition. In a day when so many academics are specialists, the missiologist needs to be a generalist, conversant in a range of topics, rarely specializing in just one field. The missiologist will integrate biblical, systematic, and historical theology. Imagine, for instance, one attempts a theological contextualization leading to a study of the doctrine of atonement. He or she needs to ask how that topic relates to other biblical motifs. One uses a theological dictionary, lexicons, concordances, bibliographies and footnotes to begin this search. Thus, a word search on "weddings" brings up other issues like marriage, sex, divorce, covenant, headship, and money.[155] Worldviews and theologies are complex, having countless interlinked pieces. This reality affects how one understands cultures and the people of the Bible. A working knowledge of the biblical languages and ancient near eastern culture is gained in order to properly exegete biblical texts and form coherent theologies. Accordingly, one can better discern error, appropriate truth, and guard against eisegesis, whereby the interpreter interjects himself or ideas foreign to the original context in order to create or defend his own non-biblical theology.[156]

In the second step, dialogical contextualization finds how one's theology contrasts with that of the local culture. An individual's theology may stress various concerns and categories of thought that are generally underappreciated by the surrounding culture. How does one choose which themes will more strongly affect contextualization? A

---

[155] Ibid., 238–39.

[156] Otherwise, we may go the way of K. K. Yeo who says, "Paul needs Confucius. Christianity needs China . . . insofar as [Chinese-Christian] identity brings the best of the Confucian tradition into the Christian story it will help revivify Christianity and compensate for biases in the western-dominated Christian self-understanding." Yeo's contextualization abandons orthodoxy because he ignores basic hermeneutic principles, barely interacts with the broader canon, and gives no defense for his theology against the vast majority of Christian writers. See Yeo, *Musing*, 431–32.

survey of contextualization literature shows a tendency to pick one over the other. A Christian may affirm the authoritative supremacy of Scripture over culture; yet, a proper doctrine of the Bible does not always ensure good missiology.[157] Theology is not equivalent to biblical truth (i.e. full revelation of all truth) because the former reflects an interpretation of the Bible, influenced by culture, bias, desires, and knowledge. While one can know much truth, no one can presume to grasp it all. Humility requires people to be open to hear what the culture is saying.

Clark rightly suggests, "Questions from cultures that have not dominated the theological world can open up new and creative lines of sight by which to criticize the categories of traditional theologies."[158] He adds, "[N]onstandard readings suggested by non-Western cultures may—I do not say *will*, but *may*—turn out to be better interpretations."[159] To admit that one's theology does not contain the whole of biblical theology concedes the possibility that culture may contain biblical truths that have been neglected or ignored. Culture can highlight truths overlooked by individual theologies. Kraft writes, "We have continually reverted to the assumption that becoming Christians means becoming like us culturally."[160]

If we are not careful, we will make a similar mistake with respect to *theology*. Robertson McQuilkin adds, "Cultural anthropology can be a missionary's best friend in opening his eyes to biblical norms he had never considered, so that he can communicate

---

[157] On the tendency to absolutize local theology, see Yung, *Mangoes or Bananas*, 63–64.
[158] Clark, *To Know and Love God*, 118.
[159] Ibid., 118. Emphasis in original.
[160] Kraft, "Culture, Worldview, and Contextualization," 384.

cross-culturally more effectively."[161] Listening to other cultures gives a fresh appreciation for potentially ignored passages or genres of Scripture, like genealogies, law, narrative, and the wisdom literature.[162] Correctives are often needed. For example, "The communal understanding of freedom in Chinese Christian theology challenges the individualistic understanding of freedom in the West as centering in personal rights and in self-service that easily ends up in self-absorption."[163] Even if people admit that worldviews are limited and that no one has perfect theology, the failure to systematically account for those errors can be fatal.

Faithful contextualization necessarily challenges and reorients prevailing worldviews. Newbigin correctly prioritizes Scripture,

> [A]uthentic Christian thought and action begin not by attending to the aspirations of the people, not by answering the questions they are asking in their terms, not by offering solutions to the problems as the world sees them. It must begin and continue by attending to what God has done in the story of Israel and supremely in the story of Jesus Christ.[164]

Accordingly, Anderson and Sleasman tell us to find out where the contextual texts and trends fit within the "story of redemption."[165] First, we try to identify "signs of creation," which are those aspects that reflect the goodness of God's creation and ultimately of God himself. Second, what cultural distinctives are "signs of the fall?" These may not be things that are inherently evil; instead, they may have become idols—good things treated as best things (e.g., one can love money, pleasure, and convenience more than God).

---

[161] Robertson McQuilkin, "Use and Misuse of the Social Sciences: Interpreting the Biblical Text," in *Missiology and the Social Sciences: Contributions, Cautions, and Conclusions* (ed. Edward Rommen and Gary Corwin; Pasadena, Calif.: William Carey Library, 1996), 169.

[162] Hiebert rightly reminds that the Holy Spirit resides in all Christians and so the priesthood of believers applies not only to individuals but to churches. See Hiebert, *Anthropological Reflections*, 91–103.

[163] Yeo, *Musing*, 430.

[164] Newbigin, *The Gospel in a Pluralist Society*, 151.

[165] Anderson and Sleasman, "Putting into Practice," 240–42.

51

Third, we must use some "imagination" to "identify the theological root error." In other words, what kind of alternative gospel is being told in the local context? How does this "gospel" describe an idealized reality, the basic human problem, the means for deliverance from that problem, and the hope to live for?[166] Contextualization involves retelling the *cultural* story in a way that illuminates the *gospel* story. Since God created the world, sustains the world, came into the world, offers salvation to the world, and judges the world, it is right to say biblical theology touches all aspects of life. A "society never existed, in East or West, ancient time or modern, which could absorb the word of Christ painlessly into its system."[167] Yet, in a *biblically* faithful contextualization, very little that is said will truly be unfamiliar. Anyone should be able to see it within the Bible itself. On the other hand, a contextualized theology will be provocative, shifting emphases and questioning priorities.

The final step in implementing a dialogical model is contextualization itself. This is a shift from analysis to synthesis. Figure 1 illustrates the process.[168] Culture and theology are in constant conversation. Newbigin plainly asserts, "We must start with the basic fact that there is no such thing as a pure gospel if by that is meant something which is not embodied in a culture."[169] Areas 3 and 4 represent matters of agreement between theology and culture. This may include the importance of family and learning. However, to distinguish theology from complete biblical truth suggests there are areas where one's

---

[166] False gospels with "functional saviors" are discussed in Mark Driscoll and Gerry Breshears, *Doctrine: What Christians Should Believe* (Wheaton, Ill: Crossway, 2011), 112, 369, 448.

[167] Yung, *Mangoes or Bananas*, 63. He cites Andrew Walls, "The Gospel as the Prisoner and Liberator of Culture," *Missionalia* 10, no. 3 (1982): 99.

[168] Note how this differs from Paul Hiebert's proposed model in which culture and Bible are separated, with theology as the intermediary. In his diagram, there is not a place for culture and Bible to overlap apart from one's theological position. See figure 2.4 in Hiebert, *Anthropological Reflections*, 47.

[169] Newbigin, *The Gospel in a Pluralist Society*, 144.

theology agrees with the prevailing culture in an unbiblical way (area 4). Everyone has

blind spots. Of course, there are biblical truths that no culture or individual gets right.

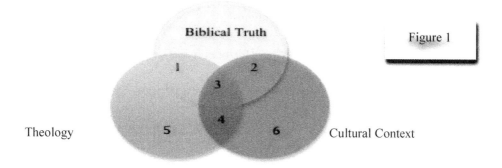

More difficult to deal with are areas 1 and 2. In area 1, one's theology is correct,

but a culture rejects the truth. In area 2, the culture has accepted biblical categories and

values (perhaps unknowingly). General revelation makes this possible. Nevertheless, the

temptation remains for missionaries to reject the culture and press hard the truths

expressed in area 1 or 5 (where one's theology is neither biblical nor intersects the local

culture). He or she might not reject the categories (of area 2) themselves as unbiblical.

For example, personal bias may cause him or her to deny uncritically the legitimacy of

the culture's insights. Consequently, that person runs the risk of contextualizing

something that is already contextualized (i.e. one's own theology).[170] *All* theologies are

contextualized to address the categories and questions of people in real situations. Clark

rightly highlights that people often distinguish so-called "theology" and "African or

Asian theology."[171] When talking about North American and European theology, one

tends to drop the adjective, simply calling it "theology." Yet, Bosch notes many instances

---

[170] Bosch, *Transforming Mission*, 428.
[171] Clark, *To Know and Love God*, 120–21.

where culture and context forever shaped Western theology.[172] Therefore, when Christians give ear to a culture, they avoid the naïve assumption that one can go directly from Scripture to application. This is because ". . . cultural perspectives guide the reasoning process by raising questions. But because the Bible is ultimate, we continually ask it to refine and judge all viewpoints."[173] From a Chinese perspective, Western theologians under-stress biblical ideas such as HS, group-identity, idolatry, and familial piety. What other theological truths go unnoticed by neglecting these vital motifs?

Contextualization is not only necessary and strategic; it is inevitable. As Clark states, "[T]he idea that one can achieve an acultural theology [is a] 'fundamental fallacy.'"[174] A person can have convictions about what is true theology and yet remain teachable or "quick to hear" (Jas 1:19). If contextualizers do not learn from the culture, then they should question the quality of their contextualization. Likewise, if the biblical narrative does not challenge the culture, one is not preaching the gospel truth.

Contextualization reverses the hermeneutical order. Normally, one first asks, "What does the Bible say?" Then, moving from text to life, "How does this apply to life?" In contextualization, one first seeks to understand people within their particular cultural context in order to appreciate their ways of thinking. What questions do they bring to the Bible and through what thought categories do they read Scripture? What are the culture's values, problems, and assumptions? Of course, Scripture may assert itself in

---

[172] See Bosch, *Transforming Mission*, 267–74 for a discussion on the Enlightenment's influence on theology. He also explores various points where individualism and anthropocentrism crept into Western theology. See pp. 216, 241–42, 267, 273, 289.

[173] Clark, *To Know and Love God*, 122.

[174] Ibid., 50. He credits this term to Richard Lints, *The Fabric of Theology* (Grand Rapids, Mich: Eerdmans, 1993), 8.

this self-discovery process. Nevertheless, this first phase is followed by a rigorous inquiry of Scripture, "What does the Bible say about these ideas, goals, systems, and ways of living?" Only then is one equipped to answer the relevant issues of a given context. An analysis of culture opens eyes to biblical concepts and insights previously unremarkable because one has been asking different questions or simply is not accustomed to certain patterns of thought.[175] For example, Western theology highlights the *legal* aspects of the atonement and justification. This language is biblical, but it is only one way Scripture depicts the work of salvation.

Imagine coming to the Bible with Eastern eyes. One reads the language of law, transgression, and judgment; yet for some reason, it sounds a bit distant and lacks the appropriate force on the conscience. For some people, other categories of thoughts and speech are common. In an Eastern context, the questions reflected on usually relate to reputation (saving, gaining, and losing face), group identity (whether ethnic or familial), and proper relationship (hierarchy, harmony, and roles). Therefore, one quickly notices the Bible's language about HS, group excommunication, and hierarchy. Such passages by definition are biblical. These are simply different ways of expressing who God is, the nature of human society, the purpose and problems of life, and the dynamics of salvation. Westerners may be tempted to read past such diction because it is foreign to their contemporary setting. Western politics, philosophies, and values emphasize individual autonomy and self-sufficiency. From that perspective, it is easy to disregard or minimize

---

[175] This is essentially the point Andrew Walls makes as he describes the expansion of Christianity into non-Western contexts: "Christian theology is expanding as it comes into contact with new areas of human experience, new accumulations of knowledge, relationship, and activity. Themes are being recognized in the Scriptures that the West had never noticed." See Andrew Walls, *The Cross-Cultural Process in Christian History* (Maryknoll, N.Y.: Orbis, 2002), 46. See also pp. 80–81.

group identity and loyalty. Jenkins argues that those in the "global South" may actually identify with the early church better than Western Christians, resulting in greater sensitivity to Biblical teaching. Many Africans greatly appreciate the supernatural and sacrificial elements of Scripture. The Gospels challenge India's caste system. James or Revelation, in particular, can capture the attention of the Third World poor.[176]

Starting with the social context does not necessitate a move towards relativism or biblical liberalism. First of all, the Bible may inspire a number of critiques and observations about the status quo. The Bible initiates and fuels the dialogue. Second, beginning with our present context aims simply at exposing reality, that is, the state of our thinking and relating. All too often, one is ignorant to the consequences of his or her assumptions and actions. As present realities and Scripture converse, blind spots are exposed. To use a medical analogy, one starts by looking at a person's body not an anatomy textbook. Third, it is worthy to note, "even the original designations [for the word 'God', *elohim* and *theos*] themselves were preexisting terms."[177] Finally, the ultimate question is never "What does culture want?" Instead, it is "What does the Bible say?" Scripture has primacy. The Bible judges theology and practice.

Order is key to contextualization. In what order does one ask questions? If people proceed from Bible to context, they naturally assume pre-set categories and may overlook an array of biblical concepts and meaning. Postmodern thinking has helped the church by raising awareness to the role of the reader in the act of hermeneutics. Readers bring assumptions and values to their task, either helping or hindering a faithful rendering or

---

[176] Jenkins, *The New Faces of Christianity*, 178–93.
[177] J. Nelson Jennings, "A Missional Theology of the Glory of God," in *The Glory of God* (ed. Christopher Morgan and Robert A. Peterson; Wheaton, Ill.: Crossway, 2010), 215.

application of a text. If readers *first* consciously analyze their context, they can make explicit what is implicit to their own verbiage and values. In this way, one gains fresh eyes to see in Scripture what is there but previously seemed merely to be style or nuance.

What must a person practically do to hold biases in check? The missionary must so identify with local people, personally and academically, that he or she genuinely begins to think their thoughts and feel their desires after them. Within a "personal" relationship, there is a sense of understanding, affection, respect, sympathy, and nearness. On the other hand, "academic" or theoretical knowledge about the local people is beneficial in giving broad descriptions and generalizations about culture. For example, Chinese tend to value hierarchy, harmony, and honor. Westerners tend to be more individualistic, seek efficiency, and value critical thinking. These broad insights direct curiosity, helping us to ask better questions and make particular observations. They suggest initial hypotheses to be tested within the real world among real people. These starting points are largely abstractions and so locals may not be cognizant of them. An East Asian person may never classify himself or herself as "collectivistic." However, the outsider status of the missionary affords a perspective with a bit of objectivity (relative to the insider), contributing to a well-rounded exchange. This approach not only gives the missionary constructive insights into the culture by which to contextualize theology; also, he or she gains credibility. After all, one has personally identified with the people, learning the language and worldview, humbly showing a contrasting perspective on the world as they know it. Accordingly, the missionary now offers some initial proposals. He or she suggests ways of reading the Bible, faithful to its original intent yet in terms well understood by the local culture. As a result, local believers more easily grasp theological meaning, give feedback, and put forward new ideas and applications. However, if they are presented with a theology that is too saturated in the missionary's cultural categories, it can be difficult if not impossible for them to analyze, critique, and correct inadequacies in the attempted contextualization. Roland Müller's warning is helpful: when the worldviews of the missionary and the non-Christian conflict, "Either we must change our listener's worldview to be more like our own, or we must find a way to communicate the Gospel so that it speaks to the listener's worldview."[178] He affirms the latter, wary of discipleship methods that *de facto* acculturate locals to the missionary's culture.[179]

What this book proposes is very similar to the manner by which the epistles were written, having varying emphases and language to fit the needs to the readers' context. Local situations dictated what content to highlight. This does not mean circumstances drive truth. This might be the only possible missiological approach to contextualization for this reason: unless the missionary's assumptions and the context's distinctives are made explicit, one cannot but import his or her *own* emphases into the teaching and application. It is critically important to distinguish between what is biblical and what are one's theological emphases (among various biblical ideas). Of the many biblical teachings, what will be emphasized and in what way?

Contextualizers decide which answers to give to the questions being asked. There are many biblical answers to the questions, "What problem does sin cause?" and "What

---

[178] Roland Müller, *The Messenger, the Message and the Community: Three Critical Issues for the Cross-Cultural Church Planter* (2nd ed.; Osler, Canada: CanBooks, 2010), 133.

[179] Ibid., 133. His affirmation does not imply that local hearers will not or should not adjust their worldview in some regard toward the direction of the missionary's. The dilemma posed by Müller should not be taken wholesale, as if one person entirely accepts the other's culture. In dialogue, one expects some philosophical give-and-take. However, Müller's point is communication. If missionaries are unwilling to speak in contextually clear ways, they *de facto* forfeit much of the potential for general revelation to act as a framework for special revelation in that particular context; effectively, the missionary "baptizes" his own culture. It is no wonder then that some would accuse missionaries of cultural imperialism.

benefit does Christ secure?" Aside from HS, the Bible uses diverse figures of speech: atonement, adoption, reconciliation, justification, redemption, marriage, saving, healing. Regarding sin, the Bible speaks of crime, alienation, slavery, exile, sickness, blindness, and death. Goheen aptly captures the way we influence our theologizing:

> Our understanding of the cross is conditioned by the questions we ask. If we ask, "How can I as an individual person be forgiven and obtain eternal life even if I am a sinner to be punished?" then the answer will be, "Because Jesus has died in my place." But if we ask, "How can God renew the entirety of the creation and the whole of human life from the pollution of sin?" then the answer will be, "Because on the cross Jesus took the power of sin and evil that threatened to destroy it." Again if we ask, "How can God create a new community that already anticipates and embodies the life of the coming kingdom of God?" then the answer will be, "Because in the death of Jesus God has acted to conquer the evil that has so corrupted the life of human kind since the time of Adam." We should be clear that *these and other possible questions and answers are not mutually exclusive.*[180]

In time, it is desirable that all Christians from every culture would know and love the range of ways in which the Bible speaks.

People must answer the question as to what has "priority" in contextualization—the Bible or culture. To do so, one can consider an analogous problem within apologetics. On the one hand, apologists say that reason justifies faith in the Bible.[181] This seems to make reason the ultimate authority, not the Bible, raising the question whether an appeal to reason is an abdication of *sola scriptura*. On the other hand, others may say the Bible should be assumed "the first premise of thought," usurping reason as the arbiter of truth.

---

[180] Goheen, *A Light to the Nations*, 104. Italics in original. Goheen is quoting N. T. Wright, *Surprised by Hope: Rethinking Heaven, the Resurrection, and the Mission of the Church* (New York, N.Y.: Harper One: 2008), 199.

[181] What follows is a summary of Clark, *To Know and Love God*, 84–85.

Gordon Clark argues that every philosophical or theological system has a beginning that "cannot be preceded by anything else, or it would not be the beginning."[182]

The argument hinges on an order fallacy. To ask whether the Bible or culture has "priority" is unclear. The idea of "priority" can refer either to temporal sequence (i.e. what comes first) or to authoritative rank (i.e. what has authority). According to the fallacy, it is supposed that whatever comes first temporally has greater authority. To the contrary, sequence is not always supreme. For example, in the apologetics debate just mentioned, one can easily see how reason *initially* has epistemological authority (over revelation) in its defense of *sola scriptura*. Related back to missiology/theology, a similar relationship exists between general revelation (i.e. culture) and special revelation (i.e. Bible). General revelation grounds and makes possible special revelation. It primes or readies the mind for what is to come. General revelation builds a framework upon which special revelation fits and flourishes. General revelation is like scaffolding; special revelation is like bricks. That which is temporally prior simply prepares the way for what has primary authority. In evangelical theology, special revelation has ultimate authority. General revelation is a broad pointer. Its relative authority is in its function to direct attention to special revelation, i.e. Scripture and Christ. Accordingly, there is no reason to conclude that one *must start* with the Bible in the contextualization process. It is possible to begin with culture without compromising the authority of the Bible.

The diverse features of a culture can direct one's attention to a plethora of existential concerns. Particular details may be ambiguous or may even obscure biblical truth; yet, collectively, the world's cultures can point to universal norms, values, and

---

[182] See Gordon H. Clark, "Classical Apologetics," *The Trinity Review* 45 (Oct 1998): 1–5.

expectations with authority that transcends time, place, and personality.[183] Missionaries

collect data from around the world. What key questions are being asked? How do

relationships, customs, and ways of speaking open one's eyes to the many topics

breached in Scripture? General revelation embedded within culture offers hints and a

preliminary structure on which to explore Scripture. All theological readings depend on

one's perception of general revelation. What are moral and epistemological norms? What

is real? These answers shape one's theology and missiology. At issue is not whether the

Bible is the "first premise . . . the first item in a linear sequence of rational thinking" but

whether it has "prime" or "fundamental, regulative" control.[184]

Does contextualization necessarily mean reading some meaning *into* the text? To

object to using culture first would be to assume that by not reading Scripture with one

cultural lens one would not bring some other worldview to the text. However, everyone

in fact brings to the Bible various experiences, cultural categories, and worldviews

largely foreign to the biblical writers. Therefore, the question is not whether one has a

slanted perspective with loaded concerns that bias one's exegesis, perhaps resulting in

eisegesis. This is simply to state the obvious. The real question is *what kind* of

perspective will be brought to the text. By diversifying cultural frames of reference, one

asks a range of questions otherwise impossible to ask from a more limited vantage point.

Contextualization is the prime venue in which one applies the doctrine of general

revelation. By analogy, consider a near-sighted man. Far things are blurry. He definitely

---

[183] One must be careful to define terms, which are loaded with implicit theological meaning. Frances S. Adeney calls gender equality a "universal value." What does "equality" and "universal" mean? Definitions may not be "universally" accepted. See his work, "Contextualizing Universal Values: A Method for Christian Mission," *International Bulletin of Missionary Research* 31, no. 1 (Jan 2007): 33–37.

[184] Clark, *To Know and Love God*, 87.

61

has the power of vision, even if his sight is deficient. Glasses themselves do not give the ability to see. They utilize what nature has given to sharpen corners, distinctions, and make colors more vivid. Likewise, cultural knowledge and general revelation give access to vast amounts of true knowledge—however limited it may be. Diverse clues point to other aspects of reality beyond immediate experience. Conversations, maps, and books may confirm suspicions. The Bible builds upon and critiques subjective human experience. One compares truth claims in "dialogue" with Scripture. This is possible because general revelation provides people with their cultural categories that are also used in special revelation. Contextualizers can value culture as an expression of God's general revelation.[185] Culture is a valid conversation partner, even if not the final authority.

In good contextualization, one expects to see something from each category of the circles in Figure 1. The goal is to make clear what the Bible says. Therefore, one first strives to learn *all* biblical truth, whether coming from area 1, 2, or 3. Problems emerge if people do not make *practical* efforts to distinguish theology from biblical truth. For instance, people can intentionally and honestly listen to a culture's critique of their faith.[186] This is another reason why interdisciplinary study is helpful. Second, people can explore how Christian theologians have responded to a given question. Third, one tries to discern the relative value of theological arguments. Not all issues are as clear as some

---

[185] To clarify again, all cultures are negatively affected by human sin. The point here is simply that cultures act as mediators of general revelation, refracting deeper level truths, even if distorted in the details. What can be known through nature and conscience is expressed in part at a collective level via culture.

[186] One interesting example is Merold Westphal, *Suspicion and Faith: The Religious Uses of Modern Atheism* (New York, N.Y.: Fordham, 1999). Westphal examines Freud, Marx, and Nietzsche's critiques of Christianity, trying to hear how Christians may fall short in expressing authentic Christianity.

leaders may assert. Contextualization may lack biblical fidelity where these points are not heeded. For example, Yung laments that many Asian Christians affirm their "Asianness" at the expense of the gospel. Maintaining a "proper tension" between theology and culture without fear "means the gospel must be incarnated into Asia soil without losing its distinctives."[187] A culture can highlight themes and doctrines that go less noticed elsewhere. As a result, conventional theologies will be challenged and improved by what is found in area 2 of Figure 1.

Theological contextualization means telling and retelling the biblical story. Hesselgrave and Rommen correctly remind us that worldviews are highly integrated systems of story and meaning. Rather than teaching in "piecemeal fashion," missionaries can be more helpful by presenting the Bible in "some sort of unitary whole." Furthermore, "The pieces of the Christian story can be expected to make sense logically only in the context of the larger biblical story."[188] Humans live within this grand story of redemption.[189] Realizing this dynamic may deter people from developing less specialized contextualizations, such as Aloysius Pieris' "theology of voluntary poverty."[190] These are actually contextualized applications or specific issue theologies. These are not contextualized *biblical theologies* that retell the entire biblical narrative, being true to the central themes of Scripture. Newbigin says the "essential Christian contribution" in a dialogue with the unbelieving world "will simply be telling the story, the story of Jesus, the story of the Bible." This in essence is the "common human story in which we are all,

---

[187] Yung, *Mangoes or Bananas*, 120–21.
[188] Hesselgrave and Rommen, *Contextualization*, 214–15.
[189] Anderson and Sleasman, "Putting into Practice," 240.
[190] Yung, *Mangoes or Bananas*, 67.

Christian and others together, participants."[191] Wright says Christian theology "includes a necessarily normative element . . . commending a way" to look at and live in the world; "It offers a rearrangement of timeless truths and propositions" while at the same time telling a "coherent" story that answers the fundamental questions of a worldview: "Who are we?" "Where are we?" "What is wrong?" and "What is the solution?"[192] Offering a *biblical theology* (not just a theology that is biblical) "subverts" prevailing worldviews in order to help people "understand everyday life: to see it as God sees it."[193] Theological contextualization is a work of "emphasis and de-emphasis."[194] One expects faithful attempts to draw mainly from areas 2 and 3, while incorporating truths from area 1 of Figure 1.

Mapping the Contextualization Process

A few principles help map a process for contextualization. First, theology must be distinguished from the Bible itself. Second, cultural context opens the conversation with Scripture. Third, the Bible regulates what ultimately is appropriate for a contextualized theology. Fourth, this is a dialogue between contextualizers, numerous cultural contexts, social sciences, and Scripture.

There is a general flow to contextualization, beginning with a person (or group of people) who catalyzes the process (illustrated in Figure 2). This person brings variegated experiences, theological impressions, and cultural assumptions. The missionary becomes increasingly aware of this background as he interacts with a foreign culture. New

---

[191] Newbigin, *The Gospel in a Pluralist Society*, 182.
[192] Wright, *The New Testament and the People of God*, 131–32.
[193] Vanhoozer, *Everyday Theology*, 56.
[194] Donald Leroy Stults, *Developing an Asian Evangelical Theology* (Manila: OMF, 1989), 148.

questions and categories of thought emerge; one tries to reconcile old intellectual paradigms with this newly broadened perspective. Inevitably, he identifies certain cultural distinctives that resonate with Scripture. This is true in two senses. Descriptively, contemporary contexts may share commonality with ancient Mediterranean cultures. Exegetically, a biblical writer may raise issues also found in the present-day but which were not common among his contemporaries. The outlined sequence does not imply the contextualizer ceases to interact with the Bible. The double arrow highlights the ongoing dialogue (between interpreter and Scripture) that shapes one's theology. Yet, in principle, one recognizes that different aspects have primacy (of attention) at different times. In the process, common themes emerge across modern and ancient contexts. Social sciences can sharpen one's understanding or the questions asked of the text.

Figure 2

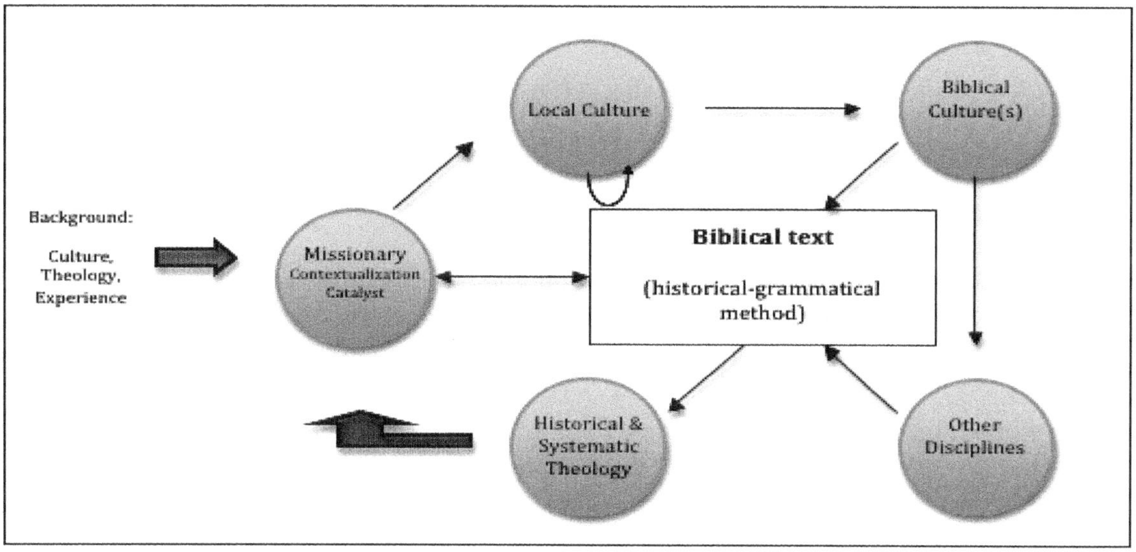

Historical-grammatical interpretation protects against reader response interpretations, effectively filtering the vast data arising from cultural study and research. Anthropology, for instance, runs the risk of two opposite errors. First, its models may be too abstract and complex, becoming too difficult to apply. Second, theories may be too particular, forcing a narrow or foreign set of parameters onto the text.[195] Before

concentrated attention is given to exegesis itself, the contextualizer notes the features

shared by cultural contexts. The goal is to find common principles and themes while

noting contrasting applications of those ideas. In one's analysis, it is critical to distinguish

between possible and necessary meanings. It is all too easy to infer too much. The

Scripture itself then adds a few layers of context. Specifically, the reader considers the

immediate pericope being interpreted. However, the canon serves as the broader literary

context in which one understands the diverse images and allusions present within any

given passage. Finally, interpreters compare their conclusions with historical and

systematic theologies. This puts the reader in dialogue with the historical, global, and

scholarly community. However, this step is last so as to allow for fresh nuances that may

challenge or concur with previous readings. Naturally, one expects certain applications to

surface from this process, providing the grounds for contextualized practice.

How Does One Argue at a Worldview Level?

A critical question must be answered in order to mediate between different interpretations

that result from contrary ways of seeing the world. How does one evaluate worldview

claims? This is not a question of how to argue *for* one worldview over another, but rather

about matters that derive from different cultural vantage points. One presumption taken

here is that all worldviews have some degree of coherency and contradiction. Therefore,

simply because there are problems and tensions does not negate the validity of a whole

system of thought. In addition, as a principle, one cannot assume two or more worldviews

---

[195] For a survey of concerns related to potential influence of anthropology and other social sciences on missiology, see Edward Rommen and Gary Corwin, eds., *Missiology and the Social Sciences: Contributions, Cautions and Conclusions* (Pasadena, Calif.: William Carey Library, 1996).

fundamentally contradict at any given point. Some contradictions may be superficial or occur at the level of *application* or *possible* inference. If one immediately tries to debate details, he may begin to set up an *either-or* scenario and feel compelled to judge right/wrong or better/worse.

Two steps can be taken to engage arguments or interpretations at the level of a worldview. First, one observes *if* and *where* the two perspectives contradict, particularly noting differences in assumptions, inferences, and conclusions. Are the differences inherent contradictions or simply questions of emphasis? Second, does the perspective (lens) under consideration fit the biblical text itself? This is *not* a question of which lens fits better than another. One asks simply whether it fits. If two lenses seem largely to fit Scripture, then one's task is to figure out how they relate.

To shift a worldview paradigm threatens one's entire epistemological orientation, causing one to wonder if choosing a cultural worldview is a question of relative and absolute truth. One might question whether a concession about a doctrine (prominent within one's worldview) essentially relativizes that truth. However, it is possible that people can wrongly contrast "relative" truth and "absolute" truth. Some concepts and statements are inherently relative by virtue of perspective, *not* because of their truthfulness. For instance, one could ask, "Am I tall?" The answer will no doubt be, "Compared to what?" If asked, "Is she right?" one may say she is be right in one respect but wrong in another. Thus, the word "relative" may refer to one's relative perspective of "absolute" truth. A number of differing relative truths may be absolutely true. Perspective does not change reality, yet conflicting perspectives are still true even if they seem irreconcilable at times. By saying "relative," one asks, "Relative to what?" As a result, the truth claim may be relative to a valid perspective and does *not* undermine truth.

Conclusions

The chapter opened by observing a common fallacy that threatens the contextualization process. To assume the gospel prior to contextualization risks not actually contextualizing the gospel, since the conclusion is presupposed. To do so immediately makes contextualization a matter of application or communication; rather than doing so, this book argues that it is more helpful to see contextualization most basically as an interpretative process. All readers come to the biblical text with worldviews that influence their ability to understand Scripture. One must not completely equate biblical truth with one's personal theology. Therefore, in order to temper subjectivity and broaden one's perspective, the contextualizer critically examines the local context and compares it with ancient biblical culture, noting commonalities and differences. The model proposed in this chapter takes seriously the influence of the reader upon an interpretation while allowing Scripture to speak for itself within its own historical and grammatical context. Moreover, one needs to mediate between two distinct worldviews, which inevitably direct how people interpret the Bible. A few criteria have been suggested to bridge the epistemological gap. The chapter demonstrates that seemingly irreconcilable viewpoints might be "relatively" true statements of "absolute" reality.

CHAPTER 3: THEOLOGIZING FOR A CHINESE CULTURE

A Chinese Context: What Needs to Be Addressed?

In order to theologize for a Chinese context, one needs to be familiar with the culture.

What are the key issues that need to be addressed? This chapter briefly sketches the

philosophical and social underpinnings of China's long history. Then, it looks at the past

and present state of Chinese Christianity. At the heart of the chapter, we seek to better

understand what is means to be "Chinese." A closer look at *guanxi* and face will bring up

the question of HS, which is discussed in the next chapter. Finally, the chapter closes by

surveying various attempts to contextualize Christian theology in China.

Chinese culture is peppered with diverse religious expressions.[1] Chinese religion

has frequently been described as pragmatic, moralistic, and syncretistic.[2] Historically,

China's most prominent religions include Confucianism, Buddhism, and Daoism, though

the last has always been "a minor school of thought."[3] Winfried Corduan rightly observes,

"Many Chinese people, if asked about their religion, will say that they are Buddhist,

though what they mean by that term has relatively little to do with textbook descriptions

---

[1] Zhibin says "as much as 80 percent of China's population may be termed 'religious' if customary beliefs and practices in the countryside are included." Zhibin Xie, "Religious Diversity and the Public Roles of Religion in Chinese Society," in *Sino-Christian Studies in China* (ed. Huilin Yang and Xinan Yang; Newcastle, UK: Cambridge Scholars Press, 2006), 230. He cites Kevin Boyle and Juliet Sheen, eds., *Freedom of Religion and Belief: A World Report* (New York: Routledge, 1997), 177.

[2] For example, Milton Wan, "Chinese Religions," *GDT*, 161.

[3] Dilin Liu, *Metaphor, Culture, and Worldview: The Case of American English and the Chinese Language* (Lanham, Md.: University Press of America, 2002), 64.

of Buddhism."[4] At a popular level, Chinese Buddhism provides a pantheon of local gods/goddesses, vague notions about nirvana, and a sense of the importance of compassion.[5] In practice, these faiths are often intermingled. Since 1949, however, the controlling Communist government has propagated atheism, which is common in urban areas and among the educated.[6] To be sure, China's vast urban population partakes in a myriad of spiritual practices.[7] Chinese religion is more concrete than abstract, focusing more on "this life" than on the next.[8] In fact, "The major Chinese philosophies all attach great importance to the physical aspects of life."[9] Therefore, religious practice aims at practical benefits that bring happiness, wealth, health, and good fortune.[10] Human relationships are emphasized more than a divine being. Countless folk religions and beliefs saturate the Chinese milieu.[11] These include the worship/veneration of ancestors and spirit/ghosts, palm reading, fortune telling, geomancy (*fengshui*), and the use of altars dedicated to "domestic deities like the 'kitchen god' and 'earth god'."[12] Traditionally,

---

[4] Winfried Corduan, *Neighboring Faiths: A Christian Introduction to World Religions* (Downers Grove, Ill.: IVP Academic, 1998), 296.

[5] Mario Poceski, *Chinese Religions: The eBook* (State College, Pa.: JBE Online Books, 2009), 131–54.

[6] Xie, "Religious Diversity," 234.

[7] Lizhu Fan and James D. Whitehead, "Spirituality in a Modern Chinese Metropolis," in *Chinese Religious Life* (ed. David A. Palmer, Glenn Landes Shive, and Philip L. Wickeri; New York, N.Y.: Oxford University Press, 2011), 12–29. The importance of China's urban spirituality is unmistakable in light of the fact that "Over 500 cities in China have more than one million people." See Glenn Shive, "Conclusion: The Future of Chinese Religious Life," in *Chinese Religious Life* (ed. David A. Palmer, Glenn Landes Shive, and Philip L. Wickeri; New York, N.Y.: Oxford University Press, 2011), 242.

[8] Pengye Li, "The Characteristics of Chinese Religion and the Development of Christianity in China," in *Sino-Christian Studies in China* (ed. Yang Huilin and Daniel H. N. Yeung; Newcastle, UK: Cambridge Scholars Publishing, 2006), 328–29. Also, Shive, "Conclusion," 244.

[9] Liu, *Metaphor*, 64.

[10] Wan, "Chinese Religions," 160.

[11] For instance, in the opinion of one Chinese theologian, "pantheistic folk religion predominates" in China, particularly in rural areas. Dong Long Yang, "Theological and Cultural Reflections on the Relationship between Church and Society in China," *CTR* (2003): 70.

[12] Quote from Wan, "Chinese Religions," 159–60. Also, Shining Gao, "The Impact of Contemporary Chinese Folk Religions on Christianity," in *Christianity and Chinese Culture* (ed. Mikka Ruokanen and Paulos Huang; Grand Rapids, Mich.: Eerdmans, 2010), 170–71.

sacrifices are offered "as a means to solicit the protection and blessing of the unseen spirit world."[13] Fan and Whitehead point out three typical "moral themes" among urban Chinese: "fateful coincidences," responsibility for personal destiny, and "the conviction that the universe is moral. No action, good or bad, goes unrecompensed."[14] The "utilitarian" nature of Chinese religion means that people will change religions and gods if they do not get the desired result; not surprisingly, Chinese faith is pluralistic and inclusive of differing, even contradictory, beliefs.[15] A well known idiom in China is 信则灵不信则不灵 (xin ze ling, bu xin ze bu ling), which suggests that faith does not have to be rational, as long as its works for a person.[16]

It is critical to note how Chinese authorities have typically viewed religion. There has not been a subordination of the state to a religious power, even when certain religions received official recognition.[17] Secular authorities have remained fearful that religion could become a political tool.[18] Therefore, Fällman rightly highlights the fact many Chinese face a dilemma of identity because they hold firmly to their religious convictions and are thus deemed "un-Chinese."[19] He adds,

> This question of identity is not to be underestimated since it also
> encompasses an issue of loyalty—loyalty first to faith or to the ruler. Any

---

[13] Covell, *Confucius*, 8–9.

[14] Fan and Whitehead, "Spirituality in a Modern Chinese Metropolis," 16–19.

[15] Qiuling Li, "The Position of Religion in Chinese Society," in *Christianity and Chinese Culture* (ed. Mikka Ruokanen and Paulos Huang; Grand Rapids, Mich.: Eerdmans, 2010), 277–79. Pingye Li, "How Do Social and Psychological Needs Impact the Existence and Growth of Christianity in Moden China?," in *Christianity and Chinese Culture* (ed. Mikka Ruokanen and Paulos Huang; Grand Rapids, Mich.: Eerdmans, 2010), 220–22.

[16] 郑明德, "关于信仰与科学关系的思考 (Reflections on the Relationship Between Religious Faith and Science)," *Social Sciences Journal of Colleges of Shanxi* 17, no. 11 (Nov 2005): 28. [in Chinese]

[17] Li, "The Characteristics of Chinese Religion," 326–27. Also, Li, "The Position of Religion," 284–85. Xie, "Religious Diversity," 237.

[18] Li, "The Position of Religion," 284.

[19] Fredrik Fällman, "A Response to Professor Li QiuLing," in *Christianity and Chinese Culture* (ed. Mikka Ruokanen and Paulos Huang; Grand Rapids, Mich.: Eerdmans, 2010), 289.

ruler is afraid of a true believer since he puts loyalty to his faith before loyalty to the ruler. The slogan among patriotic religious organizations in contemporary China, *aiguo aijiao* (love the country, love religion), puts loyalty to country first, not religion or faith.[20]

Political leaders see religion as "a tool for fulfilling their rule in the country."[21] Accordingly, on the one hand, the Chinese government claims that citizens have a "constitutionally guaranteed freedom of religious belief in China (Article 36 of the 1982 Constitution)."[22] On the other hand, reported persecution against religious groups leads some to deny freedom of *practice*.[23]

Confucianism has been called the "foundational" religion of Chinese culture.[24] It remains a significant influence in contemporary China.[25] For example, Confucian thinking influences education methodology, evaluation, and assumptions about teachers and students.[26] Humans are thought to be innately good, thus a key goal of learning is self-cultivation for the sake of "maintain[ing] harmony in the social world."[27] The Confucian doctrine of mean (*zhongyong*) entails "the disposition to view oneself as

---

[20] Ibid.

[21] Li, "The Position of Religion," 285. This perspective continues today. Li notes a 1993 comment where "Jiang Zemin, China's former President, put forward a principle 'to actively lead religions to adjust to socialist society'" (p. 286).

[22] Xie, "Religious Diversity," 238.

[23] For example, among Christian organizations, see Voice of the Martyrs Online: Online: http://www.persecution.net/china.htm; also, note Andrew Jacobs, "Chinese Christians Defend Persecuted Underground Church," *The New York Times*, May 12, 2011, Online edition, sec. World / Asia Pacific, n.p. [cited 8 Mar 2012]. Online: http://www.nytimes.com/2011/05/13/world/asia/13china.html.

[24] Huston Smith, "Chinese Religion in World Perspective," *Dialogue and Alliance* 4, no. 2 (Summer 1990): 5.

[25] Some have even sought to show this empirically, such as Sing Cheung Tak et al., "How Confucian Are Contemporary Chinese? Construction of an Ideal Type and Its Application to Three Chinese Communities," *EJEAS* 5, no. 2 (2006): 157–80. For Confucianism's influence on business, see Zhang and Baker, *Think Like Chinese*, 56–58.

[26] A broad discussion can be found in Fengyan Wang, "Confucian Thinking in Traditional Moral Education: Key Ideas and Fundamental Features," *JME* 33, no. 4 (Dec 2004): 429–47. Other studies make more specific connections, such as Carol K. K. Chan and Nirmala Rao, eds., *Revisiting the Chinese Learner: Changing Contexts, Changing Education* (Seattle, Wash.: University of Washington Press, 2010).

[27] Tak et al., "How Confucian Are Contemporary Chinese?," 167.

embedded in a social system and therefore to see things holistically and in social terms."[28] Five basic social relationships are paradigmatic for ethical decision-making: father-son, elder-younger brother, husband-wife, elder-junior, ruler-subject.[29] Hierarchy is valued. Chinese religion seeks harmony within social relationships in keeping with "a basic balance of nature."[30] Not surprisingly, "[T]he chief moral role of religion lay not in its being a premise of ethical values, but in its assistance in the enforcement of the secular moral standards."[31] The distinctively Chinese principle 礼 (li, "propriety") "delineates correct manners for all social situations."[32] Leon Stover calls li, "right conduct in maintaining one's place in the hierarchical order."[33] In *Analects* 2:2, Confucius summarizes the relationship between concrete, human relationships and spirituality, teaching, "Until you are able to serve men, how can you serve spiritual beings? Until you know about life, how can you know about death?"[34]

Smith asserts the most central problem in Chinese thinking is how people are to relate to one another, such that family has been called China's "real religion."[35] Foremost among all virtues is filial piety.[36] N. H. Ko's words may shock some,

> The conjugal relationship is considered as the least important familial relationship. This can partially explains why a man cannot stand on his

---

[28] Ibid., 167.

[29] Corduan, *Neighboring Faiths*, 294.

[30] This point is extensively argued by Smith, "Chinese Religion in World Perspective," 4–14. The quote comes from Corduan, *Neighboring Faiths*, 282.

[31] Xie, "Religious Diversity," 232. Citing C. K. Yang, *Religion in Chinese Society* (Berkeley, Calif.: University of California, 1961), 286.

[32] Corduan, *Neighboring Faiths*, 294.

[33] Leon Stover, *The Cultural Ecology of Chinese Civilization: Peasants and Elites in the Last of the Agrarian States* (New York, N.Y.: New American Library, 1974), 246. This is cited in Wenzhong Hu and Cornelius Lee Grove, *Encountering the Chinese: A Guide for Americans* (Yarmouth, Maine: Intercultural Press, 1991), 116.

[34] Herbert Fingarette, "Human Community as Holy Rite: An Interpretation of Confucius' Analects," *HTR* 59, no. 1 (Jan 1966): 54–55.

[35] Smith, "Chinese Religion in World Perspective," 5–6.

[36] Wang, "Confucian Thinking in Traditional Moral Education," 431–32.

wife's side while there is a conflict between his wife and parents. This illustrates the situation clearly that in a Confucian society, blood is indeed thicker than water as Chinese people usually say. In addition, it should be noted that, except for the relationship between friends, the relationships are vertical between superiors and inferiors.[37]

Loyalty to family further extends to the state, as Liu explains, "since state is considered one's extended family [hence] loyalty to one's local and national governments is tantamount to loyalty to one's family and ancestors."[38] Likewise, those who govern see themselves as "patriarchs" who are to set a virtuous example for others to follow.[39]

Politically, Chinese society has generally been ruled autocratically. Largely, this has come in the form of emperors representing many dynasties spanning 4,000–5,000 years.[40] For most of Chinese history, Chinese society operated under some degree of feudalism. Dillion further explains, "In the modern Chinese usage, [feudalism] describe[s], in a pejorative sense, the peasant economy controlled and exploited by the emperor, nobility and landlords."[41] In the 19th century, catalyzed by the Opium Wars (1839–42, 1856–60), Western powers subjected China to unfair trading agreements, undermining China's own sense of superiority.[42] In the "century of humiliation" that

---

[37] N. H. Ko, "Familism in Confucianism" (Paper presented at the International Conference of Women's Global Connection, San Antonio, 2004), n.p. [cited 1 Feb 2011]. Online: http://wgc.womensglobalconnection.org/pdf/11naihuako.pdf.

[38] Liu, *Metaphor*, 60. The connection between family and state continues in contemporary politcal discourse. For instance, see Antonio L. Rappa and Sor-Hoon Tan, "Political Implications of Confucian Familism," *Asian Philosophy* 13, no. 2/3 (2003): 87–102. Also, It is noteworthy that the Chinese word for country 国家(*guojia*) combines the characters for nation/state (国, *guo*) and family (家, *jia*).

[39] Liu, *Metaphor*, 60–62. Xinzhong Yao, "Confucius, the Founder of Confucianism," *Dialogue and Alliance* 12, no. 2 (Fall/Winter 1998): 21.

[40] China's "age" varies from resource to resource.

[41] Michael Dillon, "Feudalism," *DCH*, 61–62.

[42] Richard Cook, "Overcoming Missions Guilt," in *After Imperialism: Christian Identity in China and the Global Evangelical Movement* (ed. Richard R. Cook and David W. Pao; Eugene, Ore.: Pickwick, 2011), 42–44. Paul Halsall, "Chinese Cultural Studies: Concise Political History of China," ed. Alan Zisman, *Compton's Living Encyclopedia* (Carlsbad, Calif.: Compton's NewMedia, Aug 1995), n.p. [cited 5 Mar 2012]. Online: http://academic.brooklyn.cuny.edu/core9/phalsall/texts/chinhist.html. Also, Peter Hays

followed, Chinese nationalism festered, drawing calls to "wipe away the national humiliation!"[43] Finally, Communists took control of the country in 1949, establishing a one-party ruled socialist state. They limited religious exercise and reckoned Christian conversion as unpatriotic, such that a famous slogan emerged, "One more Christian, one less Chinese."[44] In some sense, recent Chinese history has created and strengthened something of an "us versus them" mentality in many Chinese minds.

For 1,500 years, Christianity never firmly rooted itself in China. Nestorian traders (578 C.E.) and then missionaries (635) first arrived but were forced out in 845.[45] A Franciscan, John of Montecorvino arrived in 1294, but it was the first Jesuits, Matteo Ricci and Michele Ruggieri (1582), who helped the Catholic Church find sustained footing within the country.[46] However, the "Rites Controversy," which concerned the proper translation for "God" and the use of ancestor rites, set the Chinese Emperor against the Pope. As a result, years of persecution followed, and Christianity was banned from China in 1724. In 1807, the first Protestant missionary, Robert Morrison, reached Guangzhou (Canton). Missionaries faced severe opposition, and Chinese could be put to death for teaching their language to foreigners.[47] Covell mentions a few of the problems that plagued Protestant missions, including "an insistence on 'rights,' an assumption of European superiority, . . . a disdain for the need to adjust to Chinese culture, . . . and a

---

Gries, *China's New Nationalism: Pride, Politics, and Diplomacy* (Berkeley: University of California Press, 2004), 47–48.

[43] In Chinese, "洗雪国耻"; Gries, *China's New Nationalism*, 43–53.

[44] The quote is well known. Cf. John Promfret, *Chinese Lessons: Five Classmates and the Story of the New China* (New York, N.Y.: Henry Holt & Co, 2006), 198. Yang, "Theological and Cultural Reflections," 72.

[45] Covell, *Confucius*, 21–24.

[46] For a survey of Chinese Catholic origins, see Ibid., 36–67.

[47] Ibid., 71.

resignation to the alliance of the gospel with worldly power."[48] Despite some success, Protestants were viewed with suspicion, since Chinese closely associated them with Western political powers. The Opium Wars and the century following only cemented the idea that Christianity was a "foreign religion used by imperialist aggressors."[49] Following the Communist victory in 1949, China has only officially sanctioned five religions (Buddhism, Daoism, Islam, Catholicism, and Protestantism), which are administrated by a governmental religious bureau that establishes "Three-Self Patriotic Movement" (TSPM) churches, temples, and mosques.[50]

Since China opened up to the outside world after 1978, Christianity has firmly fixed itself within Chinese society. The estimated number of Christians in Mainland China ranges from 21 million to 130 million.[51] The city of Wenzhou has been called "China's Jerusalem," with approximately one million Protestants and over 2,000 churches (as of 2007), despite being made an "atheistic zone" by the state in 1958.[52] Most Chinese Christians are Protestant and are a part of "house churches," though they may in fact meet in businesses, factories, parks, and apartments. A fundamental divide among TSPM and house church Christians is the question of authority, since an atheistic

---

[48] Ibid., 83.

[49] Guanzong Luo, "'Foreword'," in *Remembering the Past as a Lesson for the Future* (ed. Guanzong Luo; Beijing: Religious Culture Publishers, 2003), 1. The forward gives insight into this sort of Chinese perspective. Luo Guanzong is a director of the National CCC/TSPM Advisory Committee.

[50] Xie, "Religious Diversity," 231. The "Three-Self" language refers to the goal of national churches being self-governed, self-funded, and self-propagating.

[51] Aikman says the government's official number is 21 million, though the true number probably hits around 80 million. See David Aikman, *Jesus in Beijing: How Christianity is Transforming China and Changing the Global Balance of Power* (Lanham, Md.: Regnery, 2003), 7–8. The Center of the Study of Global Christianity estimates 70 million. Others say 130 million is a reasonable guess. See "Sons of Heaven: Inside China's Fastest-Growing Non-Governmental Organization," *The Economist*, 2 Oct 2008, World Politics section. Online edition. n.p. [cited 28 Oct 2010]. Online http://www.economist.com/node/12342509?story_id=1234509.htm.

[52] Nanlai Cao, *Constructing China's Jerusalem: Christians, Power, and Place in Contemporary Wenzhou* (Palo Alto, Calif.: Stanford University Press, 2010), 1.

government ultimately administrates TSPM churches. William Dyrness reports that suffering is an important theme in house churches because ". . . standing up to give one's testimony in China is clearly understood to be a political statement of allegiance. To become a Christian is to identify with God's work in a way that necessarily limits one's submission to the state."[53] Jackson Wu also elaborates on critical issues facing churches, including ways that collectivistic thinking may shape Chinese ecclesiology.[54] A plethora of writers recognizes the current need for theological contextualization and training.[55]

In order to contextualize theology in a Chinese context, one must ask what it means to be "Chinese." The dynamic nature of culture and particularities of people allow only for "ideal" generalizations.[56] Therefore, there will be differences between "desirable values" and those that are actually reflected in daily practice.[57] In short, how does one construct a model for understanding a Chinese worldview? Zhu Bo's taxonomy is quite representative of the relevant literature. He highlights seven Chinese cultural values: past-time orientation, respect for hierarchy, interdependence, group orientation (collectivistic), face, modesty, and harmony with others.[58] Face will receive a lengthy treatment in the

---

[53] William A. Dyrness, *Invitation to Cross-Cultural Theology: Case Studies in Vernacular Theologies* (Grand Rapids, Mich.: Zondervan, 1992), 55.

[54] Wu, "Authority in a Collectivist Church."

[55] For a representative sample, see Richard X. Y. Zhang, "Sino-Christian Theology and Nationalism," in *Sino-Christian Studies in China* (ed. Huilin Yang and Daniel H. N. Yeung; Newcastle: Cambridge Scholars, 2006), 173–95; Huilin and Yeung, *Sino-Christian Studies in China*; K. K. Yeo, *Musing*; Bruce J. Nicholls, "Contextualisation in Chinese Culture," *ERT* 19, no. 4 (Oct 1995): 368–80; Chengmian Wang, *Contextualization of Christianity in China: An Evaluation in Modern Perspective* (Collectanea serica; Sankt Augustin; Nettetal: Institut Monumenta Serica; Steyler Verlag, 2007); M. David Sills, *Reaching*, 44–45, 153, 163; Wan, "Practical Contextualization"; Wan, "Critiquing"; Cook and Pao, *After Imperialism*.

[56] By "ideal," I mean a "pure type" or abstract model that represents the major contours of Chinese culture. For more on this, see Tak et al., "How Confucian Are Contemporary Chinese?," 160–61.

[57] For elaboration, see Zhu Bo, "Chinese Cultural Values and Chinese Language Pedagogy" (Master's Thesis, Columbus, Ohio: The Ohio State University, 2008), 24–30.

[58] Ibid., 32–39.

next chapter. Otherwise, the following discussion addresses these and other features of Chinese culture.

Chinese culture is described as having a collectivistic or "relational orientation."[59] Collectivism is typically contrasted with individualism. The latter "emphasizes personal goals and boundaries between self and other, whereas collectivist cultures emphasize group goals and connectedness and ways of behavior that promote harmony among in-group members by helping each other."[60] However, Ho gives a key qualification, explaining that relational orientation

> . . . differs from collective orientation. The emphasis is put on relationships, rather than on collective interests. Loyalties based on personal relationships within a collective often contradict, even sabotage, the larger interests of the collective. It is thus important to specify the kind and quality of relationships between the individual and the group or between individuals in the group in order to assess the impact of relationships on social behavior.[61]

To some degree, one might say individual personalities are a composite of his/her social relationships.[62] This characterization does not deny the fact that changing economic and political conditions afford some degree of individualization in Chinese society.[63] Hwang captures the essence of Chinese thinking: "An individual's life can be meaningful only through coexistence with others; life may become meaningless if one loses relationship

---

[59] Kwang-Kuo Hwang, *Foundations of Chinese Psychology: Confucian Social Relations* (New York, N.Y.: Springer, 2012), 192.

[60] Carol K. K. Chan and Nirmala Rao, "Moving Beyond Paradoxes: Understanding Chinese Learners and Their Teachers," in *Revisiting the Chinese Learner: Changing Contexts, Changing Education* (ed. Carol K. K. Chan and Nirmala Rao; Seattle, Wash.: University of Washington Press, 2010), 8.

[61] D. Y. F. Ho, "Relational Orientation and Methodological Individualism," *Bulletin of the Hong Kong Psychological Society*, no. 26/27 (1991): 84.

[62] Or as Kipnis says, "one's relationships in fact constitute oneself" in *Producing Guanxi*, 8.

[63] Yunxiang Yan, *The Individualization of Chinese Society* (English ed.; New York, N.Y.: Berg, 2009). As will be seen, this individualization ironically increases relational dependency.

with significant others . . . Because there is no clear cut boundary between oneself and others, the Chinese self can be termed the *relational self*."[64]

It has been argued that this group-orientation does not generally apply to Chinese religious life.[65] Sheldon Sawatsky states, "In China, 'there has never been a central religious authority to dictate to the conscience, regulate the beliefs, and control the destiny of the individual' . . . Chinese temples have no fixed group of followers or believers."[66] However, this oversimplifies the issue. First of all, Confucianism (inasmuch as it can be regarded a humanistic "religion") fits this description. Gan Chunsong explains, "Institutional Confucianism was the basic mode in which traditional Confucianism endured. The imperial examination played a core role, and its decline was fateful."[67] In practice, Elman argues that the system favored "social mobility of lineages."[68] In addition, he reviews the examination questions, observing a "priority of 'public' over 'private' [thus leaving] little room for appeals to individual desires or private interests."[69] Finally, he ignores a few key facts. For instance, Buddhism throughout the world is individualized, not simply in China. Also, in history, privatized

---

[64] Hwang, *Foundations*, 192. He is following Ho D. Y. F. Also, Hu and Grove regard collectivism a "fundamental value" of the Chinese; cf. Hu and Grove, *Encountering the Chinese*, 5–6.

[65] Sheldon Sawatzky, "Body as Metaphor in Chinese Religious Cultures: Implications for Chinese Ecclesiology," *TJTh* 16 (1994): 106–7.

[66] Ibid., 107. Wing Tsit Chan, "The Individual in Chinese Religions," in *The Chinese Mind* (Honolulu, Hawaii: East-West Center Press, 1967), 286.

[67] Gan Chunsong, "Decline of the Imperial Examination System and the Disintegration of Institutional Confucianism [Abstract]," *Social Sciences in China* 23 (Feb 2002), n.p. [cited 22 Feb 2012]. Online: http://en.cnki.com.cn/Article_en/CJFDTOTAL-ZSHK200202009.htm; In agreement is Hai-feng Liu, "On the Development and Multiplication of the Imperial Examination System and Confucianism [Abstract]," *Journal of China University of Geosciences (Social Sciences Edition)* 45, no. 9 (Jan 2009), n.p. [cited 22 Feb 2012]. Online: http://en.cnki.com.cn/Article_en/CJFDTOTAL-DDXS200901002.htm.

[68] Benjamin A. Elman, *A Cultural History of Civil Examinations in Late Imperial China* (Berkeley: University of California Press, 2000), 245–49. Similarly, see Ronnie Littlejohn, *Confucianism: An Introduction* (New York, N.Y.: I. B. Tauris, 2010), 72–73.

[69] Elman, *A Cultural History of Civil Examinations in Late Imperial China*, 437.

religious expressions are likely to flourish better than highly organized theistic religions since the latter are seen as political threats.

This relational/collective dynamic is manifest most clearly within family life.[70] The use of metaphors is important because they indicate and shape people's worldview.[71] Therefore, as Liu points out, it is significant that two primary metaphors within Chinese language are family and eating (as opposed to sports and business in American culture).[72] Ko observes, "Confucians conceptualized the family by analogy to the human body," where each person is "distinct" yet "inseparable."[73] This picture grounds "the principle of respecting the superior, but also on favoring the intimate."[74] Smith reinforces the point by noting that in Chinese naming convention, the family name is placed first in order before one's given name.[75] The rational behind filial piety is straightforward: One honors parents since "[they] are the origins of one's life."[76] Family members are interdependent inasmuch as elders provide for the needs of their children and children honor their ancestors.[77] Since family is the ideal relationship, it is not surprising that "family" acts as the governing metaphor over other social relationships, even outside one's blood family.[78] Thus, one daily sees people address one another as family, according to age,

---

[70] "Relational" and "collective" terminology may be used interchangeably in what follows.

[71] Liu, *Metaphor*, 8.

[72] This is extensively demonstrated in Liu, *Metaphor*.

[73] Ko, "Familism in Confucianism." The body analogy is also discussed in Kwang-Kuo Hwang, "Filial Piety and Loyalty: Two Types of Social Identification in Confucianism," *AJSP* 2 (1999): 169–70. Though in ironic contrast, the Bible similarly mixes metaphors, calling the church Christ's "body" while also using family imagery (e.g. Eph 1:22–23; 3:14; 5:22, 32; 1 Tim 5:1–2). In addition, Paul uses "body" language to depict the husband-wife relationship (Eph 5:22–33).

[74] Ko, "Familism in Confucianism."

[75] Smith, "Chinese Religion in World Perspective," 8.

[76] Hwang, *Foundations*, 174.

[77] Hwang, "Filial Piety," 179; Hwang, *Foundations*, 255.

[78] Hui-Ching Chang and G. Richard Holt, "More Than Relationship: Chinese Interaction and the Principle of *Kuan-Hsi*," *Communication Quarterly* 39, no. 3 (Summer 1991): 253.

calling elders "uncle/aunt" and older peers "elder brother/sister."[79] Naturally, this

relational emphasis has pervasive implications. Liu highlights the logic: a society

conceived as a family will not be contentious but rather have harmony.[80] Hwang

concludes, "The most important principle for a person to consider when immersed in

group identity is loyalty."[81]

A clarification is needed lest some share Hwang's misunderstanding about the

relationship between Christianity, individualism, and collectivism. He begins rightly by

observing, "[T]he basic difference between Confucianism and Christianity can be traced

to their fundamental discrepancy in explaining the origin of life"; however, he continues,

> Christianity advocates the idea that each person is an *independent* entity
> created by God. An individual should strive to defend the territory of self
> that has been drawn around the immediate surface of the physical body. In
> contrast, according to Confucianism, individuals' personal lives are a
> continuity of their parents' lives, who in turn succeed their ancestors.[82]

To verify his meaning, one can note his comment in the same book, "As a cultural

product of Christianity, the self-contained individualism of Western civilization

encourages an individual to define the boundary between one and other by the immediate

surface surrounding one's body."[83] He suggests Christianity teaches that one's

ontological identity is best defined in terms of one's "physical self" rather than his "social

self" (i.e. Chinese interdependence).[84] Hwang's basic fallacy is confusing Christianity

with Western culture. Simply because the former has greatly influenced the latter does

---

[79] This is also observed by Xiang-lang Hou and Liu He, "Comparative Study of Chinese Family and American Family," *US-China Foreign Language* 6, no. 7 (Jun 2008): 67. Chang and Holt root this practice explicitly in Confucian thought. Chang and Holt, "More Than Relationship," 253–54.

[80] Liu, *Metaphor*, 57.

[81] Hwang, "Filial Piety," 180.

[82] Hwang, *Foundations*, 280–81. Emphasis mine.

[83] Ibid., 340.

[84] Ibid.

not mean they are equivalent. Christianity certainly gives value to the individual. Yet, one should not doubt various historical and social factors have forged a sort of individualism not inherent to Christian theology itself. For instance, a survey of numerous biblical texts makes the counterpoint, making much of a person's collective identity. One of the most important disputes of the NT concerned who were the children of Abraham (cf. John 8:12–59; Rom 2:25–29; 4:1–14; 9:6–7; Gal 3:14; Eph 2:11–3:6). As will be seen in the next chapter, ancient biblical cultures were quite collectivistic. These factors correct the mistaken impression that Christianity stands in contradistinction to a group orientation.

From a Chinese perspective, "Harmony is the measure of all things."[85] Some have even argued that Chinese conceptions of truth have less to do with knowledge's correspondence to a fact and more to do with ethical norms that "promote harmony."[86] The rationale behind this thinking may be the idea that morality is rooted in the nature of the universe.[87] Social harmony is achieved by maintaining hierarchical relationships built on the "inferior's respect rather than superior's domineering."[88] Of course, the use of authority is critical. Therefore, Chinese views of leadership, either in theory or practice, emphasize morality, "interpersonal competence," indirect communication, building consensus, conformity, modesty, and "contributing to society."[89]

---

[85] Covell, *Confucius*, 11. Hu and Grove call harmony a "fundamental value" and "supreme concern" in Hu and Grove, *Encountering the Chinese*, 7–8.

[86] Covell, *Confucius*, 11. Similarly, Smith, "Chinese Religion in World Perspective," 6.

[87] For a rigorous historical and philosophical treatment, see Dora ShuFang Dien, *The Chinese Worldview Regarding Justice and the Supernatural: The Cultural and Historical Roots of Rule by Law* (New York, N.Y.: Nova Science Publishers, 2007).

[88] Olwen Bedford, "Guilt and Shame in American and Chinese Culture" (PhD diss., Boulder, Colo: University of Colorado, 1994), 73. Yao-Chia Chuang, "Effects of Interaction Pattern on Family Harmony and Well-Being: Test of Interpersonal Theory, Relational-Models Theory, and Confucian Ethics," *AJSP* 8 (2005): 290.

[89] For empirical studies, see Canchu Lin, "Western Research on Chinese Culture and Leadership" (Paper presented at the Annual Meeting of the International Communication Association, New Orleans Sheraton, New Orleans, LA, May 27, 2004, [cited 6 Feb 2011]. Online: http://www.allacademic.com/

When stress on community extends to a country, nationalism and ethnocentrism easily emerges. People treasure the fact China is one of the world's oldest civilizations. As a result, Chinese culture is past-oriented.[90] Traditionalism and reverence for ancestors reflect this perspective. In their review of Chinese nationalism, Chan and Bridges assert, "Tracing back the long Chinese history of seeing itself as the 'center of the earth' (*zhongyuan or zhongtu*) and neighboring countries as admirers of and learners of this central state, it is apparent that the Chinese people have a 'great nation complex.'"[91] Covell reckons "ethnic culturalism" an "essential element" of Chinese culture.[92] This explains why some scholars are giving increasing attention to the relationship between Christian theology and Chinese nationalism.[93]

Relational interdependence is expressed in the concept of *guanxi* (translated "relationship"). Kipnis explains that *guanxi* involves reciprocity and human feelings, entails social and material obligations, and points to the web of in-group relationships within one's daily life.[94] More simply, Peter Verhezen calls it one's "social capital."[95]

---

meta/p113422_index.html; Wenquan Ling, Rosina Chia, and LiLuo Fang, "Chinese Implicit Leadership Theory," *JSP* 140, no. 6 (2000): 729–39; For a historical/philosophical perspective, see Kam-Cheung Wong, "Chinese Culture and Leadership," *IJLE* 4, no. 4 (2001): 309–19.

[90] This emphasis is evident in some contemporary business books that market "ancient Chinese wisdom," such as Chow Hou Wee and Luh Luh Lan, *The 36 Strategies of the Chinese: Adapting Ancient Chinese Wisdom to the Business World* (Singapore: Addison-Wesley, 1998).

[91] Che-po Chan and Brian Bridges, "China, Japan, and the Clash of Nationalisms," *Asian Perspective* 30, no. 1 (2006): 132. The characters for China (中国, *zhongguo*) literally means middle country/nation, hence the nickname "Middle Kingdom." The first character represents China's central place in the world. Chan and Bridges cite Lucian W. Pye, "How China's Nationalism was Shanghaied," *Australian Journal of Chinese Affairs*, no. 29 (Jan 1993): 107–33. Covell even quotes Emporer Wu's eviction of Nestorians from China, which ordered them to "return to the world." See Covell, *Confucius*, 24.

[92] Covell, *Confucius*, 7, 13.

[93] For example, Zhang, "Nationalism."

[94] Kipnis, *Producing Guanxi*, 23–27. A helpful and brief summary can be found in Wilfried Vanhonacker, "Guanxi Networks in China," *The China Business Review* (Jun 2004): 48–53.

[95] Peter Verhezen, "Guanxi: Networks or Nepotism?," in *Europe-Asia Dialogue on Business Spirituality* (ed. Laszlo Zsolnai; Garant: Antwerpen-Apeldoom, 2008), 89–106.

Whereas Western notions of "networking" are typically limited to business and common interest contacts, *guanxi* relationships have a higher degree of commitment, "suggesting in essence one of an extended family."[96] Therefore, they tend to be more personal, time intensive and holistic, not compartmentalized to one sphere of life (like business). Furthermore, Kipnis relates *guanxi* to identity, observing, "In a very real sense, when Fengjia villagers re-create their networks of relationships, they also re-create themselves."[97] Vanhonacker's clarification guards against common misunderstandings:

> To most Chinese, *guanxi* has its own moral code and serves a necessary social function. Westerners see *guanxi* as "using" others which, according to Western morality, is unethical. But in China, "using" a relationship creates an obligation to do something at a later date. As long as you eventually fulfill that obligation, you are considered ethical. It is the ethical dimension that sets a *guanxi* relationship apart from money-based or commodified transactions. *Guanxi* is not the same as corruption because *guanxi* is relation-focused whereas corruption is transaction-focused. And the relational ethic of *guanxi* implies that it cannot be bought.[98]

A key dynamic must not be missed in understanding the moral quality of *guanxi*. To enter into close relationship is to take risk. Trust therefore calls upon the other party to demonstrate "moral integrity, not expose [them] or create any vulnerability, not abuse [them or their] network, and watch out for [them]." *Guanxi* brings the risk that one side will not pay their relational debt. It is precisely in this context that virtues like love, righteousness, loyalty, and filial piety can be expressed.[99]

How then should one understand Chinese ethical thought in view of *guanxi*?

---

[96] Liu, *Metaphor*, 60.

[97] Kipnis, *Producing Guanxi*, 8.

[98] Vanhonacker, "Guanxi Networks in China," 50.

[99] These four represent a standard list of Confucian ideals. Cf. Wang, "Confucian Thinking in Traditional Moral Education," 432; also, Hwang, "Filial Piety." Hwang says loyalty proved to be more important than mere *guanxi* when assessed in management environments; see Hwang, *Foundations*, 320.

84

Hwang suggests Confucian morality distinguishes between positive duties ("duties of commission") and negative duties ("duties of omission").[100] One first notes, "The natural law of Confucian ethics is built on conceptions of natural duties and goals rather than on natural rights," which is typical of Western moral systems.[101] He concludes,

> . . . morality in Western culture of individualism is right-based as it emphasizes "negative duties" or "duties of omission." An individual should take 'respecting other's rights' as a fundamental principle for moral judgment. [Accordingly] Practicing "positive duty" is a kind of "virtue;" [yet] it is all right for an individual to chose not to practice it.[102]

Hwang then ponders, "But how can ordinary people with limited resources possibly practice the positive duty of benevolence toward all other people?"[103] In short, positive duties should be done for insiders according to priority of relationship. Two standards prevail: "intimacy/distance and superiority/inferiority."[104] Thus, while humanity is obligated to show love (*ren*) to all, priority is given to family and then those nearest in relationship.[105] Righteousness (*yi*) means "appropriateness" and governs one's conduct towards those of different social status and role.[106] Negative duties can be applied in practice across all relationships, in particular the outsider or strangers.[107] Most generally, the Chinese rule of propriety (called *li*) provides the (ideal) norm by which society operates.[108] Noting that people "tend to use different standards of justice to interact with

---

[100] See his discussion in Hwang, *Foundations*, 162–74.

[101] Ibid., 168.

[102] Ibid., 254.

[103] Ibid., 163. Confucius explained *ren* as "loving *all* men" (Hwang's emphasis; Ibid., 112.) He quotes *Analects* 22.

[104] Hwang, *Foundations*, 109.

[105] Ibid., 113. His findings confirm this in practice respective to reward allocation on pp. 200–201.

[106] Ibid., 108, 160. He cites Chapter 20 of The Golden Mean.

[107] Ibid., 163, 174. Hwang remarks, "However, there is no moral obligation to fulfill a positive duty by doing favors for strangers outside one's network" (p. 174).

[108] Ibid., 114–15.

others of various relationships in different situations," Hwang especially highlights the

"rule or *renqing*."[109] In effect, the *renqing* rule means that resources will be allocated

within one's relational network "for the sake of maintaining interpersonal harmony with a

group . . . no matter how much actual input each one of them objectively contributed

toward the [task's] completion."[110] To be sure, it must be recognized that to some degree

(1) "Reciprocity is a universal norm for social interaction in all human societies"[111] and

(2) "helping behaviors among close relationships are a universal phenomenon" and "with

only context-specific, cross-cultural variation."[112]

Despite the increasing "individualization of Chinese society," the importance of

guanxi has ironically increased over the past few decades. Yan cogently shows how the

collapse of "social trust" bolsters the value of "personal trust [which] derives from long-

term interactions with the same group of people."[113] By contrast,

> [S]ocial trust is understood as a more generalized trust in social
> institutions that will behave in accordance with the stated rules in experts
> who will guard the rules to make the institutions work well; and also the
> strangers who will work for peaceful and non-harmful social
> interactions.[114]

Yan names a few factors that undermine social trust, including China's move to a market

economy, increased social mobility, political corruption, a decrease in daily oversight by

local communist cadre, and the uneven enforcement of laws.[115] In addition, he astutely

points out that individualization depends on stable systems of education, heath care, and

---

[109] Ibid., 91–93.

[110] Ibid., 92.

[111] Ibid., 174. He cites Alvin Goulder, "The Norm of Reciprocity: A Preliminary Statement," *ASR* 25 (1960): 161–79.

[112] Hwang, *Foundations*, 203, 202.

[113] Yan, *Individualization*, 285.

[114] Ibid., 285.

[115] Ibid., 284–87.

forms of social welfare.[116] Since these are underdeveloped in China, it is essential for

individuals to secure a strong and diverse web of relationships in order to protect

themselves and their interests.[117] Not surprisingly, these dynamics not only add to

guanxi's importance but they further emphasize the in/out-group distinction and reinforce

moral relativism as the standard social perspective.[118] Yan's analysis shows how "identity"

concerns "the redefinition of the individual-group-institution relationship."[119]

Outsiders living in China may need to adjust their practice and perspective on

relationships. For example, it is critical to establish relationships in a Chinese way.[120]

Chang and Holt mention a few features of building *guanxi*, such as emphasizing

commonalities, using intermediaries,[121] and spending a lot of time with people (especially

eating together).[122] They also offer tips for maintaining *guanxi*. These include keeping

pleasant/happy facial expressions, making sure there is balance in exchanging favors, and

being sensitive to social status.[123] Of course, one must be aware as to what he or she

communicates non-verbally. In addition, because some westerners may fear falling into

social debt, they may too hastily "pay back" a favor as if *guanxi* were a mere resource

transaction. A well-timed giving/reciprocation of help (as well as receiving it) can go a

long way towards developing genuine *renqing* feelings (literally translated "human

---

[116] Ibid., 288.

[117] Ibid., 286. Yan affirms the central role of the family to Chinese identity (p. 289), yet the scope, purpose, and practices surrounding *guanxi* formation shift; for instance, from locality to common interest.

[118] Others have made this observation and projection, e.g. Hwang, "Filial Piety," 179; also, Vanhonacker, "Guanxi Networks in China," 53.

[119] Yan, *Individualization*, 288.

[120] From a business perspective, see the ideas from Zhang and Baker, *Think Like Chinese*, 99–117.

[121] Similarly, note Duane Elmer, *Cross-Cultural Conflict: Building Relationships for Effective Ministry* (Downers Grove, Ill.: IVP, 1993), 65–79; Irene Y. M. Yeung, "The Dynamism of *Guanxi* in Company Performance in China" (MBA Thesis, Burnaby, Canada: Simon Fraser University, 1995), 59–62.

[122] Chang and Holt, "More Than Relationship," 259–61.

[123] Ibid., 264–66.

emotions").[124] No doubt many westerners may be challenged by this fundamental shift in orientation, even questioning a morality that stresses the group. Graham offers philosophical rationale for collectivistic thinking:

> My carrying out my plans, whatever they are, will carry implications for other agents and their ability to carry out *their* plans. In that way, any state of affairs which represents a fulfillment of some interest of mine will impact the interests of some other people . . . while no one can deny that a distinction must be drawn somewhere between public and private behavior, the case still needs to be made for the claim that a distinction between self- and other-regarding behaviour can serve as a basis for drawing the former distinction, rather than merely providing us with a vocabulary for expressing the former distinction once it has been drawn.[125]

In short, in any culture, even so-called "private" actions have public implications.

Given the central role of legal metaphors in historical theology, it is important to understand how Chinese think of law. Naturally, one cannot assume Western notions of law when considering ideas about law in modern China. In order to understand Chinese legal thought, it is helpful, for the sake of contrast, to review briefly Western legal history. Western views trace back to ancient Greek and Roman law. Liang compares the historical development of Western and Chinese legal concepts.[126] In the West, he explains that law refers to what is universally right for all people in society, thus carrying connotations of fairness and rights.[127] Historically, conflicts between rich and poor led to the formation of legal codes aimed at bringing about order across economically disparate groups.[128] Furthermore, common law has been the primary legal philosophy in the West for over

---

[124] This emotional aspect of *renqing* is addressed in Hwang, *Foundations*, 91.

[125] Keith Graham, *Practical Reasoning in a Social World: How We Act Together* (Cambridge, UK: Cambridge University Press, 2002), 62, 64.

[126] Zhiping Liang, "Explicating 'Law': A Comparative Perspective of Chinese and Western Legal Culture," *Journal of Chinese Law* 3, no. 1 (1989): 55–92.

[127] Ibid., 56–58, 65–66.

[128] Ibid., 63–65, 79.

millennia. In this system, judges have significant law making powers in accordance with precedence; thus, law falls within the purview of the judiciary.[129]

By contrast, Chinese law has different origins and function. First of all, the idea of "law" is not a universal abstraction. Rather, laws are general norms meant to be flexible enough to apply differing contexts.[130] Liang traces the dissimilarity to the contrasting way Chinese laws developed.[131] Historically, Chinese wars were not fought along economic lines but between rival clans.[132] As a result, laws reflected the familial customs of the reigning group. Therefore, ancient Chinese laws preserved familial norms and hierarchical relationships.[133] One can easily see how in Western law "the power that rides over society" could have the opposite effect over time, weakening familial ties and dependency.[134] Significantly, Chinese law has not traditionally emphasized the judiciary;[135] instead, laws emerge out of the legislature (in modern China) or from the king (in most of Chinese history).[136] Courts and local officials have tremendous flexibility in interpreting and implementing laws, but they are not bound by precedence. As "speech acts," Cao explains legislated laws perform what they prescribe without respect for judicial warrant.[137] More simply, laws derive from the legislative authority

---

[129] Deborah Cao, *Chinese Law: A Language Perspective* (Burlington, Vt.: Ashgate, 2004), 5–6.

[130] Ibid., 94–95.

[131] Liang, "Explicating 'Law'," 79–80.

[132] Ibid., 69–79.

[133] Ibid., 72–75.

[134] This phrase comes from Ibid., 65. As has been mentioned, scholars have predicted this outcome for modern China, who increasingly formalizes and strengthens its legal system. See Vanhonacker, "Guanxi Networks in China," 179; Hwang, "Filial Piety," 53; Yan, *Individualization*, 284–87.

[135] Berring's comments are direct, "China has no historical office that corresponds to the Western idea of a judge. China lacks any history of an independent judiciary. The magistrate was an extension of the Emperor—no limits could restrain him. All comparisons with an American judge are counterproductive." See Robert C. Berring, Jr., "Rule of Law: The Chinese Perspective," *JOSP* 35, no. 4 (Winter 2004): 452.

[136] Liang, "Explicating 'Law'," 83. For more on Chinese "lawmaking as a communicative act," see Cao, *Chinese Law*, 141–60.

[137] Cao, *Chinese Law*, 122–24.

rather than court decisions. In order for a law to have validity, "it must also be issued by the right person under the right circumstance, following the specifications of the relevant convention."[138] Yet, one must recall that this high degree of formality in instituting laws is combined with tremendous flexibility with regard to implementation. A few considerations make sense of this. In the West, law has been conceived as an "impersonal" principle that protects universal "rights"; however,

> [a]s evidenced by many dynastic histories, in ancient China, theoretically speaking, there were rulers, but there were no laws of governing. Since law was only a personified tool for governing, it was dependent on and confined by its function, and therefore of extremely limited use. . . . Thus, the king issues orders. . . . Because of this process, Chinese history has always connected "law" with the strengthening of the king's authority.[139]

Yan Fu, a Chinese thinker and translator (1853–1921), draws a key implication: "the ruler then transcends [sic] above law, can intentionally use law and change law, and is not restrained by law."[140] Liang outlines the meaning of "law" (法, fa) throughout Chinese literature, concluding that it does not parallel Latin terms like *lex* and *jus* from which Western "law" derives its meaning.[141] In traditional Chinese thought, "Law is only an instrument to govern the state; its source of authority comes from the authority of the king."[142] Primary, *fa* connotes "punishment" used to enforce statutes.[143]

Fundamentally, Chinese and Western views of law have different starting points. Although both legal philosophies appeal to "natural law" as a basis for morality, their

---

[138] Ibid., 124.
[139] Liang, "Explicating 'Law'," 89.
[140] Ibid.
[141] Ibid., 56.
[142] Ibid., 83.
[143] Ibid., 61.

rationales do not converge.[144] Historically, Western legal theory dichotomizes natural law and "man-made law," seeking universal ideals of justice and good.[145] Even apart from the influence of Greek philosophy, Western "law" found grounding in Christian theology, wherein the Creator "God has created a system of natural law."[146] Berring remarks, "The point of the English Common Law was to mirror this 'natural law' as closely as possible."[147] If so, one gains important insight. Unwittingly, Western civilization may give common law a sacred status, thereby making it natural for Christian interpreters to eisegete (i.e. read back into the Bible) a view of law that may simply not hold true for ancient biblical cultures. Given the ramifications, this possibility deserves consideration.

China, on the other hand, applied a different idea of natural law. As previously noted, Confucian ethics emphasize not only rights but also duties. An illustration in point is the Chinese Constitution, which explicitly and frequently lists duties (not only "rights") required of all citizens.[148] A person's foremost duty is to maintain harmony with the world and people. One must keep in mind ". . . the development of the Chinese justice system is rooted in their cosmological worldview of the unity of man and nature. [Hence, t]he natural order is closely bound up with the moral order of human society."[149] Accordingly, Dien shows from Chinese history how filial piety and the legal system worked to preserve harmony in the family.[150] She recounts the Tang Code, which served

---

[144] Berring, Jr., "Rule of Law," 452; Liang, "Explicating 'Law'," 67.

[145] Liang, "Explicating 'Law'," 67.

[146] Berring, Jr., "Rule of Law," 452.

[147] Ibid. Other have also made this connection, such as John Witte, Jr., "Introduction," in *Christianity and Law: An Introduction* (ed. John Witte, Jr. and Frank S. Alexander; Cambridge, UK: Cambridge University Press, 2008), 6. Also, note Jude P. Dougherty, *Western Creed, Western Identity: Essays in Legal and Social Philosophy* (Washington, D.C.: Catholic University of America, 2000), 13.

[148] Cao, *Chinese Law*, 125–27.

[149] Dien, *The Chinese Worldview Regarding Justice and the Supernatural*, 6.

[150] Ibid.

as a basis for various Chinese dynasties.[151] The Tang Code made it illegal (and

punishable by death) for (grand)children to accuse their (grand)parents of a crime. In fact,

the younger generation was obligated to hide such criminal activity. She adds the Tang

Code permitted families even to help family members "evade legal sanction."[152] The

prioritization of relationships influences perceptions of contracts as well. Lei states, "The

personal dimension of *guanxi* stresses the significance of trust, which implies that moral

obligation is more important than legal contract."[153] This is because business contracts

are seen as "statements of good intention [which] represent more the long-term friendly

relationship between the parties than a simple one-off transaction."[154]

One can now better understand how Chinese relates law and shame. Confucius

directly gives the priority of shame over law in issues of morality:

> If the people are led by laws, and uniformity among them be sought by
> punishments, they will try to escape punishment and have no sense of
> shame. If they are led by virtue, and uniformity sought among them
> through practice of ritual propriety, they will possess a sense of shame and
> come to you of their own accord.[155]

In short, laws cannot change human hearts by instilling a genuine love of virtue.[156] Since

Confucius held out the "ideal of a 'no litigation' society," it is not surprising that seeking

legal settlements via the lawcourt may be "regarded as shameful and immoral conduct—

where you have the potential of losing 'face' or making your opponent lose significant

---

[151] According to Wagner and Pencak, the Tang Code was written in AD 653 and finalized in 737. See Anne Wagner and William Pencak, *Images in Law* (Burlington, Vt.: Ashgate Publishing, 2006), 40.

[152] Dien, *The Chinese Worldview Regarding Justice and the Supernatural*, 5.

[153] Duo Lei, "Guanxi and Its Influence on Chinese Business Practices," *Harvard China Review* (Spring 2005): 83.

[154] Cao, *Chinese Law*, 95–96. This is echoed in Zhang and Baker, *Think Like Chinese*, 142–43.

[155] Lunyu 2:3 as quoted in Zhang and Baker, *Think Like Chinese*, 136. They cite *Stanford Encyclopedia of Philosophy*, n.p. Online: http://plato/stanford.edu/entries confucius.

[156] This thinking resembles a number of Scriptural passages, including Rom 8:3; Col 2:23.

mianzi [face]."[157] Reconciliation outside of formal legal systems is far more desirable.[158]

Shen Deyong, appointed vice president of China's Supreme People's Court in 2008,

affirms the ongoing relevance of this thinking within modern China.[159] A deep concern

for relationships, not abstract law, regulates morality. By disregarding public standards of

decency, one "can no longer count on [his or her] network of social relationships to help

them out, for they have isolated themselves."[160]

Finally, for the sake of a contextualized soteriology, one needs to understand what

Chinese mean by "righteousness." After all, such cultural background will inevitably

inform how Chinese readers may interpret or apply various biblical passages.

"Righteousness" is typically translated, *yi* (义) both in the Bible and in Chinese literature.

From Confucius' Analects, Yu argues that righteousness (*yi*) refers both to appropriate

action and judgment.[161] Rather than an inflexible law, it is an "internalized" virtue by

which one knows how to behave in a plethora of changing contexts.[162] An important

aspect of being a righteous person is having a sense of shame; however, that discussion

must wait until the next chapter, where Chinese notions like face, honor, and shame are

explained. As ethical practice, righteousness can be cultivated. Though there is not a

---

[157] Zhang and Baker, *Think Like Chinese*, 136. The translation of *mianzi* to "face" is my addition.

[158] Berring, Jr., "Rule of Law," 453–55. In the Bible, Paul's comments in 1 Cor 6:1, 4–8 are a striking echo of this sort of thinking.

[159] Deyong Shen, "Chinese Judicial Culture: From Tradition to Modernity," *BYU Journal of Public Law* 25 (21 Oct 2009): 136.

[160] Hsien Chin Hu, "The Chinese Concepts of 'Face'," *American Anthropologist* 46, no. 1 (Mar 1944): 51. Contrast this isolation with Confucius' view in Analects 4:25: "Confucius' understanding of the socialization process is that one authenticates one's being not by detaching from the world of human relations but by making sincere attempts to harmonize one's relationship with others. Confucius says, 'Virtue does not exist in isolation; there must be neighbors'." See Yeo, *What Has Jerusalem?*, 160.

[161] This is the fundamental argument of Jiyuan Yu, "Yi: Practical Wisdom in Confucius's Analects," *JCP* 33, no. 3 (2006): 335–48.

[162] Ibid., 340, 343.

uniform Confucian position on human nature, most Chinese are optimistic, affirming the humans are good by nature.[163] What Chinese mean by *yi* is anthropological, making little or no reference to a deity as one finds in Christianity. The question remains how much of what *yi affirms* can be accepted by Christian contextualizers even while rejecting the Confucian *denial* of the Christian God. It gives concrete expression to love (*ren*) involving loyalty and consideration for others.[164] *Yi* is "a way of living" that is sensitive to other's social status or role.[165] Righteousness takes into account the good of the entire community.[166] Simply, *yi* is playing one's role in society thus satisfying one's relational obligations.

Towards a Chinese Theology: What Has Been Attempted?

Having outlined the major contours of Chinese culture, this chapter reviews various ways theologians/missiologists have attempted to construct a contextualized theology for Chinese culture. Just as there is no consensus about how to do contextualized theology, so it is not surprising to find a myriad of proposals on Chinese theology. This section highlights some of the major themes, methods, and perspectives that relate to a contextualized Chinese theology.[167]

---

[163] Peters, "Issues Confronting Evangelical Missions," 267–68.

[164] Yu, "Yi," 336, 344.

[165] Quoted from Yeo, *Musing*, 460; cf. Hwang, *Foundations*, 110–11, 160–62; Chung-Ying Cheng, "Justice and Peace in Kant and Confucius," *JCP* 34, no. 3 (Sept 2007): 354. Such relations especially include family; cf. Chuang, "Effects of Interaction Pattern on Family Harmony and Well-Being: Test of Interpersonal Theory, Relational-Models Theory, and Confucian Ethics," 275.

[166] Cheng, "Justice and Peace in Kant and Confucius," 350–51.

[167] A brief review of contextualized Chinese theology is found in K. K. Yeo, "Paul's Ethic of Holiness and Chinese Morality of Renren," in *Cross-Cultural Paul: Journeys to Others, Journeys to Ourselves* (ed. Charles H. Cosgrove, Herold Weiss, and K. K. Yeo; Grand Rapids, Mich.: Eerdmans, 2005), 104–20.

Many authors have suggested criteria for doing contextualized theology. Yung says Asian theology must meet people's felt needs, assist in evangelism and pastoral care, take seriously the culture's ways of thinking, and be faithful to Christian tradition.[168] He repeatedly stresses that theology must be practical, addressing the real problems and situations people face. Similarly, other Asian theologians try to write theologies that emphasize ethics and integrate Confucianism with Christianity.[169] Stults gives a more extensive and helpful list of seven "principles for doing theology in Asia": Contextual theology should be complete, comprehensive, properly exegeted, in harmony with the rest of Scripture, balanced, positive; in addition, it will stress message over method.[170] One should note Yung and others stress culture and the immediate context a bit more than Scripture. On the other hand, Stults' criteria are more text-based, less centered on the surrounding culture. How does one avoid these two polarities?

This chapter lays out a spectrum of approaches to Chinese contextualization. Given the lack of consensus and uniform categories on the topic, the following taxonomy is no doubt subjective. However, it represents the spectrum of views in a way that seems less arbitrary than dividing them via geography, ethnicity, denominations, or topics in systematic theology. Theological contextualization involves the Bible and culture. While all theologians/missiologists try to treat the two fairly, inevitably certain patterns and priorities concerning interpretation and application are bound to emerge. Six categories

---

[168] Yung, *Mangoes or Bananas*, 65–102.

[169] Wing-Hung Lam discusses these things when considering the indigenizing of theology in China. See Wing-Hung Lam, *Chinese Theology in Construction* (Pasadena, Calif.: William Carey Library, 1983). Also, K. K. Yeo overtly interprets Paul using Confucian philosophy as his "way of being faithful to being Chinese." See Yeo, *Musing*, 425.

[170] Stults, *Developing an Asian Evangelical Theology*, 191–93.

signify six ways of talking about and doing theology for a Chinese context. Although each has defining characteristics, this does not deny overlap and agreement between the approaches. These categories do not suppose hard and fast dichotomies. Extensive discussion will follow a brief introduction of each view. Particular attention is given to identifying each approach's view of Chinese culture, its methodological assumptions, and the doctrine of salvation. What informs these contextualized theologies?

First, a "situational" approach lays stress on the contextual issues Chinese face. Liberation theologies fall into this category. With respect to Chinese theology, C. S. Song is representative of a "situational" approach. Factors from the readers' own circumstances are given prime importance in formulating theology.[171] In practice, this emphasis on the local situation acts as a protest against the tendency to universalize Western theology.

Second, many have emphasized ethnic identity. This will be called the "Sino" approach. These thinkers repeatedly stress the utmost importance of making sure their theology is "Chinese." As a result, they may be criticized for using weak theological methods or minimizing the biblical context. "Sino-theology" is probably the best example of this perspective.[172] Especially noteworthy is Malaysian Chinese theologian, K. K. Yeo, who is quite explicit about his ambition to develop a distinctive Chinese theology.

Third, the "synchronistic" approach draws from a number of cultural concepts to communicate theological meaning. Many of the earliest missionaries to China are

---

[171] After writing this, I found another Chinese theologian who asserts, "I think the starting point for Chinese Christianity is the contemporary Chinese socio-cultural reality," after which he offers C. S. Song as an illustration. See Wenxi Zhang, "Christianity in the Chinese Cultural Context" (Paper presented at 22nd National Catholic China Conference, Nov 2006), n.p. [cited 2 Feb 2011]. Online: www.holyredeemer.cc/pdf/Zhang.pdf.

[172] For further study, see the Institute of Sino-Christian Studies. Online: *www.iscs.org.hk.*

characteristic of this view. They and others have taken seriously the importance of culture in contextualization. Typically, this method employs a prominent cultural issue, seeking to synchronize or coordinate theology and culture. Often, the chosen theme is not one of the foremost motifs found in the Bible itself. In China, this may include ancestor worship, Chinese New Year, cosmology, even the Chinese language itself.

Fourth, many evangelicals have utilized a "Scriptural" methodology. They are emphatic that the Bible directs the contextualization process; therefore, such treatments are littered with biblical references. Traditional theological topics receive special attention. A grammatical-historical method of interpreting the Bible is a common characteristic. This nomenclature in no way suggests that others ignore the Bible or do not affirm the Scripture's supreme authority; nor is it implied that others do not use a grammatical-historical method. Rather, these categories signify the aspect of contextualization most emphasized by an author. Therefore, someone like Enoch Wan has used a "synchronistic" approach to the "Tao" idea,[173] a "Scriptural" treatment of Christology,[174] and a "systematic" analysis of Western and Chinese theology.[175] Of course, some articles defy easy categorization due to a high degree of integration.[176] However, this grouping tends to use conceptual models rather than theological contextualizations themselves.

Fifth, many thinkers have only developed "systematic" frameworks for approaching the question. They are more speculative in nature. These writers engage in

---

[173] Enoch Wan, "Tao—The Chinese Theology of God-Man," *His Dominion* 11, no. 3 (Spring 1985): 24–27.
[174] Wan, "Jesus Christ for the Chinese."
[175] Wan, "Critiquing."
[176] Wan, "Practical Contextualization."

questions of meta-theory; that is, they primarily explore problems *related to* or *about* contextualization. For example, topics might include the use of metaphors, cross-cultural hermeneutics, the danger of syncretism, and the influence of worldview on contextualization. Works that demonstrate a "systematic" approach to Chinese contextualization are not themselves *theological* proposals regarding a central theme within historical, systematic, or biblical theology.

Sixth, a "soterian" approach aims at sharing with individuals how they can be saved.[177] Gospel tracts are typical of this method. It communicates the "plan of salvation," whereby one may come into a personal relationship with God. In short, sharing the gospel means helping people understand salvation. "Soterian" presentations are generally brief, less nuanced than other approaches, and are not overtly theological works. They try to communicate basic truths needed for salvation. Many of these evangelistic methods share theologies and concepts utilized in other approaches.

"Situational" Approach

Returning to the situational approach, Taiwanese theologian C. S. Song brazenly rejects Scripture as the "absolute norm" for theologizing; instead, he sees the Bible "as a pattern of type of God's salvation."[178] He suggests, "Scriptures can thus be interpreted symbolically [since] a literal interpretation of the Bible kills revelation."[179] Song finds justification for his approach in Israel's adaption of Canaanite religious practices, even going so far as saying the Bible does not condemn idolatry itself, simply treating idols as

---

[177] Here I use "soterian" as articulated by Scot McKnight in *The King Jesus Gospel.*

[178] C. S. Song, "The New China and Salvation History: A Methodological Enquiry," *South East Asia Journal of Theology* 15, no. 2 (1974): 55–56. Quoted by Covell, *Confucius*, 218.

[179] Song, *Third-Eye Theology*, 103–4.

"ultimate objects of worship."[180] Song espouses a God who changes, because "[a]n unchanging God is a metaphysical God who is removed from history . . . who maintains a stoic composure."[181] Because people all share a common humanity, he rejects "sectarian" theologies that do not "have room" for people of other religions and cultures.[182] He interprets Christ's incarnation to mean that God reveals himself in history and cares for the injustices found in the physical world. Characterizing the OT as "a *political* history of Israel," Song calls people to grasp the "biblical meaning of justice or righteousness," for "[i]t cannot be confined to a spiritual realm divorced from what is going on in the world."[183] Drawing upon Jesus' kingdom language, Christians should seek to "transform" the present world, suffering for the "*metanoia* of power" by "exposing the wickedness of the religious and political leaders," who veer from God's truth of love.[184] What drives this sort of thinking? Founded on creation, it is "the kingdom of God that links all humanity in a common kinship and blood relationship."[185] Yet, Song regards the West (and its theology) as oppressive to Asians, robbing them of their cultural identity and fragmenting God's intention for humanity.[186] He affirms, "[S]alvation is essentially an event associated with community and kinship" and "The concept of kinship is therefore fundamental to the biblical understanding of salvation."[187] This salvation will only be

---

[180] Ibid., 106–7. It is noteworthy that Song cites many verses condemning idolatry; yet, when he then redefines idolatry and excuses it, he gives no Scriptural warrant.

[181] Ibid., 196–99. Quote from p. 197.

[182] C. S. Song, "Christian Theology: Towards An Asian Reconstruction" (Paper presented at the Conference of World Mission and the Role of Korean Churches, Seoul, Korea, Nov 1995), n.p. [cited 14 Feb 2012]. Online: http://www.religion-online.org/showarticle.asp?title=128.

[183] Song, *Third-Eye Theology*, 201, 206. Emphasis in original

[184] Ibid., 222, 232, 236. *Metanoia* is the Greek word typically translated "repentance" in the Bible.

[185] Ibid., 140.

[186] James Wu, "C. S. Song," *BCEWT*, n.p.

[187] Song, *Third-Eye Theology*, 139.

possible when Christ is seen not merely through Western eyes, but in the experience of

the Asian world. After all, he contends, "Those who are not endowed with German eyes

should not be prevented from seeing Christ differently" from the views espoused by the

German reformers.[188] In short, Song sees himself as protecting the human family from a

presumptuous, younger brother (i.e. the West).

The contemporary TSPM leadership is likewise wary of "certain traditional

understanding that does not fit the situation of the age."[189] Deng Fucun, Vice-President of

the TSPM of the Chinese Christian Church, says, "[T]he Chinese church has been

rethinking its theology [in order to help] guide religions to be adaptable to the socialist

society."[190] Specifically, he dismisses "[Western] conservative theological thinking" that

separates Christians from non-Christians, "places church above the country," and

"negates rational thinking."[191] He informs the reader of the prospective direction of

TSPM theology. Deng contends, "No faith belief or church rules should go beyond the

statements in [the Apostles' Creed and the Nicene Creed]. Neither systematic theology

nor doctrinal theology should contradict them."[192] Yet, at the same time, he says

overdependence on literal interpretations of Scripture inhibit one from discerning "new

revelation from God."[193] Chinese theology should look very different since Chinese

culture is not like the "Greek dualist culture" of Western theology.[194] He adds, "[T]he

---

[188] Ibid., 11.

[189] Fucun Deng, "The Basis for the Reconstruction of Chinese Theological Thinking," in *Christianity and Chinese Culture* (ed. Mikka Ruokanen and Paulos Huang; Grand Rapids, Mich.: Eerdmans, 2010), 304.

[190] Ibid., 299, 301.

[191] Ibid., 299–300. On p. 305, he makes explicit that he refers to "Western conservative theology."

[192] Ibid., 303.

[193] Ibid., 304.

[194] Ibid.

'incarnated Jesus' was easier to be understood and accepted by the people living in the Hellenistic culture along the Mediterranean seacoast," as opposed to Chinese people.[195]

How might such an approach affect a topic like Christology? Zhang echoes the sentiments of Song and Ding when he says, "Christianity is a foreign religion imported from a fundamentally different cultural matrix. [Therefore] I think the starting point for Chinese Christianity is the contemporary Chinese socio-cultural reality."[196] Emphasizing the suffering of Chinese people, Zhang stresses "not God's suffering 'on behalf of' our suffering" but rather his "solidarity," suffering "together 'with' our Chinese and all humanity." He adds that Jesus is "a builder of a new culture and a new society," "a teacher who teaches you the wisdom of living," "the healer of body, soul, and mind," and "a reconciliatory figure of Chinese religions and a moral example."

"Sino" Approach

The "Sino" method of contextualization shares a concern about the cultural dimension of Christianity. Whereas Song strongly resists the prominence of Western culture/theology against other world cultures, this Sino-approach stresses Chinese identity in particular. Feudalism compounded by Western imperialism drove national leaders to exert their autonomy by establishing the Republic of China in 1912. Further, the TSPM in the 1950s aimed at guarding the independence of the Chinese church from Western influence.[197] By the 1920s, T. C. Chao had attempted to rid the Chinese church of "unscientific" doctrines from the West (like miracles) in favor of a kind of Christianity more sympathetic to

---

[195] Ibid., 301.
[196] Zhang, "Christianity in the Chinese Cultural Context."
[197] Sze-kar Wan, "Chinese Theology," *GDT*, 163.

Confucianism, which he thought "part of the revelation of God."[198] In short, many Chinese have long been regarded Christianity as a "foreign religion."[199]

In reaction, Chinese theologians have since sought to find a way to be distinctly "Chinese" while remaining Christian. One might categorize these efforts to contextualize Christianity according to one of three patterns. First, some theologies are "Chinese" by the fact they try to retain characteristics of Confucianism. These proposals emphasize national unity. Second, a number of contemporary scholars propose a theology based on the "Chinese" existential experience. Third, the theology typified by K. K. Yeo is "Chinese" inasmuch as it reads a Chinese context *into* biblical texts.

Some have tried to resurrect Confucian ideals as a means of saving Christianity. In a day when many were seeking "national salvation," Wan suggests a common question has spurred the Chinese church over the past 100 years: "How does one reconcile salvation by grace with social and cosmic transformation through self-effort?"[200] Denying Christ's resurrection and deity, Chao reinterprets Jesus as a "Confucian sage, a moral exemplar."[201] He appealed to the Holy Spirit as the means by which self-cultivation was possible.[202] In this way, Christianity was put in the service of national social reform. Consistent with concrete Chinese thinking, many church leaders reject the sort of escapist theology they perceive in the Western tradition. In essence, some accuse Western

---

[198] Edmond Tang, "Chinese Theologies," *DTWT*, 38.

[199] Xinzhong Yao, "Success or Failure? Christianity in China," *History Today*, 1 Sept 1994, n.p. [cited 14 Feb 2012]. Online: http://www.historytoday.com/xinzhong-yao/success-or-failure-christianity-china; Wan, "Chinese Theology," 162.

[200] Wan, "Chinese Theology," 163.

[201] G. Wright Doyle, "A Review of Reading Christian Scriptures in China," *Global China Center*, 4 Sept 2008, n.p. [cited 15 Feb 2012]. Online: http://www.globalchinacenter.org/analysis/ christianity-in-china/reading-christian-scriptures-in-china.php; Wan, "Chinese Theology," 162.

[202] Wan, "Chinese Theology," 163.

theology of a dualism that sets heaven against earth, body against spirit, thus

"depreciating the quality of this life."[203] Bishop Ding (*Ding Guangxun*), one of the most

influential voices of the TSPM Church, echoes this sentiment. Ding contends that the

gospel calls us to "transcend the personal" such that any brand of Christianity that is

apathetic to social evils and is "concerned only with personal salvation, is not a two-

legged Christianity, but a lame one."[204] In agreement with Y. T. Wu, another founder in

the TSPM, Ding adds that this privatized Christianity reflects people's ongoing need to

be "saved from our captivity by selfishness."[205] Liu, echoing Ding, compares Christianity

to Buddhism, being individualistic and having little concern for "the moral order of the

community."[206] These comments reflect more than a mere philosophical agenda. They

were driven more by nationalism than anything else.[207]

Like Confucianism, this contextualized theology routinely points to creation as

the model by which to bring harmony to society.[208] Ding is a leading representative of

this view; he states, "The goal of this creation is a world of harmony that will embrace

---

[203] Zhien Zhao, "Fifty Years of Theological Transformation in Chinese Christianity," *AJT* 15, no. 1 (Apr 2001): 137.

[204] K. H. Ting, *God is Love: Collected Writing of Bishop K. H. Ting* (Colorado Springs, Colo.: David C. Cook, 2004), 33–34. His family name is sometimes translated either "Ting" or "Ding."

[205] Ibid., 493. Wan says of T. C. Wu, "National salvation was to him more important than personal salvation." See Wan, "Chinese Theology," 163. His contemporary Wu Leichuan holds a similar opinion. Cf. Huiliang Ni, "Sinicizing Jesus in the First Half of the Twentieth Century: How Chinese Christians Understood Jesus" (PhD diss., Claremont, Calif.: Claremont Graduate University, 2008), 131–54.

[206] Chin Ken-Pa cites Xiaofeng Liu, *Hanyu Shenxue yu Lishi Zhexue* [*The Sino-Christian Theology and Philosophy of History*] (Hong Kong: Institute of Sino-Christian Studies, 2000), 49. See Ken-Pa Chin, "The Paradigm Shift: From Chinese Theology to Sino-Christian Theology–A Case Study on Liu Xiaofeng," in *Sino-Christian Theology* (ed. Pan-chiu Lai and Jason Lam; New York, N.Y.: Peter Lang, 2010), 153.

[207] This argument is well laid out in Chin, "The Paradigm Shift."

[208] K. K. Yeo explicitly grounds his hermeneutical method on a Confucian premise, "Cosmology is more important than anthropology, because anthropology is a part of cosmology. If one wishes to know anthropology, one has to know its larger context, namely, cosmology." Yeo, *What Has Jerusalem?*, 18.

both the present world and the world to come."[209] Therefore, some theologies urgently seek to close any perceived gap between Christians and non-Christians. Ding conjectures, "After all, the God who is worthy of our worship and praise is not so small as to be concerned with a few million Chinese who profess to believe in him. . . . He does not mind terribly much if many, for good reasons, do not recognize his existence."[210] Speaking to a church under the oversight of an atheistic government, Ding explicitly appeals to Confucianism in emphasizing ethics in Chinese theology.[211] Ding asserts, "Salvation and sanctification cannot be separated, and the source of all these is Love, the key that opens up all existence. . . . In the beginning, we made belief and unbelief the only question Christianity posed to humanity; only later did we realize that God's creation, salvation and sanctification are one in the cosmos and in history."[212] Against the "antisocial, sectarian tendency to elevate personal salvation above ethics," Ding sees justification by faith as a divisive doctrine employed by missionaries to remove the sense of moral responsibility.[213] He clarifies one of his previous comments about the need to "play down" the doctrine of justification:

> I said this because it is overemphasized in China, as if it is the all in all of
> Christian faith. The idea is that anyone who believes will go to heaven
> after death, and those who do not believe will go to hell. This is an idea
> that denies morality. By extension, Hitler and Mussolini, as Christians,
> would be in heaven, while Confucius, Laozi and Zhou Enlai, non-

---

[209] Ting, *God is Love*, 135.

[210] Guangxun Ding, "Religious Policy and Theological Reorientation in China," *China Notes* 18, no. 3 (Summer 1980): 124. Cited in Covell, *Confucius*, 238.

[211] Ting, *God is Love*, 512. Also observed by Jonathan Chao, "The Gospel and Culture in Chinese History," in *Chinese Intellectuals and the Gospel* (ed. Samuel D. Ling and Stacey Bieler; San Gabriel, Calif.: China Horizon, 1999), 18.

[212] As quoted by Yang, "Theological and Cultural Reflections," 68.

[213] The words quoted are Wan's in Wan, "Chinese Theology," 163. Ding speaks for himself in K. H. Ting, "Some Thoughts on the Subject of Theological Reconstruction," *CTR* 17 (2003): 116.

believers, would be in hell. This is the only logical conclusion according to this idea.[214]

In short, he thinks creation is often overshadowed by redemption, thus love is eclipsed by faith. Moreover, the stress on morality in Christian salvation is not limited to theologians who hold to a "social gospel." Wang Mingdao staunchly affirms Christ's death for sins and the traditional view of justification by faith. Nevertheless, he so emphasized the point that salvation entails sanctification that "Wang was often regarded as a moralist."[215]

A younger generation of Chinese scholars has followed their predecessor in ironic fashion. The purpose of their "Sino-theology" is "primarily serving Chinese-speakers" but "from a basis of the *existential experience* of Chinese-speakers."[216] Chin claims, "Sino-Christian theology is essentially a theology of existentialism [such that its] main concern . . . is whether a contingent individual shows his or her will of openness to the Christ event."[217] They object to using Christianity as a mere tool for nationalistic propaganda; the "modern spirit" of Sino-theology resists a "grand national narrative."[218] However, this movement should not be interpreted as a rejection of the previous generation. Frequent attempts are made to harmonize Christian faith with Marxism, which is likened to Confucianism, being focused on "this world," "rationality," "responsibility," and having "the priority of community over individuals."[219] Li remarks,

---

[214] Ting, *God is Love*, 124–25.

[215] Ni, "Sinicizing Jesus," 196–97.

[216] Qiuling Liu, "Historical Reflections on 'Sino-Christian Theology'," in *Sino-Christian Studies in China* (ed. Huilin Yang and Daniel H. N. Yeung; trans. Alison Hardie; Newcastle: Cambridge Scholars, 2006), 44, 50. My emphasis. Also see Huilin Yang, "The Value of Theology in Humanities: Possible Approaches to Sino-Christian Theology," in *Sino-Christian Theology* (ed. Pan-chiu Lai and Jason Lam; New York, N.Y.: Peter Lang, 2010), 101.

[217] Chin, "The Paradigm Shift," 153, 157.

[218] Zhang, "Nationalism," 173–95. Chin, "The Paradigm Shift."

[219] Li, "How Do Social and Psychological," 216–18. Also noteworthy is Xian Zhang, "Christianity, Marxism, and 'The End of History': An Analysis of History Strung Together with the Examples of

"Except for tension over the issue of theism and atheism, Christianity is not necessarily in conflict with Marxism; they are more similar than different, especially in aspects of ethics and value system."[220] Social unity is gained through a distinctively Chinese kind of individualism that emphasizes tolerance for the common good.

These theologians are sometimes called "cultural Christians," having an academic interest in Christianity but not necessarily claiming a personal conversion or affiliation with a church.[221] Methodologically, these Sino-theologians make use of methods found in philosophy, literature, history, and other human sciences.[222] A distinctive feature of Sino-theology is its emphasis on using *hanyu*, the majority language of Mainland China.[223] It is felt that language is a vehicle for culture even if unconsciously.[224] A survey of their work shows they give more attention to Christian tradition than exegetical or systematic theology.[225] Lai concedes that Sino-theologians are "relatively weak" in the area of biblical studies, reflected in the fact they "seldom quote the bible in their theological writing," thus raising questions about whether "Sino-Christian theology [is] to be

---

Liberation Theology," in *Sino-Christian Studies in China* (ed. Huilin Yang and Daniel H. N. Yeung; Newcastle: Cambridge Scholars, 2006), 204–21.

[220] Li, "How Do Social and Psychological," 225.

[221] Pan-chiu Lai and Jason T. S. Lam, "Retrospect and Prospect of Sino-Christian Theology: An Introduction," in *Sino-Christian Theology* (ed. Pan-chiu Lai and Jason T. S. Lam; New York, N.Y.: Peter Lang, 2010), 1–4. They note the term is unclear and controversial, but common. Some do affirm faith in Christ and prefer the name "Chinese Scholars" (p. 11). Cf. Wan, "Chinese Theology," 163–64.

[222] Lai and Lam, "Retrospect and Prospect," 8.

[223] Ibid., 7. In fact, this connection between theology and the linguistics is a common theme in Sino-theologian articles. He Guanghu's articles are examples. See his work, "The Basis and Significance of Sino-Christian Theology," in *Sino-Christian Studies in China* (ed. Yang Huilin and Daniel H. N. Yeung; Newcastle, UK: Cambridge Scholars Publishing, 2006), 120–32; He, "A Methodology," 106–119. Also see Qingxlong Zhang, "Sino-Christian Theology: The Unfolding of 'Dao' in the Chinese Language Context," in *Sino-Christian Theology* (ed. Pan-chiu Lai and Jason Lam; New York, N.Y.: Peter Lang, 2010), 123–38.

[224] For a fuller discussion, see Huilin Yang, "Theological Translation and Transmission between China and West," in *Sino-Christian Theology* (ed. Pan-chiu Lai and Jason Lam; New York, N.Y.: Peter Lang, 2010), 83–99.

[225] Anecdotally, a friend attended the TSPM's premier seminary in Nanjing. When asked about the learning process, he said they rarely studied the Bible. Instead, nearly half the time was spent studied ideas from historical theologians (especially Barth) and the other half on Chinese culture.

recognized as a Christian theology at all."[226] Alternatively, they draw liberally from

"traditional Chinese culture."[227] Therefore, a "Chinese Buddhist method of doctrinal

criticism" may be employed, since "ultimate authority does not lie in the Scriptural texts

but with the Holy Spirit, who inspired the Scriptures."[228]

With respect to soteriology, Lai Pan-chiu reflects a desire among Sino-

theologians to be inclusive rather than exclusive. He adopts Paul Tillich's understanding

of salvation as "healing."[229] This definition broadens traditional ideas about Christian

salvation to include any instance of physical, psychological, and spiritual health. Lai adds,

"In this sense, all human beings have the potential to be saviours, healers and

liberators."[230] Lai opens the article by expressing his concern for the question of identity

as it relates to being both Chinese and Christian. His agenda becomes clear when he

explains why he favors this soteriological view:

> The most important implication of Tillich's conception of salvation
> remains that it can overcome the exclusivism associated with the doctrine
> of no salvation outside the church. . . . His soteriology provides the
> concept of salvation required for an understanding of the history of
> Chinese religions as part of the history of salvation.[231]

He acknowledges but does not elaborate on a problem with this view; namely, what

"criterion" should one use to "discern salvation in the midst of ambiguities . . . ?"[232]

---

[226] Pan-chiu Lai, "Sino-Christian Theology, Bible, and Christian Tradition," in *Sino-Christian Theology* (ed. Jason Lam and Pan-chiu Lai; New York, N.Y.: Peter Lang, 2010), 163, 165.

[227] Ibid., 174. In defense, Lai says, "It is noteworthy that there is no mention of 'one Scripture' [in Eph 4:3–6]. In fact, the canon adopted by Roman Catholicism is slightly different from that of Protestantism." (p. 174)

[228] Ibid., 176. He adds, "[I]t is of no necessity that theology should be unilaterally determined by the Bible or biblical studies" (p. 176).

[229] Pan-chiu Lai, "Chinese Religions and the History of Salvation: A Theological Perspective," *Ching Feng* 40, no. 1 (Mar 1997): 25.

[230] Ibid., 25.

[231] Ibid., 26.

[232] Ibid., 28.

Sino-theology often appeals to Christ's incarnation to justify its vision for Christianity. This doctrine provides a model for contextualization that expresses "God's entering into Chinese thought."[233] Accordingly, Chen states, "[T]he main task of Christianity is not to rationalize and defend universal doctrines, but to make Christians open our minds to God's different ways of working."[234] It is therefore not surprising to find frequent appeals to "the revelation of God" in Chinese culture.[235] Christianity becomes the means to harmonize the social and supernatural.[236] No doubt, there is some degree of truth to Yang's conclusion. He suggests Christianity's contribution of "ethics and social order" to Chinese culture likely accounts "for its rapid spread on the Chinese mainland as well as the core content of its' contextualized' interpretations."[237]

An important subnarrative begins to take shape the more one reads Chinese theology. In effect, Chinese theologians overlay the Jew-Gentile story atop of the Chinese church. In particular, comparisons are commonly drawn between Israel and China. This serves a few purposes. Politically, Israel is regarded as a model in which "spiritual dedication and zealous patriotism . . . are in complete harmony."[238] On the other hand, Israel becomes a symbol pointing to China's salvation. Chinese nationalism simply

---

[233] Chin, "The Paradigm Shift," 157.

[234] Peilan Guo, *Shangdi zai Yazhou renmin zhi zhong [God in the Midst of the Asian People]* (Hong Kong: Jidujiao wenyi chubanshe, 1993), 25. This is cited in Yongtao Chen, "Christ and Culture: A Reflection by a Chinese Christian," in *Christianity and Chinese Culture* (ed. Mikka Ruokanen and Paulos Huang; Grand Rapids, Mich.: Eerdmans, 2010), 347.

[235] Chen, "The Basis for the Reconstruction," 349. Similarly, Wang Aiming, dean of Nanjing Theological Seminary, affirms, "God's revelation is gradual and progressive, as is human understanding of God." See Aiming Wang, "Understanding Theological Reconstruction in the Chinese Church: A Hermeneutical Approach," *CTR* 16 (2002): 145–46. Quoted in Gerald Anderson, "A Response to Professor Li Deng Fucun," in *Christianity and Chinese Culture* (ed. Mikka Ruokanen and Paulos Huang; Grand Rapids, Mich.: Eerdmans, 2010), 314.

[236] For instance, Xie Zhibin says, "[W]e may turn to Christianity as a religion that synthesizes the ethic system and the worship of the supernatural [in Chinese society]," in "Religious Diversity," 234.

[237] Yang, "Inculturation," 160, 162.

[238] Ting, *God is Love*, 230.

expresses the same sort of longing felt by the Jews amid their various oppressions.[239]

Covell points out there have been "many who try to equate Mao's Long March (the 'Chinese exodus') with the scriptural account of the deliverance of Israel from Egypt."[240] It may be noteworthy that the leader of the Taiping rebellion (1851–1864), Hong Xiuquan, saw his movement in light of Israel's call by God to rid herself of idolatry.[241] Chen bluntly states, "As Jesus Christ did not come to abolish Jewish culture, he will not abolish Chinese culture but fulfill it."[242] Another Chinese scholar observes Confucianism's focus on "ritual propriety [*li*] . . . resembles the Jewish-Christian tradition of God's commandments and laws."[243] No doubt other similarities could be added. For instance, Yang notes that, in the twentieth century, "ethicizing" Christianity by means of Confucianism was a means of fostering nationalism.[244] This brand of Christianity fed off a value system that sharply separated "Chinese" from "foreign." Likewise, Sino-theologians aspire to unify not only Chinese together but humanity.

Wan observes a problem in Sino-theology's exalting the Han language (*hanyu*), which only represents the majority group in Mainland China, overlooking that "Chinese is not one language but a system of languages."[245] What are we to make of the emphasis on being "Chinese" (or perhaps one could say, *not* being foreign)? Could it create a kind of chasm that divided Hellenistic Jews from those Jews who lived in their homeland?

---

[239] Zhang, "Nationalism," 190.

[240] Covell, *Confucius*, 218. He lists Raymond Whitehead as an example in his "Christ, Salvation, and Maoism." Address given at the American Society of Missiology, North Park University, Chicago, Jun 1977.

[241] Ibid., 165.

[242] Chen, "The Basis for the Reconstruction," 348–49.

[243] Paulos Huang, "A Response to He Guanghu," in *Christianity and Chinese Culture* (ed. Mikka Ruokanen and Paulos Huang; Grand Rapids, Mich.: Eerdmans, 2010), 79.

[244] Yang, "Inculturation," 153–54.

[245] Wan, "Chinese Theology," 164.

Further, does this movement potentially foster the sort of ethnocentrism that threatened the early church? Amid the potential comparisons made with the Jewish people, one can see the danger of turning Chinese Christianity into a *Judiazing* movement. One might call this *ethnicizing* Christianity.

Yeo goes well beyond others in that his theology consistently and intentionally attempts to reckon with the biblical text. In that sense, Yeo's work may be the most "theological" of the Chinese theologies we have seen. Therefore, this chapter gives Yeo's writings a more thorough treatment. He echoes a goal frequently stated among Chinese theologians, remaining *fully Chinese* while being fully Christian.[246] In actuality, "being faithful to be being Chinese" becomes the overriding standard for his interpretation of the Bible.[247] For example, he gives considerable effort to harmonize Confucianism with Pauline theology by comparing *Analects* and Galatians.[248] However, Yeo's theological method causes him to tell a very different story than that traditionally told by Christians. In his contextualized theology, neither the Bible nor the Chinese context is fully respected. Differences are grossly overlooked in order to convey a sense of (superficial) commonality. In the end, Confucian thinking wins out, and his contextualization is less than Christian.

Yeo's theological agenda is distinguished not simply by what he affirms, but in what he *denies*. He unmistakably follows E. P. Sanders and James Dunn in arguing that the Jewish law is the ethnic "badge" separating Israel from Gentiles; accordingly,

---

[246] Yeo, *Musing*, 252; cf. 425, 428–29.
[247] Ibid., 425.
[248] An entire book is dedicated to the topic, i.e. Yeo, *Musing*. He also discusses this theme in Chapter 2 of Yeo, *What Has Jerusalem?*.

Galatians and justification concern "defining the identity symbol for the people of God."[249] Yeo rightly affirms that the law (in the OT) "protected Israel from the defiling influence of the Gentiles;" thus, Galatians' discussion about justification involves ecclesiology and "racial inclusiveness."[250] Further, he correctly affirms "eschatological salvation" entails one's participation "in Christ," who acts as "a representative" for Israel and all humanity.[251]

Nonetheless, Yeo is wrong in *what he denies*. He denies that justification involves salvation.[252] Also, many Christians will reject his views on Christ's atonement and the gospel, which he reduces to symbolism merely leading to the reconciliation of ethnic groups.[253] He says Galatians is not "talking about *individual* salvation, but about group identity and what is required to be a full member of God's people."[254] Elsewhere, Yeo makes a comment, without elaboration, that seems to conflict with his larger treatment of justification. He leaves room for a more expansive view by saying, "Justification does not stop at restoring our status as acceptable to God."[255]

---

[249] Yeo, *What Has Jerusalem?*, 42.

[250] Ibid. His concern is extended beyond ethnicity, "But the problems [of church division] when one group or race perceives its traditions or emphasis as the only true one or, worse still, imposes it on others as essential to the gospel of Christ" (p. 46.)

[251] Ibid., 38.

[252] Ibid., 31. For Yeo, salvation is a sociological-relational term (Yeo, *Musing*, 249, 258–59. He does not use the term as much *theologically* as anthropologically

[253] For his treatment on the cross, see Yeo, *Musing*, 83, 109, 301. He calls the cross of Christ an "inclusive symbol" that overcomes "cultural and religious imperialism" (p. 83). For his take on the gospel, see pp. 136, 140–41, 173, 181. Cf. Yeo, *What Has Jerusalem?*, 26–42.

[254] Yeo, *Musing*, 80.

[255] K. K. Yeo, "Christian Chinese Theology: Theological Ethics of Becoming Human and Holy," in *Global Theology in Evangelical Perspective: Exploring the Contextual Nature of Theology and Mission* (ed. Jeffrey P. Greenman and Gene Green; Downers Grove, Ill.: IVP, 2012), 112. As will be seen, I suggest the issue of "status" is integral to bridging soteriology and ecclesiology within debates about justification.

Elsewhere, he appears to distinguish between "justified" and "set right."[256]

The real aim of his exegesis now comes into focus. One cannot help but see how Yeo frames this "Chinese theology" to explain how one can be a *Chinese* Christian free from Western "imperialism."[257] His antipathy is quite transparent:

> Many Protestant churches have long been guilty of using religion as opium or as escapism. They are guilty of neglecting social reform, and are only interested in saving pagan souls. TSPM has striven to maintain the more holistic approach of combining the social gospel and the personal gospel. . . . The old way to evangelize was to convert a pagan into a Westerner with Western ideas, cultural values, and ways of practicing Christian faith. . . . Chinese Christians have reacted against becoming Westernized Christians. Easterners never bow down to the god of logic, dogma, or creeds.[258]

One sees how Yeo's biographical struggle with identity[259] heavily influences his approach to contextualization, or what he calls "cross-cultural hermeneutics."[260]

Yeo argues that Galatians represents a fight against cultural imperialism. Repeatedly, Yeo claims the "basic issue" Paul addresses is how Gentiles can be "full members of the people of God," free from Jewish symbolism (which he thinks is oppressive).[261] Paul writes to explain how Christ "liberates" people from symbols of Jewish identity like the Mosaic Law.[262] Yeo absorbs the goals of Confucianism,

---

[256] Yeo, *Musing*, 207. Elsewhere, "set right" is understood "in the sense that a person or people group maintains the covenant-relation, a set-right relationship that defines [God's] people." However, he does not explain how "set right" (which implies a change) means "maintain" (implying no change). See K. K. Yeo, "Introduction," in *Navigating Romans Through Cultures: Challenging Readings by Charting a New Course* (ed. K. K. Yeo; New York, N.Y.: T&T Clark International, 2004), 14.

[257] Yeo equates "religious imperialism" with "proselytism," which he says, "is akin to the Roman ideology of conquest" (Yeo, *Musing*, 134, 149). By extension, evangelism or missions are acts of "terror" or "social control" used by outside ideologists (pp. 148–49; Yeo's terms). Finally, he juxtaposes criticism of "cultural imperial" with "the aberrations [against China] of Christian history in the West" (p. 432).

[258] Yeo, *What Has Jerusalem?*, 241.

[259] See this interspersed throughout Yeo, *Musing*, 3–25.

[260] Ibid., 10–11.

[261] Ibid., 79, 81, 83, 84.

[262] Ibid., 396.

justifying them with his own interpretation of Paul. Since Chinese philosophy is the lens through which he reads the biblical text, Yeo generally refrains from using Paul to rigorously critique *Confucius*.[263] The latter is simply assumed authoritative for exegeting Christian Scripture. Confucius' this-world, socio-political orientation saturates Yeo's reflection. His so-called Chinese theology is really an apologetic for a harmonious community. The question of *divine* authorship or intent is never taken up. "Virtue," as defined by Confucius, is more persuasive than revelation.[264] Therefore, it is not surprising to read Yeo say, "whether Christ or the law should best symbolize the identity of the people of God is ultimately to be determined by the virtuous life of the community."[265] Christ's work is thus reduced to a "divine paradigm for being a community."[266] Accordingly, he advances the Jew-Gentile analogy, though in a much different way that those we have examined. By contrast, Yeo depicts China in the role of the Gentiles excluded by those who demand conformity and deny the value of Chinese identity.[267]

While Yeo correctly sees common ground between Confucianism and Paul's writing, nevertheless, their differences are fundamental and nullify Yeo's construction. Mostly acutely, Paul and Confucius have very divergent ontologies. Confucius' concept of *tian* (天, "heaven") is quite different from the personal God who reveals himself in the Bible. In numerous places, Yeo concedes these fundamentally divergent starting points

---

[263] An exception is found on Ibid., 342. Yeo calls Confucius' view of human nature "naïve" and then uses Paul to correct it.

[264] On the Confucian concept of virtue (*de*, 德), see Ibid., 88–109.

[265] Ibid., 109.

[266] Ibid.

[267] For his exegesis and application, see Yeo, *What Has Jerusalem?*, 25–47. At times, he seems to turn the comparison back to China/Israel (pp. 259–61), however, it better resembles the sort of argument found in Rom 9–11 to the effect of saying that ethic Israel alone is not God's chosen people for Gentiles have been grafted in. Therefore, it appears that China still plays the role of Gentile even here.

radically affect their contrasting views on morality and human nature.[268] Strangely, this

difference is swept under the rug. Somehow, Yeo feels he can still reconcile two

worldviews that are built upon radically dissimilar foundations. This no doubt stems from

his hermeneutical method. He asserts that meaning does not derive from the author of a

text but rather from the interaction between reader and text.[269] He does not see the Bible

as a unified whole, recounting one grand narrative, inspired by a sovereign God, who has

supremely revealed himself in Jesus throughout all of Scripture (i.e. Luke 24:24, 44–45).

He cites Paul's use of Genesis in Gal 3:8–9. There, Paul asserts that the promise to

Abraham is the "gospel in advance." According to Yeo, Genesis is not *really* referring to

Christ. Paul simply uses the text as a convenient medium to express God's work in Christ.

Yeo claims that Paul's adaption of original intent is warrant for his own "indigenization

of the gospel of Christ into the cultural language of Confucianism."[270] Scripture must be

interpreted with Scripture. Yeo's low view of biblical inspiration undermines a holistic

biblical theology. His view is rooted in his indifference to the doctrine of the one true

God revealed in the Bible. Yeo's theology lacks a serious treatment of God. His project is

socio-political and oriented towards humans. Although he mentions topics like sin,

salvation, and the cross, they are constantly reinterpreted.

Yeo's doctrines of sin and salvation are shaped by Confucian philosophy as well.

"Sin" is essentially a break from social traditions, practices that should reflect the order

of the universe.[271] Perfection means living in harmony with what is natural, including

---

[268] Yeo, *Musing*, 115–22, 258, 270, 272.
[269] Ibid., 34.
[270] Ibid., 35.
[271] Ibid., 257.

society and the web of relationships that constitute our human identity.[272] Evil is "the occasional departure" from the universe's harmonious balance.[273] Yeo asserts, "Salvation in Galatians is essentially about different ethnic groups becoming the people of God *via* baptism and unconditional love."[274] The human predicament is social alienation.

In his reading of Galatians, Yeo uses an implication of the gospel to *replace* the main point itself.[275] Because Yeo mistakes the original intent of Paul's letter, he emphasizes social ethics at the expense of the cross, the nature of God, and human sin. Contextualization requires a respect for contextual differences and a humble search to learn whatever truth may be found. However, Yeo's proposal only retains superficial similarities, minimizing fundamental ontological and epistemological divisions. Perhaps, it is plausible to call Yeo's work a contextualization *of Confucianism*, since it is less dogmatic about philosophical categories thus allowing for borrowing from Christianity. It is far easier to contextualize Christianity within a culture than doing it with another religion. The latter tends to have too many immoveable parts. By examining Yeo's attempt at contextualization, one sees the subtle yet destructive potential of personal bias when reading and applying Scripture. Yeo's blending of contexts causes him to suppose that Paul's Christology gives us insight into the "Confucius' moral and political world."[276] Contextualization demands one know not only the biblical context and theology but also carefully examine one's *own* influences and the surrounding culture.

---

[272] Ibid., 220–21, 266.

[273] Ibid., 344.

[274] Ibid., 249. Yeo uses an entire chapter to compare the concept *li* (which he translated "rites") with law, including the "rituals" of circumcision, Sabbath-keeping, baptism, and the Lord's Supper.

[275] "Replace" is fitting, for it seems Yeo does not simply *confuse* primary and secondary points.

[276] Yeo, *Musing*, 175.

To what degree is Yeo's synthesis possible? One must be careful not to categorically dismiss his contextualization. It is possible to have right conclusions but wrong premises. Neither does a wrong conclusion necessarily invalidate all the ideas that went into it. No doubt, those familiar with recent debates concerning the so-called "New Perspective on Paul" may object to Yeo's use of Sanders or Dunn. Yet, Yeo's contextualization is not "wrong by association." Genuine dialogue means taking seriously those with whom we disagree.

Yeo's contextualization does have value. Positively, he uses Confucius to highlight key ideas largely absent in Western theology. For instance, he stresses the community over individualism and the necessity of practical love. If biblical theology does not emphasize social ethics and group identification, it is sub-biblical. This is a healthy corrective for those who accentuate otherworldly salvation and individualism at the expense of love and the church. He takes great effort to esteem individuality *without* collapsing into individualism. To be human is to be in relationship with others.[277] This is certainly a lesson drawn from Gen 1–2. God created man and women *together* in his image. Yeo says, "Becoming fully human is achieved not by detaching from the world but by making sincere efforts to harmonize one's relationship with others."[278] The Christian cannot be enslaved to autonomous individuality.[279] Yeo helpfully reminds theologians and missiologists to listen to other cultures in order that culture can expose potential blind spots in one's own theology. Finally, Yeo's major emphasis on becoming fully human is helpful in that it impresses upon readers the concept of identity. Both

[277] Ibid., 264–65, 399–400.
[278] Ibid., 346.
[279] Ibid., 392.

Christianity and culture strive to shape one's worldview. One's sense of identity is crucial in forming meaning.[280] Yeo reminds people of the propensity to identify oneself according to various contexts, whether ethnically, vocationally, or familial.

Yeo's analysis highlights aspects that can help in the development of a contextualized Chinese theology. First, he defines the Chinese *li* as a ritual or rite by which community membership is maintained or those "cultural patterns that are deemed proper or decent."[281] He then connects *li* to Jewish law:

> For first century Jews and ancient Chinese alike ritual and propriety were not simply social convention and therefore insignificant. In fact, they were *identity symbols* that express the core being of a people. Thus, "works of the law". . . for Jewish Christians were a matter of decency and honor. Paul took identity symbols not as a sociological variant, but as matters of *theological anthropology*—who we are in relation to what is sacred.[282]

Yeo agrees that the Chinese *li* and the Jewish law cannot be equated.[283] His point is simply that for Chinese and Jews respectively, both *li* and the law have social and ethnic importance. Moreover, these norms are considered to have transcendent value beyond the social. He elaborates, "Human beings participate in ritual (*li*) because they want to be formed and shaped by their sacred traditions, and because they believe that ritualized behavior constitutes the way to being more completely human and holy."[284] While each concept (*li* and Jewish Law) may say more, they do not mean less. He identifies at least some pattern of thinking between the two.

---

[280] Ibid., 405.

[281] Ibid., 191–95. Thus, Yeo asserts that Peter's behavior among the Gentiles in Galatia "does not match the *li* ([ritual] propriety) of his new conviction" (p. 204). See also his article K. K. Yeo, "Li and Law in the Analects and Galatians: A Chinese Christian Understanding of Ritual and Propriety," *AJT* 19 (Oct 2005): 309–32.

[282] Yeo, *Musing*, 76. Yeo's emphasis.

[283] Ibid., 201. Various Chinese philosophical terms carry ontological implications, for it is the *li* that helps people find "harmony with a greater, cosmic *Dao*" (p. 202).

[284] Ibid., 201.

A final and important distinction needs to be made between Yeo's hermeneutical method and the contextualization approach that this book proposes. Although there are times where Yeo's description of his methodology may sound *similar* to this book,[285] significant distinctions must be noted. For Yeo, Confucianism routinely defines the terms used in the discussion so as to delimit the scope of the inquiry. Thus, Confucianism becomes a restrictive hermeneutical lens, inevitably forcing a reading that does not fit the original context of Scripture. In the paradigm offered in this book, Chinese culture (e.g., Confucianism) does not necessarily set the agenda for theological contextualization; however, it should be a dialogue partner who poses challenging questions and raises themes for possible discussion. Therefore, the culture need not pose artificial limits. Rather, a broader awareness of cultures may bring out new questions and fresh emphases that have always been in the Scripture but simply have not been seen.

"Synchronistic" Approach

The earliest missionaries to China used what is being called the "synchronistic" approach to Chinese contextualization. The literature on the theology and history of China missions is vast and cannot be recounted here. Covell's thorough review in *Confucius, the Buddha, and the Christ* remains a standard read on the subject. For the present purpose, this section highlights the most noteworthy aspects related to these missionaries' gospel and soteriology. Using cultural symbols, philosophies, and concepts familiar to local people, they sought to make Christianity less foreign. In some way or another, they primarily tried to present themselves similar to the Chinese, whether in terminology, learning,

---

[285] K. K. Yeo, "Messianic Predestination in Romans 8 and Classical Confucianism," in *Sino-Christian Theology* (ed. Pan-chiu Lai and Jason Lam; New York, N.Y.: Peter Lang, 2010), 179.

religious practice, or clothing. Covell describes how Nestorians relied heavily on Buddhist and Daoist terminology and practices to win favor with the imperial court.[286] He adds that their theology seems to describe Jesus as a "Buddhist bodhisattva" and notes how they prayed to ancestors seven times a day as a way of expressing filial piety.[287] As a result, their movement teetered towards syncretism.

Catholic missionaries emphasized the Christian God as the one true God who created the world and was distinct from it.[288] They opted to represent themselves as Confucian scholars learned in science and philosophy.[289] Their use of natural theology aimed at appealing to the Chinese love of nature and science. The Jesuits' desire not to offend seems to have led to some form of inclusivism, as they affirm the possibility of ancient Chinese teachers inheriting salvation.[290] Naturally, many Chinese were receptive to the missionaries' stress on moral effort as a means for earning merit and avoiding God's judgment.[291] Nevertheless, Chinese continued to see Christianity as something foreign. This impression was reinforced by the fact missionaries used Greek and Latin to instruct converts.[292] In view of the Rites Controversy, Covell's conclusion seems right: "[The Pope's] authority was clearly a part of what they deemed to be the central core of the gospel."[293] Accordingly, their message took on political overtones since it essentially proclaimed the Chinese Emperor should submit to the Pope. The fact that they struggled (famously) to decide how to translate "God" suggests these missionaries could barely get

---

[286] Covell, *Confucius*, 25.
[287] Ibid., 29–30.
[288] Nicolas Standaert, ed., *Handbook of Christianity in China: 635–1800* (*vol.* 1 of *Handbook of Oriental Studies*; Leiden: Brill, 2001), 641–44.
[289] Covell, *Confucius*, 36.
[290] Ibid., 60.
[291] Standaert, *Handbook of Christianity in China*, 650–51.
[292] Yeo, "Paul's Ethic of Holiness and Chinese Morality of Renren," 108.
[293] Covell, *Confucius*, 56.

beyond a "pre-evangelistic" message;[294] in addition, their work illustrates the difficulty of sharing the gospel when there is little agreement on basic principles for contextualization.

Protestants refined the strategies of their predecessors and more directly addressed the question of salvation. Their labor spawned from a concerted emphasis on translating Scripture and other Christian literature into the local language. Overall, they were positive expositions of Christian truths, including biblical commentaries, rather than critiques of Chinese culture.[295] Rather than closely aligning Christianity to Confucianism, they tried to clarify ideas where the latter was "incomplete."[296] For instance, they affirmed the original goodness of humanity at creation and importance of morality; however, Protestant literature also presented the Christian doctrine of sin and the need for the Holy Spirit to bring about self-cultivation.[297] Special revelation, not only natural revelation, was needed for salvation. William Martin explained that Jesus showed filial piety when he "honored the King's law."[298] Similarly, Young Allen taught, "[Salvation] not only comprises spiritual regeneration but restoration of man's long lost and forfeited relationships to God, to his fellow-man, and to all created things—his primordial relationship of sonship, brotherhood, and dominion."[299] Despite this recognition of family as a core value of Chinese culture, the Protestant gospel primarily stressed the plight of the individual. In general, it did not differ significantly from what one might have read in books back in the West. Protestant missionaries did contribute to contextualization methodology. This is seen in their strategic focus on China's inland and their increased

---

[294] Ibid., 54. This is his description of Ricci's tract called "Tianzhu Shiyi."
[295] Ibid., 94.
[296] Ibid., 96.
[297] Ibid., 95–96.
[298] Ibid., 104.
[299] Ibid., 110. Citing Young J. Allen, "A Supreme Need for the work in China," in his *Missionary Issues of the Twentieth Century*, 192.

willingness to live and dress like the Chinese.[300] Nevertheless, it was foreignness that once again complicated the spread of Protestant Christianity. Martin had hoped to attract Chinese to the gospel by associating it with the West (e.g., science, economics, etc.).[301] Yet, political conflicts like the Opium Wars only turned Chinese against the missionaries who were closely identified with the Western military powers.

Some speculate why Christianity has never integrated into Chinese culture and received acceptance, as has Buddhism.[302] Covell says Buddhism, originally an Indian religion, kept much of its original forms but allowed the Chinese culture to fill them with new meaning.[303] By contrast, Christianity has generally been willing to change its forms while remaining more rigid when it comes to meaning. Covell adds a number of factors for Christianity's relative failure to be domesticated in China. In contrast to Buddhism, Chinese dismissed Christianity's exclusivism and perceived that Christianity did not theologically address the daily issues of suffering felt by the people and which were addressed in other religions like Buddhism.[304]

More recent examples of the synchronistic approach are found in C. H. Kang and Ethel Nelson's *The Discovery of Genesis*[305] and Thong's *Finding God in Ancient China*.[306] Kang and Nelson's well-known book suggests Chinese characters give indications that God revealed himself to ancient China. Supposedly, the characters reveal the sort of general revelation available prior to Gen 12. However, How Chuangchua's

---

[300] For example, one might recall Hudson Taylor.

[301] Covell, *Confucius*, 110–12.

[302] Cf. ibid., 145–49.

[303] Ibid., 145–46.

[304] Ibid., 147.

[305] C. H. Kang and Ethel R. Nelson, *The Discovery of Genesis: How the Truths of Genesis Were Found Hidden in the Chinese Language* (St. Louis, Mo.: Concordia, 1979).

[306] Thong and Fu, *Finding God*. This was previously published as Chan Kei Thong and Charlene L. Fu, *Faith of Our Fathers: God in Ancient China* (Shanghai: China Publishing Group Orient, 2005).

critique raises serious doubt as to the book's value.[307] More generally, he highlights a

potential problem with such "redemptive analogies":

> When missionaries or evangelists, consciously or otherwise, regard
> cultural elements as revelatory each time they can be used to teach the
> truths of the gospel, they are in effect conditioning people to adopt a
> particular mode of thinking about faith and culture that in long run can
> only lead to syncretism.[308]

One might add another danger of linking an authoritative message (Scripture) with a frail

medium (analogy); namely, invalidating the latter may appear to invalidate the former.

Thong takes a similar approach as Kang and Nelson. His thesis is that ancient Chinese

beliefs parallel and corroborate the events and teachings of the Bible. In particular, Thong

argues that evidence suggests early Chinese worshipped the Christian God, who was then

called *Shang Di* (上帝).[309] He appeals to archeology, Sinologists, ancient Chinese

classics, and the Bible. A significant portion of his argument relies on his finding

similarities between the Bible, numerous Chinese characters, and ancient Chinese

descriptions of God. Claiming similarity between Hebrew and Chinese blood covenants,

he concludes "that the symbolism of these ancient rites was divinely ordained to prepare

mankind for the final blood covenant . . . the shed blood of Jesus Christ on the cross."[310]

However, he adds that a person needs to accept Jesus and forsake idolatry in order to

receive eternal life.[311] Thong's book is essentially an apologetic appealing to natural

revelation to spur Chinese people to seek Christ. Yet, when it comes to contextualizing

---

[307] Chuang Chua How, "Revelation in the Chinese Characters: Divine or Divined?," in *Contextualization and Syncretism: Navigating Cultural Currents* (ed. Gailyn Van Rheenen; Pasadena, Calif.: William Carey Library, 2006), 229–39.

[308] Ibid., 238.

[309] Thong and Fu, *Finding God*, 174.

[310] Ibid., 180.

[311] Ibid., 173.

the message of salvation, Thong has little distinctive to say. G. Wright Doyle's review

points out a number of weaknesses. Although Thong does not claim China is chosen in

the same manner as Israel nor does he stress Chinese texts over the Bible, nevertheless,

Thong's comparisons are "strained" and selective.[312]

Betty Tan takes up the controversial question of ancestor veneration at Chinese

New Year. She looks for "dynamic equivalence" between Scripture and the ideas behind

Chinese cultural forms.[313] For her, contextualization seeks "to redeem the forms by

applying new meanings to them."[314] She succeeds in offering suggestions to express filial

piety in keeping with the Scriptures she cites. However, she fails to address the crux issue

of treating ancestors as if they demanded ongoing provision or have power in the world,

whether to bless or curse the living.[315] Further, honoring the *Christian* dead hardly acts as

a substitute in cultures where most people and ancestors have never heard of Jesus.[316]

Similar to that of earlier missionaries, recent contextualization efforts sometimes

center on the meaning of key terms. For instance, the Christian Union Version (CUV)

uses the word *dao* to translate the Greek *logos* concept found in John 1. Although

translating the Bible is an essential task of the church, there is a temptation to infuse

Christian meaning into the local language. Hsu's analysis confirms this suspicion. His

dissertation reviews the theology of Yuan Zhiming, who attempts to equate Laozi's Dao

with the Christian God. His conclusions are a warning:

---

[312] G. Wright Doyle, "Review of Faith of Our Fathers: God in Ancient China," *Global Chinese Center: Christianity in China*, Mar 20, 2007, n.p. [cited 19 Feb 2012]. Online: http://www. globalchinacenter.org/analysis/christianity-in-china/faith-of-our-fathers-god-in-ancient-china.php.

[313] Betty O. S. Tan, "The Contextualization of the Chinese New Year Festival," *AJT* 15, no. 1 (2001): 117.

[314] Ibid., 118.

[315] Yeo notes this dynamic in his "Paul's Ethic of Holiness and Chinese Morality of Renren," 139.

[316] In agreement, Nancy Porras sees the same weakness in other treatments of the problem. See her work, "Doing Theology in a Chinese Context," *IJFM* 4 (Jan 1987): 63.

123

It is evident that Yuan tends to interpret the whole text of the *Laozi* from a totally Christian perspective in which he rules out the traditional understandings of the Dao and the sage in the *Laozi*. The traditional perception of the *Laozi* is entangled in those metaphors, puzzles, and paradoxes used in the classic text. . . . Driven by his enthusiasm for evangelism, Yuan tends to Christianize the *Laozi* to a point that he somehow tries to make the *Laozi* adoptive to what he believes in the Christian faith, and unacceptable to many informaqts [*sic*].[317]

In short, synchronistic contextualization at times runs the risk of treating ancient Chinese classics as allegory. To give these texts some sort of Christian meaning has an added danger of implicitly affirming the divine inspiration of those works, as if they had an objective meaning from God at the time of their writing. This is the reverse of Yeo's error, since he reads the culture *into* the biblical context.

The synchronistic approach must guard against two tendencies—syncretism and superficiality. Yang's comments on contextualization are a sober warning. He reacts to the methods used by the earliest Catholic missionaries: "However, from the angle of the recipients [Chinese], the method of acceptance 'triggered' by such 'adaption' is not a corresponding 'adaption' to the party [missionaries], but rather a happy acceptance of 'adaptations' by the other party [missionaries]."[318] Quoting Nicolas Standaert, Yang says the most that certain synchronistic adaptations will achieve is "merely to make Christianity a 'useful contribution to the Confucian school of thought.'"[319] Yang's

---

[317] Evan Chen-Yih Hsu, "Yuan Zhiming's Treatment of Dao and Christian Theism: A Study of the Perceptions of Yuan's Approach to Contextualization Among Contemporary Chinese Intellectuals and Church Leaders" (PhD diss., Deerfield, Ill.: Trinity International University, 2006), 295. John Dao offers a optimistic view about synthesizing Dao and the Christian God (via the Greek *Logos* concept). However, his critique seems too uncritical of the differences between God and Dao; thus, he may overly idealize Daoist thought. See his work, "Toward a Contextual Theology for the Chinese–A Case Study from Translation and Interpretation of the Greek Logos and Chinese Dao," *Global Missiology* 2, no. 3 (Jan 2006), n.p. [cited 19 Feb 2012]. Online: http://ojs.globalmissiology.org/index.php/english/ article/view/420/1071.

[318] Yang, "Inculturation," 151.

[319] Ibid., 152. He cites Nicolas Standaert, *Inculturation: On the Gospel and Culture* (trans. Chen Kuanwei; Taibei: Kuang Chi, 1993), 18–22.

critique could be summed up by saying contextualization does not convert people if it merely becomes attractive by the superficial use of bridges.[320]

"Scriptural" Approach

A "Scriptural" approach is not to be contrasted with an unbiblical approach. In other words, this designation does not imply "synchronistic" or other methods are inherently contradictory to Scripture. The labels simply address aspects that receive the greatest emphasis in the contextualization. A distinguishing feature of this "Scriptural" approach is the particular way it relates Scripture to contextualization. Either it discusses themes that are unmistakably central to Christian theology and/or its conclusions are more obviously determined by Scripture. The Bible does not merely justify a cultural value or motif. Contextualization's product is more fully and properly called a "theology" (compared to the other approaches). Often, this is a topic within systematic theology, like sin or Christology. However, biblical theology is not excluded.

The doctrine of sin is notoriously difficult to communicate to a Chinese person. One reason for this is the word "sin" literally translates "crime" (罪, zui). Therefore, the average person responds to a gospel presentation, "I'm not a criminal!" Strand recounts a church leader who committed adultery but refused to resign because the government was responsible for zui.[321] Covell adds, "[T]hroughout the history of Christian mission in China, sin was presented as a violation of God's law demanding punishment; Jesus came as a substitute for humankind in paying the penalty for sin."[322] In addition to conveying

---

[320] Standaert, *Inculturation: On the Gospel and Culture*, 18–22.
[321] Mark Strand, "Explaining Sin in a Chinese Context," *Missiology* 28, no. 4 (2000): 427.
[322] Covell, *Confucius*, 97.

legal guilt, Corwin notes that Chinese traditionally think people are born good.[323] Moral evil is a result of ignorance, remedied by education.[324] Strand thinks another reason why Chinese struggle to understand sin is that they judge right and wrong based on social norms and negative results brought on the community.[325] No doubt there is some truth here, but not necessarily. First, one's community may be God's family, in which one shows filial piety.[326] Second, Chinese may feel they have done wrong even if there is no obvious negative result.[327] Strand gives many positive suggestions, like translating sin as *guo*.[328] Also, he suggests treating sin as a "debt" that is owed to God in the sense of familial piety, starting from Rom 3:23 where sin is falling short of God's glory (not simply social laws) and emphasizing that humans are "incomplete" or have flaws.[329] TSPM leaders like Chen Zeming add a social dimension. Covell summarizes Chen's

---

[323] Charles Corwin, "Communicating the Concept of Sin in the Chinese Context," *The Network for Strategic Missions*, n.d., [cited 28 Dec 2011]. Online: http://www.strategicnetwork.org/index.php?loc= kb&view=v&id=4588.

[324] Lit-Sen Chang, *Asia's Religions: Christianity's Momentous Encounter with Paganism* (Phillipsburg, N.J.: P & R Publishing, 2000), 45, 53.

[325] Strand, "Explaining Sin in a Chinese Context," 430–31.

[326] Strand acknowledges the familial piety as a key to contextualization in Ibid., 436. However, he does not relate people's ethnic community with their spiritual family.

[327] For example, see Bedford and Hwang's excellent study on aspects of Chinese guilt and shame. For words like *nei jiu, zui'e gan, fan zui gan, can kui, xiu kui, xiu chi*, one can feel it without others around and yet concern issues like obligations, rules, laws, and identity. See Bedford and Hwang, "Guilt and Shame." The chart on p. 135 is helpful. The focus on "result" is repeated relative to Japanese culture by Boyle, "Communicating the Gospel in Terms of Shame."

[328] He makes a good case for this translation, showing that *guo* is broad enough to fit the Greek word for sin and transgression. *Zui* is too narrow, and Chinese are more willing to admit they have *guo* as opposed to *zui*. See Strand, "Explaining Sin in a Chinese Context," 432–33. Typical translations of *guo* is "mistake," "fault," "error," "oversight," or "wrong."

[329] He equates "complete" with "perfect" on p. 434, using "*wanquan*." On the same page, he translates "incomplete" with *bu wanmei de ren*, meaning "not perfect." The decision depends on whether the distinction carries problematic connotations to the listener. He uses *quehan* for "flaw" or "failing."

126

belief, "[Chen] suggests that sin is not so much a rebellion against a sovereign God as it is a violation of God's will in human relationships, especially failure to attain the *summum bonum* of social justice within the community."[330]

Corwin puts forth his own Chinese adaption of the Four Spiritual Laws. His contextualization recommends first speaking of sin as not attaining to a *junzi*, the Confucian notion of an ideal person, therefore "man is in chaos [and] we are separated from the source of our life-God."[331] He attempts to connect other Chinese ideas about human nature by explaining humanity's being created good, in the image of God. He concludes, "To restore our relationship with God, we must receive Jesus Christ as Savior and Lord."[332] This explanation of sin raises a few simple questions, like "Does the average person grasp or care about the ancient concept of *junzi*?" and "Is this substantively distinct for Chinese culture?"

Maureen Yeung helpfully explains what is means to be "in Christ" in terms of ethnic identity. She begins with the premise, "The identity of a person is always defined in relation to others," adding that Christian identity trumps ethnic identity.[333] Observing the social and ethnic aspects of Jewish Law, she suggests the problem Paul confronts in the NT is that Jews wanted Gentiles "to live like Jews before they could be completely saved."[334] Ultimately, this becomes an issue of loyalty, whether one's identity is "in Christ" or in ethnicity. Yeung concludes, "Ethnic expressions are acceptable to retain so

---

[330] Covell, *Confucius*, 240.

[331] Corwin, "Concept of Sin."

[332] Ibid.

[333] Maureen W. Yeung, "Boundaries in 'In-Christ Identity': Paul's View on Table Fellowship and Its Implications for Ethnic Identities," in *After Imperialism: Christian Identity in China and the Global Evangelical Movement* (ed. Richard R. Cook and David W. Pao; Eugene, Ore.: Pickwick, 2011), 154, 156.

[334] Ibid., 162–63.

long as they are not regarded as conditions for salvation." On the other hand, ethnic diversity can bring more glory to Christ so long as it is not idolatrous but rather magnifies the unity of the *one people* of the "same Lord [who] is Lord of all."[335]

Frank Thielman questions whether Western missionaries have "export[ed] the individualism of their culture" to other places like China and thus "place an unnecessary stumbling block in the way of accepting the Gospel."[336] His essay strikes at the center of Chinese culture and theology. Wary of overcorrection, Thielman contends that Paul's soteriology gives considerable attention to the individual such that no one should trust in his or her ethnic identity in order to gain God's approval.[337] In short, he warns that excessive emphasis on the collective can prevent the salvation of individuals, whom God will *individually* hold accountable. One needs to observe a few points in his exegesis. First, he interprets Paul's oscillation between singular and plural verbs as an indication that Paul "was thinking of a group of *individuals.*"[338] However, Chinese typically view identity in terms of their relationships.[339] Shifting the stress, one could just as well speak of individual *group* members or persons *belonging* to a group. Therefore, Thielman may press an ontological distinction too strongly. After all, simply because one can *analytically* distinguish individuals from groups does not prove a fundamental individualist orientation within Paul.

---

[335] Ibid., 165. He cites Rom 10:12.

[336] Frank Thielman, "The Group and the Individual in Salvation: The Witness of Paul," in *After Imperialism: Christian Identity in China and the Global Evangelical Movement* (ed. Richard R. Cook and David W. Pao; Eugene, Ore.: Pickwick, 2011), 136.

[337] For his fuller argument, see Thielman, "The Group and the Individual."

[338] Ibid., 143. His emphasis

[339] For example, Hwang, *Foundations*, 340; Yeo, *Musing*, 266; Kipnis, *Producing Guanxi*, 8.

Thielman categorically states, "No one will be able to hide behind his or her group identity."[340] Although right about ethnic groups in particular, the statement may say more than Paul intended. Has Paul really left the group-idea for an individualist orientation? The point Paul makes repeatedly is that Christ "is our peace, who made us both one [through his death] that he might create in himself one new man in place of the two" (Eph 2:14–15; cf. Rom 4:16–17; Gal 3:14, 28–29). Paul simply shifts his categories from Jew and Gentile to those "in-Christ" and those who are not. Confusion arises because, until Jesus, "Israel" represented both an ethnic people *and also those who were God's people.* His argument presumes that having a concern for individuals would prevent one from having a more collectivistic concern, namely, "Who belongs to the people of God?"[341] Yet, this is a non sequitur. It simply does not follow that Paul's concern for individuals makes questions of group identity less central. In fact, the very nature of Paul's argument in Romans and Galatians *presumes* that Paul is addressing a fundamental question raised by the *individual,* namely, "To which *group* do I belong?" Thielman forges false dichotomies that make this more difficult to see. He states, "Although much of the boasting Paul has in mind is boasting in one's ethnic identity, he does not stop there. As we saw above in our study of Galatians, Paul implies that the movement of a Gentile Christian into Judaism through accepting circumcision entailed placing confidence in the law rather than Christ."[342] Without explanation, he dichotomizes group identity and law. By assuming this division, Thielman then ensures

---

[340] Thielman, "The Group and the Individual," 149.
[341] Ibid., 144.
[342] Ibid., 146.

that he will arrive at the traditional idea that justification is about an individual's "good works" (as if distinguished from group identity).[343]

The way Chinese relate the individual and community is difficult to understand and leads to confused assertions. The claim so far made about Chinese culture is not that individuals are not important and are to be ignored. Sawatsky is correct, "Both individual and community exist in a relationship of mutual dependence."[344] However, he makes a mistake that could have dramatic theological consequences. He charges, "At the same time, a strong sense of individualism pervades the Chinese world view with emphasis on the self-cultivation of the individual to attain moral perfection and immortality."[345] In Sawatsky's discussion, he makes rather untenable inferences about the "greater primacy of the individual" based on a line from Confucius' *The Great Learning* (*daxue*), which states of the ancients, "Wishing to regulate their families, they first cultivated their persons."[346] He over reads the word "first" (*xian*, 先), making the text sound individualistic. However, in context, very obvious parallelism clarifies the issue:

> The ancients who wished to illustrate illustrious virtue throughout the kingdom, *first* ordered well their own states. Wishing to order well their states, they *first* regulated their families. Wishing to regulate their families, they *first* cultivated their persons. Wishing to cultivate their persons, they *first* rectified their hearts. Wishing to rectify their hearts, they *first* sought to be sincere in their thoughts. Wishing to be sincere in their thoughts, they *first* extended to the utmost their knowledge. Such extension of knowledge lay in the investigation of things.[347]

---

[343] Ibid. As will be shown later, "group identity" is precisely the context for these "good works."

[344] Sawatzky, "Body as Metaphor," 106.

[345] Ibid., 113.

[346] Ibid., 106. He cites James Legge's translation in his James Legge, trans., "The Great Learning and the Doctrine of the Mean," in Vol. 1 of *The Chinese Classics* (Oxford: Clarendon Press, 1893), 357–58 [cited 22 Feb 2012]. Online: http://ctext.org/liji/da-xue. The Chinese is: "欲齊其家者，先修其身."

[347] The emphasis is mine. See Sawatzky, "Body as Metaphor," 106. Confirmed by Chinese Text Project, n.p. [cited 22 Feb 2012]. Online: http://ctext.org/liji/da-xue.

Sawatsky interprets this to mean, "According to Confucian ethics, the individual owes duties to the communities of the family, the state and the world, but one's primary obligation is the cultivation of his own person."[348] He fails to see that a process is being suggested, not an ordering of importance. By analogy, one today might say, "Wishing to get a good job, one first goes to college. Wishing to go to college, one first makes good grades in school. Wishing to make good grades, one must first learn to read." Sawatsky does not distinguish ends from means. The highest goal (that which has primacy) is the wellbeing of "the kingdom."[349] Logically, this entails certain antecedent events. Simply because these happen first in time does not make then the distinct features of a culture. After all, all cultures must first learn to eat and think before forming culture. If Sawatsky were to continue this logic, he would interpret the text to say attaining esoteric knowledge has primacy, not individualism, since that is where the process begins. Yet, as has been seen, scholars agree that Chinese thinking is generally concrete and socially oriented, not esoteric or individualistic. In short, he overlooks the fact that in Confucian thinking, "self-cultivation of a person must be conducted in the context of developing social relationships."[350] It is not a private affair.

Wan has written numerous articles on contextualization and Chinese theology. In "Tao—The Chinese Theology of God-Man," he defines Christian theology as "theologizing in Chinese concepts within the Chinese cultural context that the Gospel

---

[348] Ibid.

[349] Interestingly, we see nearly the exact same ordering from Wu Leichuan, a Confucian turned Christian scholar. Ni shows Wu saw Jesus' mission as being "social reform," thus, "He regarded individual reforms as a preparation for social reform." See Ni, "Sinicizing Jesus," 139.

[350] Chung-Ying Cheng, "The Concept of Face and Its Confucian Roots," *JCP* 13 (1986): 337. Likewise, Li, Wang, and Fisher say, "This moral aspiration is not envisioned as solely an individual undertaking but as a process embedded in one's daily social existence" in "Shame Concepts," 769.

131

may take root in the soul and soil of the Chinese."[351] He briefly suggests that Tao (or *dao* as above) is a potential symbol to contextualize theology. What makes Wan different from Yuan, whom we considered above? First of all, Wan does not equate the Tao with the Christian God. Rather, he uses the underlying ways of thinking about Tao [e.g., harmony between heaven and man]. He is then able to examine similar paradoxes and concerns found in the Bible (e.g., then incarnation). This avoids the impression that other religious texts might be placed beside the Bible as authoritative revelation. Wan's qualifiers and use of Scripture ensure "Tao" is regarded no better than an analogy.

How might Christology be both biblical and Chinese? Wan argues that Chinese theology must embrace "both-and" ways of thinking, in contrast to tradition Western theology's "either-or" approach.[352] Accordingly, there is no need to reconcile systematically seemingly contradictory actions, roles, or aspects of his nature. He especially highlights Jesus' work as a "go-between." So, Jesus brings a "reconciled relationship vertically with God and relationship horizontally with fellow man." Wan does not explain *how* Jesus accomplishes this. Problems in the created order are the consequence of human's "misuse of the gift of human free will." Wan does not use the word "sin" here. He explains, "Jesus Christ is both the shame-bearer for sinners and honor-winner for believers." He continues to discuss the *results* of sin and salvation, but never explains *how* HS might explain sin, atonement, or justification.

---

[351] Wan, "Tao," 24.
[352] The citation in this paragraph come from Wan, "Jesus Christ for the Chinese"; cf. Wan, "Critiquing."

"Systematic" Approach

The "systematic" approach takes a step away from theologizing to deal with methodological concerns related to Chinese contextualization. In the examples already discussed, even when doctrines were proposed, extensive discussion centered on methodology. There remains a need to advance beyond these considerations to the actual task of theologizing.

David Lee argues that it does not compromise *sola Scriptura* to "construct a Chinese theology that regards Chinese culture as an interpretive tool or communication vehicle that may be 'allied' with the Bible."[353] He agrees with Vanhoozer that contextualization "is not primarily a matter of communication: decoding the essential components of truth from the host culture and encoding it in a new culture."[354] Instead, he says, contextualization is theologizing in a particular context, which must also be interpreted. As Lee sketches a Christology using the Chinese concept of wisdom, he does not adopt the precise meanings found in Chinese philosophy. Rather, he simply notes the chief concerns represented within larger philosophical concepts. For instance, the desire to see the transcendent expressed in imminence finds Christian expression in the incarnation and the believer's Spirit-transformed life. Accordingly, Lee concludes, "To be a Chinese Christian, it is not necessary to take an antagonistic attitude against the Western theological heritage [nor] to identify Western theology as the norm or totality of

---

[353] David Y. T. Lee, "Chinese Contextual Theology: A Possible Reconstruction," in *After Imperialism: Christian Identity in China and the Global Evangelical Movement* (ed. Richard R. Cook and David W. Pao; Eugene, Ore.: Pickwick, 2011), 193.

[354] Ibid., 206.

the Christian tradition."[355] He is not saying Christ and the Spirit are identical to Confucian wisdom; simply, they satisfy the deeper categories of inquiry.

A high priority in Enoch Wan's writings is making Christianity less "foreign" to the Chinese people.[356] He repeatedly suggests constructing a theology in HS.[357] He states his meaning in clear terms and contrast:

> The message of the Gospel within the Chinese cultural context should be characterized by the emphasis on honor, relationship, and harmony, which are at the core of traditional Chinese cultural values. It should be different from [traditional Western theology's] overemphasis on the forensic nature of the Gospel, the legal dimension of Christ's penal substitution and divine justification.[358]

In the same article, Wan asserts, "The rationalistic argument, lineal logic, and abstract proclamation of [traditional western theology] in evangelism are less appealing to relationally-oriented, co-relational thinking, and pragmatically-inclined Chinese."[359] Chinese people are not inclined to a gospel message that speaks mainly of being saved from hell in the next life; rather the typical Chinese person wants a message that "is something that can be declared clearly, demonstrated powerfully and experienced daily." In addition, he warns that the Chinese desire not to offend people will often lead people to insincere professions of faith. A high emphasis on individual decisions and immediate

---

[355] Ibid., 219.

[356] He helps the reader understand how Christians have long been perceived in Wan, "Christianity in the Eye Of Traditional Chinese."

[357] For examples, see Wan, "Jesus Christ for the Chinese"; Wan, "Practical Contextualization." Wan, "Theological Contributions."

[358] Wan, "Practical Contextualization." Wan feels Chinese value for relationship and face is so strong that he warns: "Instantaneous and individualistic decision-making (especially telephone evangelism) and public professions of faith (by coming forward) are not to be imposed on the Chinese. They are non-committal to salesman-style pressure, they may have problems in making instantaneous decision out of their fear of social ostracism. Some Chinese may hastily say 'yes' when pressured to receive Christ. They do so out of politeness, being courteous or respectful to the one sharing the Gospel who happens to be his/her superior. But this kind of conversion is not deeply rooted and stands no test at all."

[359] Ibid.

response may convey pressure that is simply counterproductive. Others like Bruce

Nicholls agree that HS should help frame a contextualized Chinese theology.[360]

In pairs, Wan charactorizes traditional Chinese/Western values and ways of

thinking: Grace/Gifts, Life Quality/Ministry Productivity, Faithfulness/Fruitfulness,

Character/Career, Servanthood/Leadership, Solidarity/Individuality, People-

Oriented/Program-Oriented.[361] He affirms and relativizes each aspect in turn. For

instance, of the sixth pair, he writes, "The doctrine of the Church gives *primacy* to the

solidarity of the body of Christ, the household of God, etc. over individual members *but*

not without the latter. True spirituality gives priority to collective solidarity over

individual persons *but not without the latter*."[362] In this way, Wan does not take an

"either-or" approach to the "Chinese-foreign" dilemma.

Similarly, Wan translates "rational" theology into "relational" terms. Instead of

using terms such as theology-proper, anthropology, soteriology, ecclesiology, and

eschatology, respectively, Wan suggests talking about the "Fatherhood of God," "sonship

of Christians," "membership of the family," "the brotherhood of all Christians," and "the

reunion of family members."[363] Elsewhere, he develops and applies this motif.[364] Filial

piety can accord with a biblical view of God. Traditional Chinese thinking asserts that

people need only to take care of their own family. In contrast, Wan argues that

---

[360] Nicholls, "Contextualisation in Chinese Culture," 373–75.

[361] Enoch Wan, "Exploring Sino-Spirituality," *Global Missiology* 1, no. 1 (Oct 2003), n.p. [cited 20 Feb 2012]. Online: http://ojs.globalmissiology.org/index.php/english/article/view/440/1135.

[362] My emphasis.

[363] He makes a similar parallel in reference to the Trinity, since one could either analyze how three-in-one nature of God or (he prefers) think in terms of how the three persons relate to one another. Wan, "Theological Contributions."

[364] What follows is drawn from Enoch Wan, "家的文北化传流: 华人基督徒的信仰及实践," *地球华人宣教学期刊* 8 (Apr 2007), n.p. [cited 29 Nov 2011]. Online: http://www.enochwan.com/chinese/simplified/(1.5)%20articles.html.

justification brings people into one family. Therefore, God can use cultural themes while challenging any related shortcomings of such emphases. Chinese long for loyalty, filiality, and love; yet, these are found only within the family of God. To be a family, the church cannot concern itself with numbers alone; in addition, it must attend to character growth, i.e. quality. Just as Chinese care about protecting their family name, so Christians live together so as to protect the name of God our Father.

Nicholls says a contextualization needs to reflect the Chinese mindset, "which involves thinking concretely, practically, using symbols, analogies, and stories."[365] C. S. Song agrees, arguing at length that theology must be done through stories, not texts.[366] By "texts," he seems to mean systematized or philosophical books on theology; thus, one should not treat the Bible as "text" since God in fact has revealed himself in the form of stories, which include life testimonies.[367] One reads stories differently than one does highly systematic works, which tend to fragment stories, rearrange details according to the reader's preference, and lull the imagination of the reader.[368]

Nicholls sketches other ideas that he thinks contribute to a faithful Chinese contextualization. He suggests the Kingdom of Heaven/God motif in Scripture may find resonance with ancient Chinese perspectives on heaven and monotheism.[369] Given Chinese culture's anxiety about death, he applies the resurrection to issues like ancestor worship and the continuity between the present life and next.[370] Although some people

---

[365] Nicholls, "Contextualisation in Chinese Culture," 369; Also, cf. p. 378.
[366] C. S. Song, "In The Beginning Were Stories, Not Texts," *Madong* 14 (Dec 2010): 7–16.
[367] Ibid., 8–12.
[368] Ibid., 8–10.
[369] Nicholls, "Contextualisation in Chinese Culture," 372–73.
[370] Ibid., 375. Porras agrees in her "Doing Theology in a Chinese Context," 53.

have proposed criteria to assess Chinese theologies, they tend to have more to do with contextualization in general than with *Chinese* contextualization in particular.[371]

"Soterian" Approach

Having examined in length various ways of theologizing for a Chinese context, this section considers how Christians practically communicate theology in China. Gospel tracts may be the most common places to find "soterian" contextualizations. However, other popular strategies like T4T ("Training for Trainers"), C2C ("Creation-to-Christ"), and the Four Spiritual Laws are tools widely used used among the Chinese. Designed for practitioners, like missionaries and laypersons, these evangelistic methods contain very simplified theologies. It is important to consider any differences and similarities between what is suggested above and what is actually being communicated in practice.

One of the most influential methodologies in China is T4T.[372] Steve Smith says plainly, "Lesson one is the gospel."[373] Upon examination, this first lesson is titled, "The Assurance of Salvation." It actually presupposes that the reader is already a Christian.[374] An equation is given, "The redemption of Jesus + your faith + repentance = salvation." By believing that "God has done what he wants to do (death and resurrection)" and

---

[371] For examples, see Porras, "Doing Theology in a Chinese Context." Also, see Winston Crawley, "Interpreting the Bible in Chinese Context," *Taiwan Baptist Theological Seminary Annual Bulletin* (Sept 2005): 29–39.

[372] The following draws from Steve Smith and Ying Kai, *T4T: A Discipleship ReRevolution* (Monument, Colo: WIGTake, 2011); Steve Smith, "Gospel Presentations Used in T4T Packages" (www.t4tonline.org, 2011), n.p. [cited 21 Feb 2012]. Online: http://t4tonline.org/wp-content/uploads/2011/02/3d-Gospel-Presentations-Used-in-T4T-Packages.pdf.

[373] Smith and Kai, *T4T*, 53. Repeated in Smith, "Gospel Presentations Used in T4T Packages." The latter contains the six primary lessons of T4T. Translated lessons can also be found online: http://t4tonline.org/media-tags/classicsixlessons/.

[374] Under the title is the greeting, "Congratulations, you are a child of the Heavenly Father (Acts 17:28–29)! From this point on, you can have a new relationship with God and receive all of His promises. Here's how you can know Him." Then the first section adds, "Let us *review* how we receive eternal life through Jesus" [my emphasis].

having "done what you need to do (believe and repent)," the reader is told, "you are saved!" Salvation and eternal life are treated as synonyms. Eternal life entails not only living forever but also being "able to live a life of holiness, righteousness, kindness, and strength." In addition, "We will receive forever the blessings of God," including peace and happiness. In *T4T: A Discipleship ReRevolution*, Smith two times gives a direct definition to the "gospel."[375] First, he says, "It is specifically the good news that Jesus Christ provided redemption for us and that we can be saved through faith in Him." After citing Luke 24:45–48[376] and 1 Cor 15:1–6, he rephrases the gospel, "It is the truth about Jesus dying for our sins, being buried, yet raising again to prove His claims AND that through Him all people can be saved, through repentance and faith."[377]

C2C is a memorized set of stories meant to introduce the gospel to someone who has not heard, especially non-literates.[378] It begins by asserting that "the Most High God . . . *created us to have a wonderful relationship with Him forever!*"[379] Immediately, the presentation explains how demons were cast out of heaven. For people, "*Disobeying God's command is sin.* God is righteous and holy. He must punish sin. God cast the man and the woman out of the garden, and their relationship with God was broken." Moreover, "The result of sin is eternal punishment in hell. *We cannot live forever with God as we were designed.*" Later, people were not able to obey 10 commandments; the problem is then solved by means of "sacrifice," in which "the blood of a perfect animal" was shed. However, the listener is warned, "[P]eople kept sinning and the sin sacrifice

---

[375] Both are found in Smith and Kai, *T4T*, 216.

[376] In the book *T4T*, he mistypes "Luke 25:45–48," but the words come from Luke 24.

[377] Smith's emphasis.

[378] An overview of C2C is found in Smith, "Gospel Presentations Used in T4T Packages."

[379] All emphasis in this C2C paragraph are C2C's emphasis.

138

became a ritual rather than something from their heart. God became tired of their insincere acts. People were still separated from God. *We cannot come back to God on our own no matter what we do.*" Next, the story explains that Jesus is more powerful than anything, loves people, and never sinned so as to deserve punishment. Because Jesus is "perfect," he can act as a "substitute" for us. The resurrection is mentioned in passing but not fully developed.[380] Finally, the Prodigal Son story leads to an invitation, "Do you want to let Jesus bring you back to God?"

The Four Spiritual Laws (4SL) is a primary tool for Cru, one of the largest mission organizations in the world and in China.[381] Corwin is correct to observe the Chinese version of 4SL is not contextualized at all, being translated literally from the English version.[382] According to Wan, this "propositional conceptualization and impersonal presentation of Jesus Christ and salvation [has] less appeal to the traditional Chinese" than it does for Westerners.[383] Cru has written an internal training document that explicitly outlines the theology behind 4SL.[384] It aims to correct "misconceptions about salvation"; such as, "rigorous discipline may attain perfection and thus unity with

---

[380] Having personally received this training, I personally have copies of the entire training material. In the actual written out story to be memorized, only one line points to the resurrection, "On the third day Jesus rose from the dead!" (in Part 6); in Chinese, "第三天, 耶稣复活了!"

[381] As of 2011, "Cru" is the official name for the former Campus Crusade for Christ. See online: http://www.ccci.org/about-us/donor-relations/our-new-name/qanda.htm#0.

[382] Corwin, "Concept of Sin." An English-Chinese parallel version of 4SL can be found online at: Online: http://4laws.com/laws/downloads/ ChnEng4pWB04Jul.pdf.

[383] Wan, "Jesus Christ for the Chinese."

[384] Cru, "The Theological Background of the Four Spiritual Laws," *There is Hope Ministries*, Nov 2005, n.p. [cited 21 Feb 2012]. Online: http://www.hope365.co.za/sites/hope365.co.za/files/ i%20FN%201S01B%20$%20Theology%20of%20the%20Four%20Spiritual%20Laws.pdf; There is Hope Ministries works under or was trained by Cru, as evidenced by researching the name of training listed on the document. It is called "The Great Commission Ministry Training," which is a training provided by Cru in places like The Great Commission Academy (cf. their website at http://academy.weebly.com/about-us.html). Further, this training is linked to Cru via Campus Crusade-South Africa (http://www.cccsa.org.za/ministry.php?id=3) and on orientation materials posted online: http://www.hope365.co.za/sites/hope365.co.za/files/c%20FN%201M00A%20$%20Call%20to%20Reach%20Your%20World.pdf.

God," "doing good works . . . will merit God's favor," and "a philosophy of life . . . will impress God." 4SL opens by "communicating God's love to the *individual*."[385] Jesus' interaction with the Samaritan woman (John 4) is the paradigm guiding the explanation of 4SL. Sin is described as going one's "own independent way." The non-Christian is urged to "turn from self to Christ" and ask God, "Take control of the throne of my life." The theology of 4SL has an unmistakable legal tone. Appealing to Romans, readers are told that law and works justify no one. The illustrations given make clear this "law" is juridical, not royal. Also, God's "justice" and "righteousness" are contrasted against his love and presented as the reason for God's wrath against sin. Because we cannot "pay for past sins," we need "Jesus Christ" to be a "substitute." "Animal sacrifices" point to the "Messiah" in whom "God has given us His righteousness as a free gift apart from works." These titles are not explained. One is assured of salvation if she "responds by faith through prayer to Christ's invitation." Salvation is "eternal life," rather than "eternal judgment."

Other short presentations abound and even parallel 4SL's approach. Corwin develops his own Chinese version of 4SL; however, it seems only to switch verbiage without making substantive changes.[386] John Jamison contrasts his method with 4SL by explaining how the notion of "law" leads Chinese to misunderstand the gospel, especially since "our concept of sin has an essentially legal definition."[387] Jamison writes,

> In contrast to "rule of law" in the West, Chinese society has the "rule of person." The leader decides the standards according to his desires and

---

[385] My emphasis.

[386] Corwin, "Concept of Sin."

[387] John Jamison is a pseudonym. He works for the IMB in China. This resource was made widely available for IMB workers in China. The document was 15 Feb 2007 and was available on the East Asia Region's website.

what he thinks the masses will tolerate. The experience of many Chinese through history is leaders who create laws and manipulate the system to their own advantage. So no matter what we say about how much God loves them and seeks to bless them, when we explain sin as violations of God's law, their only frame of reference is a system where leaders too often abuse the laws to take advantage of the masses. This is not good news.

Finally, he puts forth six principles for Chinese evangelism: 1. "There is a most high God." 2. "The most high God desires to have an intimate and loving relationship with us." 3. "We have offended God, our relationship is broken and we cannot do anything about it." 4. "Jesus is our go-between, our mediator." 5. "If we want Jesus to intercede for us forever, he demands our loyalty forever." 6. "Becoming a Christian means joining God's family. It is not a private decision. You need to enter into relationship with others."

Finally, gospel tracts are common ways that people begin learning about salvation. Many tracts are simply translations of English materials.[388] The booklet *Discovering God in Chinese Characters* interprets numerous Chinese characters to introduce Christian concepts like guilt, sacrifice, blessed, eternal, and righteousness.[389] The tract says the ancient character meaning "guilt/sin" (罪, *zui*) was "made of self (*zi*) + bitterness (*xin*)."[390] An ancient character for righteousness (*yi*) contains a lamb symbol and the character for "I/me." Therefore, the tract explains, "When I do not accept the sacrifice of the Lamb of God for me, 'I' remain separated from Him."[391] In order to gain salvation, the tract concludes, "We receive Jesus Christ *by* faith *through* prayer."[392]

---

[388] For example, Josh McDowell, *Deception or Reality* (Ephrata, Pa.: Multilanguage Media, n.d.). The tract can be found online at: http://www.multilanguage.com/css/Default.htm. This tract simply translates chapter 10 of McDowell's *Evidence that Demands a Verdict*.

[389] *Discovering God in Chinese Characters* (Langley, BC, Canada: Intercultural Network Canada, 2007). The tract can be bought online at: http://interculturalnetwork.com/resources/discovering-god/.

[390] Ibid., 19.

[391] Ibid., 29.

[392] Ibid., 33. Tract's emphasis. No text is given to support the clause "through prayer."

Two Singaporean pamphlets include *Ancient of Days* (古人的上帝) and *Gospel Bridge* (福音侨).[393] In *Ancient of Days*, half of the tract recounts ancient Chinese history. It concludes that Tao/Dao can be equated with Jesus, "the incarnation of God." As God's creation, we are "sons and daughters of God." Therefore, "[W]e should in turn revere Him just as we honour our parents." Also, "Jesus Christ brought eternal salvation to man . . . for man's sins to be forgiven." However, the tract never explains sin. It merely assumes both an understanding of sin and the reader's acknowledgement of being a sinner. The tract then warns, "We should not imagine we can be saved on the merit of our good deeds alone." Salvation is "everlasting life in God's eternal kingdom" and "[o]nly the sacrifice of Jesus" makes this possible. The resurrection "proves [Jesus'] supreme status and impeccable innocence . . . His guiltless purity." Accordingly, the reader is urged to accept the Tao "whom Laozi knew vaguely" by praying and receiving eternal life. Finally, *Gospel Bridge* contrast "[the way of] works or [the way of] salvation" (办法 与救法).[394] Sin is never explained but it is described as "evil thoughts" (*e'nian*), which are inward, despite outward appearances. Jesus "became a 'sacrifice' for mankind" and his resurrection proves his deity.[395] One is "assured" of "eternal life" since "you have been released from Satan's power and have become a child of God."[396]

A number of patterns emerge from a survey of "soterian" attempts to contextualize salvation. Without question, they are fundamentally law-oriented and

---

[393] Joe Wong, *Ancient of Days* [古人的上帝] (Singapore: Singapore Every Home Crusade Co., 2002); *Gospel Bridge* [福音侨] (Singapore: Bible Society of Singapore, 2000).

[394] *Gospel Bridge* [福音侨], 27. The brackets are added to clarify the meaning in Chinese.

[395] Ibid., 20–23.

[396] Ibid., 37.

directed at individuals. Therefore, the primary way of framing the salvation message is diametrically contrary to the Chinese way of categorizing human experience. Not only this but the traditional way Chinese people understand concepts like "righteousness" differs drastically from the usage in the tracts. Accordingly, this leaves many presentations either open to misinterpretation or unintelligible altogether. Although Chinese emphasize the importance of personal moral effort, this value has never been theocentric and is entirely oriented towards his or her community. Therefore, it is curious to see how pervasive is the theme of "doing good works" in order to be saved. Sin is either left assumed or treated as a breech of law.[397] For that matter, the tracts have a common solution to the sin problem, but it is never clearly explained why or how Jesus' perfect sacrifice actually deals with an individual's sin. Jesus is often depicted as a "sacrifice" but this is rarely explained with clarity. This is especially true of C2C. The sacrifice motif is central within C2C yet it simply assumes the biblical concept of sacrifice will make sense to the listener, whose tribe or culture may have a very different notion of sacrifice. Unintentionally, these presentations may reinforce a sort of payment or bribery theology where God is bought off in the same way someone might think of human sacrifice. Uniquely, C2C emphasizes the origin of demons, no doubt to address the questions of animistic peoples. However, in history, the theology behind that topic has always been highly speculative and never an issue of salvation.

Typically, the "soterian" approach is more systematic than narrative, ignoring nearly all the OT beyond Gen 3 and relying primarily on Pauline epistles. These presentations say nothing of Israel, which is ironic given the importance of the Jew-

---

[397] In Cru, "The Theological Background," sin is depicted as "traffic violation."

Gentile controversy in Paul's writing. Jesus' Jewish title "Christ" is used everywhere (sometimes even "Messiah"); however, it is never defined and so appears to be nothing but a family name. The most prominent way of describing salvation is in terms of time, as evidenced by the repetition of words like "eternal," "forever," and "everlasting." The goal seems rather otherworldly, not being overtly related to society or communal identity. The resurrection is mentioned in passing and always as some sort of proof that Jesus spoke truth. The individual is pressed to choose between heaven and hell. Again and again, one reads that God's blessings are assured "by faith through prayer."

Conclusions

This chapter begins to build a conceptual framework for developing a contextualized theology in Chinese culture. Because cultures are fluid abstractions, the chapter highlights the most enduring and pervasive themes that mark the Chinese context. Yet, for the purpose of contextualization, the chapter intentionally seeks to find areas where culture and theology intersect. In the examination of six approaches to Chinese contextualization, writers across the theological spectrum do agree on a number of the significant features that must shape a theology for China. This is significant. It is more difficult to find common ground on methodology. This is despite the fact most of the publications surveyed overwhelmingly deal with questions about why and how to do contextualized theology in China. This has resulted in very little *theologizing* of Scripture itself. Rather, theological output is generally limited to a few popular themes like ancestors and the Tao/Dao. Much discussion focuses on general revelation, theology proper, and preparation for the gospel. It is not surprising therefore to see little extensive writing in terms of soteriology, ecclesiology, biblical theology, and the like.

144

What features of Chinese culture need to be addressed in order to develop more fully a holistic, Chinese theology? This chapter sets aside the topic of "face" for later discussion, but one can anticipate that HS will play a major role. In this chapter, China is described as a relationally oriented or collectivistic culture. Individual identity is defined in terms of relationships (*guanxi*), according to group identification. Loyalty and social harmony are unquestioned values. This Confucian social emphasis idealizes family. Hierarchy, pragmatism, and solidarity maintain social order. Moral decisions are made in relation to one's role and situation. Fittingly, Chinese philosophy and religion seek to find unity in transcendence, imminence, nature, and the ethical. Numerous historical considerations have solidified two basic ways of demarcating people—those who are "Chinese" and those who are "foreign." This way of dividing the world (i.e. inside/outside, East/West, etc.) is no mere abstraction. For a Chinese person, theology without some group-face orientation is like learning and speaking a language without regard for context. It is like reading words without grammar, which governs the relationship between the various words and phrases. Chinese can hardly conceive of themselves, not to mention God, apart from their web of relationships, since their identity and all that is significant is relational. Fundamentally different assumptions about the world lead to divergent conceptions of law, righteousness, God, authority, and ethnicity.

The second half of the chapter is an extensive review of previous efforts to contextualize theology in this Chinese milieu. The various writers confirm the prior findings as to what typifies the culture. Remarkably, their proposals continually return to the question of how one can be both "Chinese" and "Christian." Those who make ethnic identity an explicit theological concern routinely turn to Paul's discussion on Jews and

Gentiles. Naturally, they lay great stress on narrative passages and OT Israel. Furthermore, these theologians give great attention to social and ethical topics. Peculiarly, many who take a "scriptural" or "soterion" approach also appeal to Paul but reaffirm Western interpretations that emphasize the legal motif, the individual, and the impossibility of earning merit with God through good works. Cultural symbols are generally regarded as bridges to help Chinese make sense of these biblical (and coincidentally Western) ways of categorizing the world.

Finally, a number of other insights may significantly advance the work of Chinese contextualization. Wan's stress on "both-and" rather than "either-or" can spur a fresh reexamination of one's assumptions. For instance, the question perhaps is not whether some idea is true or wrong; instead, the issue might be *how* and *when* one's understanding is right. How might a change in perspective influence the plausibility of a certain interpretation? No doubt, if Wan's suggestion is taken seriously, a number of misunderstandings could be rectified. For illustration, consider the assertion that right and wrong are "relative." The conservative evangelical may initially be alarmed, reaffirm the historical-grammatical method of interpretation, and hold fast to the absolute truths declared within theological tradition. However, what if the point being made is simply that circumstances and relationships must be considered when making ethical decisions? Given human limitations, people must make hard choices to do one good action instead of another. How did Paul himself answer the question of whether it was right or wrong to eat certain foods (cf. Rom 14; 1 Cor 8)? In effect, he says, "It depends." "Right" requires people to ask, "Who is around? What about conscience? What is loving in this instance?"

In the process of contextualizing theology, one must be careful not to "decontextualize" human behavior.[398]

The cultural background of Chinese theologians enables them to raise a number of legitimate and important themes that are not always prioritized within a typical Western worldview. The concern for ethnic identity gives new fuel to contemporary debates about the "New Perspective of Paul." Ding and Song complain that Western Christians lose sight of creation theology amid the push to call attention to redemption. Even if one does not do this formally, might this happen in actual practice? The current chapter highlights the importance of metaphors, whether cultural or biblical, for theological contextualization. How might cultural factors take the lead and alter our reading of Scripture to provide new but legitimate biblical interpretations?[399] Certainly, the increased use of narrative can correct some kinds of theologizing. This would likely mean a shift towards biblical theology though not leaving systematic theology. Not only does story have a way of challenging people more holistically within their context, but it guards against "proof texting" one's assumptions and fosters greater respect for the entire canon.

---

[398] This word comes from Hwang who references social sciences, like psychology, that often neglect to factor situational and cultural influences that affect human behavior (Hwang, *Foundations*, ix).

[399] This is an important methodological point Sheldon Sawatsky tries to illustrate in his "Chinese Ecclesiology in Context," *TJTh*, no. 5 (1983): 161.

CHAPTER 4: HONOR AND SHAME IN CONTEXT

The array of definitions given to honor and shame (HS) has an intriguing degree of

overlap.[1] Broadly, honor refers to the value given to a person or thing according to some

public norm.[2] Malina, drawing from Julian Pitt-Rivers' benchmark essay, suggests,

"Honor is the value of a person in his or her own eyes (that is, one's claim to worth) *plus*

that person's value in the eyes of his or her social group. Honor is a claim to worth along

with the social acknowledgement of worth."[3] Conversely, one is shamed by not

conforming to that standard of good, bad, right, and wrong.[4] In practice, HS is complex

and nuanced. HS is a human phenomenon,[5] though the label has particularly described

cultures of the Middle and Far East.[6] It involves concepts like reputation, glory, name,

---

[1] John Pilch, *Handbook of Biblical Social Values* (updated ed.; Peabody, Mass.: Hendrickson, 2000), 106–7. Unni Wikan says HS is complex, and studying them can lead to much imprecision and abstraction across cultures. Yet, regardless of exact "rules," honor and shame each involve the same key issues, namely, worth and identity with reference to some public. Cf. his work "Shame and Honour: A Contestable Pair," *Man* 19, no. 4 (Dec 1984): 635–52. Huber notes that "the sanction of 'shaming' is designed to withhold basic psychological and social needs (in particular, acceptance, belonging, honor, relatedness, or significance) and to point out failure to attain desired personal attributes (such as, dignity, strength, or adequacy)." Lyn Bechtel Huber, "The Biblical Experience of Shame/Shaming in Biblical Israel in Relation to Its Use as Religious Metaphor" (PhD diss., Madison, N.J.: Drew University, 1983), 205.

[2] Neyrey, *Honor and Shame*, 15. Malina, *The New Testament World*, 30–35. For classic treatment on HS, see Julian Pitt-Rivers, "Honour and Social Status," in *Honour and Shame: The Values of Mediterranean Society.* (ed. Jean G. Peristiany; Chicago, Ill.: University of Chicago Press, 1966), 19–77. A. C. Hagedorn, "Honor and Shame," *DOTHB,* 497.

[3] Malina, *The New Testament World*, 30. Julian Pitt-Rivers' treatment is a standard text in the field of anthropology in regards to HS. See Pitt-Rivers' definition in "Honour and Social Status," 21–22.

[4] David A. deSilva, "Honor and Shame," *DOTWPW,* 288.

[5] As such, see William Lad Sessions, "Honor and God," *The Journal of Religion* 87, no. 2 (Apr 2007): 206–24. His "concern is for the potential use of the concept of honor in theology, as a monotheistic concept" (p. 207); Alloway, Lacey, and Jewett, *The Shame Factor.*

[6] For instance, Tennent, *Theology in the Context of World Christianity*, 79. Roland Müller, *Honor and Shame: Unlocking the Door* (Bloomington, Ind.: Xlibris, 2001). Of course, geographic and national

---

148

boasting, "face," and one's group identity.[7] In terms of experience, Flanders' comments are important:

> Scholars generally acknowledge that the basic distinction between these two experiences is the role of self-attribution. . . . Thus, guilt involves a more articulated condemnation of a specific behavior (i.e., "what I *did*"). . . . The focus in guilt is on the specific act that remains external to the self. Shame, in contrast, involves a global negative evaluation of the self (i.e., "who I *am*"). . . . That is, what one does is not abstracted and externalized but is appropriated as an inherent part of the self. The focus in shame is on the resulting inadequacy of the self. . . . Since shame is about falling short, corrective action must be different than that associated with guilt. Punishment will not help nor will simple absolution or forgiveness. Instead, the proper corrective measure must involve a remaking or renovation of the self in some way. There must be a true change by healing or transformation of the shamed self.[8]

In short, HS speaks to identity and worth in the context of relationships.[9]

Shame is often contrasted with guilt. Thus, it is imperative to rectify possible misunderstandings. Guilt and HS have both objective and subjective aspects.[10] A person can be guilty (objectively) and/or feel guilty (subjectively). Many are familiar with HS's subjective side such that one may say, "He is ashamed." Yet, one can be honorable or shameful, i.e. have honor or bear shame, apart from a psychological experience. S. J. DeVries adds, "In the objective sense, shame is the disgrace which a sinner brings upon

---

marker is not determinative; cf. Daphna Oyserman, Heather M. Coon, and Markus Kemmelmeier, "Rethinking Individualism and Collectivism: Evaluation of Theoretical Assumptions and Meta-Analyses," *Psychological Bulletin* 128, no. 1 (2002): 3–72.

[7] David A. deSilva, *Honor, Patronage, Kinship & Purity: Unlocking New Testament Culture* (Downers Grove, Ill.: IVP, 2000), 23–42. Within missiological literature, Christopher L. Flanders, "Fixing the Problem of Face," *EMQ* 45, no. 1 (Jan 2009): 12–19. In broader anthropology, Brooklynn Weldon, "Restoring Lost 'Honor': Retrieving Face and Identity, Removing Shame, and Controlling the Familial Cultural Environment through 'Honor' Murder," *JAPSS* 2, no. 1 (2010): 384–85. F. Gerald Downing, "Honor," *NIDB*, 884.

[8] Christopher L. Flanders, "Shame," *GDT*, 814. Emphasis in original. Similarly, see Robert J. Priest, "Shame," *EDWM*, 870–71; Thomas, "The Gospel for Shame Cultures: A Paradigm Shift," 284–90.

[9] Neyrey, *Honor and Shame*, 27–28.

[10] This is widely noted, as in G. B. Funderburke, "Shame," *ZPEB* 5:372–73.

149

himself and those associated with him."[11] HS need not imply total relativism.[12] Just as guilt is relative to a law, so HS is measured within some public context. Thus, Christians call guilt, honor, or shame "absolute" when it is *relative to* God and his people. "Absolute" does not imply existence apart of God. "Right" and "good" are as relative as honor.[13]

Social science typically describes HS as either ascribed or achieved.[14] For instance, one is *ascribed* honor by virtue of one's position, title, birth, or relationship to others. People *achieve* honor through individual deeds and virtues. To be clear, not only the word "honor," but also "glory" [δοξα] can have social import.[15] Social status might be symbolized in one's clothing, language, or ritual.[16] These dynamics govern the rules of social interaction and moral conduct.[17] Accordingly, "Honor is analogous to a contemporary society's credit rating."[18] Not surprisingly, "honor cultures" are more

---

[11] S. J. DeVries, "Shame," *IDB*, 306.

[12] Rafael Zaracho implies as much when he says of shame-based conceptions of sin, "Morality therefore becomes eminently external and superficial," in "Communicating the Gospel in a Shame Society," 272–73. Unfortunately, overlooking the objective sense and treating shame as only a psychological term is typical. Such approaches tend not to do exegesis and extensive theologizing. For examples, Pruyser, "Anxiety, Guilt, and Shame in the Atonement." In the same volume, James Armstrong calls Pruyser's article "an attempt to illustrate the bearing of psychology upon theology." See his work, "A New Look at Some Old Problems," *ThTo* 21, no. 1 (Apr 1964): 9. Similarly, see Nicholls, "Contextualisation in Chinese Culture," 374; Hesselgrave, "Missionary Elenctics and Guilt and Shame"; Binau, "When Shame is The Question, How Does The Atonement Answer?".

[13] J. H. Bavinck's warning in *An Introduction to the Science of Missions* (Phillipsburg, N.J.: P & R Publishing, 1992), 261 is apt: "It sometimes seems that God is lost behind the moral order which he himself supposedly established. The moral order, with its numerous commands and prohibitions, is then hypostatized into an independent entity, and God is made to be an appendage, a supplement, who appears to punish or to reward."

[14] For elaboration, see deSilva, *Honor, Patronage*, 23–42. A brief introduction to HS within a biblical context is Halvor Moxnes, "Honor and Shame," *BTB* 23, no. 4 (1993): 167–76. In Chinese culture, see David Yau-fai Ho, "On the Concept of Face," *AJS* 81, no. 4 (1976): 870.

[15] Ben C. Blackwell, "Immortal Glory and the Problem of Death in Romans 3.23," *JSNT* 32, no. 3 (Mar 2010): 286–87.

[16] Neyrey, *Honor and Shame*, 21–27.

[17] For an ancient Mediterranean context, see Bruce Malina and Jerome H. Neyrey, *Portraits of Paul: An Archaeology of Ancient Personality* (Louisville, Ky.: Westminster John Knox Press, 1996), 76–78, 153–201. Ng makes these connections within Chinese culture. See Ng, "Internal Shame as a Moral Sanction"; Bedford and Hwang, "Guilt and Shame."

[18] David M. May, "'Drawn from Nature or Common Life': Social and Cultural Reading Strategies for the Parables," *RevExp* 94 (1997): 203.

collectivistic as opposed to individualistic.[19] Loyalty to one's in-group is of uttermost importance. The group head represents the honor of the group, whether a family, tribe, or nation.[20] HS are thus shared by group members.[21]

Honor and Shame in the "Face" in Chinese Culture

This section specifically considers how face, honor, and shame function within a Chinese cultural framework. "Face" is a Chinese way of talking about HS.[22] Thus, Cheng states,

> The positive value of gaining [face] is a [sic] honor—an honor of recognition of personal credit and worth. The positive value of keeping or saving [face] is the acknowledgement of affirmation of one's personal status and prestige in face of challenge or disgrace. . . . The negative value of losing or breaking [face] is a disgrace due to allowance and depreciation of one's social status and prestige and calls forth wrath, shamefulness, resentment, and even hatred.[23]

This section clarifies the meaning of "face" within a Chinese context by exploring HS's relationship to other concepts such as group-orientation, identity, and morality.

---

[19] Malina's essay addresses both ancient and modern expressions of collectivism. Bruce Malina, "Collectivism in Mediterranean Culture," in *Understanding the Social World of the New Testament* (ed. Dietmar Neufeld and R. E. DeMaris; New York, N.Y.: Routledge, 2010), 17–28. Also, Malina and Jerome H. Neyrey make very clear comparisons in Appendix 2 in *Portraits of Paul*, 225–31. Anthropologists have made this same observation across the world, as in Agneta H. Fischer, Antony S.R. Manstead, and Patricia M. Rodriguez Mosquera, "The Role of Honour-related vs. Individualistic Values in Conceptualising Pride, Shame, and Anger: Spanish and Dutch Cultural Prototypes," *Cognition & Emotion* 13, no. 2 (Mar 1999): 149–79.

[20] Pitt-Rivers, "Honour and Social Status," 35–36; Malina, *The New Testament World*, 44. Within recent socio-politic discourse, O'Neill discusses this relative to "national honor" in Barry O'Neill, *Honor, Symbols, and War* (Ann Arbor, Mich.: University of Michigan Press, 2001), 87–90.

[21] The propriety of this dynamic is debated, yet the phenomenon is noted across social sciences. Cf. Peter Forrest, "Collective Guilt: Individual Shame," *Midwest Studies in Philosophy* 30 (2006): 145–53; Joel Feinberg, "Collective Responsibility," *The Journal of Philosophy* 65, no. 21 (7 Nov 1968): 674–88.

[22] Hsiang even "argues that the term *mianzi* is now synonymous with the term 'honor'." Quoted from Chang and Holt, who cite T. C. Hsiang, *Research on Chinese Charactoristics* (Taipei: Shang-wu Publishing, 1974), 52 [in Chinese]. See Hui Ching Chang and G. Richard Holt, "A Chinese Perspective on Face: A Inter-Relational Concern," in *The Challenge of Facework: Cross-Cultural and Interpersonal Issues* (ed. Stella Ting-Toomey; Suny Series in Human Communication Processes; Albany, N.Y.: State University of New York Press, 1994), 95–96. In their discussion, they note objections to the correlation. These will be addressed below.

[23] Cheng, "The Concept of Face and Its Confucian Roots," 334.

A number of scholars have given definitions to "face," despite Lin Yutang's

contention that face is "impossible to define."[24] Hu and Grove regard face as a person's

"claim" to identity; in every relationship and situation, everyone claims to be a certain

kind of person.[25] For Ho, face refers to one's social "standing" or "status."[26] Hwang

suggests, "one's situated identity." Finally, Stover calls it, "other-directed self esteem."[27]

Far from being limited to China, face is a universal human phenomenon, a fundamental

consideration in social interactions.[28] In fact, face must be protected and given in order to

maintain harmony in a group.[29] In different contexts, the rules and signs for recognizing

face may differ. A person loses faces when he or she claims to have certain

characteristics but others do not acknowledge that claim. Yan explains, "Social labeling

is important because it defines the individual's rights, status, and identity in society."[30]

One's face is contingent on one's role within a group and the expectations of the

community.[31] This is why Ho says, "A concern for face . . . is indicative of other

directedness, that is, having sensitivity to how one appears in the eyes of others and a

tendency to act in ways which meet their approval."[32] Every group will give praise and

criticism according to its distinctive values. It follows that face is lost when a person

---

[24] Yutang Lin, *My Country and My People* (New York, N.Y.: Reynal & Hitchcock, 1935), 202. Cited in Ho, "On the Concept of Face," 867.

[25] Hu and Grove, *Encountering the Chinese*, 111–12.

[26] Ho, "On the Concept of Face," 867–72.

[27] Stover, *The Cultural Ecology of Chinese Civilization*. Cited in Ho, "On the Concept of Face," 868.

[28] Many have recognized this, including Li, Wang, and Fischer, "Shame Concepts," 768; Hu and Grove, *Encountering the Chinese*, 111, 114–15. Ho, "On the Concept of Face," 867, 881–82. Hwang, *Foundations*, 292. Cf. Karen Tracy, "The Many Faces of Facework," in *Handbook of Language and Social Psychology* (ed. Howard Giles and W. P. Robinson; New York, N.Y.: John Wiley and Sons, 1990), 219.

[29] Ho, "On the Concept of Face," 872.

[30] Yan, *Individualization*, 281.

[31] Ho, "On the Concept of Face," 872, 874.

[32] Ibid., 875.

compromises group distinctives.[33] Cheng therefore differentiates between "subjective" *mianzi* and "objective" *mianzi*. Subjective *mianzi* is "a personal claim of social authority, while in the objective sense [*mianzi*] represents a recognized authority of social importance."[34] Face concerns one's perceived public value.

Naturally, people are more sensitive to face-concerns in more group-oriented cultures. They pay great attention to hierarchy, social formalities, and indirect communication.[35] Ho illustrates, "In particular, the individual's face and the good name of his family . . . were virtually inseparable in traditional Chinese society."[36] By contrast, individualistic societies (e.g., in many Western countries) tend to be more egalitarian, informal, and direct in communication.[37] Therefore, traditional societies are likely to attach greater value to face than highly mobile cultures where change is the norm.[38]

The concept of shame permeates every aspect of Chinese life.[39] Membership in a group bequeaths an identity with a certain degree of HS. This collectivism marks modern China. For instance, the Chinese commemorate "National Humiliation Day,"[40] whereby nationalistic pride is stoked by recalling the sense of shame China previously endured by foreign powers.[41] In addition, family honor and unity is perpetuated through "the most essential religious sentiment underlying the entire Chinese family system—remembrance

---

[33] Hu and Grove, *Encountering the Chinese*, 117.

[34] Cheng, "The Concept of Face and Its Confucian Roots," 332.

[35] Also, see Hwang, *Foundations*, 290–91; Hu and Grove, *Encountering the Chinese*, 116–17.

[36] Ho, "On the Concept of Face," 880.

[37] Hu and Grove, *Encountering the Chinese*, 116–18.

[38] Ibid., 116.

[39] Li, Wang, and Fischer, "Shame Concepts," 769. The entire essay is exceptional in showing the systemic impact of HS on the Chinese language.

[40] Formally, the day is called "National Defense Education Day," being established in 2001.

[41] William C. Callahan, "History, Identity, and Security: Producing and Consuming Nationalism in China," *BCAS* 38, no. 2 (2006): 179–208. In this article, he observes, "Indeed, the theme of the 2004 National Defense Education Day was 'Never forget national humiliation, strengthen our national defense'" (p. 180). See his work, "National Insecurities: Humiliation, Salvation, and Chinese Nationalism," *Alternatives: Global, Local, Political* 29, no. 2 (Mar-May 2004): 199–218.

of one's ancestors."[42] In childrearing, parents frequently compel obedience and preserve family honor by shaming their children. In this way, a person's name lives in perpetuity by one's bloodline, traced back through one's ancestors and extending forward in one's children. Not surprisingly, for the average Chinese person, one's honor or reputation is "more important than life itself."[43] A familiar idea in Chinese culture is expressed in the phrase "to owe face" (*qian mianzi*, 欠面子). Honor is owed to one's superiors. Proper decorum ensures the reciprocal exchange of honor and the avoidance of shame. Relationships require an ongoing, conscious sense of obligation or reciprocity. Favors are direct and equal repayments of social debt.[44] Yeo argues that Confucianism "does acknowledge mutual indebtedness as the basic human condition," yet, one can never repay the debt owed to parents. Having received life from their parents, children are ever obligated to give them honor, loyalty, and thanksgiving.[45]

Collectivism, honor, and shame have an inherently public nature. Shameful behavior deserves public, objective retribution. Keeping social obligations are key to right relationships and a good reputation. In this environment, trust has a more heightened importance compared to law-oriented cultures.[46] However, the dynamics of trust and distrust are complicated by a collectivist value on interdependence and the fact that people have identities within different groups (e.g., family, friends, job, state).

---

[42] Christian Jochim, *Chinese Religions* (Upper Saddle River, N.J.: Prentice-Hall, 1986), 169.

[43] Zhang and Baker, *Think Like Chinese*, 22–23.

[44] Takie Sugiyama Lebra, "Compensative Justice and Moral Investment among Japanese, Chinese, and Koreans," in *Japanese Culture and Behavior: Selected Readings* (ed. Takie Sugiyama Lebra and William P. Lebra; 2d. ed.; Hawaii: University of Hawaii, 1986), 43–60.

[45] Yeo, *Musing*, 199–200, 302.

[46] The contrast is between collectivistic, HS cultures and stereotypical, Western culture with its emphasis on law. In a law-oriented culture, trust is less integral to social relationships in that laws establish rights that protect against breaches of trust. In China, trust's function and effect are more pervasive.

Chinese have something of an absolute regard for human relationships (*guanxi*, 关系).[47]

Trust expresses itself in social practices. Li Liu explains that trust must be regulated in order to overcome the risk and anxiety that arise when group loyalties compete. A consequence for modern China is an increasing trust in money over people.[48] To secure their "spiritual and emotional ballast,"[49] many not only grope for capitalism, but also seek honor in nationalism and a renewed Confucianism with socialist characteristics. An "ideological vacuum" erodes the sense of trust needed for a flourishing Chinese society.[50]

To identify with a group implies an acceptance of its face standards. Membership bestows the individual with certain privileges and obligations. Face functions as a social control, regulating moral behavior.[51] Lack of conformity to communal norms raises doubts about one's group identity. Loss of face brings a sense of isolation. Still, there is a sense in which someone may have multiple identities inasmuch as he or she belongs to different contexts and groups. For this reason, Tracy suggests, "[I]t is important to be more specific than saying that people want to be appreciated and approved of by selected others. The face wants individuals pursue are different in different contexts. Thus, communicators need to decide which aspect of another's identity it is appropriate to

---

[47] On *guanxi*'s contemporary relevance, see Thomas Gold, Doug Guthrie, and David L. Wank, eds., *Social Connections in China: Institutions, Culture, and the Changing Nature of Guanxi* (Cambridge: Cambridge University Press, 2002).

[48] Li Liu, "Filial Piety, Guanxi, Loyalty, and Money: Trust in China," in *Trust and Distrust: Sociocultural Perspectives* (ed. Ivana Marková and Alex Gillespie; Charlotte, N.C.: Information Age Publishing, 2008), 51–73.

[49] Ibid., 71.

[50] Communist leaders have a well-known mantra that refers to socialism "with Chinese characteristics." On how they try to use Confucianism to fill the ideological vacuum and ensure social stability, see Jiawen Ai, "The Refunctioning of Confucianism: The Mainland Chinese Intellectual Response to Confucianism since the 1980s," *Issues&Stud* 44, no. 2 (Jun 2008): 29–78. Also, Wu Zhong, "Beyond Confucius and Communism," *Asia Times*, 3 Oct 2007, Online Edition edition, sec. Greater China Section. n.p. [cited 6 Nov 2010]. Online: http://www.atimes.com/atimes/China/IJ03Ad02.html.

[51] Ho, "On the Concept of Face," 873, 882.

orient to" as well as which face (of their own) to portray to others.[52] As roles and relationships change so do the rules of face.

Hwang makes a key point lest one divide too sharply the individual from the group. He notes, "[T]he uniqueness of Chinese face is that an individual would take actions not only for the face of 'one self' [*sic*] but also for the face of 'greater self.'"[53] By "greater self" (*dawo*), Hwang refers to self "extended to include other family members," even ancestors.[54] This is why students are sometimes motivated to make good grades, in order that they may honor their parents and ancestors.[55] To be clear, it is not that the individual is supposed to sacrifice his or her face for the sake of the group; rather, it is never acceptable for someone to lose face *because* that would mean the entire group would be shamed. Ultimately, identity is found in the "greater self."[56]

Authors sometimes distinguish two kinds of face, *mianzi* and *lian*. Hu describes *mianzi* as one's prestige or reputation due to "high position, wealth, power, ability, through cleverly establishing social ties to a number of prominent people"; yet, it is "dependent at all times on his external environment."[57] *Mianzi* mainly concerns conformity to "social conventions" rather than "integrity of character."[58] On the other hand, *lian* "is the respect of a group for a man with a good moral reputation."[59] Cheng adds that to lose *lian* "... means dishonor and disgrace, while to lose [*mianzi*] means

---

[52] Tracy, "The Many Faces of Facework," 218.

[53] Bedford and Hwang, "Guilt and Shame," 280.

[54] Hwang, *Foundations*, 168.

[55] Ibid., 255.

[56] In fact, Zou and Wang suggest this is the ideal result of Confucian thinking. See ZhiMin Zou and DengFeng Wang, "Guilt Versus Shame: Distinguishing the Two Emotions from a Chinese Perspective," *Social Behavior & Personality: An International Journal* 37, no. 5 (Jun 2009): 602.

[57] Hu, "The Chinese Concepts of 'Face'," 45, 61.

[58] Ibid., 56.

[59] Ibid., 45.

merely that one's honor is not honored or honor is not recognized. It does not mean that one loses ground for claiming one's honor."[60] *Lian* involves the community's "confidence" that a person will behave according to basic moral standards.[61]

Hu and Ho each examine how the words are used and give examples to distinguish these ideas.[62] *Mianzi* can simply mean one is well known or has impressed others, regardless of moral grounds (e.g., athletes, singers, CEOs). A poor person could have *lian* but little *mianzi*. Cheng says of *lian*, "It can never be lost or broken without suffering a disgrace in the eyes of others or oneself; it is therefore identified with the sense of honor, integrity, and shame of a person. Everyone is expected to protect his [*lian*] at all times, though not everyone is expected to have [*mianzi*] or have it all the time."[63] Hu rightly points out that modesty, by which one appears not to have or want face (*mianzi*), is actually a protection of face (*lian*) since it is a moral value not to express pride over others.[64] To be sure, a sharp distinction should not be pressed too far.[65] However, these comments point to historical developments in the concept, which may remain latent within common thinking and usage.

Face can be gained or lost. Hwang shows how highly fluid and complicated face can become: "In order to maintain one's status in his/her interpersonal network, an individual in Confucian society has to passively protect one's own face from loss and

---

[60] Cheng, "The Concept of Face and Its Confucian Roots," 335.

[61] Hu, "The Chinese Concepts of 'Face'," 45, 50, 55.

[62] Ibid., 46–64; Ho, "On the Concept of Face," 869–81.

[63] Cheng, "The Concept of Face and Its Confucian Roots," 334–35.

[64] Hu, "The Chinese Concepts of 'Face'," 48–49. Similarly, Hwang says being "thin skinned" (in Chinese) is considered a good quality because a person will be more aware of other people's opinions. "Thick skinned" people care less about social judgment. See Hwang, *Foundations*, 279.

[65] Hwang says this distinction relates to Mandarin, not Cantonese. See Hwang, *Foundations*, 268.

also actively adopt every action to promote his/her social status."[66] Face changes in accordance with expectations, whether social or self asserted.[67] To make a promise or boast that one does not live up to would result in a loss of face. Ho's comments are noteworthy, "Strictly speaking, the opposite of gaining face is a process of erosion [of face] . . . 'Losing face' is an expression, which properly used, refer only to *public, discrete* events."[68] There are many ways to lose face. Some are minor, like forgetting words to a song or tripping while walking. Any number of bad habits can make people lose face.[69] Other reasons are more serious. One study shows having mental illness, disease, or getting tested for AIDS (not necessarily having it) can cause a loss of face leading to a loss of relationships, discrimination, even a denial of medical care.[70]

Hwang adds a distinction between "real face," based on actual success, and "virtual face," which "use[s] some symbolic decoration, action, or language" to make up for "the lack of competency to live up to the honor."[71] A person can also "borrow" face (*jie mianzi*) by appealing to some other relationship with a person who has face.[72] "Name dropping" and job references are examples. One recent report tells of Chinese companies hiring "white foreigners" as pretend employees in order to give a company face.[73] The article quotes Zhang Haihua as saying, "Because Western countries are so developed,

---

[66] Ibid., 278.

[67] See discussion in Ho, "On the Concept of Face," 870–72; Hwang, *Foundations*, 272–80.

[68] Hwang, *Foundations*, 871.

[69] Ibid., 278.

[70] Lawrence Hsin Yang and Arthur Kleinman, "'Face' and the Embodiment of Stigma in China-The Cases of Schizophrenia and AIDS," *Social Science and Medicine* 30 (2008): 1–11.

[71] Hwang, *Foundations*, 279–80.

[72] Ibid., 335–36.

[73] Lara Farrar, "Chinese Companies 'Rent' White Foreigners," *CNN.com*, Jun 29, 2010, U. S. edition, sec. Business. [cited 23 Feb 2012]. Online: http://www.cnn.com/2010/BUSINESS/06/29/china.rent.white.people/index.html.

people think they are more well off, so people think that if a company can hire foreigners, it must have a lot of money and have very important connections overseas. So when they really want to impress someone, they may roll out a foreigner." Thus, they borrow a foreign face.

The Meaning of Morality in Relationship to Face

What is the relationship between face and morality? Cheng reminds us that political stability and social harmony depend on the ability of people, especially leaders, to relate well with others.[74] Further, "If social interaction is unavoidable, then so is mutual concern for face."[75] Thus, giving face or honor to someone acknowledges one's relationship [*guanxi*] to the other party; to withhold face or to shame someone is to deny or break relationship.[76] Many behaviors are rooted in a concern for face, whether one's own or another's. These include using manners, telling "white lies," giving compliments, showing modesty, and choosing conversation topics, clothing, and wording.

Since family is thought to be the ideal community, then society is to be patterned after the family. In that case, Cheng says, "[T]here need not be any explicit regulations or any legislations among family members. Trust, understood virtue, and need for harmony are sufficient for the give-and-take in the Chinese family."[77] He echoes the previously cited quote from Confucius to the effect that law is an inadequate basis for a harmonious society. This is because true virtue grows out of a sense of shame.[78] Accordingly, "Face

---

[74] Cheng, "The Concept of Face and Its Confucian Roots," 337.
[75] Chang and Holt, "A Chinese Perspective," 95.
[76] Ibid., 107, 125.
[77] Cheng, "The Concept of Face and Its Confucian Roots," 340–41.
[78] *Analects* 2:3. The passage can be found at *Stanford Encyclopedia of Philosophy*, n.p. [cited 7 Mar 2012]. Online: http://classics.mit.edu/Confucius/analects.1.1.html.

is both the goal and the means for strengthening and expressing the harmonization of human relationships among men in society."[79]

Conventional Chinese-Confucian thought grounds morality and social order on the pursuit of honor and the avoidance of shame. "Saving face" acts to "preserve affiliations in groups and maintain congenial social relations and only secondary to achieve certain goals which have a personal reference for the individual involved."[80] Thus, whereas a legal orientation tends towards an insistence on individual rights, HS prioritizes communal harmony. The group's security and interconnectedness are maintained via hierarchal relationships, built upon mutual obligation and loyalty.[81] Bedford and Hwang suggest, "For Chinese, maintaining one's place or identity in the social hierarchy is a duty which is connected to moral belief since the social hierarchy is part of the natural cosmic order."[82] Identity and honor have a near religious significance.

Since face both produces and signifies one's identity or group membership, it is natural that face implies shared moral responsibility between group members.[83] In other words, face is moral precisely because it is public not private. Anytime one gives or receives face, he or she implicitly abides by some shared moral standard. Mutual identification means that the members of a group can share face. This is why children might sometimes be ashamed of the conduct of parents and why politicians quickly disavow any relationship with certain people who have lost face via some verbal or moral mistake. Association is often linked with approval. As a result, "Social others, whether

---

[79] Cheng, "The Concept of Face and Its Confucian Roots," 340.
[80] Stewart, *American Cultural Patterns: A Cross-Cultural Perspective*, 69–70.
[81] Hu and Grove, *Encountering the Chinese*, 122–23.
[82] Bedford and Hwang, "Guilt and Shame," 139.
[83] Bedford and Hwang agree and offer an excellent discussion on identity and morality in relation to shame and guilt. See Bedford and Hwang, "Guilt and Shame."

specific individuals or the society as large, have a stake in the individual's maintenance

or protection of *mianzi*"; likewise, "one is expected to protect the *mianzi* of the whole

family or the ingroup."[84] Someone might object by saying everyone should mind his or

her own business. From what has been said, it makes rational sense why the Chinese

might disagree with that perspective:

> Any individual's failure to act appropriately implies that the associated
> social circle (e.g., parents, teachers, even an entire village) has not
> provided proper guidance. [Therefore] Everyone in a network supervises
> the actions of others and these standards of obligation are internalized as
> following one's heart and mind.[85]

Given that shared face means shared responsibility, one can understand people's differing

reactions to others' moral offenses. A mom may feel no loss of face when she sees a

stranger's child acting disobediently. However, she might feel appalled or give into her

own child's temper tantrum for fear of what other people may think. Hwang's study gives

empirical data to confirm this dynamic.[86]

This group-orientation leads some to think face should not be equated with honor,

which they think is "individually owned."[87] Ho lists "the knights of medieval England"

and the samurai of Japan as examples of this individualistic honor.[88] However, this

dichotomy is unnecessary and grounded on an extremely narrow conception of honor. A

person does not mean the same thing by honor in each of the following sentences: "It is

an honor for us to receive this award," "Thank you for honoring our family with your

---

[84] Chang and Holt, "A Chinese Perspective," 100–1.

[85] Yang and Kleinman, "'Face' and the Embodiment of Stigma in China," 3.

[86] Hwang found Taiwanese students, in contrast to American students, tend to be more critical of the wrongdoing of outsiders (with whom they did not share face) but were more willing to excuse illegalities of family members (with whom they shared face). See Kwang-Kuo Hwang, "Moral Face and Social Face: Contingent Self-Esteem in Confucian Society," *IJPsychol* 41, no. 4 (2006): 280.

[87] For discussion on this point, see Chang and Holt, "A Chinese Perspective," 96, 99–100.

[88] Ho, "On the Concept of Face," 877.

attendance at the party"; and "I will defend the honor of my wife after what happened to her." In the last comment, honor connotes a sense of dignity. This sort of husband might be called an "honorable man." However, this meaning is not inherent to the first two sentences. What they all *do* have in common however is they each conveys a sense of public worth. Honoring someone expresses or upholds his or her value before others.[89] In summary, two aspects consistently appear in face/honor discourse. First, face/honor is social or public. Second, face/honor expresses worth or status. To return to Ho's examples, knights and samurais act in accordance to the values of their community. They vindicate their worth on the basis of a stable moral standard. Yet, to give or have honor can issue from other reasons, such as a name, title, talent, or achievement. Therefore, to have honor in the sense of a "medieval knight" is just as individualistic *and collective* as face, which can also be discussed from both a personal and group perspective.

Those who live in collectively oriented communities recognize the moral implications of the relationships they develop. Face is highly contextual and relational, therefore when relating to others who are sensitive to face, one must take seriously the time and emotional commitment needed to get to know and identify with them. Group members expect more from those inside their group than from outsiders. By way of favors, material assistance, and giving or protecting face, one firms up his or her insider status. *Mianzi* has been compared to "a form of currency," like a "credit card."[90] The cost of face in relationships is reciprocity. This is both normal and normative.[91] Yet, the sobriety of Chinese thinking is in the awareness that all people have limited resources

---

[89] Since "face" is not merely an eastern concept but a human dynamic, it is not appropriate to contrast "face" with "western honor."

[90] Chang and Holt, "A Chinese Perspective," 122.

[91] Hwang, "Moral Face," 93.

162

available to them, whether money, food, time, *as well as* face. Mencius' answer to this question has had lasting influence on Chinese ethical thinking.[92] Bryan Van Norden explains, "[W]e frequently think of benevolence as a virtue that, when fully developed, extends equally to each human being, while Mencius thinks that a fully virtuous person will have more concern for, and special ethical obligations to, those tied to him or her by kinship and certain social roles."[93] The Bible expresses this priority with normative force. For instance, Gal 6:10 says, "So then, as we have opportunity, let us do good to everyone, and especially to those who are of the household of faith." Similarly, Paul charges, "But if anyone does not provide for his relatives, and especially for members of his household, he has denied the faith and is worse than an unbeliever" (1 Tim 5:8).

Face is a moral concern inasmuch as someone cares about other's opinions and social well-being. To have no regard for any other people's feelings of anger or sadness would be deemed immoral. At a broad level, shame is a loss of face, especially *lian*.[94] To have a sense of shame is to regard face as important, especially moral face (i.e. *lian*). Accordingly, there is another way which face is a moral concept. One group of scholars summarizes, "In Chinese culture, if a person is perceived as having no sense of shame,

---

[92] This problem of allocating limited resources among relationships has been shown to be an integral factor in people's actual moral decision making. Cf. Kwang-Kuo Hwang, "Two Moralities: Reinterpreting the Findings of Empirical Research on Moral Reasoning in Taiwan," *AJSP* 1 (1998): 211–38. He particularly asks this question with respect to "positive duties," thing we *ought* to do, not simply actions we should not do. See Hwang, *Foundations*, 163.

[93] Bryan W. Van Norden, "The Emotion of Shame and the Virtue of Righteousness in Mencius," *Dao: A Journal of Comparative Philosophy* 2, no. 1 (Winter 2002): 47.

[94] If shame is narrowly defined, then a loss of face is not necessarily shame in *every* sense of the word. Van Norden interacts with other scholars over the impossibility of giving an exact definition to shame. Yet, he agrees with Kekes, "It shades into embarrassment, humiliation, chagrin, guilt dishonor, regret, remorse, prudishness, disgrace, etc. To attempt to list necessary and sufficient conditions for shame is arbitrary to simplify a naturally complex experience." These are John Kekes' words in his "Shame and Moral Progress," *Midwest Stud Philos* 13, no. 1 (1988): 283. Kekes is cited in Van Norden, "The Emotion of Shame," 58. At a general level, any loss of face signals at least a mild level of shame in the form of lost social respect, compromised credibility, or exposure of previously hidden weaknesses. In the total picture, which is fluid, there is an adjustment in "who you are."

that person may be thought of as beyond moral reach, and therefore is even 'feared by the devil'. Thus, shame to the Chinese is not a mere emotion but also a moral and virtuous sensibility to be pursued."[95] If a person has no regard for right conduct, people might say, "*ta buzhi lianchi*," or literally "he does not know how to hide shame."[96] This gives some rational for shaming as a discipline in Chinese parenting. In addition, concern for other people's opinions is inherent and thus necessary for cultivating humility.[97] The individual who is not sensitive to shame is a threat to others. Not only that, Mencius adds, but also "Whoever has no sense of shame is not human."[98]

Given the importance of shame in Chinese culture, one needs to understand its meanings, philosophically and empirically, including how it differs from guilt. This lays groundwork for answering some theological questions that are frequently framed in terms of guilt not shame. Van Norden helpfully delineates two kinds of shame, "conventional shame," and "ethical shame."[99] The former refers to the judgment or feeling that comes "when we believe those whose views matter to us look down on us (or on those with whom we identity), on the basis of a standard of appearance we share." Ethical shame, on

---

[95] Li, Wang, and Fischer, "Shame Concepts," 769.

[96] "不知廉耻." "廉" etimologically links to 簾 in 窗簾 ("curtain"), connoting to hide/cover. Also possible is that 廉 has the meaning "integrity/honesty" such that one does not know honestry or shame.

[97] Van Norden, "The Emotion of Shame," 62.

[98] B. J. Yang, *Mengzi yizhu [Translated notes on Mencius]* (Beijing: Zhonghua Book Company, 1960), 80. This translation is cited by Wang, "Confucian Thinking in Traditional Moral Education," 439.

[99] See his discussion at Van Norden, "The Emotion of Shame," 60–62.

the other hand, occurs "when we believe that we (or those with whom we identify) have significant character flaws." Essentially, this distinction mirrors the discussion on *mianzi* and *lian* respectively. Therefore, shame increases in proportion to one's being "deficient" relative to some standard of worth he or she has in a group context.[100]

Empirically, shame is shown to have varying significance across cultures. An extensive study by Li et al. demonstrates that the meaning of Chinese shame terms are generally divided into two categories, those focusing on one's own shame experience and those primarily focuings on "consequences of and reactions to shame directed at others."[101] Shame terms that are self-focused refer to individual's experiences, yet the reason for shame feelings are still community oriented. This is because this sort of shame occurs "When failing to live up to the expectations set by themselves and others for their [social] roles."[102] Concerning other-focused shame terms, researchers summarize, "[T]his category represents people casting a negative judgement [*sic*] on others who behave in a way deemed shameful."[103] Either way, shame has a collective orientation.

Since shame is highly related to morality, it is not entirely accurate to sharply distinguish guilt and shame, particularly in human experience.[104] Though not exclusively, shame is a moral category in Chinese culture. "Shame" in this respect is not simply about public exposure—others thinking poorly of us. It essentially involves our identity,

---

[100] Ibid., 58–59. Citing Kekes, "Shame and Moral Progress," 286. Likewise, Cassie Striblen, "Guilt, Shame, and Shared Responsibility," *Journal of Social Philosophy* 38, no. 3 (Fall 2007): 478.

[101] See their full study at Li, Wang, and Fischer, "Shame Concepts." They map the meaning of 144 Chinese shame-related words through a process of interviews with 82 Mandarin speakers who explained and helped categorize nuances within each word.

[102] Ibid., 785.

[103] Ibid.

[104] The present discussion concerns subjective shame and guilt. Objective shame is the shame cast onto others due to a reason that is regarded as "shameful." Guilt feelings arise because of the impression that one is or might have been "guilty" (objectively) in the sense of actually doing something wrong.

whether or not our claim to some status or character is warranted. The study by Li et al found participants at times were unable to separate the two concepts.[105] One might say guilt is felt where shame is a loss of *lian*. Yet, even if shame and guilt are experienced similarly and simultaneously, this does not minimize very important differences.

Perhaps the most fundamental distinction between guilt and shame is their respective point of reference. Flanders' explanation of shame is already cited above. In agreement, many scholars explain guilt in terms of actions, shame in terms of identity.[106] Subjectively, guilt is the feeling in response to wrongdoing; shame is the response to bad character. Objectively, guilt points the *wrongdoing itself* as opposed to shame, which highlights the *kind of person* who does such conduct. From this perspective, one easily sees that both involve value or moral judgments.[107] The standard for both is external to the individual. Guilt comes from breaking an internalized public rule. Shame reflects a perceived status relative to others. Previously, face was described as a claim of worth/value in a social context. Here the meaning of shame is specified with respect to identity (i.e. social) and morality (i.e. value).[108] The move from value or worth to morality is easy to see. What one attributes worth to becomes the measure of what is considered good or bad. At various points, people move from good/bad judgments to

---

[105] They state this bluntly, "Thus, shame and guilt sometimes may operate interchangeably in such a way that shame is just as heavily related to moral issues as guilt is" (p. 788). See their discussion on guilt in Li, Wang, and Fischer, "Shame Concepts," 787–88.

[106] In addition to those cited with Flanders above, note Van Norden, "The Emotion of Shame," 52; Bedford and Hwang, "Guilt and Shame," 127–28; Zou and Wang, "Guilt Versus Shame," 601–2.

[107] Ho's comments could be misleading. Because he only speaks of shame in the broadest sense, it would seem he considers guilt a moral category, but not shame (since one could feel shame for non-moral reasons, like appearance). However, upon closer reading, he simply sees shame as a larger category, which *includes* the moral dimension. This agrees with what is said here. See Ho, "On the Concept of Face," 876 fn #3; For a defense of collective guilt whereby an individual can rationally assume guilt simply due to his or her identification with a group, see Striblen, "Guilt, Shame, and Shared Responsibility."

[108] Shame is discussed this way in Bedford and Hwang, "Guilt and Shame."

declarations of right/wrong. Right and wrong then become the basis on which people make laws. This natural process begins with an attribution of worth to a person, object, or circumstance. Finally, one more distinction is noteworthy. Guilt focuses on the non-relational punishment or penalty associated with wrong actions; in contrast, shame focuses on relational problems like becoming isolated from others or losing respect.[109]

Bedford and Hwang trace these two types of orientation: guilt/individual versus shame/collective.[110] They ground individualism in the "Judeo-Christian perspective" that says individuals are created equal in God's sight.[111] This leads to individual autonomy, an emphasis on rights, and freedom from social restraints. However, this oversimplified explanation is problematic. As was seen in the last chapter, the stress on equal rights originates back at least to the Greek and Roman civilization, apart from Judeo-Christian influence.[112] In addition, their analysis wrongly infers that God's creating individuals theologically entails the primacy of the individual over the group. Simply because some may use this theological idea to justify individualism does not mean Christians *must be* individualistic rather than group-oriented.

Having observed the inner logic behind face exchange, one must not be naive to problems. Face may be used as a means of flattery in order to secure limited supplies and goods.[113] Businesses, among other groups, may be slow to change since doing so might imply previous mistakes or weaknesses.[114] In addition, concern for face can result in the

---

[109] Jun Gao, Aimin Wang, and Mingyi Qian, "Differentiating Shame and Guilt from a Relational Perspective: A Cross-Cultural Study," *Soc Behav Personal* 38, no. 10 (2010): 1403.

[110] Bedford and Hwang, "Guilt and Shame," 130–41.

[111] Ibid., 130.

[112] Liang, "Explicating 'Law'."

[113] Relating face exchange and *guanxi*, see Gold, Guthrie, and Wank, *Social Connections*, 70–74.

[114] For illustration, see Sheh Seow Wah, *Chinese Leadership: Moving From Classical to Contemporary* (Tarrytown, N.Y.: Marshall Cavendish, 2009), 132–33.

avoidance of conflict, stifling of creativity, slow types of learning,[115] induce political tension,[116] as well as problems related to discrimination and health care.[117] These challenges are not unique to HS cultures, but the details in how they manifest may differ.

When disputes do occur, how do HS influence matters of reconciliation and forgiveness in China? The legal system is not the preferred way of handling problems.[118] Since harmony is of utmost importance, it is not surprising that Chinese prefer to avoid open conflict.[119] In fact, many problems can be avoided simply by using indirect communication.[120] On the whole, Chinese show a great deal of reluctance to extend forgiveness, as has been verified in numerous empirical studies.[121] For one reason, to openly discuss the problem leads to someone losing face. Secondly, some suggest Chinese relationships have higher expectations and emphasis on sacrifice than do many other cultures. This results in greater hurt when there are serious fissures in relationship.[122] Not surprisingly, studies show Chinese people carry greater long-term resentment than other countries.[123] These dynamics explain why certain new businesses

---

[115] Xiaoxin Wu, "The Dynamics of Chinese Face Mechanisms and Classroom Behaviour: A Case Study," *Evaluation and Research in Education* 22, no. 2–4 (Nov 2009): 87–105.

[116] Gries, *China's New Nationalism*, 13–29.

[117] L. Li et al., "Stigmatization and Shame: Consequences of Caring for HIV/AIDS Patients in China," *AIDS Care* 19, no. 2 (Feb 2007): 258–63. Yang and Kleinman, "'Face' and the Embodiment of Stigma in China."

[118] Zhang and Baker, *Think Like Chinese*, 136–38.

[119] For example, see Pamela Koch, "Conflict, Collectivism and Confucianism: A Study of Interpersonal Relationships in Hong Kong Organizations" (Paper presented at the Annual Meeting of the International Communication Association, New York, N.Y., 5 May 2009), [cited 6 Feb 2011]. Online: http://www.allacademic.com/meta/p14066_index.html.

[120] Practical suggestions for conflict management in an honor-shame context are given in Elmer, *Cross-Cultural Conflict*, 65–79.

[121] Katherine P. H. Young and Anita Y. L. Fok, *Marriage, Divorce, and Remarriage: Professional Practice in the Hong Kong Cultural Context* (Hong Kong: Hong Kong University Press, 2005), 92–93. See also Regina Paz, Felix Neto, and Etienne Mullet, "Forgiveness: A Chinese-Western Europe Comparison," *The Journal of Psychology* 142, no. 2 (2008): 147–57.

[122] Young and Fok, *Marriage, Divorce, and Remarriage*, 92.

[123] Paz, Neto, and Mullet, "Forgiveness: A Chinese-Western Europe Comparison," 154.

have sprung up in China. Customers hire companies in order to apologize on their behalf to another party with whom they want reconciliation.[124]

Hwang's discussion provides a comprehensive model for conflict resolution.[125] He echoes the opinion of other scholars in claiming the most common strategy for reconciling parties is the use of a mediator.[126] Hwang says Chinese use mediators to resolve conflicts more than Japanese.[127] Practically, this means a mediator will have face and relationship (*guanxi*) with both parties. Therefore, when the mediator appeals for reconciliation, his own face is at risk. Hwang and others explain that to deny this request would be a breach in the relationship between the mediator and the individual party. The mediator is typically someone of higher status than the disputing parties.[128] Preferably, these conflicts are to be managed within the in-group. Leaders step in to find communal goals where everyone can save face; this approach is in contrast to forcing a resolution upon those in conflict.[129]The greatest influences on why Chinese people typically forgive others are not religious, not a desire for personal peace, nor to protect one's own face; instead, the desire for relational harmony and the preservation of the *other person's* face highly affects whether or not forgiveness is given.[130] For smaller grievances, people tend

---

[124] Elisabeth Rosenthal, "Chinese Distaste For Apologies Means Business: Companies Ask Forgiveness, Lose Face, for San Francisco Chronicle," *www.SFGate.com* (San Francisco, Calif., Jan 7, 2001), sec. Business. [cited 24 Feb 2012]. Online: http://www.sfgate.com/cgi-bin/article.cgi?f=/c/a/2001/01/07/MN152070.DTL.

[125] Hwang, *Foundations*, 327–67.

[126] Hu, "The Chinese Concepts of 'Face'," 60. Chang and Holt, "A Chinese Perspective," 116–20. Zhang and Baker, *Think Like Chinese*, 145. Kat Cheung and Ling Chen, "When a Confucian Manages Individualists: A Study of Intercultural Conflict Between Chinese Managers and Western Subordinates" (Paper presented at the Annual Meeting of the International Communication Association, New York, N.Y., May 5, 2009), [cited 6 Feb 2011]. Online: http://www.allacademic.com/meta/ p13416_index.html.

[127] Hwang, *Foundations*, 333.

[128] Ibid., 359–60. Chang and Holt, "A Chinese Perspective," 117.

[129] Cheung and Chen, "When a Confucian Manages Individualists."

[130] Hong, Watkins, and Hui suggest that forgiving out of a desire for inner peace or one's own face would be more consistent with an individualist mentality of self-preservation. See Fu Hong, David Watkins,

simply not to talk about problems, choosing to move on like nothing happened. To ask

for forgiveness or otherwise compel an apology would result in a greater loss of face.[131]

However, when a serious offense occurs, greater effort is demanded. Forgiveness does

require the offender to show some emotion that expresses his or her sense of shame.[132]

How does shame relate to the Chinese idea of righteousness (*yi*)? Van Norden

charactorizes the tradition view of *yi* as "an ethical sense of shame."[133] Mencius could not

be more direct when he says, "The feeling of shame and dislike is the principle of

righteousness."[134] In terms of honor, an ancient Chinese text states, "Honour virtue and

delight in righteousness, and so you may always be perfectly satisfied."[135] In addition,

"Righteousness is the accordance of actions with what is right, and the great exercise of it

is in honoring the worthy."[136] Elsewhere, one reads a dialogue between two men

regarding whether righteousness will bring the desired honor. In particular, Tsze-kang

---

and Eadaoin K. P. Hui, "Personality Correlates of the Disposition towards Interpersonal Forgiveness: A Chinese Perspective," *IJPsychol* 39, no. 4 (2004): 305–16. See also Fu Hong, David Watkins, and Eadaoin K. P. Hui, "Forgiveness and Personality in a Chinese Cultural Context," *IFE PsychologIA* 16, no. 1 (2008): 9–11; cf. Young and Fok, *Marriage, Divorce, and Remarriage*, 93.

[131] For example, Chang and Holt, "A Chinese Perspective," 114.

[132] Li, Wang, and Fischer, "Shame Concepts," 771. Also, compare the face dynamics in recent politics, such as Robert Marquand, "US 'Sorry' Heard in Beijing as an Apology," *Christian Science Moniter*, Apr 12, 2001, [cited 23 Feb 2012]. Online: http://www.csmonitor.com/2001/0412/p1s2.html. Also, Sunny Lee, "Beijing Suspicious of Japan's War Crime Apology," *The National* (Beijing, Apr 13, 2010), sec. Asia Pacific, [cited 24 Feb 2012]. Online: http://www.thenational.ae/news/world/asia-pacific/beijing-suspicious-of-japans-war-crime-apology. In the latter article, a Japanese professor discusses reconciliation after World War II. "Germany's apology was very easier to do [*sic*] one group [the Nazis] took the responsibility. But for Japan, *all the Japanese have to take responsibility* for its colonial and World War Two wrongdoings" [my emphasis].

[133] Van Norden, "The Emotion of Shame," 63. Cf. Xiao Yang, "Trying to Do Justice to the Concept of Justice in Confucian Ethics," *JCP* 24 (1997): 535, 549; Kwong-loi Shun, *Mencius and Early Chinese Thought* (Palo Alto, Calif.: Stanford University Press, 1997), 25.

[134] Mencius, "The Works of Mencius, Book 2, Part 1: Kung-sun Ch'au," n.p. [cited 1 Dec 2011]. Online: http://nothingistic.org/library/mencius/mencius12.html. In Chinese: "羞恶之心, 义之端也" [*xiu'e zhi xin, yi zhi duan ye*]. A near identical comment is found in Mencius, "The Works of Mencius, Book 6, Part 1: Kai Tsze," n.p. [cited 1 Dec 2011]. Online: http://nothingistic.org/library/mencius/ mencius42.html.

[135] Mencius, "The Works of Mencius, Book 7, Part 1: Tsin Sin," n.p. [cited 1 Dec 2011]. Online: http://nothingistic.org/library/mencius/mencius49.html.

[136] Confucius, "The Doctrine of the Mean, Chapters 18 to 20," n.p. [cited 1 Dec 2011]. Online: http://nothingistic.org/library/confucius/mean/mean03.html.

(*Zhuangzi*, 庄子) questions, "Why do you not pursue a (righteous) course? . . . [I]f you look at the matter from the point of reputation, or estimate it from the point of gain, a righteous course is truly the right thing."[137]

Saving Face, Doing Works, and Implications for Chinese Theology

What are some key implications of Chinese face for contextualizing Chinese theology? A host of contrasts have emerged between Chinese and Western cultures. Given the great influence of the West on traditional theology, harmonizing Chinese thinking and Western theology appears difficult. As has been seen, Western individualism and guilt-orientation are reflected in Western theology's stress upon legal language, individual salvation, and the danger of doing works in order to earn God's favor. By contrast, Chinese culture emphasizes face (i.e. HS), relationships, and group identity. How one tries to reconcile these contrasting worlviews will have systemic effects on his or her theology.

Consider the function of works within Chinese society as opposed to Christian theology. In Western theology, moral works are the major foil for faith in the attempt to earn salvation. Yet, what if typical Chinese people do not think in terms of law or good works as a way of overcoming sin? If their basic question is not "What good works must I do to be saved," then will traditional gospel presentations (like those seen in the last chapter) fall on deaf ears? Are these salvation messages intelligible within a Chinese cultural framework? If not, does that imply Chinese Christians need first to convert *culturally* to Western ways of categorizing their experience?

---

[137] Chuang Tzu, "The Writings of Chuang Tzu, Book 29: The Robber Kih," n.p. [cited 1 Dec 2011]. Online: http://nothingistic.org/library/chuangtzu/chuang87.html.

A person's sense of identity influences how he or she thinks about works. One's identity can be understood from different perspectives, as demonstrated by the Chinese distinction between a person's "big self" (*dawo*) and "little self" (*xiaowo*). Views about guilt and HS will largely depend on whether one appeals to an "independent self-concept" or "*inter*dependent self-concept." Gao et al explain, "The independent self-concept emphasizes one's abilities and unique attributes *which distinguish oneself from others*. The interdependent self-concept emphasizes one's relationships with others and one's membership or status in a group."[138] These categories are helpful since identity involves similarities and differences. It is simply wrong and reductionistic to reckon one illegitimate compared to the other.

By way of analogy, imagine a fifty-piece jigsaw puzzle of China, completed and set on a table. What does one see? The first person sees "one thing," a picture of China. A second person disagrees, claiming it is "really" fifty pieces put together. Who is right? Naturally, some will answer, "It depends," or "Both are right." Both opinions are just as "right" as the other but from different perspectives. What are the implications for theologizing? These two perspectives represent fundamentally different starting points when one reads Scripture and the world.[139] If theologians prioritize an individualistic perspective over a collectivistic view, what Scriptural insights would be lost? Embracing a "both-and" way of thinking may open interpretive doors otherwise inaccessible with rigid "either-or" processing.

---

[138] Gao, Wang, and Qian, "Differentiating Shame and Guilt," 1406. Emphasis added.
[139] Some introductory reflections on this matter can be found in Dennis Hiebert and Edmund Neufeld, "Me and Jesus? Countering Individualism with a More Collectivist Reading of Scripture" (Paper presented at the Annual Meeting of the Evangelical Theological Society, Chicago, Ill., Nov 1994).

From the vantage point of the "independent self," the world is basically made up of a collection of individuals, each having equal value and moral responsibility for his or her conduct. This requires very clear principles that should be internalized in order to maintain social order and protect the rights of individuals. Publically, these standards commonly take the form of laws. A person's conscience is especially critical here, for it arbitrates between right and wrong decisions. Actions then are regulated by the use of guilt, the sense in which one has transgressed a universal principle. Aware of wrongdoing, there is fear of punishment. The wrong action and the guilt need to be remedied in some corresponding way, whether by punishment, compensation, or various other external measures.

From the perspective of the "interdependent self," a different story is told, using different categories to describe the same reality. The world is made up of many different kinds of groups, including families, nations, ethnicities, businesses, clubs, classes, and others. Their members have varying degrees of responsibility to the group, as a whole and to particular members. No one exists apart from some network or intersection of groups. Depending on one's role, his or her obligations, privileges, and expectations are adjusted. By virtue of identification with others, members are responsible for the well being of their own group in particular. No one person can take care of everyone's needs. Choices must be made. Choices about how one relates to others are the heart of morality. To dishonor those with whom one identifies signals a compromise in-group values, an infraction which threatens one's acceptance by the group. A sense of shame regulates actions, since they symbolically affirm the values that come with any given identity. People fear isolation. The loss of identity amounts to non-existence.

Contrasting views on identity and works lead one to ask the question: Do people, at a basic level, more earnestly seek merit or *mianzi*? Do they care more about law or *lian*? Kipnis illustrates how specific actions signal and even define certain identities in China. In the town of Fengjia, "Residents who wished to construct themselves as nonpeasants tried to avoid situations that required bows and *ketou*."[140] Conversely, having seemingly contradictory identities leads to confusion as to what actions are appropriate. Personal and communal tension can result. Therefore, "[o]nly after accepting their classification and creating something positive within it, could they act properly as subjects of a certain identity."[141] Finally, he reports that during the Cultural Revolution, authorities prohibited people weeping at the funeral of people outside their class in order to prevent "the formation of interclass relationships."[142] In short, Kipnis demonstrates that "the production and reproduction of human relationships—by means of 'guesting' and 'hosting,' attending and giving banquets, giving and receiving gifts, and a variety of other methods—was a primary activity for most villagers."[143] Hwang makes the same conclusion about Chinese in general. Personal identities are formed by ". . . the ways in which the individual follows a certain moral order, takes action, or reacts to others' actions in systems of social relationships. [This identity construction happens] with reference to the cultural logic, rules, and values, as well as their own recognition of reality."[144] Action and identity, law and honor are interwined.

---

[140] Kipnis, *Producing Guanxi*, 174. A *ketou* is an ancient Chinese expression of deference by an inferier lying prostrate before a superior.
[141] Ibid., 178.
[142] Ibid., 1.
[143] Ibid., 1, 3.
[144] Hwang, *Foundations of Chinese Psychology*, 125, 193. The quote is repeated on both pages.

One concludes that identity is shaped by both *achieved* and *ascribed* face (i.e. HS status). Just as guilt and shame are present in all cultures, so also people everywhere perceive and/or strive for achieved and ascribed face. Still, the degree of emphasis and explicit awareness of each category varies. A stress on achieved face corresponds to the goal of establishing individual self. Value is chiefly placed on unique achievement. On this basis, individuals merit the approval of others. On the other hand, ascribed face constitutes the *inter*dependent self. One's works construct and reflect relationships, hence identity. Based on associations and likeness to others, honor is imputed to the individual.

Theologically, Western Christians have overwhelmingly constricted their attention to the narrower question of *achieved* face. In the last chapter, the review of different contextualization attempts made this point quite evident. Inasmuch as a person perceives his or her independent self, matters of guilt, meritorious works, punishment, and un-contextualized principles will gain a hearing. However, this is not how "works" operate within an HS, *guanxi*-oriented culture. The primary goal is to get, maintain, and protect face. This happens one of two ways—achievement and ascription. Both have value since both contribute to identity. Many Chinese would be just as glad to get status through ascription as through achievement. In many respects, a Chinese person is well aware that having *guanxi*, being associated with certain people or having particular titles or names will cover over a multitude of flaws, vices, and limitations. This is not simply due to unjust manipulation of rules. Rather, it is quite typical that judgments, actions, and impressions are made in accordance to someone's relationships, position, name, or role.[145] People share the face of those with whom they identify. What does this imply? It cannot be assumed that individuals functionally try to save themself via moralistic works. Contrary to the presumption of much Western theology and many missionaries, the average Chinese person is not striving to do enough good works to merit God's approval. There are people in the world, like the Chinese, who define themselves not so much by what they do as whom they know. In Chinese culture, *guanxi* is the leading functional savior. Giving and receiving face is the way to enter, sustain, and strengthen relationships. In like fashion, God says to Israel, "A son honors his father, and a servant his master. If then I am a father, where is my honor? And if I am a master, where is my fear? says the LORD of hosts to you, O priests, who despise my name" (Mal 1:6). In even the most basic and important relationships, this *guanxi*-face principle holds true. Properly speaking, identity is gained through face, not merely by works.

These contrasting dynamics raise theological questions that spur a reexamination of how worldviews practically affect the way one interprets Scripture, relates to others, and thinks about contextualization. It cannot be presumed that one's view of self corresponds to those of biblical authors. As noted, this is not an either-or, since one's sense of identity is comprised of the ways one is different *and* similar to others. Since cultures can put differing degrees of stress on one facet over another, readers will need to use contextual clues. Things like metaphor, repeated motifs, and subject matter have to be considered. One naturally asks whether some theological quandaries presume an

---

[145] Change and Holt, ("A Chinese Perspective on Face: A Inter-Relational Concern," in *The Challenge of Facework: Cross-Cultural and Interpersonal Issues* (ed. Stella Ting-Toomey; Suny Series in Human Communication Processes; Albany, N.Y.: State University of New York Press, 1994), 119–21), give the illustration of an intermediary who has face and thus influence based on position or status, e.g. a boss or grandfather.

individualistic orientation where a relational-collective approach fits better because it matches the perspective of the original writer. Taking readers and their culture seriously does not have to collapse in relativism; even from a reader's limited points of view, he or she can see a biblical author's original intent. However, one will need a world of help. Therefore, a cross-cultural lens can provide this sort of help in seeking greater clarity on the doctrines of salvation, in particular Christ's atonement and justification.

Honor and Shame in Scripture

The scholarship is vast regarding the theme of HS in the Bible. This short summary will show that HS are not peripheral categories in Scripture. Rather, they and related concepts are central. Remarkably, there is tremendous overlap between the Bible and Chinese culture. On this common ground, one can pursue a contextualized soteriology that fits Eastern cultures without denying the legal motif familiar to Western theology.

The Bible's use of HS language offers a wealth of insight.[146] An objective sense of honor-glory is nicely illustrated in Heb 3:3, "For Jesus has been counted worthy of more glory than Moses—as much more glory as the builder of a house has more honor than the house itself." Notice that a *house*, not a person, possesses honor.[147] Similarly, without a self-feeling of shame, people, things, and actions can be regarded as shameful.[148] Also noteworthy is that Heb 3:3 treats glory (δόξης) and honor (τιμὴν) as

---

[146] The most common Greek and Hebrew words for "honor" are τιμή, δόξα, כָּבוֹד‎, כבד‎, and cognates; for "shame," αἰσχύνη, ἐντροπή, בוש‎, בֹּשֶׁת‎, and cognates.

[147] Similarly, see 1 Pet 3:6, where the emotion of fear is objectified, "do not fear anything that is frightening" [μὴ φοβούμεναι μηδεμίαν πτόησιν]. The latter phrase speaks of what some regard as worthy of fear. Similarly, Bultmann speaks of shame and fear, "'Shame' is 'fear of the *aischron* [shameful thing] and therefore of one's *doxa* [reputation].'" Quoted in deSilva, *The Hope of Glory*, 176. Original citation from Rudolph Bultmann, "*Aidos*," *TDNT* 1:170.

[148] For instance, see Jer 3:24; 1 Cor 14:35; Eph 5:12; Titus 1:11.

equivalent terms. Jesus' verbal contrast reiterates the point: "Jesus answered, 'I do not have a demon, but I honor my Father, and you dishonor [ἀτιμάζετέ] me. Yet I do not seek my own glory [δόξαν]; there is One who seeks it, and he is the judge'" (John 8:49–50). Glory and honor are conceptual synonyms.[149] This reflects scholarly consensus.[150] In keeping with previous discussions, HS language concerns public value. For instance, Heb 11:24–26 notes, "By faith Moses, when he was grown up, refused to be called the son of Pharaoh's daughter, choosing rather to be mistreated with the people of God than to enjoy the fleeting pleasures of sin. He considered the reproach of Christ greater wealth than the treasures of Egypt, for he was looking to the reward." Moses' disgrace or lack of honor is a type of "wealth" [πλοῦτον].[151] Finally, Hab 2:16 contrasts shame and glory: "You will have your fill of shame [קלון] instead of glory [כבודך]. Drink yourself, and show your uncircumcision! The cup in the LORD's right hand will come around to you, and utter shame [קיקלון] will come upon your glory [כבודך]!"[152]

Recently, there has been a renewed interest in using God's glory as the overarching theme to unite biblical theology. Theologians have long affirmed the centrality of God's glory, but few have extensively defended this thesis. Glory and honor are virtually synonymous terms in Scripture.[153] As was mentioned, Edwards famously

---

[149] Even where glory may refer to "being bright or shining," the fact remains this glory-manifestation displays worth or beauty, which thus brings God honor. It is the reification of honor. Cf. Walter Bauer et al., "δόξα," BDAG. BDAG lists Exod 40:34 as an example.

[150] For instance, T. Desmond Alexander and Brian S. Rosner, eds., "Honour," NDBT 1:559. Xavier Leon-Dufour, "Glory," DBT 1:201–5. M. R. Gordon, "Glory," ZPEB 1:730. H. Hüber, "τιμή," EDNT 3:357–59; H. Hegermann, "δόξα," EDNT 1:344–48. Schreiner explains "glory" with "honor" in Thomas Schreiner, Romans (Grand Rapids, Mich.: Baker Academic, 1998), 87.

[151] deSilva, The Hope of Glory, 167.

[152] The LXX reads, "πλησμονὴν ἀτιμίας ἐκ δόξης πίε καὶ σὺ καὶ διασαλεύθητι καὶ σείσθητι ἐκύκλωσεν ἐπὶ σὲ ποτήριον δεξιᾶς κυρίου καὶ συνήχθη ἀτιμία ἐπὶ τὴν δόξαν."

[153] This simply repeats a previous point. However, a few biblical references may be illustrative, such as Ps 8:5; Rom 2:7, 10; 1 Tim 1:17; 1 Pet 1:17; Rev. 5:11–12; 21:26, among others. For a more

argues that God's central passion in all he does is his own glory and honor. Recent authors like John Piper, Tom Schreiner, and Jim Hamilton have put forth theologies that have God's glory as the "centre of Biblical theology."[154] God works on behalf of those "whom I created for my own glory . . . for how should my name be profaned? My glory I will not give to another" (Isa 43:7; 48:11). The long recognition of this fundamental theme (i.e. glory) suggests a relationship between HS and other biblical themes.[155]

A number of books draw extensively from socio-historical research, tracing the importance and role of HS in the Bible and its historical context. Malina persuasively shows how HS and group identity governed the life of a typical citizen of the Mediterranean world.[156] He summarizes, "Honor, then, is a claim to worth *and* the social acknowledgement of that worth."[157] That HS is inherently public is evident in Prov 25:10, which advises against revealing someone else's secret "lest he who hears you bring shame upon you, and your ill repute have no end." Scholars agree that honor is either

---

exhaustive treatment how glory and honor are so used, see John Piper, "How Is God's Passion for His Own Glory Not Selfishness?," *Desiring God*, 24 Nov 2007, 237–41, [cited 4 Jan 2012]. Online: http://www.desiringgod.org/resource-library/articles/how-is-gods-passion-for-his-own-glory-not-selfishness.html, including editorial footnotes. Accordingly, whenever we speak of God's glory, we will somehow be able to talk about God's honor or the basis for God's having a name.

[154] See James Hamilton Jr., *God's Glory in Salvation through Judgment: A Biblical Theology* (Wheaton, Ill.: Crossway, 2010); James Hamilton Jr., "The Glory of God in Salvation through Judgment: The Centre of Biblical Theology?," *TynBul* 57, no. 1 (2006): 57–84; Thomas Schreiner, *New Testament Theology: Magnifying God in Christ* (Grand Rapids, Mich.: Baker Academic, 2008). Anything by Piper reflects this idea. In addition to *God's Passion for His Glory*, see his work, *God Is the Gospel: Meditations on God's Love as the Gift of Himself* (reprint; Wheaton, Ill.: Crossway, 2011); Piper, *Desiring God*; John Piper, *Let the Nations Be Glad!: The Supremacy of God in Missions* (Grand Rapids, Mich.: Baker, 1993); John Piper, *The Pleasures of God* (Colorado Springs, Colo.: Multnomah Books, 2000).

[155] Also noteworthy is Christopher Morgan and Robert A. Peterson, eds., *The Glory of God* (Wheaton, Ill.: Crossway, 2010) ; W. Robert Cook, "The 'Glory' Motif in the Johannine Corpus," *JETS* 27, no. 3 (Sept 1984): 291–97; David A. Glatt-Gilad, "Yahweh's Honor at Stake: A Divine Conundrum," *JSOT* 26, no. 4 (Jun 2002): 63–74. Hamilton, in "The Glory of God" (p. 59), also mentions Daniel Fuller's work *The Unity of the Bible: Unfolding God's Plan for Humanity* (Grand Rapids, Mich.: Zondervan, 1992).

[156] Malina, *The New Testament World*.

[157] Ibid., 31.

ascribed or achieved.[158] Again, the former primarily refers to one's genealogy, kinship or

group membership; the latter pertains to the honor won by virtue of accomplishments.

Neyrey not only shows how HS controls much of the narrative in Matthew's Gospel but

also that the pursuit of honor was the basis for ancient rhetorical theory.[159] Exegetically,

others have confirmed the essential function of HS within the biblical narrative. For

example, Lyn Bechtel shows how shame was used as a social control in biblical Israel.[160]

In fact, Bechtel argues that in biblical Israel, "Shaming was used so extensively that it

became necessary to attempt to limit its use in the judicial system and among the general

public."[161] David Glatt-Gilad surveys the ways in which Yahweh upholds Israel for the

sake of his honor.[162] Other interpreters defend the link between HS and covenant in

ancient Israel.[163] Finally, Hagedorn asserts that Deut 21:18–21 is not primarily about

child rearing, but rather protecting family honor.[164] In NT studies, Neyrey has already

been mentioned.[165] In addition, deSilva suggests honor discourse is integral to NT

exegesis.[166] For example, Moxnes and deSilva apply this approach to Romans and

---

[158] In addition to Malina, see deSilva, *Honor, Patronage*, 28–29, 158–65, 206–12. Also, see Neyrey, *Honor and Shame*.

[159] Neyrey, *Honor and Shame*, 6–7, 14–34, 70–89. The reason for citing this is to show the importance of theme across diverse historical spheres, to include the political.

[160] Lyn M. Bechtel, "Shame as a Sanction of Social Control in Biblical Israel: Judicial, Political, and Social Shaming," *JSOT* 49 (1991): 47–76.

[161] Ibid., 75.

[162] Glatt-Gilad, "Yahweh's Honor at Stake," 63–74.

[163] Saul M. Olyan, "Honor, Shame, and Covenant Relations in Ancient Israel and Its Environment," *JBL* 115, no. 2 (Sum 1996): 201–18. Also, T. R. Hobbs, "Critical Notes: Reflections on Honor, Shame, and Covenantal Relations," *JBL* 116, no. 3 (1997): 501–3.

[164] Anselm C. Hagedorn, "Guarding the Parents' Honour—Deuteronomy 21.18–21," JSOT 88 (Jun 2000): 101–21.

[165] F. Gerald Downing's objection that honor in only an "occasional" concern in Scripture ignores the argument by Neyrey and others that even things like wealth and poverty are simply symbolic expressions of one's public honor. In addition, Neyrey's larger point is that Christian conversion entailed one's changing group loyalties, thus a change in HS standards. For Downing's full argument, see F. Gerald Downing, "'Honor' and Exegetes," *CBQ* 61 (1999): 53–73.

[166] deSilva, *The Hope of Glory*.

Hebrews respectively.[167] Robert Jewett's massive Romans commentary incessantly presses the question how HS shapes Paul's letter.[168] There is no room here for a detailed review of the literature. Suffice to say, HS has been integral to numerous studies of the NT and in theology.[169]

These scholarly observations give some context for biblical interpretation. In Scripture, one sees a stress on group identity and authority. The head of one's group embodies the honor of its members.[170] Accordingly, Malina explains,

> [T]he *head* of the group is responsible for the honor of the group with reference to outsiders and symbolizes the group's honor as well. Hence members of the group owe loyalty, respect, and obedience of a kind that commits their individual honor without limit and without compromise[; it follows,] whenever the honor of another is bound up with an individual's honor, that individual is required to defend and represent the honor of all bound up with him.[171]

The inferior owes a debt of honor and respect to a patron and especially parents, who bore responsibility for his or her existence and sustenance.[172] Scripturally, these ideas are quite evident. For example, a major NT controversy concerns who is a child of Abraham and belongs to Israel, God's chosen people. Moreover, in Romans, Paul summarily argues that whereas all humans are in Adam, only those "in Christ" are righteous.[173]

---

[167] Moxnes, "Honour and Righteousness," 61–77. Also, see David A. deSilva, "Despising Shame: A Cultural-Anthropological Investigation of the Epistle to the Hebrews," *JBL* 113 (1994): 439–61.

[168] Jewett, *Romans*. This book does not necessarily agree with Jewett's conclusions.

[169] In addition to those already referenced, David Watson, *Honor Among Christians: The Cultural Key to the Messianic Secret* (Minneapolis, Minn.: Fortress Press, 2010); Peter W. Gosnell, "Honor and Shame Rhetoric as a Unifying Motif in Ephesians," *BBR* 16, no. 1 (2006): 105–28. Some have explored ways the atonement deals with shame. Two examples include Tennent, *Theology in the Context of World Christianity*, 105–34; Baker and Green, *Recovering the Scandal of the Cross*, 153–70.

[170] See 1 Cor 11:3–15 on head/honor. Also, 1 Chr 29:12; Eph 1:22; 4:15; 5:23; Col 1:18; 2:10, 19.

[171] Malina, *The New Testament World*, 44, 53.

[172] Ibid., 103, 153. Also, Neyrey, *Honor and Shame*, 110, 130.

[173] See Rom 5–6. A parallel is drawn in Rom 4 and Gal 3 between being "in Christ" and a "son of Abraham," such that whatever is true of the superior is true for those after him. Romans 4:11–18 makes this identification logic clear with the purpose clause. The purpose of the sign of circumcision was "to make him the *father* of all who believe without being circumcised *so that* righteousness would be counted to

Finally, a person's social status is put at risk by accruing a social or monetary debt. Financial debt poses the threat of enslavement, forfeiting honor and status.[174] Thus, sin is called a "debt" that needs to be forgiven (Matt 6:12; 18:27–34; Luke 7:41–43; 16:5; Col 2:14).

This backdrop helps one see a clearer picture of Scripture's grand narrative. At creation, "God made man in his own image" (Gen 1:27). Appropriately, humans "represent" God in the world, ultimately by being conformed to Christ.[175] Meredith Kline rightly notes that to be the image of God means mankind is to glorify God as sons.[176] All creatures owe a debt of honor to God, their Creator and Father. When people are called to "Pay to all what is owed [ὀφειλάς] to them . . . honor to whom honor is owed" (Rom 13:7), this certainly includes God above all. In the least, honor entails obedience. In Scripture, debt is not merely an unfortunate consequence of sin, for Paul adds in Rom 13:8, "Owe [ὀφείλετε] no one anything, except to love each other." Gravely, however, "all have sinned and fall short to the glory of God" (Rom 3:23). Now, a new debt is owed—one's very life (Rom 6:23). Sin is not merely the breaking of law. At its heart, sin is publically shaming God. So one reads in Rom 2:23–24, "You who boast in the law dishonor God by breaking the law. For, as it is written, 'The name of God is blasphemed

---

them as well" for the promise was to Abraham and his offspring (4:11, 13; emphasis mine; cp. v. 16–18). The offspring share in the inheritance promise of the father, thus identification with father Abraham is crucial. Galatians 3:7, 26, 29 echo this logic: Having faith like father Abraham makes people "sons of Abraham" or "Abraham's offspring," which is the same as saying that "in Christ Jesus you are all sons of God through faith."

[174] Malina, *The New Testament World*, 100. Neyrey, *Honor and Shame*, 52, 80.

[175] Anthony Hoekema, *Created in God's Image* (Grand Rapids, Mich.: Eerdmans, 1986), 13–14, 23–24, 67.

[176] Meredith Kline, *Kingdom Prologue* (Overland Park, Kans.: Two Age Press, 2000), 44–46. In addition, Richard Gaffin points out that Paul explicitly says that man "is the image and glory of God." See Richard B. Gaffin, "The Glory of God in Paul's Epistles," in *The Glory of God* (ed. Christopher Morgan and Robert A. Peterson; Wheaton, Ill.: Crossway, 2010), 133–34.

among the Gentiles because of you.'" The main (and only) Greek verb in v. 23 is

"dishonor" (ἀτιμαζεις). A preposition conveys the means, "by breaking the law."[177]

Within the context of humanity's unspeakable disgrace, one can understand the

rest of the OT, which recounts God's covenant with Abraham as played out in the history

of Israel.[178] God promises to grant Abraham offspring through whom all nations will be

blessed.[179] Throughout the biblical canon, the Abrahamic covenant becomes a paradigm

in which God works in the world.[180] As confirmation, in Gen 15, God undertakes a self-

maledictory oath, in essence, invoking a curse upon himself if he does not keep his

promises.[181] God seems to face a dilemma. To uphold his honor, he should justly inflict

punishment upon all of sinful humanity. Yet, in his covenant with Abraham, God

identified with mankind, attaching his name, via his promises, to the fate of all the

nations. As they go, so goes the cosmic reputation of God. If he condemns sinful

---

[177] In Greek: διὰ τῆς παραβάσεως τοῦ νόμου.

[178] I am aware of the debates concerning the content of the Abrahamic covenant, recorded in Gen 12, 15, 17, and 22. Space does not allow for a full excursus on the topic. Nevertheless, for our purposes, the "Abrahamic covenant" refers to the collection of promises made to Abraham, mainly consisting in land, offspring, and blessing to all nations. They are intertwined. In Gen 18:18, 22:18, and 26:4, it is through Abraham's offspring that "all the nations of the earth shall be blessed" (cf. Gen 15:5; 22:17). Also, besides the fact the promise of abundant offspring recalls the original passage in 12:1–3, the number of offspring, more than the stars in the sky, implies Abraham will have a family of nations. Abram's new name, Abraham (Genesis 17) foreshadows that he will someday be the "father of a multitude of nations."

[179] "Blessing" means more than just material or temporary benefit. It includes total salvation and restoration. This is how Paul interprets it in Gal 3:7–16. In Gal 3:8, Paul calls Gen 12:3 the "gospel." Romans 4:13 and Heb 11:15–16 only substantiate the point.

[180] Compare Neh 9:7–8; Ps 47:8–9; Jer 33:23–26; Mic 7:18–20; Luke 1:71–73; Rom 4 and Gal 3.

[181] This ceremony appears somewhat common in the Ancient Near East. Walking through the dead animals symbolized the punishment that would be due the one who did not keep covenant. A similar instance is found in Jer 34:18. For scholarly commentary, see Gerald L. Keown, Pamela J. Scalise, and Thomas G. Smothers, *Jeremiah 26–52* (WBC; Dallas, Tex.: Word Books, 1995), 189. In addition, see J. A. Thompson, *The Book of Jeremiah* (NICOT; Grand Rapids, Mich.: Eerdmans, 1980), 612–13. Finally, see Victor P. Hamilton, *Handbook on the Pentateuch* (Grand Rapids, Mich.: Baker, 1982), 105. Hittite documents attest to this practice as well. See Bill T. Arnold and Bryan E. Beyer, eds., *Readings from the Ancient Near East* (Grand Rapids, Mich.: Baker, 2002), 96–103. In the treaty between Ashurnirai V and Mati'-ilu, the agreement states, "If Mati'-ilu should sin against this [treaty], so may, just as the shou[lder of this spring lamb] is torn out and [placed in . . .], the shoulder of Mati'-ilu, of his sons, [his magnates] and the people of his land be torn out and [placed in [. . .]" (p. 101).

humanity, he would be unfaithful to his word. If God righteously keeps his promise regarding the nations, it would seem he forsakes justice and denies himself. This narrative provides the backdrop for Christ's atonement and justification.

Contextualizing Theologies of Honor and Shame

How have people previously connected HS and contextualization? A number of missiologists have raised the issue, but few have explored it with great depth. In the last chapter, Wan and Nicholls both highlight the importance of HS for contextualization in China. This section specifically focuses on contextualization attempts that use HS as a central motif. They come both from Chinese and non-Chinese contexts.

Enoch Wan's proposal is consistent with a Chinese view of HS.[182] He suggests, "The focus in salvation is 'yong-ru-jiu-en-lun (荣辱救恩论)' (Christ's shame-bearing death and honor-gaining resurrection) for honor is very desirable and shame is to be shunned at all cost by the Chinese."[183] He groups other themes together with HS, including the need for a mediator, which he links both to Chinese culture and ultimately to Jesus. Using Wan's terms, Christ is a "go-between" (*zhongbao*) who reconciles (*fuhe*) our relationship (*guanxi*) with God by being our "debt-payer" (*shu zui zhe*). However, Jesus restores a "harmonious relationship" not only between God and humans but also with each other. Originally, "Man was created in the image of God" but Wan adds, without defense or clarification, "[Man's] misuse of the gift of human free will brought in

---

[182] The following draws specifically from his representative article "Practical Contextualization: A Case Study of Evangelizing Contemporary Chinese," *Global Missiology* 1, no. 1 (Oct 2003), n.p. [cited 27 Dec 2011]. Online: http://ojs.globalmissiology.org/index.php/english/issue/view/27.

[183] Two corrections should be noted. First, Wan mistypes "yong-ru-jiu-en-lun," as the Chinese characters clarify. It should read, *rong*-ru-jiu-en-lun." Second, he does not give a literal translation, which would otherwise simply say, "Theology of Honor-Shame Salvation." In effect, however, he offers a sort of dynamic equivalence translation to convey his own intention.

sin and severed his relationship with God and the created order." Broadly, he explains salvation in three points, listing verses for each: Glory (pre-fall), Shame (post-fall), and Glorification (post-fall). He also says the Chinese values of family, honor, and harmony should produce a gospel message that corrects the "overemphasis on the forensic nature of the Gospel, the legal dimension of Christ's penal substitution and divine justification."

For Nichols and Strand, shame seems simply to be a subjective feeling that *results* from sin.[184] Nichols summarily says of human shame, "Their self-image was broken." He alternates in the way he speaks about "guilt." Sometimes "guilt" is subjectively "a sense of sin against a righteous and just God," yet in the same paragraph guilt has an objective sense in that "guilt demands a propitiatory sacrifice."[185] In context, he implies that shame in Chinese religion is "man-centered." He sees shame as a category primarily directed at other humans. Salvation is possible because "In [Jesus'] shameless and sinless life he made a sufficient atonement for the whole world on the cross." Clearly, although Nichols says Jesus takes away shame, salvation is fundamentally associated with guilt, which he treats objectively. Strand appears to make similar conclusions. Following Boyle, Strand depicts shame as "the result of having disobeyed the one we ought to honor, our father." Within the same essay, Strand describes sin as dishonoring God as well as "failure to live up to some fixed standard." For some reason, he does revise his view of shame (from being a subjective concept) despite his relating honor objectively with sin.

---

[184] The following quotations in this paragraph come from Strand, "Explaining Sin in a Chinese Context," 430, 437; Nicholls, "Contextualisation in Chinese Culture," 374.

[185] Elsewhere, he says shame has an objective aspect but does not elaborate. Cf. Nicholls, "The Role of Shame," 235.

Glen Francis' application to a Taiwanese context begins with the family motif.[186] Salvation means being adopted into God's family and rescued from shame.[187] He links shame to numerous biblical concepts, such as the Fall (Gen 2:25; 3:7), repentance and forgiveness (Ezra 9:6; Ezek 16:54, 59–61). Francis does not explicitly define sin but agrees *zui* is a misleading translation and the effect of sin is a broken relationship with God and others. As a result, people are all like Adam and Eve who "were trying to save face by covering themselves, hiding themselves, and then shifting the blame onto someone else."[188] He immediately adds, "The head of the family (God) is the only one who can restore this brokenness." He concludes with a proposal of his own "Four Spiritual Laws."[189]The first two laws hinge on the themes of adoption, filial piety, and loss of face. However, it is telling that his last two laws depart sharply from what he has presented and quickly returns to the familiar language of Western theology. Law Three says, "The only way back to God the Father is to become a righteous people." Law Four concludes, "The only way to become a righteous person is to come to the man on the cross." He gives no indication that "righteousness" has an alternative HS connotation.

Contextualizations for Japanese culture echo the themes so far presented. When Boyle uses a familial metaphor, he treats all humanity as God's children. He explains that as creator and father, God must take responsibility for his children and his creation.[190] While Boyle is right that God pursues harmony, he misses the fundamental possibility that humans have become outsiders, even God's enemies (Rom 5:10; Phil 3:18). In that

---

[186] Glen R. Francis, "The Gospel in a Sin/Shame Based Society," *Taiwan Mission Quarterly* 2, no. 2 (Oct 1992): 5–16.
[187] Ibid., 5–8.
[188] Ibid., 10.
[189] Ibid., 15.
[190] Boyle, "Communicating the Gospel in Terms of Shame," 44–45.

case, Boyle's analogy crumbles. He forces the anthropological imagery to do more than Scripture allows. He simply begins with a wrong starting point. As is typical, he only discusses man's needing to have restored face, not God's need to vindicate his own glory.

Krause grounds salvation in the view that humans are made in the image of God, thus shame finds an objective basis in relationship to God.[191] He makes stronger claims than others by arguing that shame is more fundamental than guilt. Krause directly states, "[R]elationships and ideals will be more important and persuasive than law and punitive threats."[192] However, his revulsion for law language pushes him to an extreme of denying penal substitution.[193] He mentions the debt motif but only speaks of it in terms an "accounting office . . . in order to satisfy the moral requirements of God's law."[194] Finally, he claims, "No payment such as a 'debt of justice' can balance accounts and thus restore lost honor. Neither can substitutionary compensation expiate shame."[195] This assertion is a key premise of his argument.

A large collection of articles on contextualization for HS cultures comes from the Islamic world. Müller's book *Honor and Shame* has stirred discussion in missiological circles.[196] Drawing from Genesis, he claims all cultures have some blend of three worldviews: guilt-based, fear-based, and shame-based.[197] He does not set up one against the others; however, he does think people tend to emphasize one to the neglect of others. Historically, Christians are typically guilt-based in orientation. In a flurry of metaphors,

---

[191] Kraus, "The Cross of Christ: Dealing with Shame and Guilt." He says this article is a condensed version of his related chapters in the now revised C. Norman Kraus, *Jesus Christ Our Lord: Christology from a Disciple's Perspective* (New York, N.Y.: Wipf & Stock, 2004).
[192] Kraus, "The Cross of Christ: Dealing with Shame and Guilt," 224.
[193] Ibid., 225.
[194] Ibid.
[195] Ibid., 224.
[196] Müller, *Honor and Shame*. His first book become a section in his second book, *The Messenger*.
[197] Müller, *The Messenger*, 98–119.

he explains sin in terms of being "defiled," exposed naked before God, and "expelled" from his presence. In salvation, God grants "the ultimately honorable position of joint-heirs with Christ."[198] Müller is quite clear that the gospel touches all three worldviews and so "Cross-cultural contextualization of the Gospel is simply knowing how to start the Gospel message from a place of common understanding with our audience."[199] In the end, reconciliation is the primary expression he uses for an HS presentation,[200] as reflected in his gospel tract filled with Scripture passages.[201]

DeVries' essay soberly assesses others who have ventured to use HS to contextualize the gospel for Muslims. In the end, DeVries thinks Müller does very little to explain what it means that Jesus bears human sin.[202] DeVries' observation applies for the other examples that have been considered. These approaches emphasize the effect of sin and the use of HS language for salvation, but with little exegesis. The various writers do not explain precisely how this is accomplished. While DeVries does not offer a full presentation of his own, his analysis is helpful. He offers a few key principles, "First, honour and shame affects not just the content of the message, but also the method of its delivery."[203] This entails knowledge of local manners and a strong grasp of the local language. He adds, "Secondly, explaining the atonement in the key of honour and shame is essentially a local task."[204] By this, he urges flexibility to account for context specific expressions of HS. Finally, he lays out key parts to an HS gospel presentation. To the

---

[198] Ibid., 158–63.

[199] Ibld., 208.

[200] Ibid., 205. For fear, he suggests propitiation of God's wrath; for guilt, redemption satisfies God's justice.

[201] The "Shame Tract" can be found at his website. See Roland Müller, "Shame Tract," *rmuller.com*, n.p. [cited 25 Feb 2012]. Online: http://www.rmuller.com/ShameTract.pdf.

[202] DeVries, "Explaining the Atonement," 51.

[203] Ibid., 54.

[204] Ibid.

ideas offered by others, he adds that a good starting point is the character of God, from which the doctrine of sin can be understood more clearly.[205]

A few other HS contextualizations are worth mentioning.[206] Significantly, Parsons' brief treatment on the subject introduces an important idea. He recommends following the pattern of early Christians by "plac[ing] a major emphasis on the vindication of Jesus' honor."[207] Not only that but, according to Parsons, the NT may hint that this point preceded and served as the basis for later teaching about substitutionary atonement, which would be clarified once people were Christians. Unlike others, Bill Musk actually explains *what sin is* using HS language, briefly calling it "the violation of honour."[208] He also contributes, "The ultimate test of Jesus' loyalty to his Father is couched precisely in terms of the violation of [Jesus' own] honour."[209] He poses the possibility that for many people, it will be easier to begin with God's glory than his love.[210] Finally, Nicholls has two articles directed at a Muslim context.[211] He mentions the importance of God's oneness, such that God does not share people's loyalty with idols.[212] Also, he stresses the importance of God's prophets to preserve God's honor, even at the expense of shame. Ultimately however, God will rescue them from shame.[213] Lastly, Nichols reminds the

---

[205] Ibid., 55.

[206] An exhaustive review of all attempts would indeed be exhausting and unnecessary. Much of the existing literature repeats ideas. Some articles seem to aim simply at awareness, like Thomas, "The Gospel for Shame Cultures: A Paradigm Shift," 284–90. Jewett comments on Korean culture. Jewett, "Shame and Atonement." However, the next chapter interacts with his ideas when talking about salvation.

[207] This short treatment on honor is found in Martin Parsons, *Unveiling God: Contextualizing Christology for Islamic Culture* (Pasadena, Calif.: William Carey Library, 2006), 218–19.

[208] Bill A. Musk, "Honour and Shame," *ERT* 20, no. 2 (Apr 1996): 162.

[209] Ibid., 163.

[210] Ibid., 166.

[211] Nicholls, "The Role of Shame"; Nicholls, "The Servant Songs of Isaiah in Dialogue with Muslims."

[212] Nicholls, "The Servant Songs of Isaiah in Dialogue with Muslims," 170, 174.

[213] Ibid., 171.

reader that God is in fact King and Creator over the world, thus his "justice for the nations" is an important aspect of God's honor.[214]

Mbuvi's opening comments in "African Theology from the Perspective of Honor and Shame"[215] give insight to the way HS is treated among theologians and missiologists. Unlike legal motifs, he describes HS as a "social science model."[216] He gives a fitting adaption of Descartes' dictum in order to characterize the thinking of HS cultures: "I am, because we are; and since we are, therefore I am."[217]

Zaracho tries to use HS to communicate the gospel in a Latin American context.[218] He suggests, "The terms 'sin' and 'sinful' are defined by public revelation of one's 'bad' actions. For this reason, people are more concerned about 'losing face' than about the 'bad action' itself and its consequences. Keeping up appearances is paramount."[219] Inasmuch as he applies these words to HS cultures in general, his description is a caricature at best, wrong and insulting at worse. Throughout the article, Zaracho seems to fall into the trap of assuming the motives and thoughts of people in Scripture or in an HS culture.[220] This habit leads to eisegesis and misunderstanding.

Lastly, Wiher's dissertation on conscience, guilt, and shame makes a contention regarding soteriology:

> The justification model is appropriate for shame and guilt-oriented individuals depending on the concept of righteousness and justice used. When righteousness means conformity to covenant and community behaviour, it is a shame-oriented concept. God reinserts man back into the

---

[214] Ibid., 169.

[215] Mbuvi, "African Theology from the Perspective of Honor and Shame."

[216] Ibid., 280. The problem is not that the statement is false but rather that this epithet is rarely if ever applied to legal images. Yet, law is as much an aspect of social science as HS.

[217] Ibid., 288–89.

[218] Zaracho, "Communicating the Gospel in a Shame Society."

[219] Ibid., 272–73.

[220] For example, see his depiction of Jesus with the Pharisees in Ibid., 278.

190

covenant community and brings him into the honourable status of a covenant partner. When justice means that God pays back man's debt through Jesus' sacrifice, it is a guilt-oriented concept. . . . When the justification model is presented to shame-oriented people in a guilt-oriented manner, it is misunderstood.[221]

Wiher also suggests that shame-oriented cultures easily turn traditional presentations of justification into what Bonhoeffer calls "cheap grace . . . grace without discipleship, grace without the cross."[222] Therefore, justification is better understood when explained in terms of harmony and a "restoration of righteousness."[223] A discussion on justification follows in the next chapter. For now, it is enough to say that his second assertion linking repayment of debt and guilt-orientation is questionable. As previously noted, face-oriented cultures like China have a strong appreciation for a debt metaphor; however, this is largely seen as social/relational debt. Certainly, those from a Chinese culture can well understand sin as debt, since this notion is more personal than an economic metaphor.

Conclusions

The purpose of this chapter is to give an orientation to the meaning of HS across cultures. Primarily, attention is given to understanding how "face" works within the Chinese cultural framework. Face is a complicated concept that permeates all of Chinese society. Not only does it concern both HS, face also unites and clarifies one's understanding of other concepts like Chinese collectivism and morality.

In addition, this study considers the historical and cultural contexts that make up the background of the biblical narrative. There is tremendous thematic overlap between

---

[221] Wiher, "Understanding Shame and Guilt," 318–19.

[222] Ibid., 319. He cites Dietrich Bonhoeffer, *Nachfolge* (ed. Hg. Martin Kuske and Ilse Tödt; München: Kaiser, 1989), 29.

[223] Wiher, "Understanding Shame and Guilt," 319.

Chinese culture and ancient biblical cultures. They are not equivalent. Each has its distinctive manifestations of group-identity, honor, and shame. Nevertheless, the echoes are unmistakable. In terms of broad categories, the preceding description of Chinese culture closely resembles the ancient biblical context.

CHAPTER 5: A SOTERIOLOGY OF HONOR AND SHAME

This chapter uses an honor-shame (HS) perspective to explain Christ's atonement and the doctrine of justification. The interpretation offered does not presume to exhaust the meaning of these two concepts. However, a few observations give reason to expect Chinese cultural categories may contribute significantly towards a more comprehensive soteriology. First, the Bible has transcultural relevance. Second, no single culture represents the totality of human existence. Third, many features of Chinese culture greatly overlap with the contexts of biblical writers. To say this does not infer that Chinese culture is equivalent to the Ancient Near East (ANE). Neither does it infer that Chinese culture is equivalent to the culture of the God's consummated kingdom. All cultures fall short of God's kingdom. Nevertheless, many categories are not simply cultural but human. Some aspects of human life are more prominent in one place and time than in others. The interpretations offered here neither exclude nor absolutize any one culture over another. The goal of this chapter is to find how Chinese culture adds to an understanding of salvation. Accordingly, the interpretations affirmed here do not necessarily deny views held by non-Chinese writers throughout history. In the process, the insights from previous chapters will come into dialogue with theological scholarship.

The Gospel of the King of Glory: The Story of Salvation

Theology depends on the metaphors of Scripture. They frame the way one reads and applies the Bible.[1] They regulate the interpretive process such that readers, when studying a particular metaphor, tend to use one set of texts rather than others. Interpreters who recognize potential limitations with any metaphor will seek ways to relate the manifold ways Scripture talks about salvation. Each metaphor tends to emphasize aspects of salvation not stressed as strongly, if at all, in other figures of speech.

Naturally, people from different cultures have varied understandings about the significance of particular metaphors, resulting in all sorts of contextual theologies. Interpreting Scripture often comes down to differing opinions about emphasis. Matters of emphasis can easily solidify into controversies with dichotomized options. In that case, it is quite difficult to argue that one option is a major emphasis and not merely a minor point. Thus, one can easily sacrifice truth in battles over emphasis. Readers may confuse a renewed stress on the one idea as an attack on their own preferred emphasis.

One task of contextualization is to sort through different themes and, if needed, oppose popular readings that minimize or deny the importance of a particular motif. Defending an "emphasis" is harder than defending a truth. To do so, interpreters must do four things: (a) demonstrate the theme's *presence*, (b) argue for the *probability* the writer does emphasize that motif, (c) discuss its *priority* relative to other emphases, (d) and attempt to *placate* fears the interpretation is not denying some other important idea.

Theological conclusions should explicitly be grounded in exegesis. Any insights

---

[1] Gary Anderson rightly says, "How we talk about sin . . . influences what we will do about it." See his work, *Sin: A History* (New Haven, Conn.: Yale, 2009), 13.

gained from cultural anthropology do not trump the words and context of a biblical author. One cannot assume *a priori* that ancient rhetorical theory can in any instance answer interpreters' questions. That said, those who favor a traditional emphasis on law can likewise recognize that law is every bit an anthropological, culturally laden category as HS. Exegesis cannot *a priori* privilege *any* metaphor, regardless of interpretive precedent or the preponderance of a theme in other extra-biblical documents. An author's words and flow of thought are primary factors confirming the possible readings suggested by cultural-historical research. This chapter shows that interpretations giving primacy to HS need not be relegated to mere rhetorical theory and anthropology, as if they were distinct from mainstream exegetically based theology.[2] Contemporary cultures raise questions that highlight legitimate biblical themes, which otherwise may be neglected in the broader theological guild. By implication, one must take seriously the potential contributions of non-traditional, contextual theologies from around the world.

The metaphors one uses provide a framework for understanding the biblical narrative wherein God creates, sustains, and relates to the world. However, one is wary of absolutizing any particular framework's nuances and emphases. In evangelism, the gospel gets reduced to abstracted essentials as if they could be understood out of context. Consequently, these few truths may even distort the larger context.[3] If one is not careful, the word "gospel" becomes a catchword for almost anything related to theology.[4]

---

[2] Cf. Richard N. Longenecker, *Introducing Romans: Critical Issues in Paul's Most Famous Letter* (Grand Rapids, Mich.: Eerdmans, 2011), 330–37. He says HS readings stem from rhetorical theory.

[3] For a discussion on the effect of metaphors on the atonement, see McKnight, *A Community Called Atonement*, 35–43. Dean Flemming rightly adds, "[We] must learn to think not just in contextual, but also *transcultural* categories" in his *Contextualization*, 312. Emphasis in original.

[4] For example, see Tan, "Chinese New Year," 125. She refers to Hung's suggestion that we find a substitute for ancestor worship: "He used old Chinese saying or proverbs that illustrate biblical truth, to

Since the gospel is "the power of God for salvation" (Rom 1:16; cf. Eph 1:13), it is not surprising that soteriological language influences the way people talk about the gospel. However, inasmuch as the gospel and soteriology are not coterminous, it is important to clearly state how they relate.[5] One is saved *through* the gospel (cf. Rom 10:9–17). As discussed in ch. 1, the "gospel," in biblical and ancient contexts, carried significant royal connotations. Specifically, the "gospel" message announces the victory and reign of Jesus as king (cf. Rom 1:1–4; 1 Cor 15:1–4, 24–28). This gospel is "according to the Scriptures," and so recalls the entire biblical narrative and the justification of "all the nations" (Gal 3:8).[6] Paul's survey of the gospel in Romans pulls from a plethora of OT passages to show how the gospel reveals the righteousness of God (Rom 1:17). Therefore, one naturally expects a robust soteriology to draw from various texts throughout the canon and give insight into the story of Israel within the context of God's kingdom over the world. Such a soteriology would apply to but transcend the "individual," finding particular relevance to the "group." The gospel challenges collective identity and its boasting. It calls every nation to give allegiance to Christ who saves people from shame, brings them into God's family, and gives them his own glory.

Atonement: God's Honor in Christ's Shame

Broadly, "atonement" refers to the reconciling of two parties whose relationship needs restoration due to some offense.[7] Some wrong needs to be made right. At this point, to

---

contextualize the gospel with regard to ancestor worship with his illiterate mother" in Daniel M. Hung, "Mission Blockade: Ancestor Worship," *EMQ* 19, no. 1 (Jan 1983): 37.

    [5] On framing the gospel and the difference between soteriology and gospel, see Scot McKnight's *The King Jesus Gospel.*

    [6] On contextualizing the *story* of the Bible, see Flemming, *Contextualization,* 296–322.

    [7] Among possible examples, see Bruce Demarest, *The Cross and Salvation: The Doctrine of God* (Wheaton, Ill.: Crossway, 2006), 166–67; Thomas F. Torrance, *Atonement: The Person and Work of Christ*

define atonement with more specificity runs the risk of prematurely arguing for the supremacy of one atonement metaphor over others. In Christian theology, the atonement refers to what Jesus accomplished in his life and death, atoning for human sin, thereby restoring humanity's broken relationship with God. Historical debates often miss a fundamental question, "What did Jesus' life and death do *for God*?"

What Does the Atonement Do for God?

In God's covenant with Abraham, God identifies with humanity, casting his lot with "all nations." The cross saves the God's "face" from the shame of his people. Were he to reject the people whom he promised to save, God would deny himself, shamed for all eternity. He ceases to be God. Hence, one concludes *Jesus died for God*. Since God by grace first committed himself to mankind, his covenantal obligations are not externally "binding" God. He freely initiates his covenant. Thus, Hebrews makes much of God's promises, guaranteed by oath, showing "the unchangeable character of his purpose" (Heb 6:17–18). Christ shows "God's truthfulness, in order to confirm the promises given to the patriarchs and in order that the Gentiles might glorify God for his mercy" (Rom 15:8–9).

The atonement is *necessary* and not merely for the sake of human salvation. This claim says *more* than just God wants to glorify himself. Rather, it states that if Christ did not die, God would not be righteous. In that case, God lacks honor. God is shameful. The atonement is a *God-centered* act. It is true that Christ's death vindicates God's justice so

---

(Downers Grove, Ill.: IVP Academic, 2009), 137–44; Louis Berkhof, *Systematic Theology* (Grand Rapids, Mich.: Eerdmans, 1996), 373; Niels-Eriek A. Andreasen, "Atonement/Expiation in the OT," *MDB*, 76–77; Robert E. Burks, "Atonement/Expiation in the NT," *MDB*, 75–76.

197

that he is able to save his people.[8] Yet, one must not get the order backwards. God's glory is not an obstacle to his main goal, i.e. saving sinners. Saving sinners is a *means* to his main goal. Therefore, atonement theology does not terminate simply on human salvation. That is not the end for which God does all things.

The OT saints knew the most basic motive for which God atoned for sin. In Lev 9:6, Moses made certain why the Israelites made atonement by way of sacrifice. He told the congregation,

> "This is the thing that the LORD commanded you to do, *that the glory of the LORD may appear to you.*" Then Moses said to Aaron, "Draw near to the altar and offer your sin offering and your burnt offering and *make atonement for yourself and for the people,* and bring the offering of the people and *make atonement for them,* as the LORD has commanded."

After the shedding of blood, "the glory of the LORD appeared to all the people. And fire came out from before the LORD and consumed the burnt offering and the pieces of fat on the altar, and when all the people saw it, they shouted and fell on their faces" (Lev 9:23–24). The psalmist also appeals to God, "Help us, O God of our salvation, *for the glory of your name*; deliver us, and *atone for our sins, for your name's sake!*" (Ps 79:9; my emphasis). In Num 25:11, 13, God commends Phinehas and atonement is made for Israel because Phinehas "was jealous with my jealousy . . . for his God." Fundamentally, atonement is contingent on God's honor being publically upheld where sin brings disrepute.

Both Jesus' life and death inform a biblical theology of atonement. Jesus explains how he honors his Father, "I glorified you on earth, having accomplished the work that

---

[8] This is argued in John Piper, "The Demonstration of God's Righteousness, Part 3," *Desiring God*, May 23, 1999, n.p. [cited 19 May 2012]. Online: http://www.desiringgod.org/resource-library/sermons/the-demonstration-of-gods-righteousness-part-3.

you gave me" (John 17:4). As in Rom 2:23–24, obedience is a means to the end of God's honor. Jesus represents humanity and is called "the image of God" and "the firstborn of all creation" (2 Cor 4:4; Col 1:15). Christ's obedience perfectly glorifies God, satisfying the debt mankind owes God (Heb 4:15; 1 Pet 2:22; 1 John 3:5).[9] Jesus' prayer also makes plain the reason he dies. Rather than asking to be saved from the cross (John 12:27), he prays, "Father, glorify your name" (John 12:28). Thus, by Jesus' dying on the cross, the Father glorifies his own name. The design of the cross reveals the purpose of atonement, namely, that people "boast in the Lord" (1 Cor 1:18–31; cf. Rom 3:24–28)

Jesus' sinless life not only gives significance to his death, but his death gives his life its full value. His death completes the life that manifests God's name by doing the work given to him (cf. John 17:4, 6). Accordingly, Paul highlights Jesus' "obedience unto death" so that "God has highly exalted him and bestowed on him the name that is above every name, so that at the name of Jesus every knee should bow, in heaven and on earth and under the earth, and every tongue confess that Jesus Christ is Lord, to the glory of God the Father" (Phil 2:9–11; cf. Rom 5:12–21).[10] The cross perfects Jesus' God honoring life since not even death compels Jesus to forsake and thus shame his Father.

It is *imperative* for salvation that God gets glory in order that his people might be saved. If God their king lacks honor, they too will be ashamed. Yet, God is righteous;

---

[9] Contrary to some people's concerns, Emile Nicole's conclusion is undeniable when he says that several occurrences of כפר–group "indisputably link it to the notion of compensation." See his argument at Emile Nicole, "Atonement in the Pentateuch," in *The Glory of the Atonement: Biblical, Theological & Practical Perspectives* (ed. Charles E. Hill and Frank A. James III; Downers Grove, Ill.: IVP Academic, 2004), 47. In addition, it is entirely appropriate to appeal to Christ's life when speaking of his death and the cross. First of all, Christ's perfect obedience includes his submitting to the cross. Second, his life is what qualified him to be a substitute such that his death has any value. Cf. Leon Morris, *The Apostolic Preaching of the Cross* (3d. ed.; Grand Rapids, Mich.: Eerdmans, 1965).

[10] See N. T. Wright, *Climax of the Covenant* (Minneapolis, Minn.: Fortress Press, 1993), 38–40, 91–92.

therefore, he keeps his promises. This is why Romans twice quotes Isa 49:23, "Everyone who believes in him will not be put to shame" (Rom 9:33; 10:11). Numerous texts show God's honor is bound up with his people.[11] For that reason, to defy Israel was to defy the Lord. God's own reputation was at stake when the Philistine defied Israel, "the armies of the living God" (cf. 1 Sam 17:26, 36–37, 45–47). When Paul quotes Joel 2:32, "everyone who calls on the name of the Lord will be saved" (Rom 10:13), one might ask, "saved from what?" Joel 2:26–27 twice repeats the point that God's people "shall never again be put to shame." Their honor depends on the honor of the one true God, who dwelled among them, to do kindly "as the Lord has said" (Joel 2:26–27, 32b).[12] Those who believe will be honored; the disbelieving are put to shame (1 Pet 2:6–7). If God's name is scorned, those who bear his image shall likewise bear reproach forever.

In death, Jesus sets up God's kingdom so as to defeat all God's enemies, the "last" of which is death (1 Cor 15:20–28). Wright argues the Gospels portray Jesus' death in royal terms.[13] Accordingly, Wright aptly states, "'The ruler of this world' has been overthrown; the powers of the world have been led behind Jesus' triumphal procession as a beaten, bedraggled rabble. *And that is how God is becoming king on earth as in heaven.*"[14] The implications extend into every arena of public life where allegiance to Christ is expressed in the face of authorities who demand people conform to convention.

---

[11] Deuteronomy 4:7, 34; 33:29; 2 Sam 7:23–24; 1 Chr 17:20–22; Ps 147:20; Isa 63:14; Jer 13:11; 32:20; 33:9.

[12] Also notice vv. 26–27, 32 come in the context of Joel 2:28–29, quoted by Peter at Pentecost, foretelling Jesus' coming. Many passages explicitly claim God's people will not be "put to shame" because they trust in God. Thus, their honor depends on God's having honor. If God were shown unable or unwilling to keep his promises to his people, they would be disgraced. Note Rom 9:33; 10:11; 1 Pet 2:6 all cite the same text. Also, see Ps 22:5; 25:2, 20; 31:1, 17; 37:19; 71:1; 119:6, 31, 46, 80, 116; Isa 49:23.

[13] For his argument in brief, see N. T. Wright, *How God Became King: The Forgotten Story of the Gospels* (New York, N.Y.: HarperOne, 2012), 138–53 and more fully in pp. 156–248.

[14] Ibid., 162. Emphasis original.

What Did Jesus Accomplish for People? (Objectively)

What does Jesus accomplish *for people*? This question is multifaceted, complicated by the fact that theologians have especially focused on this aspect. This section explains how the atonement brings people into communion with Christ because objectively he is both a penal substitute and an honor-substitute. In addition, the atonement necessarily has a subjective side. The word "objective" refers to what Christ achieves independent of or "outside" a person. "Subjective" indicates what he accomplishes "inside" of people (e.g., nature, behavior). In the end, the conclusions offered in this section both fit an HS context and cohere well with traditional interpretations of the atonement.

The cross of Christ brings people into union with him. Theologians customarily connect "union with Christ" with justification.[15] The most common language Paul uses to express this union is "in Christ" (ἐν Χριστῷ) or "in the Lord" (ἐν κυρίῳ). This union signifies the mutual identification of Christ with his people. Accordingly, what is true of Christ becomes true of his followers. In Christ, there is a sharing of life, death, honor, and shame. This reading fits the most common texts about union with Christ (Rom 6:3–8; 8:1–2; 1 Cor 15:18–22; Gal 2:19–20; Col 3:3–4). Loyalty unto union with Christ constitutes a new identity (Gal 3:26–29). Relationship brings both benefit and responsibility (1 Cor 1:30; Gal 3:14; Phil 3:8–11). Jesus himself used this sort of language about his relationship to both the Father and his followers (John 14:10–11; 15:4, 7–16; 17:20–23). Second Samuel 19:41–43 [2 Sam 19:42–44, LXX] is important because it uses the same phraseology found in the NT yet without referencing Christ. It says,

---

[15] Theologians have long recognized the relationship between justification and union with Christ. The concept is typically indicated by phrases like "in Christ" or "with Christ." For example, see Murray, *Redemption*, 161–73. He says, "Union with Christ is the central truth of the whole doctrine of salvation" (p. 170). For a survey of this doctrine, see Demarest, *The Cross and Salvation*, 313–44.

Then all the men of Israel came to the king and said to the king, "Why have our brothers the men of Judah stolen you away and brought the king and his household over the Jordan, and all David's men with him?" All the men of Judah answered the men of Israel, "Because the king is our close relative. Why then are you angry over this matter? Have we eaten at all at the king's expense? Or has he given us any gift?" And the men of Israel answered the men of Judah, "We have ten shares in the king, and in David also we have more than you. Why then did you despise us? Were we not the first to speak of bringing back our king?" But the words of the men of Judah were fiercer than the words of the men of Israel.

In verse 43 [v. 44, LXX], the men affirm their allegiance by claiming to be "in David" (ἐν τῷ Δαυιδ). This reflects the verbiage of the NT (e.g., ἐν τῷ Χριστῷ, Eph 1:10).

For Paul, this identification is both collective and individual. More plainly, "What is true of the individual is also true of the community. Indeed, it is questionable whether Paul separated the two concepts in his own mind."[16] Christ as the "image of God" represents humanity (2 Cor 4:4; Col 1:15). Others suggest that Christ, as messianic king, typifies Israel and the Servant in Isa 53.[17] This identification principle is primary and fits within HS cultures. As the group head, Christ is both the representative and a substitute on behalf of his people.[18] This idea is clearly conveyed in 1 Cor 15:22–23, 45 and Rom 5:12–21. In Adam, death comes to all through sin. Those who are "in Christ . . . belong to Christ," are righteous, and share in his glory. These passages accord with collectivistic thinking, in which the community is more fundamental than an individual. The whole group shares moral responsibility, praise or blame. Only when individuals are the

---

[16] Demarest, *The Cross and Salvation*, 327. He cites Donald Guthrie, *New Testament Theology* (Leicester: IVP, 1981), 651.

[17] Especially see N. T. Wright, *Jesus and the Victory of God* (Minneapolis, Minn.: Fortress Press, 1996), 477–539. Also, Dan McCartney, "Atonement in James, Peter, and Jude," in *The Glory of the Atonement: Biblical, Theological & Practical Perspectives* (ed. Charles E. Hill and Frank A. James III; Downers Grove, Ill.: IVP Academic, 2004), 180–89. Each offers numerous Scripture citations.

[18] Charles Hill, "Atonement in the Old and New Testaments," in *The Glory of the Atonement: Biblical, Theological & Practical Perspectives* (ed. Charles E. Hill and Frank A. James III; Downers Grove, Ill.: IVP Academic, 2004), 30.

fundamental social unit does responsibility rest solely on the offender.[19] This initial value

assumption determines whether or not one thinks corporate identification is morally just.

Reflecting on Gal 3:8–9, 14, Wedderburn ties Paul's use of "in Christ" language

to OT language about Abraham (e.g., Gen 12:3; 18:8; 22:18).[20] Israel saw God's blessing

coming "in Abraham" to all who are "associated with" Abraham since God "views

Abraham as their representative."[21] This background sheds light on ethnic tensions within

Scripture, since God's blessing was closely linked to identification with Abraham's

national family. Paul's "in Christ" motif demands a shift in loyalty since one is justified

by virtue of identification with Christ not by ethnic identity (1 Cor 6:11).[22] Some Jews no

doubt wondered what it meant to be both "Christian" and "Jewish."[23] Moxnes

summarizes that Paul undermines competitive notions of honor, making identification

with Christ the standard for honor. In time, all will publically see "the revealing of the

sons of God" (Rom 8:19). For now, one loves others by honoring them without regard to

merit or social status, even when shamed by those who are "in Adam."[24]

In view of HS, what is biblical faith? Faith recognizes the worth of God. A

change of identity is an exchange of HS standards. The shame endured in this age is of no

comparison to the glory to be revealed to God's children (cf. Rom 8:18; 2 Cor 4:17).

Faith is necessarily public, not private. Why? First, genuine faith inevitably expresses

---

[19] Mark R. Reiff, "Terrorism, Retribution, and Collective Responsibility," *STP* 34, no. 2 (Apr 2008): 209–42. For example, some terrorists think any American is responsible for what "America" does.
    [20] A. J. M. Wedderburn, "Some Observations on Paul's Use of the Phrases 'in Christ' and 'with Christ'," *JSNT* 25 (Oct 1985): 88–91.
    [21] Ibid., 90.
    [22] Mark Garcia well develops a similar line of thinking in his work, "Imputation as Attribution." He calls justification "a matter of *status-in-relation*" (p. 426).
    [23] Likewise, many Chinese ask how one can be "Christian" and "Chinese." For a helpful essay on implications of the "in Christ" doctrine for ethnic identity, see Yeung, "Boundaries in 'In-Christ Identity'."
    [24] Moxnes, "Honour and Righteousness," 74. He appeals to Rom 12:9–10.

itself. Second, one glorifies what one trusts in. Faith publicly communicates, "It is dependable. It is great. It satisfies me!" Romans 4:20–22 says of Abraham, "No distrust made him waver concerning the promise of God, but he grew strong *in his faith as he gave glory to God*, fully convinced that God was able to do what he had promised. That is why his faith was 'counted to him as righteousness'" (cf. Heb 11:11, 19). In Matt 13:57–58, the unbelief of Jesus' hometown and family is expressed in terms of their *not* honoring him. Real faith makes much of God. In Num 20:12, Moses' lack of faith is equated to his not "upholding [the Lord] as holy in the eyes of the people of Israel" (cf. Num 27:14). Everyone has faith, even if the object of faith differs. Pursuing reputation and identity is the antithesis of faith. Faith magnifies God's name, his character.[25] Naturally, honoring Christ through faith is expressed *publicly* through obedience, which is essentially one's proclamation that God is faithful to his promises.[26]

Key biblical words for "faith" (אמנה/אמונה, πίστις) entail the meaning of "loyalty" or "faithfulness."[27] To have faith in Christ is to pledge loyalty to him, repenting of other forms of identification. A "real Jew" has faith like Abraham.[28] Thus, union with Christ also means sharing in the covenant promise of identification, "I will be their God,

---

[25] Daniel Block's exegesis is illustrative. He suggests the commandment not to take the Lord's name in vain (Exod 20:7) is less about speech and more about "wearing the name of Yahweh as a badge or a brand of ownership." Also, Zeba Crook, "Reconceptualizing Conversion: Patronage Loyalty, and Conversion in the Religions of the Ancient Mediterranean" (PhD diss., Toronto: University of St. Michael's College, 2003), 333.

[26] For an excellent exposition explaining how God's glory-honor relates to his promises, our faith and obedience, see Scott J. Hafemann, *The God of Promise and the Life of Faith: Understanding the Heart of the Bible* (Wheaton, Ill.: Crossway, 2001). For a representative summary, see pp. 86–105.

[27] See Bauer et al., "πίστις," BDAG. Also, *HALOT*, "אמנה/אמונה." For example, see Luke 12:42, where Jesus asks, "Who then is the faithful [ὁ πιστὸς] and wise manager, whom his master will set over his household, to give them their portion of food at the proper time?" Also see Matt 25:21, 23; 1 Cor 10:13; Heb 3:6; 10:23.

[28] Hafemann, *The God of Promise*, 230. He cites Rom 2:25–29; Gal 3:14, 5:6; Phil 3:3; Col 2:11–15. In addition, we could add Matt 8:10–11; Rom 4; Heb 6:12–13; Jas 2:21–23.

and they shall be my people" (Heb 2:10b). Zeba Crook's dissertation, drawing from many biblical and extra biblical texts, argues "that at times loyalty was the dominant characteristic that πίστις was describing."[29] Loyalty is inherently public. Within an ancient Mediterranean setting, patron-client systems were prevalent.[30] Niels Lemche's analysis suggests that ANE covenants, the חסד-concept, and God-king relationship each reflect known patron-client patterns.[31] This background raises awareness to other themes related to faith/loyalty. For instance, demonstrations of faith-loyalty "functioned to honour a patron."[32] As Geert Hofstede points out, loyalty "is an essential element of the collectivist family [which is] partially kept in order by the threat of shame."[33] Thus, even if one were to disagree with particular theories of social scientists, the connection between faith-loyalty and group identification is evident. In Crook's interpretation,

> Conversion, a change in the patronal relationship, would have involved simultaneous acts of disloyalty and loyalty—disloyalty to a former patron [*or group*], loyalty to a new patron [*or group*]. Each of these can be understood analogously with honour and dishonour—disloyalty is dishonouring, loyalty honouring, and thus, the stakes in conversion were high.[34] [additions mine]

Christian faith consummates union with Christ wherein one shares in his HS, life, and death. Within the context of God's kingdom, faith recognizes the right and reality of his reign, rejoices in Christ's kingship, and responds in action. Accordingly, union is expressed by loyal obedience (Acts 6:7; Rom 1:5; 10:16; 16:26; Gal 5:6–7; Heb 11:8).

---

[29] Crook, "Reconceptualizing Conversion," 286. Her fuller discussion is on pp. 270–93.

[30] Watson, *Honor Among Christians*, 43–46.

[31] Niels Peter Lemche, "Kings and Clients: On Loyalty Between the Rule and the Ruled in Ancient 'Israel'," *Semia* 66 (1994): 119–32.

[32] deSilva, *Honor, Patronage*, 95–120. Crook, in agreement, stresses the point, "Loyalty is measured in one way and one way alone—externally" in her "Reconceptualizing Conversion," 324.

[33] Geert H. Hofstede, *Culture's Consequences: Comparing Values, Behaviors, Institutions, and Organizations Across Nations* (2nd ed.; Thousand Oaks: Sage, 2001), 229. The first part of the quote was initially noted by Crook, "Reconceptualizing Conversion," 326.

[34] Crook, "Reconceptualizing Conversion," 333.

How does group-identification relate to concepts like righteousness and covenant? Covenants no doubt involve "law"; yet they also indicate the terms of a relationship.[35] One's honor depends on maintaining proper relationships. Fidelity in relationship brings honor. A break in relationship brings shame. Thus, God's honor is at stake when he covenants to "be their God." Placing inordinate stress on the legal motif within the covenant concept leads to impersonal abstraction. Legal language is a mere explication of a relationship (i.e. how parties relate), including how to be honorable and avoid shame in relation to God their true King. "Law" in many regards is an impersonal concept. "Impersonal" need not necessitate unloving; nonetheless, it is not the natural language of family relationships. This does not imply that close, intimate relationships have no rules. Indeed they do, but it is offensive to speak of one's marriage vows as mere "laws." While it is possible to speak this way, the abstraction to law-language masks the fundamental nature of the relationship. One must not lose what is essential only to keep what is merely legitimate.

The God who cares about his name upholds and displays his glory precisely by entering into relationships. His honor is most vividly seen in identifying with humanity, via covenant. He shows faithfulness, love, grace, power and justice, precisely by taking on the disgrace that comes by identifying with people. Ironically, the pain of the incarnation and the shame of death actually manifest the glory of God in such a unique manner otherwise impossible outside of relationship.[36] This explains why Jesus endured

---

[35] For some introductory remarks on this, see Adrian M. Leske, "Righteousness as Relationship," in *Festschrift: A Tribute to Dr. William Hordern* (ed. Walter Freitag; Saskatoon, Canada: University of Saskatchewan, 1985), 125–37.

[36] This can address potential Muslim objections that God would not let his prophet endure shame.

shame. God's honor depended on it. In this way, God righteously keeps his covenant by identifying with his people.

How does this sort of relationship bring about atonement? Traditionally, Protestants affirm *penal substitution*, wherein God's wrath against sin is satisfied by Christ's death. Christ pays the debt humans owe for sin by dying in their place. Demarest summarizes, "According to this view sin, which is primarily a violation of God's law, *not his honor*, results in the just penalty of death."[37] The interpretation suggested in this book rejects Demarest's bifurcation and affirms that sin *is most basically a violation against God's honor*. Averting God's anger is not most fundamental. Law is but one sphere within HS. A penalty points towards something more basic at stake. How is God's wrath appeased?[38] Why is it right for God to pour wrath against sin? This is not merely an abstract principle of justice righting a wrong through punishment. Rather, the reason why it is right to punish is that humans defame God's name. The punishment accords with the measure of the offense. To offend an infinitely glorious God deserves the ultimate retribution.[39] However, sin brings more than a penal consequence against the sinner. Sin also raises the need for God's own vindication. God's vindication involves the manifestation of his supreme worth in all the earth. God's character is more than simply a

---

[37] Demarest, *The Cross and Salvation*, 158. Emphasis mine.

[38] God's wrath and atonement are clearly linked in Num 16:46–47; Ps 78:38. Cf. Prov 16:14.

[39] This argument is seen in Jonathan Edwards, *Sermons and Discourse, 1734–1738* (vol. 19 of *Works of Jonathan Edwards Online*; ed. M. X. Lesser; New Haven, Conn.: Yale University Press, 2000), 342. n.p. [cited 19 July 2012]. Online: http://edwards.yale.edu/. God vindicates the worth of his honor via retribution. This is deSilva's point regarding Heb 10:26–31. See his work, "Despising Shame: A Cultural-Anthropological Investigation of the Epistle to the Hebrews," 454–55. Also, see deSilva, *Honor, Patronage*, 161, note 60. Also, see Deut 32:35–36; Job 40:10–11; Ps 149:5–19; Isa 59:9–19 (esp. vv. 18–19); 66:5–6; Jer 5:9, 29; 9:9; Ezek 38:16–18; Rom 9:22–23; Rev 15:1–8, 19:1–2. Also, compare Rom 12:19, 1 Thess 4:6. In Ex 34:5–7, God's glory and name is found in his punishing iniquity (v. 7b).

cause for punishment. The honoring of God is an end in itself about which penalty for sinners is but a corollary.

There is a second facet of the atonement, *honor substitution*. Reconciliation is possible because *God's honor is restored* through retribution.[40] Morris explains that "propitiation" in essence is a "compensatory payment," a "ransom," "by the offering of a suitable gift," *resulting in* the averting of God's punishment and obtaining a reconciled relationship with God.[41] Malina explains from the perspective of NT culture,

> This process of restoring the situation after the deprivation of honor is usually called satisfaction or getting satisfaction. To allow one's honor to be impugned, hence taken is to leave one's honor in a state of *desecration*—vitiated, profaned, debase—and this would leave a person socially dishonored. On the other hand, to attempt to restore one's honor, even if the attempt is unsuccessful, is to return one's honor to the state of the sacred, to resanctify it and reconsecrate it, leaving one socially honored and honorable.[42]

This accords with Rom 3:25–26 where God's honor is vindicated in Jesus' death. God does not punish based on irrational or misplaced anger. Rather, his anger is justified because his name is defamed. Ezekiel repeats that God's wrath is poured out in order to vindicate God's honor (Ezek 6:3–14; 30:17–26; 38:17, 23; 39:7, 13, 21). Also, in Gen 9:5–6, capital punishment is based on the fact that "God made man *in his own image*."

---

[40] See Deut 32:35–36; Job 40:10–11; Ps 79:9–10; 149:5–19; Isa 59:9–19 (esp. v. 18–19); 66:5–6; Jer 5:9, 29; 9:9; Ezek 38:16–18; Rom 9:22–23; Rev 15:1–8; 19:1–2. Also, compare Rom 12:19, 1 Thess 4:6. In Exod 34:5–7, God's glory/name is exalted in punishing iniquity (v. 7b). These passages contradict those who say penal substitution does not address shame, e.g. Kevin Vanhoozer, "The Atonement in Postmodernity: Guilt, Goats, and Gifts," in *The Glory of the Atonement: Biblical, Theological & Practical Perspectives* (ed. Charles E. Hill and Frank A. James III; Downers Grove, Ill.: IVP Academic, 2004), 377. There is no need to dichotomize shame and guilt as Vanhoozer seems to do.

[41] Morris, *The Apostolic Preaching of the Cross*, 144–213. Although Morris emphasizes "propitiation" and atonement as the "the removal of wrath," this misses *how* this is accomplished, that is, the sacrifice God satisfies God demand for honor.

[42] Malina, *The New Testament World*, 39. Emphasis in original.

Another aspect of honor substitution deserves attention, namely that Christ gives his honor to his people. One might say his honor is reckoned or imputed. Jesus intercedes for his followers, "The glory that you have given me I have given to them, that they may be one even as we are one" (John 17:22). So, "those whom he justified he also glorified" (Rom 8:30). In Rom 5:15–18, one righteous man's obedience made many sinners righteous. The honorable faithfulness of Christ supersedes the shameful unfaithfulness of God's people.[43] Because Jesus is worthy of "glory and honor," being without the shame of sin, he brings "many sons to glory" (Heb 2:9–10; 4:15). The gospel calls us to "obtain the glory of our Lord Jesus Christ" (2 Thess 2:14). Paul persevered so that others "may obtain the salvation that is in Christ Jesus with eternal glory" (2 Tim 2:10; cf. Titus 2:13). In Scripture, salvation is often linked to honor and judgment with shame.[44] Saving faith seeks honor.[45] Extra-biblical literature makes similar connections,

> These, then, who have been consecrated for the sake of God, are honored [τετίμηνται], not only with this honor [τιμῇ], but also by the fact that because of them our enemies did not rule over our nation, the tyrant was punished, and the homeland purified—they having become, as it were, a ransom [ἀντίψυχον] for the sin of our nation. And through the blood of those devout ones and their death as an atoning sacrifice [ἱλαστηρίου], divine Providence preserved [διέσωσεν] Israel that previously had been mistreated [προκακωθέντα]. (4Ma 17:20–22, NRSV)

The writer thus relates honor, atonement (using the same word used in Rom 3:25),

---

[43] In Heb 3:1–6, Christ is counted worthy of glory because of his faithfulness. If one were to see phrases like "πίστεως Ἰησοῦ Χριστοῦ" (Rom 3:22; cf. 3:26; Gal 2:16, 20; 3:22; Eph 3:12; Phil 3:9) as a subjective genitive, meaning "Christ's faithfulness" rather than the objective genitive ("faith in Christ"), then the present argument would only find further support.

[44] See a sampling of verses. For honor, see Ps 37:17–19; 62:7; 85:9; 91:15; Zech 12:7; for shame, Ps 35:4; Isa 44:9–11; 45:16–17; Jer 20:11–12; 51:51; Dan 12:2; Joel 2:25–26; together, Ps 4:1; Hos 4:7; 1 Pet 2:6–7. Scholars have noticed, "Shame and judgment are juxtaposed so frequently that 'to be put to shame' is recognized as an idiom meaning to come under God's judgment." See Leland Ryken, Jim Wilhoit, and Tremper Longman, eds., "Shame," *DBI*, 780. Likewise, Blackwell, "Immortal Glory," 294.

[45] John 5:44; Rom 2:7; Heb 12:2.

ransom, and salvation from shame (via mistreatment).[46]

In the atonement, God glorifies himself by taking away human shame. Hence, in Ezek 16:62–63, God says, "I will establish my covenant with you, and you shall know that I am the LORD, that you may remember and be confounded,[47] and never open your mouth again because of your shame, when I atone for you for all that you have done, declares the Lord GOD."[48] OT sacrifices "provided atonement for the unintended affronts against God's honor (Lev 4:2–4; 5:5–6)."[49] Jesus endures shame on behalf of his people (Heb 12:2; cf. Ps 22:6–7; 69:19–20; Isa 52:14–53:12; Phil 2:8). Thus, they are not put to shame (Rom 5:8; 10:11; Phil 1:20; 1 Pet 2:6). Instead, the cross brings disgrace on those who spurn him (Mark 8:34, 38; Luke 9:22–26; 1 Cor 1:18, 23, 27; Col 2:14–15).

Glory or glorification via identification with Christ entails God's adopting people as children (Rom 8:14–19). Christians exchange familial and relational loyalties for the sake of being a part of Abraham's family (cf. John 8:31–58; Gal 4:22–31). Jesus "is not ashamed to call them brothers" who are willing to forsake natural "brothers or sisters or mother or father or children" (Mark 10:29; Heb 2:11; cf. Matt 25:40). Jesus said, "If anyone serves me, the Father will honor him" (John 12:26). Packer calls adoption "the *primary and fundamental* blessing of the gospel."[50] Trevor Burke argues that adoption historically would have been seen as bestowing extraordinary honor upon the believer.[51]

---

[46] In agreement, Calvin Porter translates the last phrase "rescued Israel, which had been shamefully treated." See his work, "God's Justice and the Culture of the Law: Conflicting Traditions in Paul's Letter to the Romans," *Enc* 59, no. 1–2 (1998): 146–47.

[47] The LXX uses αἰσχυνθῇς to translate ובשׁת; both typically mean "ashamed" or "put to shame."

[48] "Shame" translates ἀτιμίας (LXX)/כלמתך (MT). "Atone" renders ἐξιλάσκεσθαί (LXX)/בכפרי.

[49] David A. deSilva, "Honor and Shame," *DOTP*, 435.

[50] Packer, *Knowing God*, 206.

[51] Trevor J. Burke, *Adopted into God's Family: Exploring a Pauline Metaphor* (Downers Grove, Ill.: IVP Academic, 2006), 152–76.

As the second Adam, the perfect "image of God," Christ pays the original debt owed by every human—honor to God.[52] Honor substitution is an essential aspect of atonement theology, balancing a one sided emphasis on penal substitution. *Substitution,* not merely penal substitution, is central to the atonement. The atonement's effect on God parallels the effect of justification on people. Taking away sin in justification corresponds to Christ's restoring God's honor via death. However, nothing in conventional understandings of the atonement undergirds the notion of a person's being righteous (i.e. justification). Unless one sees *both* humanity's honor-debt and the Son's perfectly glorifying the Father, then one has not addressed the problem that justification presumes relative to God. His demand for honor is satisfied via Christ's obedience and his death, which pay both debts owed to God, that of honor and death.[53] Hence, Christ's death is not so much a "bribe" as it is "restitution" (cf. Lev 5:16; Num 5:8).[54]

What Does Jesus Accomplish for People (Subjectively)?

The cross also brings about a subjective change that is *necessary* if people are to be reconciled with God. Someone might object to talking about the atonement's "subjective" side, perhaps fearful that it would diminish the cross' "objective" achievements.[55] However, for reasons of theology and context, one must not overlook what the atonement

---

[52] Wright makes a similar point in discussing Jesus as the last Adam, "[Jesus'] role was that of obedience, not merely *in place of* disobedience but in order to *undo* that disobedience." Jesus' "obedience unto death [is] the task by which the old Adamic humanity is redeemed" in Wright, *Climax*, 38.

[53] Anderson, *Sin*, 3–54. Unfortunately, he dichotomizes satisfaction and punishment, overlooking the point here that each simply has a different reference and thus they not mutually exclusive (p. 197–98).

[54] Morris, *The Apostolic Preaching of the Cross*, 169, 211. He seems unaware how to reconcile the "unworthy and crude" idea of a bribe with the idea of "payment," which he affirms elsewhere.

[55] Sadly, J. I. Packer treats the atonement as a mere linchpin for life-changing theology. He does not speak of the atonement itself as being *efficacious* for godly living. See J. I. Packer, "The Atonement in the Life of the Christian," in *The Glory of the Atonement: Biblical, Theological & Practical Perspectives* (ed. Charles E. Hill and Frank A. James III; Downers Grove, Ill.: IVP Academic, 2004), 409–25.

accomplishes *subjectively*, that is, what Christ achieves "inside" a person.

First, Jesus died on the cross to inaugurate the new covenant.[56] To ignore this would be to minimize some of what Christ achieved and pose a false "either-or" dilemma—either "objective" or "subjective." Although Jesus' blood established the new covenant, many overlook some of its essential blessings, fixating only on forgiveness (Heb 8:12). For example, Jesus' death means that God puts his law into people's hearts (Heb 8:10b). Second, a holy and harmonious community is established (Heb 8:11). Third, God identifies with his people saying, "I will be their God, and they shall be my people" (Heb 8:10c). Ezekiel 36:26–27 adds, "I will give you a new heart, and a new spirit I will put within you . . . And I will put my Spirit within you, and cause you to walk in my statutes and be careful to obey my rules." Jesus' death is not merely a moral example to follow; it is the *efficient cause* of Christians' honoring Christ practically in their daily lives. This point must not be underestimated. Good works do not atone for sin. Rather, by way of the cross, Christians receive circumcised hearts "by the Spirit" (Rom 2:29; cf. Phil 3:3; Col 2:11). That faith (i.e. a new heart) is a necessary condition is not to turn faith into a meritorious work. This sort of confusion creates innumerable disputes about the role of faith and the "basis" in the salvation practice. Being female is a necessary but not sufficient basis on which a man marries a *wife*. Having a heart that loves God is essential for reconciliation. It is unthinkable to say a person could be reconciled to God while at the same time he or she still hates God. Thus, the subjective achievement of Christ's

---

[56] Matthew 26:28; Mark 14:24; Luke 22:20; 1 Cor 11:25; cf. 2 Cor 3; Heb 8–10; 12:24; 13:20. Linking atonement and the new covenant, see Michael J. Gorman, "Effecting the New Covenant: A (Not So) New, New Testament Model for the Atonement," *ExAud* 26 (2010): 26–59. He states categorically that no well developed "model of the atonement" centers upon the new covenant (pp. 26–31).

blood is critical to understanding reconciliation; it is not a mere logical consequence.[57]

A second reason to emphasize the subjective side of the atonement is cultural context. All human cultures deal with HS and guilt to some degree. A key distinction between guilt and shame consists in how each is experienced. Flanders explains, "guilt involves a more articulated condemnation of a specific behavior (i.e., 'what I *did*') [whereas shame] involves a global negative evaluation of the self (i.e., 'who I *am*')."[58] Thus, guilt cultures resolve the perceived problem by emphasizing the external, yet punishment does not alleviate shame; "Instead, the proper corrective measure must involve a remaking or renovation of the self in some way."[59] This constitutes a new identity, thus restored value. Second, contexts like China want religion to have practical relevance. As a result, any contextualization must apply to *this life*. Theology must reflect the fact that Christ explicitly did *not* pray that God take people out of the world (John 17:15). Because of what the cross effectually accomplished, people are genuinely transformed such that "the name of our Lord Jesus may be glorified in you, and you in him" (2 Thess 1:12). Therefore, it is reductionistic to suggest that what Jesus achieved was *only* objective or that Christ died *only* as a good example. Instead, contextualized theology affirms that Jesus in fact changed the way people love others, suffer criticism, work a job, train a child, play, spend money, and use words. These practical aspects of

---

[57] Demarest for instance separates his section "Exposition of the Doctrine of the Atonement," where he discusses the objective aspect of atonement, from his section on its "Practical Implications," which deals with the "subjective" side. See *The Cross and Salvation*, 196.

[58] Flanders, "Shame," 814.

[59] Ibid., 815.

life are emphasized in Chinese thinking and in Scripture (1 Cor 10:31; Phil 2:12). Christ does not merely transform culture; rather, he forms a culture, a community of whom God says, "And no longer shall each one teach his neighbor and each his brother, saying, 'Know the Lord,' for they shall all know me, from the least of them to the greatest" (Jer 31:34). Therefore, Jesus promises,

> Truly, I say to you, there is no one who has left house or brothers or sisters or mother or father or children or lands, for my sake and for the gospel, who will not receive a hundredfold now in this time, houses and brothers and sisters and mothers and children and lands, with persecutions, and in the age to come eternal life. (Mark 10:29–30)

The cross creates an HS culture among God's people. No issue is more practical than the community with whom one lives. God's people find their identity not as individuals, but rather in the sharing of God's honor.

What does it mean to be this new covenant community? The atonement creates a people zealous to manifest God's glory in the world.[60] To be a part of this covenant community, to have one's sin atoned for, is more than a changed status or position (in a mere legal sense). Familial language was standard covenant terminology in both the ANE and the Bible.[61] Hence, Mal 1:6 asks, "A son honors his father, and a servant his master. If then I am a father, where is my honor? And if I am a master, where is my fear? says the LORD of hosts to you, O priests, who despise my name." In covenant language, "servant" and "son" are synonymous.[62] To be a "son of" is to take up the father's favor and honor.

---

[60] Goheen makes a similar argument. See Goheen, *A Light to the Nations*.

[61] Richard Patterson, "Parental Love as a Metaphor for Divine-Human Love," *JETS* 46, no. 2 (Jan 2003): 205–16. This can also include marital language (i.e. Jer 31:32). This includes the new covenant: See Jer 31:1, 9, 32 and Dennis J. McCarthy, "Notes on the Love of God in Deuteronomy and the Father-Son Relationship Between Yahweh and Israel," *CBQ* (Apr 1, 1965): 144–47.

[62] Sarah J. Dille, *Mixing Metaphors: God as Mother and Father in Deutero-Isaiah* (New York, N.Y.: T&T Clark, 2004), 33. For a more thorough exegesis of Deuteronomy, see J. W. McKay, "Man's

In addition, this sort of language invokes loyalty. In ANE covenants, including those in the Bible, "to love" is to be loyal, to honor, show reverence, serve, and obey as a son to a father. Love is commanded. To disobey the suzerain king is to "hate" him.[63] Jesus redefines his family in this way, "whoever does the will of my Father in heaven is my brother and sister and mother" (Matt 12:50). These considerations give background for הֶסֶד, occurring over 250 times in the OT. It has been translated "steadfast love," "loving kindness," or "covenant loyalty."[64] In Exod 33:12–34:9, God proclaims that he abounds in הֶסֶד. It is God's "essential nature," indeed "his name and glory," to express הֶסֶד.[65] Yet, this word is unequivocally "relational or covenantal."[66] Covenant love as loyalty or duty does not exclude "tenderness," but rather grounds it. Why does God delight in his children? Piper answers, "At root, what God delights in about us is that we delight in him."[67] The psalmist rejoices, "[T]he LORD takes pleasure in those who fear him, in those who hope in his steadfast love" (Ps 147:11). Likewise, the worshipper cries, "So I have looked upon you in the sanctuary, beholding[68] your power and glory. Because your

---

Love for God in Deuteronomy and the Father/Teacher-Son/Pupil Relationship," *VT* (1 Oct 1972): 426–35. Cf. 1 Sam 24:13; 2 Sam 19:6–7; 2 Kgs 16:7.

[63] Kline, *Kingdom Prologue*, 62–66. McCarthy, "Notes on the Love of God," 146. William L. Moran, "The Ancient Near Eastern Background of the Love of God in Deuteronomy," *CBQ* 25 (Jan 1, 1963): 77–87. Sandra L. Richter, *The Epic of Eden: A Christian Entry into the Old Testament* (Downers Grove, Ill.: IVP, 2008), 79. Also, see the parallelism in Exod 20:5–6, "those who hate me" are contrasted by "those who love me and keep my commandments." These authors strongly show that covenantal love in Scripture carries the same meaning as in ANE political treaties.

[64] Sandra L. Richter expresses it as "covenant loyalty." See Richter, *Epic of Eden*, 79.

[65] John Piper, *The Justification of God: An Exegetical and Theological Study of Romans 9:1–23* (2nd ed.; Grand Rapids, Mich.: Baker Academic, 1993), 88–89.

[66]Demarest, *The Cross and Salvation*, 71.

[67] John Piper, "Why God Tells Us He Delights in His Children," *Desiringgod.org*, 23 Aug 2006, n.p. [cited 19 Nov 2010]. Online: http://desiringgod.org/resource-library/taste-see-articles/why-god-tells-us-he-delights-in-his-children.htm.

[68] The Hebrew here for "beholding" (לִרְאוֹת, a qal infinitive construct) occurs 82 times in the OT, most often suggesting some purpose or intention, as the context suggests here. Thus, v. 2 might be translated, "So I have looked upon you in the sanctuary *in order to behold* your power and glory."

steadfast love is better than life, my lips will praise you" (Ps 63:2–3). In short, covenant love seeks to honor God.[69]

The atonement has practical, subjective consequences for God's new covenant people.[70] They are characterized by steadfast love. In Matthew's Gospel, Jesus teaches that ethical righteousness consists in showing mercy, that is, "abounding in steadfast love."[71] Scholarly debate whether people can show "steadfast love" to God or only to other people may miss an obvious point.[72] For God's people to show covenant love or faithfulness *to him*, they must show mercy *to others*, imitating their Father, "who practices steadfast love, justice, and righteousness in the earth. For in these things I delight, declares the LORD" (Jer 9:24). In covenant, each person is a "son of God," invested with God's image thus are obligated to wholeheartedly love him by obeying God's design for man "to reproduce in himself on his image-glory level the likeness of the God he loves."[73] This sort of life is no mere incidental yet independent result of an objective, "more basic" achievement. Reconciliation with God requires a subjective change of heart in his people, necessarily causing them to honor God with their lives.

Christian soteriology unequivocally emphasizes human life lived here and now.

---

[69] Dille's chapter on Isa 43:1–7 in *Mixing Metaphors* does an outstanding job illustrating and synthesizing all that has been said about honor, identification, covenant, kinship, and even substitution. In addition, she helpfully comments on Yahweh as "redeemer," "a flesh-and-blood" relative "who acts to ensure or restore family honor" by redeeming a "*debt* slave." See Dille, *Mixing Metaphors*, 74–101.

[70] Gorman, "Effecting the New Covenant," 27–28, 32. He cites David A. Brondos, *Fortress Introduction to Salvation and the Cross* (Minneapolis, Minn.: Fortress, 2007), 182–84.

[71] Mary Hinkle Edin, "Learning What Righteousness Means: Hosea 6:6 and the Ethic of Mercy in Matthew's Gospel," *WW* 18, no. 4 (Fall 1998): 362.

[72] Compare Robin Routledge, "*Hesed* as Obligation: A Re-Examination," *TynBul* 46, no. 1 (May 1995): 193–95. Also, Katharine Doob Sakenfeld, *The Word* Hesed *in the Hebrew Bible: A New Inquiry* (Missoula, Mont.: Scholars Press, 1978) as reviewed by Yehoshua Gitay, "Review of Katharine Doob Sakenfeld, 'The Meaning of Hesed in the Hebrew Bible: A New Inquiry'," *JBL* 98, no. 4 (Dec 1979): 583–84. The reason for this has to do with whether *hesed* implies the commitment of a higher to a lower, or if it infers the meeting of one's relational (covenantal) obligations.

[73] This summary, including phraseology, comes from Kline, *Kingdom Prologue*, 42–46, 62–66.

The atonement necessarily brings about a change in disposition. How does the cross bring about this transformed daily life? Vanhoozer's thesis is succinct: "[T]he saving significance of Christ's death consists in making possible God's gift of the Holy Spirit."[74] Christ's "blood of the covenant" hastens the Holy Spirit's coming, in fulfillment of God's promises, causing one to obey, to the glory of Christ.[75] God grants the Spirit because those who are "in Christ" have been adopted as sons (Rom 8:12–17; Gal 3:23–4:7). His presence signifies all who are genuinely God's people, whose hearts are circumcised and whose "praise is not from man but from God" (Rom 2:28–29; cf. John 12:26; Phil 3:3). The Spirit forms a community, the temple wherein God's Spirit dwells without regard for ethnicity.[76] He sanctifies a people who "have become obedient from the heart" (Rom 6:17).[77] Hafemann rightly argues that the Spirit's power is decisive in salvation history. Previously, God's people "transgressed the law because it lacked the power of the Spirit to put it into practice. . . . The problem was that the law was given apart from the transforming work of the Spirit to a hardened and resistant people."[78] The Spirit, whose mission is to glorify Jesus (John 16:14), is essential for Christian salvation.[79]

---

[74] Vanhoozer, "The Atonement," 398–99. He adds, "Jesus' death saves because it enables a new *objective* situation, namely, the end of exile and the construction of a new kind of temple, indwelt by God's Spirit. The cross saves, not by bequeathing an example, but by bequeathing to the church the same power that enabled Jesus to lay down his life for others: the Spirit of self-giving love" (pp. 400–401).

[75] On how the Spirit honors Jesus, see John 16:7–15 (cf. 14:15–31). Paul's contrasts the old and new covenants in 1 Cor 3, centering on the Spirit. On fulfillment, see Acts 2:1–21. Also, see the Spirit as God's promise of old in Acts 2:33 and Gal 3:14. In addition, we see the new covenant promise in Ezek 11:19–20; 36:26–27 and Joel 2:28 such that the Lord would be their God, them his people, with the law written on their hearts (Jer 31:31–34).

[76] On community, see Acts 10:45; Gal 3:14, 28; Eph 2:11–3:21 is a lengthy passage connecting this theme with the "temple" motif. On temple, see 1 Cor 3:16; 6:19–20.

[77] I am linking Rom 6:17 with the Rom 8, especially vv. 2–4. Also, note Acts 5:32; 1 Pet 1:2.

[78] Tom Schreiner, "Review of Scott Hafemann, 'Paul, Moses, and the History of Israel: The Letter/Spirit Contrast and the Argument from Scripture in 2 Corinthians 3'," n.d., n.p. [cited 19 Nov 2010]. Online: http://www.sbts.edu/documents/tschreiner/review_Hafemann2Cor3.pdf.htm.

[79] Prior to Jesus' ascension, the Spirit was still needed for regeneration (cf. Jesus' conversation with Nicodemus in John 3). Otherwise, I label "Christian" the salvation that follows Jesus' departure.

How does this contextualization relate to other views of the atonement? Schreiner puts it in a correct, albeit incomplete, manner: "The theory of penal substitution is the heart and soul of an evangelical view of the atonement."[80] It is more fitting just to say "substitutionary atonement," to include honor-substitution. This formulation could answer Boyd, who is unclear "how the penal substitution motif can be integrated with (let alone central to) most other aspects of Jesus' life."[81] McKnight rightly suggests that a principle of "*identification for incorporation*" best "embraces all the models of atonement."[82] By "incorporation," he means how "we gain access to everything [Jesus] is." One enjoys what is "properly" his, including his righteousness, love, freedom, blessings, and joy.[83] Unfortunately, he limits it to the incarnation, by which "God knows what we go through . . . by participating in our condition."[84] Instead, one should include "vested interest" wherein this identification determines mutual fortunes. Two parties share stakes in one other. Theoretically, this depicts a marriage. In life, death, honor and shame, one can "[r]ejoice with those who rejoice, weep with those who weep" (Rom 12:15). Their joy is our joy; our name is their name. McKnight cites Heb 2:14–18 "to be thematic of the entire scope of the atonement."[85] However, he misses the honor idea expressed in vv. 11–13: "For he who sanctifies and those who are sanctified all have one source. That is why he is not ashamed to call them brothers, saying, 'I will tell of your

---

[80] Schreiner, "Penal Substitution View," 67.

[81] Gregory A. Boyd, "'Christus Victor Response' to Penal Substitution View," in *The Nature of the Atonement: Four Views* (ed. James Beilby and Paul R. Eddy; Downers Grove, Ill.: IVP Academic, 2006), 99.

[82] McKnight, *A Community Called Atonement*, 107–14. The quotation comes from p. 110. He defends this claim against the major historical models. Emphasis in original.

[83] Ibid., 109–10. Recall Garcia's comment that what is "properly" Christ's is "improperly" ours.

[84] Ibid., 108.

[85] Ibid., 107.

name to my brothers; in the midst of the congregation I will sing your praise.' And again, 'I will put my trust in him.' And again, 'Behold, I and the children God has given me.'"

Via identification, Christ is not ashamed to call them family. It is Jesus who is worthy of all honor, to whom everything is put in subjection, who is "crowned with glory and honor" and is "the founder of their salvation" (Heb 2:7–10). In this way, Jesus represents his people, acts as a substitute, honors God as humans do not, and defeats death and evil. Omitting either the objective or the subjective facet limits the atonement. This view of atonement gives teleological unity to other schemes, for the *goal* of salvation is the glory and honor of God.[86]

Summary

Christ's atonement centrally concerns the honor of God and the shame of man. Salvation preserves God's honor and takes away human shame. God keeps his promises made in the OT, foremost to Abraham. Jesus' death therefore vindicates God's name. Therefore, God's people will not be put to shame. Christ perfectly honored the Father, who then reckons worthy of honor all who, by faith, are united to Christ. Even common theological categories like covenant have a communal, honor-orientation. Jesus is a substitute in that he pays the honor-debt and the life-debt owed by sinful creatures. In both China and the

---

[86] Interestingly, in a message given by Greg Gilbert, at the Together for the Gospel Conference (2010), he says that if we look at the various metaphors for atonement and salvation, we can find the most basic metaphor and dynamic if we keep asking "why?" Why adoption? Why healing? Why redemption? Gilbert claims these questions all point finally to penal substitution. This is only *half* right. Substitution is needed. A penalty must be paid. However, ask the question again of penal substitution: Why does Christ have to die? Why this substitution? Not only because we need someone to bear the penalty for sin; we also need someone who, representing humanity, perfectly glorifies God publically through obedience, even unto death. Unlike us, Christ satisfies the demand of God for supreme glory. This advances atonement theology from "mechanics" to purpose. Greg Gilbert, "What is the Gospel?" (Breakout Session presented at the Together for the Gospel, Louisville, Ky., Apr 2010), n.p. [cited 12 Mar 2012]. Online: http://t4g.org/media/2010/04/what-is-the-gospel/.

biblical world, HS are attributed in relation to the moral values of the community. Being adopted by the Father changes one's standard of honor. Jesus' death ushers in a new covenant. The Spirit calls forth and indwells a people from every nation who honors God in daily practice. This community is ascribed honor relative to its head—Jesus the Christ. Since God makes for himself a name, his people share his honor. In Christ, they "will never again be ashamed or humiliated" (Isa 45:17, NASB).

Justifying Honor and Restoring a Right Perspective

This section offers an interpretation of Paul's doctrine of justification through the lens of HS. First, it reviews key concepts and background related to the doctrine. Second, an exegetical overview of Romans roots the interpretation in the biblical text itself. The third part systematically relates HS and righteousness. The discussion demonstrates how HS helps readers to appreciate the collectivistic aspects of justification.

Righteousness in an Honor and Shame Context

Scholarly precedence exists for relating righteousness to honor and glory, though it is quite underdeveloped.[87] Robinson's lexicon explains Δικαιόω to mean, "to vindicate, to approve, to honour, to glorify; Pass. to receive honour, etc."[88] Kuyper says justification is "to restore him to honor as a righteous person," a "declaration of being a man of

---

[87] As will be argued, righteousness is too intertwined with HS to say it is distinct from HS. Nevertheless, it is interesting to compare Paul's use of the δικ-stem (i.e. righteousness language) and of explicit HS terms (using the τιμ- and δοξ-stems). Granting that statistical analysis has limited value, it can indicate tendencies that raise questions about emphases. He uses the δικ-stem 150 times; the HS stems 145 times. Both themes are most concentrated in Romans, though HS has more of an even distribution in his letters. Paul does not use the δικ-stem in Ephesians. It should be noted that this count does not factor important words within the same semantic range, like "boast," "name," "exalt," "profane," etc.

[88] Edward Robinson, "δικαιόω," *A Greek and English Lexicon of the New Testament* (Boston, Mass.: Crocker and Brewster, 1836), 199.

honor."[89] In addition, "man's righteousness refers to his honor[ing] God as his sovereign Ruler, to acknowledge God as God, and to bow before his majesty."[90] The number of instances where Jonathan Edwards links these ideas fills a book.[91] Baxter speaks of both divine and human justification in terms of glory.[92] Harrelson's entry on "Honor" states, "A man's honor must be employed in the maintenance of wholeness (שָׁלוֹם) within the life of the community. Thus honor is closely connected with justice, righteousness, and peace—key terms in the covenant vocabulary of the OT. Dishonor, accordingly, is equally closely connected with sin."[93] Elsewhere, "glory" is understood in terms of righteousness.[94] Seifrid explains the Hebrew [צֶדֶק] and Greek [δόξα] combine the two notions of "righteousness" and "justice" as distinguished in English. Thus, this "single word group" in part "signifies a right order, that is, the proper distribution of goods and honour, including retribution for evil."[95] In talking about the image of God, Jervell says, "[G]lory emerges as a 'double-referent' for righteousness [and] the imprint of the justified status."[96] Furthermore, the glory of Christians is their righteousness, not merely in a forensic sense but effectually.[97] Arguing for "[t]he correspondence of δόξα and δικαιοσύνη τοῦ θεοῦ," Kaseman adds, "To put it more precisely, the δόξα τοῦ θεοῦ is

---

[89] Abraham Kuyper, *The Work of the Holy Spirit* (trans. Henri De Vries; New York, N.Y.: Funk and Wagnalls, 1900), 367, 368.

[90] Ibid., 445.

[91] See nearly every chapter of Craig Biehl, *The Infinite Merit of Christ: The Glory of Christ's Obedience in the Theology of Jonathan Edwards* (Jackson, Miss.: Reformed Academic Press, 2009).

[92] Richard Baxter and William Orme, *The Practical Works of Richard Baxter: With a Life of the Author and a Critical Examination of His Writings by William Orme* (London: J. Duncan, 1830), 12:580–81.

[93] W. Harrelson, "Honor," *IDB* 2:639–40.

[94] Gordon, "Glory," 733.

[95] Mark Seifrid, "Righteousness, Justice, and Justification," *NDBT*, 740.

[96] Jacob Jervell, *Imago Dei. Gen 1, 26 f. im Spätjudentum, in der Gnosis und in den paulinischen Briefen* (Göttingen: Vandenhoeck & Ruprecht, 1960), 181–82. My translation.

[97] Ibid., 183.

δικαιοσύνη within the horizon of the restoration of paradisiacal perfection, while conversely δικαιοσύνη is the divine δόξα within the horizon of controversy with the world."[98] Many others make similar suggestions, especially regarding Romans.[99]

Apocryphal writings frequently link righteousness to HS,[100] illustrating ways people thought within ancient Judaism. There is a striking parallelism in *Apoc. Mos.* 20:1–2, "And in that very hour my eyes were opened, and forthwith I knew that I was *naked of the righteousness with which I had been clothed* (upon), and I wept and said to him: 'Why have you done this that you has deprived me *of the glory with which I was clothed?*'"[101] Referencing *Apoc. Mos.* 21:2, 6, Preston Sprinkle says, "The term glory here may connote a number of ideas including 'honour/status' [and] 'righteousness'."[102] God glorifies the righteous, who receive "everlasting honor" (Wis 10:13–14; 18:7–9).[103]

---

[98] Ernst Käsemann, *Commentary on Romans* (ed. Geoffrey W. Bromiley; trans. Geoffrey W. Bromiley; Grand Rapids, Mich.: Eerdmans, 1980), 95.

[99] More significant scholarly works will be cited in the coming discussion. For now, note H. Hegermann, "δόξα," *EDNT* 1:344–48. Martin Luther, *Lectures on Romans: Glosses and Scholia.* (vol. 25 of *Luther's Works*; ed. Hilton C. Oswald; trans. Walter G. Tillmans and Jacob Preus; St. Louis, Mo.: Concordia, 1972), 248; Ryken Leland, Jim Wilhoit, and Tremper Longman, eds., "Honor," *DBI* 1:398; Lester Jacob Kuyper, "Righteousness and Salvation," *SJT* 30, no. 3 (1977): 248; M. Welker, "Righteousness and God's Righteousness," *PSB* 1, no. suppl. (1990): 132, 136–37; Piper, *The Justification of God*; Torrance, *Atonement*, 134.

[100] Also noted by Gerhard Kittel, "δόξα," *TDNT* 2:246–47.

[101] Käsemann, *Romans*, 94–95; Preston Sprinkle, "The Afterlife in Romans: Understanding Paul's Glory Motif in Light of the Apocalypse of Moses and 2 Baruch," in *LebendigeHoffnung–ewiger Tod?!: Jenseitsvorstellungen im Hellenismus, Judentum und Christentum* (ed. Manfred Lang and Michael Labhan; Arbeiten zur Bibel und ihrer Geschichte 24; Leipzig: EvangelischeVerlagsanstalt: 2007), 205–6. Translated text comes from Gary A. Anderson, trans., *Apocalypse of Moses*, n.p. [cited 2 Jan 2011]. Online: http://www2.iath.virginia.edu/anderson/vita/english/vita.gre.html#per20. The Greek reads, "Καὶ ἐν αὐτῇ τῇ ὥρα ἠνεῴχθησαν οἱ ὀφθαλμοί μού καὶ ἔγνων ὅτι γυμνὴ ἤμην τῆς δικαιοσύνης ἧς ἤμην ἐνδεδυμένη καὶ ἔκλαυσα λέγουσα· τί τοῦτο ἐποίησάς μοί ὅτι ἀπηλλοτριώθην ἐκ τῆς δόξης μού ἧς ἤμην ἐνδεδυμένη;" Also, Blackwell notes that the Armenian translation actually replaces "righteousness" in 20:1 with "glory." See Blackwell, "Immortal Glory," 288. Blackwell (290) also notes other passages linking glory and righteousness, including 4 Ezra 7:116–31; 2 Bar 15:1–19:8; 54:13–21. At Qumran, 1QS 4:22–23 (cf. 1QS 4:6–8); 19 CD 3:19–20; 1QH 4:14–15 [17:14–15]. *1 En.* 50.1; 62.13–16; 104:1–6; 108:11–15; 1QH 15:22–25; 1QS 4:6–8; *T. Benj.* 10:6–8; *4 Ezra* 7:38–42, 75–101 (esp. 95–98); 8:51–54; 9:31–37; *2 Bar* 48:49–51:12; 54:14–22; He adds, "and possibly" Wis 3:4–8 and *T. Mos* 10:9."

[102] Sprinkle, "The Afterlife," 205.

[103] A similar interplay of words is in Wis 4:7–8, 16–18; 5:15–18; 9:10–12.

222

Even more so than other books, Sirach relates honor, shame, and righteousness. Sirach 10:28–29 advises, "My son, glorify yourself with humility, and ascribe to yourself honor according to your worth. Who will justify [δικαιώσει] the man that sins against himself? And who will honor the man that dishonors his own life?" The writer urges an honorable sense of shame, "Observe the right time, and beware of evil; and do not bring shame on yourself. For there is a shame which brings sin, and there is a shame which is glory and favor" (Sir 4:20–21), later listing rules by which one should be ashamed (Sir 41:12–23).[104] Baruch 2:6 echoes the contrast made in Dan 9:7, "Righteousness belongs to the Lord our God, but confusion [αἰσχύνη] of face to us and our fathers."[105] Sprinkle summarizes how *2 Bar.* 49:48–51:7 speaks of the righteous, "Glorification, then, is a necessary qualification for membership in the future heavenly world."[106] Also remarkable is 1 Macc 2:50–52, which says, "Now, my children, show zeal for the law, and give your lives for the covenant of our fathers. Remember the deeds of the fathers, which they did in their generations; and *receive great honor* [δόξαν] *and an everlasting name.* Was not Abraham found faithful when tested, and *it was reckoned to him as righteousness?*" Gathercole's survey of Second Temple Judaism concludes, "sin leads to dishonor [but] honor is the result of a righteous life, and this honor is again the affirmation of others rather than personal confidence."[107] Other works could be listed.[108]

---

[104] Other relevant passages are Sir 7:3–7; 9:16; 10:19–31; 13:22; 17:12–14; 27:8; 29:6; 31:5; 30:13; 35:3–8; 39:6–8; 42:1–2; 44:1–23; 45:26; 47:20.

[105] Also, Bar 2:17–18; 5:2–4, 9.

[106] Sprinkle, "The Afterlife," 210.

[107] Simon J. Gathercole, *Where Is Boasting?: Early Jewish Soteriology and Paul's Response in Romans 1–5* (Grand Rapids, Mich.: Eerdmans, 2002), 190–93. He adds to the above list 1 Macc 2:64; *Sentt. Syr. Men* II 52–55; 4 Macc 11:5–6; *Ep. Arist.* 266, 272; *Pss. Sol.* 5:16–17; *Jub.* 7:34; 35:2–3.

[108] See also 4 Esr 7:98–99; 16:52–53 [cf. Rom 3:23]; Pr Azar 1:3–5; *1 En.* 22:14–15; 38:4; 50:4.

Old and New Perspectives on Justification

This section highlights a few key topics related to the "New Perspective on Paul" (NPP) in order to give historical and theological context to Paul's doctrine of justification. Fuller treatments and summaries of the NPP are noted in footnotes.[109] A distinguishing mark of the NPP is the belief that Paul's doctrine did not rebut a legalism whereby Jews attempted to gain salvation via works-righteousness. Rather, NPP thinkers say Paul struggles primarily with problems of ethnocentrism, e.g., some Jews' exclusion of Gentiles. In large measure, justification has more to do with ecclesiology than soteriology. God's people do not need to be circumcised nor do any such works that act as "ethnic badges." Accordingly, the NPP understands "law" in Romans and Galatians mainly to refer to the Mosaic Law. Righteousness often is a covenantal category for Paul. Leading spokesmen for the NPP include E. P. Sanders, James Dunn, and N. T. Wright. By contrast, the traditional view of justification is often dubbed the "Old Perspective." It refers to the most common interpretation coming out of the Protestant Reformation. In essence, traditional interpreters argue that Paul rejects the idea that justification comes

---

[109] For helpful and concise summaries, see Stephen Westerholm, "The 'New Perspective' at Twenty-Five," in *The Paradoxes of Paul* (ed. D. A. Carson, Mark A. Seifrid, and Peter T. O'Brien; vol. 2 of *Justification and Variegated Nomism*; Grand Rapids, Mich.: Baker Academic, 2004), 1–38. Although the NPP is not monolithic, a few key representative works include E. P Sanders, *Paul and Palestinian Judaism: A Comparison of Patterns of Religion* (Philadelphia, Pa.: Fortress Press, 1977); James D. G Dunn, *The New Perspective on Paul* (Grand Rapids, Mich.: Eerdmans, 2008); N. T. Wright, *Justification: God's Plan & Paul's Vision* (Downers Grove, Ill.: IVP Academic, 2009); N. T. Wright, "The Paul of History and the Apostle of Faith," *TynBul* 29 (1978): 61–88. Criticism of the NPP can be found in D. A. Carson, Mark A. Seifrid, and Peter T. O'Brien, eds., *The Complexities of Second Temple Judaism* (vol. 1 of *Justification and Variegated Nomism*; ed. D. A. Carson, Mark A. Seifrid, and Peter T. O'Brien; Grand Rapids, Mich.: Baker Academic, 2001); D. A. Carson, Mark A. Seifrid, and Peter T. O'Brien, eds., *The Paradoxes of Paul* (vol. 2 of *Justification and Variegated Nomism*; ed. D. A. Carson, Mark A. Seifrid, and Peter T. O'Brien; Grand Rapids, Mich.: Baker Academic, 2004); Gary L. W. Johnson and Guy Prentiss Waters, *By Faith Alone: Answering the Challenges to the Doctrine of Justification* (Wheaton, Ill.: Crossway Books, 2006). For more mediating treatments, see Michael Bird, *The Saving Righteousness of God: Studies on Paul, Justification and the New Perspective* (New York, N.Y.: Wipf & Stock, 2007); Michael Bird, "What Is There Between Minneapolis and St. Andrews? A Third Way in the Piper-Wright Debate," *JETS* 54, no. 2 (2011): 299–310; Francis Watson, *Paul, Judaism, and the Gentiles: Beyond the New Perspective* (rev. and exp. ed.; Grand Rapids, Mich.: Eerdmans, 2007).

through legalistic obedience to God's commands. His Jewish interlocutor is simply the quintessential human struggling with self-righteousness. "Law" is typically understood to mean God's rules in a broader sense. These scholars do not deny the Jewish context of Paul's letters. They assert justification is primarily a soteriological doctrine concerning one's standing before God. It is no mere social doctrine. Moo's comment aptly summarizes the concern of the "Old Perspective" with the NPP: "At the center of the new paradigm is a rotation of Paul's central theological axis from a vertical to a horizontal orientation. . . . The basic thrust of Paul's justification teaching is also shifted from a vertical to a horizontal concern."[110] Righteousness is mainly an ethical category referring to one's being or doing what is right according to God's absolute standards.

The interpretation proposed in this chapter draws from both perspectives. An HS lens may even help to reconcile some points of dispute between the two groups. In HS language, the traditional view lays stress on "achieved" righteousness whereas the NPP emphasizes "ascribed" righteousness. Each interpretation offers a limited perspective inasmuch as it focuses on only one means of pursuing justification. Ascribed righteousness largely concerns one's relationships and group membership.[111] Achieved righteousness refers to that which is gained through individual distinctives like good moral works. Both the Old and New Perspective tell only half the story.

Rudolf Bultmann illustrates the ease by which one arrives at a half-truth. He claims that,

> . . . the striving of the Jews is basically motivated by the need for
> recognition, and that in this connection this need to be recognized means
> fundamentally not seeking to be accepted in the sight of other humans
> (though this will always be a concomitant of it), but rather to be accepted

---

[110] Douglas J. Moo, "Israel and the Law in Romans 5–11: Interaction with the New Perspective," in *The Paradoxes of Paul* (ed. D. A. Carson, Mark A. Seifrid, and Peter T. O'Brien; vol. 2 of *Justification and Variegated Nomism*; Grand Rapids, Mich.: Baker Academic, 2004), 186–87.

[111] Philip Esler explicitly calls righteousness an "ascribed honor" that affects one's group identity in his *Conflict and Identity in Romans* (Minneapolis, Minn.: Fortress Press, 2003), 167, 186–88.

in the sight of God. . . . A specifically human striving has merely taken on a culturally and historically specific form in Judaism. For it is in fact a universal striving to gain recognition of one's achievement; and this generates pride.[112]

Many agree that the Jews' problem had been their pursuit of recognition. Bultmann however overly narrows the means of getting honor to their *achievements*. He demonstrates a problematic tendency typical of traditional interpretations. He argues that what is true for the Jews is true for all humans such that the distinctive features of Paul's context are "merely . . . a culturally and historically specific form." Schreiner builds upon this foundation, claiming, "We do not deny that Paul distinguished between moral norms of the law and laws which separate Jews from Gentiles. What we deny is that he has this distinction in mind when he uses the phrase 'works of law'."[113] The Bultmannian premise results in a reductionistic reading of Paul.

One cannot overlook the importance of a particular context for discerning the universal significance of Paul's doctrine. In Christian theology, the universal finds embodiment in the particular. If contemporary debates about justification were mapped over onto Christology, arguably the two sides would debate reductionistically for and against Christ's divine and human nature. The collective does not contrast the individual; rather, it is the context for individuals. These considerations cause one to reconsider the role of works and representation in a particular context. A proper reading of Paul's doctrine highlights the significance of group identity. Conceptually, justification as an expression of honor can either be achieved or ascribed.

---

[112] From Watson, *Paul, Judaism, and the Gentiles*, 34. Citing Rudolf Bultmann, "Christ and the End of the Law," in *Essays Philosophical and Theological* (English trans.; London: SCM Press, 1995), 43.
[113] Thomas Schreiner, "'Works of Law' in Paul," *NovT* 33, no. 3 (1991): 227 fn #31.

The Meaning of "Righteousness"

At a basic level, "righteousness" is that which is right. Yet, its meaning is highly dependent on the context and form of the word.[114] Even within ancient Hebrew, Greek and Roman cultures, "ideals of righteousness" varied.[115] The idea may carry ethical, royal, covenantal, creation, and legal overtones.[116] P. J. Achtemeier adds that

> . . . righteousness is in the OT the fulfillment of the demands of a relationship, whether that relationship be with men or with God. . . . [T]he demands may differ from relationship to relationship; righteousness in one situation may be unrighteousness in another. Further, there is no norm of righteousness outside of the relationship itself. When God or man fulfills the conditions imposed upon him by a relationship, he is, in OT terms, righteous.[117]

Leske and Carl Graesser agree, "[R]ighteousness is certainly a relationship term."[118] Different relationships entail differing expressions of righteousness. This relational aspect makes sense of why Judah says of Tamar, "She is more righteous than I, since I did not give her to my son Shelah" (Gen 38:26). Christopher Bryan argues from Plutarch,"

---

[114] This is evidenced in the sheer volume of scholarly writing attempting to explain and summarizes the various nuances. For cases in point, see the extensive dictionary entries in P. J. Achtemeier, "Righteousness," *IDB* 4:80–99; John Reumann, "Righteousness," *ABD* 5:724–73.

[115] R. H. Kennett, Adela Marion Adam, and H. M. Gwatkin, *Early Ideals of Righteousness: Hebrew, Greek and Roman* (Edinburgh: T&T Clark, 1910).

[116] To read contemporary literature, it seems safer to affirm a particular meaning of righteousness than to deny one. At times, scholars deny one meaning as an overarching meaning, perhaps giving the impression that one must choose one or the other. It may sometimes be the case that authors overstate their opponent's case. For an example, Seifrid adjudicates between "norm," "rectification" or restoration, and "proper relation" as possible meanings for righteousness, yet even within Seifrid's own Creator-righteousness interpretation, the Creator is restoring the world back to a proper relationship/norm, relative to himself. Therefore, claiming that righteousness means "proper relation" is not reductionistic. See Mark Seifrid, *Christ, Our Righteousness: Paul's Theology of Justification* (New Studies in Biblical Theology 9; Downers Grove, Ill.: IVP, 2000), 41. For a few condensed summaries, see Achtemeier, "Righteousness"; Peter Toon, "Righteousness," *BTDB*, 687–88; N. T. Wright, "Righteousness," *TNDT* 1:590–92.

[117] Achtemeier, "Righteousness," 80.

[118] Leske, "Righteousness as Relationship," 134. Carl Graesser, "Righteousness, Human and Divine," *CurTM* 10, no. 3 (1983): 134. Bird, *Saving Righteousness*, 10–12. Likewise, Moore suggests "all the *dikai*-words in Romans and Galatians should be understood relationally." Quoting A. B. du Toit, "Forensic Metaphors in Romans and Their Soteriological Significance," *Verbum et Ecclesia* 24, no. 1 (2003): 56. He cites D. A. Campbell, "The Meaning of *Pistis* and *Nomos* in Paul: A Linguistic and Structural Perspective," *JBL* 111, no. 1 (1992): 91–103.

[Righteousness has] no function in relation to oneself or to a part of oneself, but only in relation to others."[119] A range of metaphors is needed to interpret this contextually relative concept. The righteous person does what is right in a given relationship and circumstance.

God acts rightly in relation to himself. Bavink warns, "It is thus a fatal error when a person hypostatizes the norm, and pushes God into the distance. Such an act results solely in breaking the norm into an endless number of commands and prohibitions, but its deepest meaning, its relationship to God, is thereby lost."[120] Righteousness is Trinitarian. Coppedge says, "Righteousness is established on relationship between the persons of the Trinity. This in turn is expressed in right relationships with others. This righteous way of relating becomes the standard for all person-to-person relationships and this is the standard for all morality and laws."[121] God is not bound by independent abstract norms.

God's righteousness is often understood as a righteousness from God gifted to believers (particularly in Romans),[122] as his own covenantal faithfulness for the salvation of his people,[123] and as his sovereign kingship over his creation whereby he sets the world in "right order."[124] These options are not mutually exclusive but instead depend on relationship and context. His own character is the measure of right within creation. Bird

---

[119] Christopher Bryan, *A Preface to Romans: Notes on the Epistle in Its Literary and Cultural Setting* (New York, N.Y.: Oxford University Press, 2000), 69, 77.

[120] Bavinck, *An Introduction to the Science of Missions*, 264.

[121] Allan Coppedge, *The God Who Is Triune: Revisioning the Christian Doctrine of God* (Downers Grove, Ill.: IVP, 2007), 187. He suggests, "Understanding righteousness in relation to the Trinity shifts the focus from primarily being a legal term to being a relational category." Notice Jesus' own appeal in John 17:25, "O righteous Father, even though the world does not know you, I know you, and these know that you have sent me."

[122] Thomas Schreiner, *Paul, Apostle of God's Glory in Christ: A Pauline Theology* (Downers Grove, Ill.: IVP, 2001), 188–209.

[123] Wright, *Justification*, 64–71.

[124] Seifrid, *Christ*, 38–44. Quote from page 40.

helpfully shows there is no tension between God's covenant righteous and his righteousness as Creator: "The covenant people were also God's instrument to extend righteousness to all of creation. . . . Consequently, 'creation' and 'covenant' are parallel spheres in the operation of God's righteousness and not competing paradigms."[125] Precisely because God covenanted to use Israel for the rescue of his creation, one cannot polarize the meaning of righteousness. What is righteousness for God to do in one relationship may not apply to another relationship. Thus, because of Jesus, it is righteousness for God both to save his children and to judge the unrepentant rebel.[126]

Is it true that no one is righteous because no one is perfectly obedient?[127] Certainly, righteousness has ethical dimensions.[128] Yet, the very obvious objection remains that the biblical writers are quite comfortable calling imperfect people "righteous."[129] In fact, Ps 14, which Paul cites in Rom 3:10 ("None is righteous, no, not one"), actually refers to God's righteous people in Ps 14:5. Therefore, to be "righteous" does not *necessarily* mean one is "perfect."[130]

---

[125] Bird, *Saving Righteousness*, 38–39. N. T. Wright elaborates as well in *Paul: In Fresh Perspective* (Minneapolis, Minn.: Fortress Press, 2009), 21–39. A lengthier treatment is found in M. S. C. Nwachukwu, *Creation-Covenant Scheme and Justification by Faith: A Canonical Study of the God-Human Drama in the Pentateuch and the Letter to the Romans* (Tesi Gregoriana, Serie Teologia 89; Rome: Editrice Pontificia Università Gregoriana, 2002). Psalm 74 blends righteousness, creation and covenant.

[126] It is unfortunate that Seifrid does not see this dynamic, for within a page he categorically denies it. Claiming that righteousness refers to "the concept of a 'norm', an order within the world," he then states, "'Righteousness' therefore cannot be reduced to the idea of a 'proper relation', as often has been done in recent interpretation." See Seifrid, *Christ*, 41. What he mistakes is the fact that relationships have norms, ways in which it is *right* to act. In his way of thinking, he simply stresses a particular relationship, that of Creator and creation.

[127] This common view is defended in Thomas Schreiner, "Is Perfect Obedience to the Law Possible? A Re-examination of Galatians 3:10," *JETS* 27, no. 2 (1984): 160.

[128] Benno Przybylski, *Righteousness in Matthew and His World of Thought* (Cambridge: Cambridge University Press, 1980); D. A. Hagner, "Law, Righteousness, and Discipleship in Matthew," *WW* 18, no. 4 (1998): 364–71; Brendan Byrne, "Living Out the Righteousness of God: The Contribution of Rom 6:1–8:13 to an Understanding of Paul's Ethical Presuppositions," *CBQ* 43, no. 4 (Oct 1981): 557–81.

[129] Noah (Gen 6:9); Abraham (Rom 4); Also, Ps 37:29–30; Isa 26:2, 7; Jas 5:16; Rev 19:7–8.

[130] To affirm this does *not* deny God's requirement that we be without sin. Sin dishonors God and must be dealt with in Christ. The key point here is that we must not press the word "righteousness" to say

God's "righteousness" has "positive" and "negative" connotations, though the former "appears more frequently."[131] Regarding people, righteousness can point to one's faithfulness or right standing within a relationship.[132] Respective to God, it may refer to his character, expressed in right action, such as covenant faithfulness.[133] Thus, "God's righteousness" is sometimes short for his acts of salvation.[134] On the other hand, "God's righteousness" can infer judgment (Rom 2:5), although even that "punishment is an integral part of the restoration" of the Creator's world.[135] God saves his people by condemning their enemies, who ultimately include sin and death.

"Righteousness" frequently has covenantal overtones.[136] Leske comprehensively illustrates how Scripture and Rabbinic Judaism conceived of righteousness within a

---

more than it does. As we will see, it is evident "righteous" and "perfect" are not synonyms. Not being synonyms does not make overlap impossible in certain usages. To minimize the distinction inevitably leads to misreading or eisegeting Scripture.

[131] Seifrid, *Christ*, 43. He estimates that "references to God's saving righteousness appear[s] roughly four times as frequently as those to his retributive justice" (p. 44). Regarding God's righteousness as "divine victory," Seifrid speaks of salvation "presupposing" judgment. In addition, "Retribution remains on the 'backside' of divine acts of righteousness" (Mark Seifrid, "Paul's Use of Righteousness Language Against Its Hellenistic Background," in *The Paradoxes of Paul* (ed. D. A. Carson, Mark A. Seifrid, and Peter T. O'Brien; vol. 2 of *Justification and Variegated Nomism*; Grand Rapids, Mich.: Baker Academic, 2004), 44. Even if God's righteousness were to refer to God's rulership as Creator, this should not be too sharply bifurcated from salvation, as even he himself seems to suggest in Seifrid, *Christ*, 45.

[132] Achtemeier, "Righteousness," 80–81, 94–95.

[133] Wright, "Righteousness." Leske, "Righteousness as Relationship," 126, 136.

[134] Douglas Campbell, *The Deliverance of God: An Apocalyptic Rereading of Justification in Paul* (Grand Rapids, Mich.: Eerdmans, 2009), 688–702; Seifrid uses the language, "salvation from injustice" in "Righteousness, Justice, and Justification," 740. Elsewhere, Seifrid rejects a general equivalence, yet concedes overlap in meaning; cf. "Paul's Use of Righteousness," 42. For a small selection of passages that identify God's righteousness with salvation, see Ps 51:14; 65:6; 98:1–3; Isa 46:13; 56:1; 61:10–62:2.

[135] Achtemeier, "Righteousness," 83; Seifrid, "Righteousness, Justice, and Justification," 741–42.

[136] Brian Vickers, *Jesus' Blood and Righteousness: Paul's Theology of Imputation* (Wheaton, Ill.: Crossway, 2006), 182. Vickers affirms the connection with such comments: "A problem, however, arises when someone says that God's righteousness *is* his covenant faithfulness" [his emphasis]; then, he rightly adds the footnote, "I suspect that in some cases the problem is semantic. One could say that God's righteousness *is* his covenant faithfulness but not mean it categorically" (p. 182). Against a strong relationship between the two concepts, see Mark Seifrid, "Unrighteous by Faith: Apostolic Proclamation in Romans 1:18–3:20," in *The Paradoxes of Paul* (ed. D. A. Carson, Mark A. Seifrid, and Peter T. O'Brien; vol. 2 of *Justification and Variegated Nomism*; Grand Rapids, Mich.: Baker Academic, 2004), 423–25. He sees righteousness foremost as a creation concept. For relating the two, see Wright, "Righteousness." He

covenant relationship.[137] In Rom 4:11, Paul makes an explicit correlation. He quotes Gen

17:11, but replaces the original word "covenant" [διαθήκης] in "a sign of the covenant."

Instead, he says "[Abraham] received the sign of circumcision as a seal of the

righteousness that he had by faith."[138] Also, Wright connects Phinehas' justification (Ps

106:31) to God's covenant with him (Num 25:10–13) concluding, "'[R]eckoned as

righteous' . . . is about the establishment of a covenant with that person and their

descendants."[139] A number of other passages confirm that righteousness results from the

coming of the Spirit, promised to God's people by covenant.[140]

Righteousness is often associated with kingship.[141] The point is important in order

not to flatten its meaning as a legal metaphor, perhaps due to cultural bias.[142] Moshe

Weinfeld and Bernard Jackson offer exegetically dense arguments asserting that for a

king to exercise righteousness was not merely as a judge impartially enforcing laws;[143]

---

argues, "the covenant is there to solve the problems within creation" in Wright, *Paul*, 24. For balance, see Bird, *Saving Righteousness*, 35–39.

[137] Leske, "Righteousness as Relationship."

[138] N. T. Wright, "Justification: Yesterday, Today, and Forever," *JETS* 54, no. 1 (2011): 56. Gen 17:11, "καὶ ἔσται ἐν σημείῳ διαθήκης ἀνὰ μέσον ἐμοῦ καὶ ὑμῶν." Rom 4:11, "καὶ σημεῖον ἔλαβεν περιτομῆς σφραγῖδα τῆς δικαιοσύνης τῆς πίστεως τῆς ἐν τῇ ἀκροβυστίᾳ."

[139] Ibid., 55–56.

[140] Isaiah 59:21; Ezek 11:19; 36:26–27 (cf. Jer 31:31–34); Rom 8:2–11; 14:17; Gal 3:14–15.

[141] J. N. Oswalt, "Justice and Righteousness," *DOTHB*, 606. Campbell, *The Deliverance of God*, 688–702.

[142] Seifrid (in "Paul's Use of Righteousness," 42) rightly notes the kingly context of righteousness but asserts "that the usage bears a forensic dimension." While he is right about usage, a reader may interpret "forensic" in different ways. Elsewhere, he rightly notes the overlap between "legal activity" and royal legislation and ruling; however, this seems underdeveloped or less explicit in his writing. See his work, "Righteousness Language in the Hebrew Scriptures and Early Judaism," in *The Complexities of Second Temple Judaism* (ed. D. A. Carson, Mark A. Seifrid, and Peter T. O'Brien; vol. 1 of *Justification and Variegated Nomism*; Grand Rapids, Mich.: Baker Academic, 2001), 422. Cao's insight, drawing from other legal theorists, may explain a key influence on Western theology. She suggests a common feature of places like the West (where common law has long been standard practice): "As is pointed out, common law jurists often deny that legislation is law at all, although they accept that legislation is a possible source of law. The prevailing view is: law is just what the courts do." Cao, *Chinese Law*, 6.

[143] For a very typical summary of justification from this latter perspective, see Thomas C. Oden, *The Justification Reader* (Grand Rapids, Mich.: Eerdmans, 2002), 53–58.

especially importantly was the responsibility to "legislate" or "create the laws and care for their execution."[144] This important nuance critically shifts metaphors from a mere juridical courtroom (with a judge or jury) to a king's court. In short, righteousness is not only legal but also regal. Not only do the prophets stress the point that God is the king who establishes righteousness for his people; even Romans intertwines righteousness and royal language. Having opened the letter announcing the kingship of Jesus the Christ (Rom 1:1–4), Paul compactly employs δικαι-words within a kingship metaphor (Rom 5:14–21; 6:7–20; cf. 14:17; 2 Thess 1:5–6).[145] The association is also clear in Matt 5:10, 20; 6:33; 13:43; 21:31–32.

Isaiah regards the declaration that God, "the King of Jacob," is "righteous" as tantamount to a "gospel" announcement (Isa 41:21, 26–27). God recalls that he chose "the offspring of Abraham" and then foretells that he will "put to shame" and "trample on the rulers" who oppose him (Isa 41:8, 11, 25). Isaiah asks,

> Who declared [הִגִּיד] it from the beginning, that we might know, and beforehand, that we might say, "He is right [צַדִּיק]"? There was none who declared it [מַגִּיד], none who proclaimed, none who heard your words. I was the first to say to Zion, "Behold, here they are!" and I give to Jerusalem a herald of good news [מְבַשֵּׂר].[146]

In the LXX, the repeated verb נגד is translated by the verb ἀναγγέλλω, which can convey the same meaning as its cognate εὐαγγελίζω ["to preach the gospel"], as evidenced by 2

---

[144] Moshe Weinfeld, "'Justice and Righteousness': *mshpt wtsdqh* the Expression and Its Meaning," in *Justice and Righteousness* (Sheffield: JSOT Press, 1992), 246. In addition to this essay, see his fuller treatment in *Social Justice in Ancient Israel and in the Ancient Near East* (Publications of the Perry Foundation for Biblical Research in the Hebrew University of Jerusalem; Minneapolis, Minn.: Magnes Press, 1995). Likewise, Bernard S. Jackson, "Justice and Righteousness in the Bible: Rule of Law or Royal Paternalism?," in *ZAR* 4 (1998): 218–62.

[145] The slave-master imagery in Rom 6 specifically pictures a king's ruling over his slave. See also the dense and explicit preceding pericope in Rom 5. In Rom 6:14, Paul uses "βασιλευέτω."

[146] The LXX typically translates בשׂר with the εὐαγγελ–word group (meaning "gospel" or "to preach the gospel"). A few well known examples include Isa 40:9; 52:7; 61:1.

232

Sam 1:20, 4:10.[147] The psalmist even goes on to say, "I have preached the gospel of [God's] righteousness in the great congregation" (my literal translation of Ps 40:9).[148] Finally, the context suggests that this gospel is in essence a declaration of montheism (Isa 41:7, 21–24, 29; cf. Acts 14:15–17; 17:24–31).

Justification as Achieved and Ascribed Righteousness

As a declarative statement, the verb δικαιόω concerns one's public status. It is sometimes but not always a legal status. In baptism, tax collectors "declared God just" and "wisdom is justified by all her children" (Luke 7:29, 35; cf. Matt 11:19).[149] People do not make God righteous. Deeds and words do not make wisdom to be wisdom. In Rom 2:13, the parallel phraseology sheds lights on the meaning of δικαιόω: "For it is not the hearers of the law who *are* righteous before God, but the doers of the law who will be justified." Those who are justified are righteous before God. The ensuing context (esp. v. 16) makes clear that God's declaration reveals the reality that remains unseen "on that day when, according to my gospel, God judges the secrets of men by Christ Jesus." In each case, there is recognition of change or regard.

Some explain justification as "the pardoning act of the supreme Judge of all," "the opposite of condemnation," and "a judicial act by which God declares the sinner free from guilt—acquitted!"[150] Even if righteousness carries legal connotations, one must still guard against over generalizing. Righteousness within a relationship entails normative

---

[147] In 2 Sam 4:10, the messenger [ὁ ἀπαγγείλας] εὐαγγελίζω the gospel [εὐαγγέλιον].

[148] In the LXX, "εὐηγγελισάμην δικαιοσύνην ἐν ἐκκλησίᾳ μεγάλῃ" (Ps 39:10 LXX). The next verse, Ps 40:10, makes clear v. 9 refers to God's righteousness. The parallelism in v. 10 elucidates the meaning of God's righteousness when it speaks of God's "faithfulness," "salvation," and "steadfast love." In the near context, cf. Isa 43:9, 45:21, where God's righteousness is "announced" [נגד, ἀναγγέλλω].

[149] Also, see Rom 3:4 (quoting Ps 51:4); 1 Tim 3:16; Jas 2:21, 24, 25. Perhaps, Isa 43:26; 45:25.

[150] Oden, *The Justification Reader*, 36, 37, 53.

behavior. Yet, the mere presence of a "rule" does not dismiss the relational context. A "rule" within marriage differs from a rule given to a servant by a king. Persistently using "law" in a general sense can easily decontextualize Scripture and obscure its original meaning. A law context is not the only sphere with a standard that governs behavior.

Justification publicly acknowledges one's identity. A legal setting is but one instance where an announcement effectively determines identity. When parents adopt a child, a judge approves. That approval changes the child's public identity. If a widely esteemed person praises us in public, people look more highly on us. The speaker's status can determine our status. This public regard is precisely the hinge that can explain how justification can both confer a change and yet state what is already true. The change is both legal and familial. "What is already true" refers to the fact that everything has been satisfied which constitutes having this status. Fulfilling the criteria is the objective basis for the new identity; however, public recognition is essential if it is to have any meaning. Law is inherently public, but one should notice that other contexts also determine identity. In a community, some people have special authority or honor, like an elder, parent, or famous figure. When they speak, they change a person's reputation or status.

A righteous judge cannot see that the requirements are met and *at the same time* deny a child membership in the family. Here the problem is with human analogies. Human judges have limited perspective. Though all the criteria are satisfied, a judge may not yet know it. They first gain awareness of objective facts, only then reckoning the child as officially having a new status. However, God is not confined to human analogy. Upon seeing what Christ's work and one's faith in him, God *at that moment* regards one as righteous, as one of his children. It is only analytically possible to separate the requirements being met, God's recognition and his declaration of fact. In other words, when speaking of God, it is simply a category mistake to separate sharply *what is true* from *the declaration that changes identity*. To return to earlier examples (Luke 7:29, 35), wisdom was wisdom before its justification; it simply was not yet recognized. God was just prior to being declared just, yet it was not yet acknowledged. Justification ascribes status to people because it publicly recognizes how people are regarded.

These reflections are consistent with the OT, where justification can mean vindication. As a result of the exile, the nations mocked Israel, saying God could not rescue them. The situation raised the question whether God keeps his promises or whether Israel truly was his people (cf. Ps 79:10; Isa 49:14; Jer 7:29; Ezek 8:12; 9:9; Joel 2:17). In this context, one sees how God's justifying work of deliverance signifies who his people are. Isaiah 50:7–8 says, "But the Lord GOD helps me; therefore I have not been disgraced; therefore I have set my face like a flint, and I know that I shall not be put to shame. He who vindicates [ὁ δικαιώσας] me is near. Who will contend with me? Let us stand up together. Who is my adversary? Let him come near to me." Thus, God's actions authenticate who are the true people of God.[151]

Scholars have found it difficult to agree on precise nuances behind the Hebrew and Greek words that denote "justification/righteousness" or "to justify." Decisions about the meaning of justification as a concept begin at the level of the words themselves; the meaning of the original terms will drive one's theological conclusions.[152] The varied explanations for words like δικαιόω are not mutually exclusive but rather reflect differing

---

[151] See 2 Chr 6:23; Isa 54:10–17; Jer 51:9–10; cf. this theme in Rev 3:8–9.

[152] Douglas Campbell, "The Interpretation of Paul's *dikaio* Language" (presented at the Beyond Old and New Perspective, London, 17 Dec 2011), n.p. [cited 14 Mar 2012]. Online: http://gcitv.net/dl/MiscVid/2011CampbellConf/Day2PMSession1.mp3.

emphases and perspectives on the same general idea. Tracing out the interrelationship between various proposed meanings will help to avoid false dichotomies and understand how HS contributes to an understanding of righteousness.

At one level, there is consensus that the basic idea of δικαιόω is "to declare righteous." Yet this bare assertion does not convey important connotations or make clear the context in which the action takes place. This declaration appeals to some relational norm. While all agree that δικαιόω can carry forensic overtones, beyond this point, scholarly opinions diverge about potential presuppositions and implications.

Theoretically, the one who "justifies" people actually regards them as being in the right. Hence, the corrupt judge who acquits the guilty is deemed unrighteous. The verb δικαιόω can presume a prior action that rectified some wrong behavior or accusation. On the other hand, to justify someone has some very important implications. For example, inasmuch as justification suggests vindication, it could take two forms. First, to justify people can mean to *show* them to be in the right, to validate a claim of identity or honor. Second, the justifier may actively work on someone's behalf to set things right that were wrong. Accordingly, the word "justification" may be understood as vindication.

The critical point to note here is that one must be careful not to privilege one particular facet of justification at the linguistic level since the verb itself may reasonably connote different things in different contexts yet without contradiction. In a particular context, writers may want to highlight one aspect of justification over another. In any case, the effect of one's being justified is unmistakable. There is some change in how others regard the person (whose reputation lay under a shadow of doubt and accusation); hence, a person's identity is at stake in justification.

These considerations show how righteousness can be both achieved and ascribed, depending on context. If a person does some deeds deemed right and good, others affirm the person as being "right" or "righteous." This is *achieved* righteousness. Yet, we can also say one is *ascribed* righteousness. This is because "being justified" points to how he or she is regarded, implying status or identity within a particular context. After all, ascriptions of rightness inherently depend on the context and whom it is that does the judging. For instance, in Rom 1:32, some people are approved for practicing sin; yet, Rom 2:1–2 makes clear God condemns them. How one is regarded always depends on one's relational context. What is assessed as right and good in one situation by one set of people may be despised in another. In this respect, justification confers a status or honor and so determines identity within a group. Therefore, at a very basic linguistic level, to justify a person is dependent both on their actions and context.

In Phil 3:2–9, Paul illustrates how one can see justification primary in terms of group identity, not simply good works. There are two aspects to his identity claim (i.e. his assertion to be one of God's people). First, he recalls circumcision, lineage, and position (v. 5). These are examples of *ascribed* honor. They marked him out as a "Hebrew of Hebrews." Second, he mentions works that typify *achieved* honor (v. 6). Identity or group membership involves both aspects. No doubt individual Jews differed in whether he or she emphasized *achieved* or *ascribed* honor. Yet, variance in accent does not change the fundamental fact that justification or "being righteous" marks a person's identity in a group. Paul disputes the *criteria* for justification not the *meaning* of justification (membership in God's people). Some distinctive(s) mark every group. Paul's Jewish opponents appealed to identification with Israel by way of Jewish works. Paul however

237

said God's people are those who had faith in the Christ. This criterion is the true mark of membership. The identity claim of v. 3, being "the circumcision, who worship by the Spirit of God" is defined in v. 9 as those who have "righteousness from God." The bigger issue in Paul's argument is *who he is* and hence how that is reflected.[153]

Theologically, complications arise from the fact God revealed himself in the Mosaic Law, which was given in a particular historical and cultural context. It is difficult to sort out the universal from the contingent. Consequently, there is a natural tendency towards two flawed options. Either people emphasize the cultural context, under appreciating that these are God's commands or else highlight the universal relevance of God's law to the point of overlooking the significance of its cultural setting. One sees the complications involved in doing theology in context. The Mosaic Law is one way that God contextualizes his self-revelation. Theology and contextualization are essentially identical processes coming from different perspectives. Learning contextualization means learning to do theology and vice versa. Theology is especially conscious of the meaning of biblical texts, whereas contextualization more explicitly reckons with the influence of the reader's context on his reading of Scripture. Yet, since all theology is contextualized theology, the two concepts are only separated in abstraction not practice.

The importance of what has been said is apparent in view of the tendency of writers to debate whether justification "makes" people righteousness or simply "declares" them so.[154] Traditionally, the former is associated with Roman Catholicism and that of

---

[153] Bird echoes Seifrid saying, "[T]he status of the individual before God and the status of individuals within a group are not mutually exclusive categories." He notes Mark Seifrid, *Justification by Faith: The Origin and Development of a Central Pauline Theme* (NovTSup 68; Leiden: Brill, 1992), 63.

[154] Cf. Daniel L. Akin, David P. Nelson, and Peter R. Schemm Jr., *A Theology for the Church* (Nashville, Tenn.: B & H, 2007), 750–53. Henri A. Blocher, "The Luther-Catholic Declaration on

infused righteousness wherein a person actually is enabled to do and so be righteous. Protestants typically use "declaration" language, claiming a person is not righteousness in himself, but rather in Christ he is declared righteous. The unrecognized problem may be that *both* positions seem to imply a change of some sort, in either one's nature or status. However, δικαιοω typically denotes the truth of some reality-in-fact, even if connoting a change. Hence, it means to prove, demonstrate, vindicate, etc.[155] Thus, the objection is raised against the Protestant position that God's declaration is a "legal fiction." After all, in view of Prov 17:15, how can God declare one righteous contrary to reality? Further, many theologians recognize a sort of future justification, wherein God's declaration at the final resurrection vindicates believers as actually being his people.[156] Protestants answer by describing justification as a transaction wherein a status is conferred. The reality of righteousness is found in Christ. Those who believe in him are truly righteousness inasmuch as Christ is righteous, yet believers' righteousness is a conferred status and not having an identical nature as Christ's personal righteousness.

When God justifies people, he declares that he regards them as righteous as Christ is righteous, which is to say they both are *in actual fact* "in Christ" and included among God's people. All who are in Christ are included in the new covenant inaugurated by his blood (Luke 22:20; Heb 8–10). Thus, being "in Christ" and "in his covenant people" refer to the same reality but from two different perspectives. *This group* is rightly regarded as the people of God.

Justification," in *Justification in Perspective: Historical Developments And Contemporary Challenges* (ed. Bruce L. McCormack; Grand Rapids, Mich.: Baker, 2006), 197–217; David A. Brondos, *Redeeming the Gospel: The Christian Faith Reconsidered* (Philadelphia, Pa.: Fortress, 2010), 108–13; Philip Graham Ryken, *Justification* (Wheaton, Ill.: Crossway, 2011), 10–12.

[155] Cf. Bauer et al., "δικαιόω," BDAG; Johannes Louw and Eugene Nida, eds., "δικαιόω," *L&N*.

[156] One of the better presentations of this view is G. K. Beale, *A New Testament Biblical Theology: The Unfolding of the Old Testament in the New* (Grand Rapids, Mich.: Baker, 2011), 469–526.

"Righteousness" and "Law" as Honor-Shame Concepts

Law and HS do not stand in tension, but rather have overlapping domains. A clear example of this is Rom 2:23–24, "You who boast in the law dishonor God by breaking the law. For, as it is written, 'The name of God is blasphemed among the Gentiles because of you.'"[157] Law is a *means* to (dis)honor. That is, the main action is indicated by the lone verb "dishonor," expressed by the verbal noun "breaking the law." The ground clause in v. 24 highlights HS as the central concern (not law).[158] In Rom 1:18–32, Paul describes unrighteousness in HS terms not in legal language. Sin is fundamentally a lack of glory (Rom 3:23).[159] Sin is not glorifying to God because it does not express trust in him (cf. Rom 4:20; 14:23). The point can be missed that sin is not merely a matter of "law" breaking;[160] the aim of obedience is honoring God.[161] Job laments with a clear conscience, "If I am guilty, woe to me! If I am in the right, I cannot lift up my head, for I am filled with disgrace and look on my affliction" (Job 10:15). Jeremiah prefers not being born over shame, asking, "Why did I come out from the womb to see toil and sorrow, and spend my days in shame?" (Jer 20:18). People across cultures can grasp the moral significance of shame in Zeph 3:5: "The LORD within her is righteous; he does no

---

[157] ὃς ἐν νόμῳ καυχᾶσαι, διὰ τῆς παραβάσεως τοῦ νόμου τὸν θεὸν ἀτιμάζεις· τὸ γὰρ ὄνομα τοῦ θεοῦ δι᾽ ὑμᾶς βλασφημεῖται ἐν τοῖς ἔθνεσιν, καθὼς γέγραπται . . . .

[158] Note too Blackwell subordinates righteousness to glory as the *telos*: "Paul does not use glory and righteousness synonymously as he does with honour and incorruption. Rather, based on their close association we can say that righteousness is a necessary condition for experiencing glory." See his work, "Immortal Glory," 298.

[159] Jervell, *Imago Dei*, 181; Blackwell, "Immortal Glory," 297–98; Käsemann, *Romans*, 95.

[160] See Rom 2:12, 25; 5:13; Gal 5:7. 1 John 3:4 does say that sin is lawlessness. However, such a statement works within a legal metaphor or in the instance where God is depicted as king. The point is that a change of metaphors makes changes the way sin is discussed. If honor is the broader category, the law is one way to talk about dishonor. However, a person could dishonor a father, in which no "law" has been broken. In Scripture, God is variously described both as King and as Father. Sin can be explained in terms other than law, yet the explanation remains biblically faithful.

[161] Prov 14:31; 30:19; Matt 5:16; 1 Cor 10:31. In this sense, ethical living expresses a "faithful relationship with the Father and reflect his glory. Cf. Leske, "Righteousness as Relationship," 133.

injustice; every morning he shows forth his justice; each dawn he does not fail; but the unjust knows no shame."[162] HS is a prime concern, not simply guilt/innocence.

Every society has HS standards. It is honorable and not shameful to obey various rules, whether written or unwritten. As was stated, not all rules are laws. Law language functions only within a certain kind of metaphorical discourse. Such a world may include a judiciary, legislators, kings, and the like. One does not typically call it a crime when children break rules of dinner etiquette. Clearly, a person can break a rule but not law. All rules reflect some sort of value system by which one is ascribed honor if he or she conforms to it. In most cultures, respecting elders is honorable. Murder is shameful. In theory, governments use these values to establish laws; crimes are considered disgraceful conduct. The point is that laws are means and expressions of HS standards, yet legal language suits a narrow socio-political sphere. It is completely natural that much righteousness language in Scripture is within a law-sphere. In short, even law language depends on a relational context that presumes a *who* before a *what*.

Theologically, righteousness should mark *God's* people, who rejoice in and give expression to God's character. In other words, they are to have God's perspective of HS. Accordingly, righteousness is both theological and collectively normative. The church stands in glorious contrast to the surrounding world culture. This "peculiar people," in a sense, embodies God's glory in the world, mediating his presence in the world.[163]

---

[162] For the last phrase, the Hebrew is ולא־יודע עול בשת; in LXX, οὐκ ἔγνω ἀδικίαν ἐν ἀπαιτήσει καὶ οὐκ εἰς νεῖκος ἀδικίαν.

[163] The phraseology comes from Rodney Clapp, *A Peculiar People: The Church as Culture in a Post-Christian Society* (Downers Grove, Ill.: IVP, 1996). On mediating God's presence in the world, we could think of Col 1:18–24 or 1 Pet 2:9–10.

"Righteousness" is an HS word. In Scripture, righteousness is often paired with honor-glory but contrasted with shame. The evident parallelism is seen in Ps 97:6, "The heavens proclaim his righteousness, and all the peoples see his glory."[164] In Ps 85:9–13, the "glory [that] may dwell in the land" is defined in terms in "righteousness." This does not mean that righteousness and honor are exactly interchangeable in all contexts. It is more appropriate to understand the word "righteousness" as conveying a particular aspect of honor just as patience and kindness are two expressions of love.[165]

---

[164] Other examples include Ps 4:1–2; 112:9; Prov 8:18; Isa 62:1–2.

[165] E.g., loyalty/faithfulness to his people or power/wrath against evil (cf. Rom 9:14, 17, 22–23).

Faith, Works, and Group Identity

What does it mean that God regards a person as righteous? Romans 4 explains by using

λογίζομαι, variously translated as "to count," "impute," "credit," "consider," or "reckon."

People dispute whether the word is an accounting metaphor, confers a status, or speaks of

incorporation.[166] Broader connotations aside, it means to either "regard as right" and/or

"treat rightly."[167] Λογίζομαι refers to *an assessment of worth or evaluation*, thus quite

relevant to HS. In the LXX, one calculates the value of a field (Lev 27:18–23), God's

servant is reckoned "stricken, smitten by God, and afflicted" (Isa 53:2–4), and God's

people, "worth their weight in fine gold[,] . . . are regarded as [ἐλογίσθησαν] earthen pots"

(Lam 4:2). This valuation idea is explicitly tied to honor in Dan 4:34–35 (via contrast),

> At the end of the days I, Nebuchadnezzar, lifted my eyes to heaven, and
> my reason returned to me, and I blessed the Most High, and praised and
> honored him who lives forever, for his dominion is an everlasting
> dominion, and his kingdom endures from generation to generation; all the
> inhabitants of the earth are accounted as nothing [ὡς οὐδὲν ἐλογίσθησαν].

Whereas God is esteemed, humans by comparison are reckoned or valued "as nothing."

In Rom 8:18, Paul says, "For I consider [Λογίζομαι] that the sufferings of this present

time are not worth comparing with the glory that is to be revealed to us." Paul ascribes

---

[166] For contending viewpoints across this spectrum, see John Piper, *Counted Righteous in Christ: Should We Abandon the Imputation of Christ's Righteousness?* (Wheaton, Ill.: Crossway, 2002). Vickers, *Jesus' Blood and Righteousness*; D. A. Carson, "The Vindication of Imputation: On Fields of Discourse and Semantic Fields," in *Justification: What's at Stake in the Current Debates* (ed. Mark Husbands and Daniel J. Treier; Downers Grove, Ill.: IVP, 2004), 46–78; Wright, *Justification*. Don B. Garlington, "Imputation or Union with Christ? A Response to John Piper," *Reformation & Revival* 12, no. 4 (Fall 2003): 45–113; Robert H. Gundry, "The Nonimputation of Christ's Righteousness," in *Justification: What's at Stake in the Current Debates* (ed. Mark Husbands and Daniel J. Treier; Downers Grove, Ill.: IVP, 2004), 17–45; Bird, *Saving Righteousness*.

[167] E. C. Blackman, "Justification, Justify," *IDB*, 1028. Perhaps, some of the cause for debate as to whether justification is about *who is already one of God's people* or *how one enters God's covenant* is a result of confusing the declaration with the reason for the declaration. Thus, if God declares a person "righteous," from one perspective, this is accurate inasmuch as he or she already is in union with Christ. Yet, as an announcement, justification changes public status. Thus, as shall be seen more fully, there is no inherent contradiction between the two positions, if one recognizes the contrasting points of reference.

value to his present circumstance according to the standard of coming glory. Other literature, like Wis 14:18–20, is rather pronounced:

> . . . the craftsman impelled even those who did not know the king to intensify their worship. For he, perhaps wishing to please his ruler, skillfully [*sic*] forced the likeness to take more beautiful form, and the multitude, attracted by the charm of his work, now regarded as [ἐλογίσαντο] an object of worship the one whom shortly before they had honored [τιμηθέντα] as a man. (RSV)

In fact, a number of Apocryphal writings overtly relate λογίζομαι to honor.[168]

Why then does Paul oppose "works?"[169] Doing works of (Jewish) law signified who was a Jew; hence, "if one *does* these works then one will *become* a Jew."[170] These actions expressed loyalty to God and thus identification with God's people. Fidelity to God and group were inseparable. The Jew's effort to retain his "inherited privilege" or status within the covenant amounted to a "personal achievement"; as such, "Generally speaking works of the *Torah* are just as much *ethical* as they are *ethnic*."[171] In short, works were a means of gaining and retaining identity. One responded to God by being Jewish, one of his people. Conversion was an act of national allegiance.[172] Of course, all of this depended on God's election of Israel. In this scheme, works are necessary, though such actions as circumcision have no inherent merit. However, *not* to keep Torah would

---

[168] Examples include Wis 3:17; 5:4; 7:8–10; 14:20; Sir 40:19.

[169] It is interesting how people sometimes talk differently about faith and work. The two are consistently juxtaposed. One view argues Paul rejects works as a "basis" for salvation. Yet, the same people may feel uncomfortable speaking of faith as a "basis," even though the latter is clearly put in direct contrast. Few are willing to argue that Jews held to a legalism apart from God's grace. If so, then even in the traditional reading works act as a relative (not an absolute) means of justification. That being so, why are people so reticent to speak of faith as a "basis," even if a relative basis? The key criticism of course is that works should not be view synergistically, as having merit that diminishes grace. No one wants to make faith to be meritorious. However, this shift in language may actually create problems when it comes to discerning what faith does, whether it is a badge of membership, or if it has some salvific role to play. Therefore, in overplaying the charge of legalism (as if works did not need grace), we may inadvertently create obstacles to understanding faith, which parallels while yet contrasting works.

[170] Cf. Bird, *Saving Righteousness*, 88–112. Quotation comes from p. 99. Emphasis in original.

[171] Ibid., 99–100. Emphasis in original.

[172] Ibid., 99.

be a definite break with God and his people. Bird summarizes, "What Paul attacks is the view that one must do-Judaism in order to join the people of God and thus be *justified* as the eschaton. That is tantamount to saying that one must become a Jew in order to be a Christian."[173] Identification with God's people is essential.

How then does faith determine collective identity? Phinehas ". . . stood up and intervened, and the plague was stayed. And that *was counted to him as righteousness*[174] from generation to generation forever" (Ps 106:30–31). Why was he justified? In Num 25:11, 13, it is because "he was jealous with my jealousy among them . . . because he was jealous for his God." Such jealously publicly manifested his faith, revealing what he values or honors. Therefore, works function as public affirmations of loyalty to God and group. One could easily confuse the honor *ascribed by God* and that which is *achieved by maintaining group norms*. In either respect, collective identity remains a central concern.

Justification distinguishes between those who boast in personal or collective distinctives (to their shame) and those who faithfully seek to glorify their Father (to their honor). Those who trust him will not be put to shame. Since HS are inherently public/group terms, to share others' HS immediately orients a person within some community that shares that perspective of HS. Naturally, the adoption theme is located in those letters where justification is emphasized (Rom 8:15, 23; Gal 4:5).[175] Burke shows adoption in the ancient world ascribed honor to the child who "inherited 'the family name

---

[173] Ibid., 116. Emphasis in original. Bird's exegesis of Rom 4:1–15 is also helpful. Ibid., 71–80. Cf. Wright, "Justification: Yesterday," 54.

[174] Ps 105:31 (LXX): ἐλογίσθη αὐτῷ εἰς δικαιοσύνην; Hebrew, וַתֵּחָשֶׁב לוֹ לִצְדָקָה; this language is used of Abraham in Gen 15:6, ἐλογίσθη αὐτῷ εἰς δικαιοσύνην (LXX); Hebrew, וַיַּחְשְׁבֶהָ לּוֹ צְדָקָה.

[175] Ephesians 1:5 may not be an exception in view of an HS reading since a main motif in Ephesians is the reconciliation of Jews and Gentiles into one family under "the Father, from whom every family in heaven and on earth is named," (Eph 3:14–15; cf. Eph 1:2, 3, 17; 2:18; 3:5; 4:6). See also Burke, *Adopted*, 152–76.

245

and *honour* and obligations that go with them'."[176] He concludes that Paul

> . . . could quite easily stress his own Jewish credentials (Gal 1:13ff.) to emphasize his acquired honour, but chooses instead to point to the greater honour ascribed by God's call . . . Fully cognizant of the consequences that a fractionalized household in the ancient world would cause, Paul's adoption metaphor is a rhetorical tool he employs to stress the need for acceptance between Jews and Gentiles and the shared honour of being members of the one household of God (cf. Rom 8:15; 9:4).[177]

Vanhoozer bridges honor and the law metaphor. In asking the question, "Might it be that the law court in which the justifying verdict is read out is also an *adoption* court," he proposes, "One might even say that adoption *imputes* filial status."[178] Adoption "in Christ" bestows honor via justification by incorporating "the forensic and the familial."[179]

Putting Justification in Perspective

The following syllogism summarizes how *Paul's Jewish interlocutor* thought about justification. For each point, scholars will interpret the wording differently.

> (1) Justification (being justified) implies doing works of the Law.
> (2) Doing works of the Law implied one was a Jew.[180]
> (3) Thus, justification (being justified) implies that one is a Jew.

As will be seen, this logic is quite explicit in Rom 3:28–30. The NPP emphasizes line 3. The traditional view stresses line 1. Stated abstractly, people agree on line 2; however, this is where people debate definitions of terms. The NPP reduces works to those that mark ethnicity. The traditional view generalizes the Jew to typify anyone who is self-righteousness. Thus, the meaning of works is broadened beyond the Mosaic Law.

---

[176] Ibid., 134. He quotes S. Dixon, *The Roman Family* (Baltimore, Md.: Johns Hopkins, 1992), 111.

[177] Burke, *Adopted*, 175–76.

[178] Kevin Vanhoozer, "Wrighting the Wrongs of the Reformation? The State of the Union with Christ in St. Paul and the Protestant Soteriology," in *Jesus, Paul and the People of God: A Theological Dialogue with N. T. Wright* (ed. Nicholas Perrin and Richard B. Hays; Downers Grove, Ill.: IVP, 2011), 256.

[179] Ibid.

[180] By this, I could include either the native born Jew or the Gentile convert.

An HS perspective helps resolve any seeming dichotomy between ethnic and ethical works. Doing works either *presumes* or *achieves* identity.[181] Works have no meaning outside of relationship(s). Some works have significance inside a relationship or status that would be meaningless apart from that relationship status. For first century Jews, doing the works of law signified identification with Israel. Ethnic identity was not incidental. It was essential if one hoped to win God's approval. To minimize the ethnic context of Paul's doctrine discussion limits honor to only that which is achieved. Such oversight does not see the way works center on the matter of identity. Identity is not only achieved; it is also ascribed inasmuch as HS are ascribed. It is true that someone might do works of the law in order to achieve honor in the sight of God; yet, this presumes that those works identified him with God's people. Accordingly, membership warrants a matchless but *ascribed* honor. This interpretation is free of the false dilemma that sees works as either ethical mandates or ethnic markers. This solution does not deny ethical legalism when it affirms the essential, *not peripheral*, place Paul gives to ethnic identity. Moralism can be an expression of ethnic confidence.

From the viewpoint of Paul's interlocutor, "works" only have *ethical* value inasmuch as they identified a person with an *ethnic* [Jewish] people. If one does not stress group/ethnic identity, he or she is not talking about justification the way Paul talked about it. It is a proper application of Paul's teaching to say to someone, "You can't do good works to earn God's acceptance." However, this is not Paul's precise point. One

---

[181] For example, saluting a flag and wearing certain clothing can express solidarity. In American passports, one reads that citizenship is lost if a person renounces it before an official authority. However, by *not* renouncing it, one would not normally speak in terms of that non-action "earning" citizenship. The point here is both doing works and not doing works are determined by the question of identity within a context. Works are done either *because* of one's identity or *for the sake of* attaining some identity.

247

must not confuse right application with right interpretation. Overlooking his point makes it more difficult to discern broader implications and applications. The traditional perspective is right in that Jews did not see themselves justified simply because they were Jews *qua* Jews, apart from law keeping. Similarly, the problem Paul challenges is not doing good works *qua* good works. He is not talking about morality in the abstract, but within the particular context of a historical people to whom God chose to revel himself. One must not imagine that in ancient Palestine some Gentile might have been in a cave circumcising himself as a work to earn God's favor apart from loyalty or identification with the Jewish people.[182]

Paul's teaching on justification speaks more to the problem of people pleasing than that of working to earn God's favor.[183] Justification ultimately comes down to the matter of whose acceptance one wants. The person seeking justification wants to know whether he or she will gain God's favor, be right, and attain salvation by belonging to this or that group. In short, "Which group's acceptance best signals the measure by which God himself will accept people?" There is a subtle shift in emphasis when changing the way one asks questions related to justification. Instead of asking, "*What* must I do to gain acceptance?" a better question is "*Who* do I want to accept me?" These are obviously related questions; however, the second question determines how to answer the first. Whom one regards as honorable, right, and good determines which works are judged to be honorable or shameful. The "who" question is inherently relational and group-oriented.

---

[182] For a modern analogy, no one presumes that by developing a skill in a sport, he or she then may participate in the Olympics apart from joining the national team.

[183] Emphasizing one does not deny the other. For example, when I say, "She is a wife," I am speaking more to her marital status than that she is a female. Yet, emphasizing the former does not deny the latter. Similarly, if I say, "She is *his* wife," I am speaking more to his relationship to the woman than that she is married. Yet, again, emphasizing the former does not deny the latter.

Works point to that group whose standard of HS one accepts as his or her own. It is within a particular group that works are reckoned as either right or wrong. Justification is more concerned with the issue of whom one wants to please than the question of what one must do to be accepted. For Paul, justification declares that glory, honor, immortality, and eternal life are found among those who have faith in Christ (cf. Rom 2:6–10).[184]

Who can be God's people and *what* one must do to be a member of God's people are not the same question. In one respect, the what-question determines the answer to the who-question. However, a person's identity is not entirely explained in terms of their actions. It largely derives from circumstance and relationships, irrespective of an individual's choices. Neither works nor context entirely dictates identity. Identity consists both in how one is the same and different from others. Justification challenges both the individualist *and* the conformist. The apparent tension is not an "either-or," nor simply a "both-and." Rather, it is a "with-in"—*with* works *in* Israel.

This *who* question gets to the heart of the matter. In Gal 4:17–18, for example, the root problem behind the justification debate seems to be that people wanted to "be made much of" by others. The reason one practices certain works and not others is that he or she wants to be accepted by one group over another. Even *repentance* is inherently social, for it entails a changing of value standards and thus group identity. Why then do people ask, "What do we do?" It is because people recognize that something is awry about their HS compass. The purely ethical question ("what" does one do) can decontextualize people's life, abstracting them from their relationships. Relationships are the context for

---

[184] Bird summarizes well, "[Circumcision] is thus the *social* and *soteriological* function of the law. . . . The question that permeates Romans 4 is 'who are the people of God and on what condition shall they be justified?'" See Bird, *Saving Righteousness*, 74.

moral living. The traditional formulation may put the cart before the horse. As a result, people don't recognize the influence of their peers and family, that is, the group in which they belong. Their sense of identity does not change because the traditional presentation seemingly says little about group identity. When behavior is abstractly connected to God apart from context, relationships become an afterthought.

Interpreting Romans from an Honor-Shame Perspective

Romans gives evidence that what has been stated represents Paul's argumentation. This interpretation explains a range of disputed passages related to justification. Traditionally, Paul is understood to use inductive logic; that is, neither Gentiles nor Jews are justified by works, concluding "by works of the law no human being will be justified in his sin" (Rom 3:20). In fact, Paul actually uses *deductive* logic throughout Romans. He categorically denies the relevance of ethnicity for justification. Paul undermines the Jewish presumption that God shows partiality to Israel.[185] *As a corollary*, Paul also undercuts the idea that the Mosaic Law justifies people. Likewise, inasmuch as Paul shows the futility of law keeping, he also undermines confidence in national identification.[186] Precisely because God's absolutely authoritative Law is given to Israel, one can say Paul undercuts Jewish ethnocentrism but does so without relativizing God's ethical standards. A deductive argument fits the text more naturally than an inductive argument. HS logic moves from the collective to the particular. Although the interlocutor presumes that a person's being righteous implies one does works of the law (R→W), this

---

[185] Given Rom 11, we can include Gentile presumption as well.

[186] If one does find any inductive arguments at work in Paul, this does not overturn the deductive nature of Paul's letter, since a premise in a deductive argument can be disproven inductively, that is, by finding a particular instance which denies the consequent of an if-then clause (i.e. *modus tollens*).

statement needs to be broken down further into two propositions: (1) Being declared

righteous by God implied one is a Jew (R➔ J), i.e. ascribed honor; (2) Being a Jew (in

any meaningful sense) would imply doing works of the law (J➔W), i.e. achieved honor.

Paul at times undermines claims of achieved righteousness via law keeping (~W), as in

Rom 2:28–29; 4:5–8. He also uses theology rather than ethics to show righteousness is

not exclusively ascribed to Jews (cf. Rom 3:28–30; 4:13–16; 5:12–21, et al).

A complete exegesis of Romans with HS in view is impossible here.[187] Literature

addressing HS within Romans is scant but significant.[188] Jewett's work is representative.

He has been accused of "imposing the honor and shame scheme upon the situation in

Rome"[189] and minimizing sin for the sake of the social.[190] To be sure, Jewett's attention

to social conditions generates highly anthropocentric interpretations, seeming to make

God a peripheral focus.[191] Some could get the impression that law is the language of

---

[187] To my knowledge, no one save Jewett, *Romans*, has attempted a full exegesis in terms of HS. His volume has 1140 pages. Ben Witherington and Darlene Hyatt, *Paul's Letter to the Romans: A Socio-Rhetorical Commentary* (Grand Rapids, Mich.: Eerdmans, 2004) take the theme seriously but it is not as pervasive in their commentary as in Jewett. Cf. Downing, *NIDB*, 884.

[188] Jewett, *Romans*, has been mentioned. He has also written Robert Jewett, "Honor and Shame in the Argument of Romans," in *Putting Body and Soul Together: Essays in Honor of Robin Scroggs* (ed. Virginia Wiles, Alexandra R. Brown, and Graydon F. Snyder; Valley Forge, Pa.: Trinity Press International, 1997), 258–76; Robert Jewett, "Aimed at Overcoming Shameful Status-Romans as a Missionary Letter," *Hong Kong Theological Seminary Newsletter*, Aug 2008 edition; Jewett, "Shame and Atonement." Moxnes directly relates honor, righteousness and Romans. See Moxnes, "Honour and Righteousness"; Halvor Moxnes, "Honor, Shame, and the Outside World in Paul's Letter to the Romans," in *Social World of Formative Christianity and Judaism* (Philadelphia, Pa.: Fortress Press, 1988), 207–18; Halvor Moxnes, "The Quest for Honor and the Unity of the Community in Romans 12 and in the Orations of Dio Chrysostom," in *Paul in His Hellenistic Context* (ed. Engberg-Pedersen, T.; Minneapolis, Minn.: Fortress Press, 1995), 203–30; Halvor Moxnes, *Theology in Conflict: Studies in Paul's Understanding of God in Romans* (Leiden: Brill, 1980); Halvor Moxnes, "Paulus og den norske vaerematen': Skam' og 'aere' i Romerbrevet," *Norsk Teologisk Tidsskrift* 86, no. 3 (1985): 129–40. Also, note Jayson George's important article Georges, "From Shame to Honor." Also, see Blackwell, "Immortal Glory."

[189] Thomas Schreiner, "Review of Romans: A Commentary. Robert Jewett," *BBR* 19 (2009): 446–48.

[190] Matt O'Reilly, "Robert Jewett, Romans: a Commentary," *PTR* 14, no. 39 (Fall 2008): 119.

[191] For instance, in Rom 1:18, the "revelation of wrath" has more to do with broken social relationships than with *God's* wrath. In Rom 3:23–26, Jewett stresses the fact that Christ's "blood covers both shameful discrimination and the guilt of groups" caused by social barriers. Jewett, *Romans*, 150–53, 287. He reiterates his view of atonement in Jewett, "Shame and Atonement."

theology whereas HS is just a sociological model. Of course, law, HS, adoption, and family all act as metaphors. There is danger is privileging one of multiple overlapping metaphors, which are essentially contextually sensitive maps of cultural experience.[192] Qualifications aside, Jewett's excesses do not negate the legitimacy of exegeting Romans in view of HS.

Moxnes finds explicit HS terminology in all but two chapters of Romans.[193] He says, "These concepts also determined the way in which [Paul] spoke of justification and righteousness."[194] Moxnes is far more theologically oriented (than Jewett); thus, his view of justification has both horizontal and vertical dimensions. Justification is mainly a soteriological category with overwhelming social implications.[195] The key issue of discord in Romans, Moxnes asserts, is one of status—who are the true children of God; yet, by boasting in Jewishness, the Jews ceased to have God as their measure of honor.[196] Justification by faith alleviates competition for achieved honor; instead, it entails exchanging cultural standards of HS for God's.[197] He adds, "Thus, the question of honour and shame is now a question of their relationship to Christ. Christ now defines what is honour and what is shame."[198] In Christians' humility, suffering and love, God is glorified and grants (i.e. ascribes) them honor.

Being justified by faith "is to have such glory and honor restored, not as an

---

[192] Jewett, "Shame and Atonement."
[193] Moxnes, "Honour and Righteousness," 63–64, 77. Romans 7, 14 are the exceptions. The count is conservative, limited to extant terms not HS concepts.
[194] Moxnes, "Honor, Shame, and the Outside World," 210.
[195] Moxnes, "Honour and Righteousness," 63.
[196] Ibid., 64, 68, 71–72.
[197] Ibid., 74–75.
[198] Ibid., 72.

achievement but as a gift."[199] Jewett says, "'Righteousness,' 'honor,' and 'glory' can be used as virtually synonymous terms."[200] Justification is an inherently public notion. Eschatologically, just as the resurrection vindicates Christ, so also his people will be publically justified at his return. Jewett adds a social implication: "To privatize this [restoration of righteousness] is to reduce the impact of conversion to the sphere of individual conscience, leaving social relations untouched."[201] The gospel reveals God's righteousness by challenging and transforming social groupings and identity.[202] This is necessary because "The competition for human honor that assaults the honor and glory of God leads to shameful behavior by the entire human race. Sin is therefore redefined to refer to the universal human involvement in distorted, prevaricating systems of honor and shame."[203] Georges then posits, "[S]alvation in Romans is consistently presented as inclusion into the group of God's honored people."[204] One glorifies God by boasting in the one true God, not social distinctives, by "no longer depend[ing] on culture for honor," but instead gaining "a new honor code for the Christian community."[205]

Romans 1:1–3:26: Exchanging Glory for Shame

Romans 1–4 is full of overt claims and contrasts concerning Jews and Gentiles. In Rom 1:3–5, 13–14, Paul opens by identifying Jesus as Israel's king and introducing Paul's own mission to evangelize the Gentiles. He explicitly gives priority within the gospel message when he says, "it is the power of God for salvation to everyone who believes, *to the Jew*

---

[199] Jewett, "Honor and Shame," 270. By "such," he refers to the "glory of God" in Rom 3:23.
[200] Ibid., 270.
[201] Jewett, *Romans*, 281.
[202] Jewett, "Honor and Shame," 262.
[203] Ibid., 268.
[204] Georges, "From Shame to Honor," 302.
[205] Ibid., 302.

first and also to the Greek" (Rom 1:16; cf. Rom 2:9, 10). It appears Rom 15:8–9 acts as an interpretive bookend to this introduction, "For I tell you that Christ became a servant to the circumcised to show God's truthfulness, in order to confirm the promises given to the patriarchs, and in order that the Gentiles might glorify God for his mercy." One of Paul's major tasks in Romans is to explain how salvation comes through the Jews yet without implying ethnocentrism (whereby salvation is restricted to Israel).

In Rom 2, traditionalists rightly observe an emphasis on God's ethical demands (Rom 2:1–10). This section prepares the way for Paul's theological conclusion in Rom 2:11, "For God shows no partiality." This raises the question, "God is not partial between whom?" Jew and Greek (and Gentiles more generally). The repetition of these groups in Rom 2:9–10 suggests that one regard these—not the individual—as Paul's most basic categories in the ensuing discussion (cf. Rom 1:16). One might object the ὦ ἄνθρωπε ["O man"] suggests Paul is not talking about cultural or ethnic collectives. However, as will become increasingly evident, Paul can use this language precisely because he wants to overcome collective demarcations that cause boasting and division.[206] One must not confuse Paul's solution with the problem he deals with.

A collective orientation fits the immediate context. In Rom 2:13, 17, 28–29, the issue is who will be justified, who is a "real" Jew. Romans 2:10b–14 clearly contrasts the

---

[206] For now, note Caroline Johnson Hodge, *If Sons, Then Heirs: A Study of Kinship and Ethnicity in the Letters of Paul* (Oxford: Oxford University Press, 2007), 49, 54–55. Her observation is importation: "[Paul's] totalizing language [i.e. terms like 'Gentile,' 'uncircumcised,' 'barbarian'] does not de-ethnicize these people, but strategically constructs and highlights a particular facet of identity, the fact that they are not Jews. . . . The oppositions [e.g. between Gentile and Jew] are crucial because Paul formulates the gentile [*sic*] problem—alienation from God—in terms of ethnic differences between Jews and non-Jews" (p. 49). Also, she says of the term "gentile": "It is a label applied by Jews to all others; it lumps all non-Jews into one category and effectively masks all differences among them. . . . This use of 'gentile' is pejorative, and it marks ethnic and religious 'others.' Thus 'gentiles' serves both as a term of address for his readers and a label of 'otherness' against which the [Jews] are defined" (p. 54–55).

Jews who have the law and Gentiles who do not (v. 12). Significantly, v. 13 begins with a ground clause, "for" (γὰρ). Therefore, in v. 13, Paul rebuts the very presumption that justification implies ethnicity (*expressed* by Jewish law keeping). Even if keeping the law is involved, the context makes certain these works demarcate one's belonging to the Jews. The point is made even clearer by v. 14 since the "for"-clause (γὰρ) indicates that v. 14 grounds vv. 12–13.[207] Verse 14 combines the phrasing from vv. 12–13, thus clarifying that those without the law are "Gentiles." Verse 14 has a φύσει between two clauses: "Gentiles, who do not have the law," and "do what the law requires." Typical translations echo the ESV, "For when Gentiles, who do not have the law, *by nature* [φύσει] *do* what the law requires."[208] However, a number of clues suggest another translation, "For when the Gentiles, who do not *have the law by nature*, do what the law requires."[209] At issue is whether φύσει modifies what comes after it (doing the law) or prior to it (not having the law). Wright observes Paul's parallel usage of φύσει in Rom 2:27, where it unambiguously signifies ethnicity. Paul writes, "Then he who is physically uncircumcised [ἐκ φύσεως ἀκροβυστία] but keeps the law will condemn you who have the written code and circumcision but break the law. For no one is a Jew who is merely one outwardly, nor is circumcision outward and physical" (Rom 2:27–28).[210] In both Rom 2:14 and Rom 2:27, Paul describes Gentiles in exactly these terms; namely, they do not have the law/circumcision "by nature" precisely because they are not Jews "physically." Galatians 2:14–16 is insightful. In a context paralleling Romans, Paul writes,

---

[207] N. T. Wright, *Romans*, 440–41.

[208] N. T. Wright argued this translation convincingly in *Romans*, 441–43. The following line of argument draws from Wright.

[209] In Greek, ὅταν γὰρ ἔθνη τὰ μὴ νόμον ἔχοντα φύσει τὰ τοῦ νόμου ποιῶσιν, οὗτοι νόμον μὴ ἔχοντες ἑαυτοῖς εἰσιν νόμος.

[210] The last phrase ἐν σαρκὶ ["physical"] is also found in Eph 2:11ff "in the flesh" where it signifies ethnic group and is functionally equivalent to φύσει. Thanks to Ian Lawrence for this observation.

> . . . I said to Cephas before them all, "If you, though a Jew, live like a Gentile and not like a Jew how can you force the Gentiles to live like Jews?" We ourselves are Jews *by birth* [φύσει Ἰουδαῖοι] and not Gentile sinners; yet we know that a person is not justified by works of the law but through faith in Jesus Christ.

In Rom 2, justification identifies God's people, those who are Jews "inwardly . . . by the Spirit, not by the letter" (Rom 2:29). Thus, Paul's argument shows that his opponents made group distinctions according to ethnic markers (e.g., works of law, like circumcision). In contrast, Paul explains that Jewish works do not signify the true people of God, for "circumcision is a matter of the heart" (Rom 2:29). The difference between Paul and his interlocutor's view of justification is simply what constitutes genuine group membership.[211]

---

[211] Against this view that Rom 2:12–15 concerns ethnic identification, see Thomas Schreiner, "Did Paul Believe in Justification by Works? Another Look at Romans 2," *BBR* 3 (1993): 144–47. My position is a minority interpretation as Rom 2:14 is often interpreted to speak merely of a moralistic "law" rather than a "Jewish" law (ethnic marker). First, Schreiner says v. 14–15 defends v. 13a (saying that v. 15 is parallel to "hearing" the law by the Jews). He rejects the idea that vv. 14–15 defends v. 13b, "doing the law," even though "doing" is explicitly mentioned in v. 14 and "hearing" has to be read into the words "written on their hearts." It would be far more natural to recognize this as very familiar OT language (law in heart), the fulfilling of the new covenant (NC). Thus, Rom 2:14–15 talk about Gentile Christians. This is because they by faith are fulfilling the law, which was God's promise in Ezek 36:26. Why should we be surprised that in the new reality ushered in by Christ that Paul would look for NC fulfillment, like the law written on hearts such that they observe God's commands? Second, Schreiner contends, "To say that the Gentiles "are a law to themselves" would be an odd way of describing God's law written on the heart" (p. 146). However, this is too speculative to be conclusive. Just as reasonable is that the Gentiles act in a way consistent with the Mosaic Law but without implying ethnic conformity. Certainly, one could agree that having the law written on human hearts (Jer 31:31–34; Ezek 36:26–27) does not mean keeping those aspects of the law that separate Jew from Gentile (like circumcision and food regulations). Keep in mind Ezekiel says we will observe God's commands. By denying a NC reading, Schreiner seems not to allow Paul to speak of "law" in any sense except that which connotes ethnicity. Strangely, on p. 151, regarding Rom 2:26–29, Schreiner thinks the passage talks about Gentiles who have the Spirit and obey the law. I don't know why he does not then see this also in Rom 2:14–15, where the keeping of the law by Gentiles is first mentioned. In Rom 2:28–29, Paul simply elaborates how these Gentiles keep the law in Rom 2:14. Having already said the law is written on their heart, he now adds to the picture with another aspect of the NC—the giving of the Spirit. From Rom 2:14–29, Paul simply gives an exposition how the new covenant promises have come true among Gentiles, to the surprise and dismay of some Jews. Finally, Schreiner asserts the accusing conscience of Rom 2:15 indicates these Gentiles do not have salvation (p. 147). His point is that these Gentiles are accused (not defended) on the day of judgment. This reading has two problems. First, it does not take seriously the verb "defending" (ἀπολογουμένων) that is paired with "accusing" (κατηγορούντων). The conflicting occurrence of accusation and defense raises questions about whom it is the conscience is responding. Could it be that Gentile Christians are responding to accusations laid against him by God's enemies? Second and more important, the text does not say God accuses them

Unlike in Rom 1, the Gentiles of Rom 2:14 are those who are "inward" Jews "do[ing] what the law requires."[212] That Paul contrasts the categories "Jew" and "Gentile" is reinforced in the ensuing discussion in ch. 3 (cf. Rom 2:9–10). Romans 2 uses ethics to undermine *ethnic* claims to privilege (not simply individualistic claims). Paul is not merely giving a negative argument, rebutting Jewish legalism and exposing the Jewish sinner. Positively, Paul argues that Gentiles can be regarded as righteous (cf. Rom 2:9–10, 13–14, 26–29). Paul's train of thought is illuminating. If Paul were *only* making the inductive argument that all people are sinners, he has absolutely no reason to consider so extensively the *Gentile* who "keeps the law [and is] a Jew . . . inwardly" (Rom 2:27, 29). If Paul simply wants to prove the Jew is a lawbreaker, then affirming the possibility of Gentiles being justified does not advance his point. Paul does more by arguing deductively. Logically, he categorically *denies* any ethnic presumption that justification implies being Jewish.

In Rom 3, Paul defends God's faithfulness to the Jews whom he has favored (vv. 1–5) while also undermining ethnic boasting (vv. 27–30). Chapter 3 is often seen as the point where "the scope of Paul's argument broaden[s] to include all humanity, or more

---

but rather that their *conscience* accuses and defends them. We cannot read too much into the actions of the conscience, especially that an accusing heart indicates a lack of salvation (p. 146–47). Consider elsewhere how Paul talks about conscience (e.g. Rom 13:5; 1 Cor 8:7, 10, 12; 10:28), none of which imply that a bad conscience indicates a lack of salvation. In fact, 1 Cor 8:11–13 makes quite clear that the person with a wounded conscience is a brother who stumbles by doing what his conscience rejects. Further "to accuse" is not a statement of fact, for people even "accused" Paul and Jesus. As in 1 Cor 8, consciences are not perfect. This is why Paul in 1 Cor 4:3–5 says that his lack of judging himself does not mean he is innocent. In fact, 1 Cor 4:3–5 parallels Rom 2:15–16 in the respect that God's judgment will come, revealing secrets of the heart. However, in 1 Cor 4:5, this result in "commendation" [ἔπαινος], not condemnation! It is peculiar that Schreiner implicitly affirms that these "works" marked them out as Jews: "It should be noted that Paul's main purpose in Rom 2:12–16 is to convince the Jews that possession of the law is of no salvific advantage" (p. 147). Yet, if Paul thinks the Jews' confidence is based on possessing the law (rather than just doing), then Paul is not entirely rebutting a Jewish moralist. He is refuting Jewish ethnocentrism. Also, cf. Schreiner, "'Works of Law' in Paul," 237 fn #63.

[212] Even if one does not agree that Rom 2:14–15 refers to Gentile Christians who have the law written on their heart, Paul in Rom 2:25–29 categorically challenges the idea that only Jews are righteous.

properly here, each and every person."[213] Does Paul set the ethnic-collectivistic question aside for a more individualistic focus? Importantly, the chapter seven times mentions God's righteousness or his being justified (vv. 4, 5, 21, 22, 25, 26 twice). Verses 1–3 pose the interlocutor's objection that Paul's theology seemingly makes God unfaithful to his word given to the Jews. Paul's denial of this possibility in 3:4–8 is often misconstrued due to a misinterpretation of v. 4, "By no means! Let God be true though every one were a liar, as it is written, 'That you may be justified in your words, and prevail when you are judged.'" In his sequence of thought, Paul references God's "faithfulness," being "true," "righteousness," and "glory" showing, in this context, they conceptually act as near synonyms. Paul's quoting Ps 51:4 (Ps 50:6 LXX) and Ps 116:1 (Ps 115:2 LXX) is traditionally read as referencing God's penal justice wherein he righteously judges sin.[214]

A closer reading of Psalms gives evidence that God's being justified in Rom 3:4–5 does not refer to his punishing "liars" but rather his being "true."[215] Conventionally, the mistaken interpretation comes from a misreading of Ps 51:1–4 where David writes,

> [1] Have mercy on me, O God, according to your steadfast love; according to your abundant mercy blot out my transgressions. [2] Wash me thoroughly from my iniquity, and cleanse me from my sin! [3] For I know my transgressions, and my sin is ever before me. [4] Against you, you only, have I sinned and done what is evil in your sight, so that you may be justified in your words and blameless in your judgment.

---

[213] Seifrid, "Unrighteousness," 137.

[214] Cf. Demarest, *The Cross and Salvation*, 367; Leon Morris, *The Epistle to the Romans* (Grand Rapids, Mich.: Eerdmans, 1988), 155–56; Robert H. Mounce, *Romans* (*TNAC* 27; Nashville, Tenn.: B & H, 1995), 105; John Murray, *The Epistle to the Romans* (Grand Rapids, Mich.: Eerdmans, 1997), 95–96; Schreiner, *Romans*, 151–59; Similarly, cf. David Hill, *Greek Words and Hebrew Meanings: Studies in the Semantics of Soteriological Terms* (London: Cambridge University Press, 1967), 158; Seifrid, *Christ*, 58.

[215] In Ps 116, three observations should be noted. First, the context of v. 11 does not suggest the psalmist being judged by God for sin. Second, the psalmist actually appeals to God's righteousness (v. 5) for his rescue. Third, v. 11 appears to reflect a false accusation made against the psalmist. On point #3, see R. C. Sproul and Keith A. Mathison, eds., "Commentary on Ps 116:11," in *The Reformation Study Bible: English Standard Version* (Orlando, Fla.: Ligonier Ministries, 2005), 841. Just as the psalmist wants vindication, so in Rom 3:4, God also wants to be vindicated.

The final clause in 4b is seen as an elaboration on David's confession in v. 4a. Yet even traditional interpreters see the difficulty with this view. Most critical is the fact "so that" in v. 4 translates לְמַעַן in Hebrew and ὅπως ἄν in the LXX; both typically denote purpose.[216] Using the traditional reading, it appears David sins *in order to* show God is a righteous to condemn him.[217] It makes better sense to connect Ps 51:4b with vv. 1–2, which contain the main verbs in David's petition: "Have mercy," "blot out," "wash me" and "cleanse me."[218] Verse 3 simply explains the occasion of David's need—his sin (note the ὅτι in Greek and כִּי in Hebrew).[219] The purpose of v. 4b is to appeal to God to

---

[216] The NET Bible commentary on Ps 51:4 says לְמַעַן ". . . normally indicates purpose ("in order that"), but here it introduces a logical consequence of the preceding statement. (Taking the clause as indicating purpose here would yield a theologically preposterous idea–the psalmist purposely sinned so that God's justice might be vindicated!)." See *The NET Bible Version 1.0* (3rd; Electronic Version for BibleWorks 7.0; Bible Studies Foundation, 2005). Likewise observing the purpose clause, see Morris, *Romans*, 156 fn #22; Schreiner, *Romans*, 151–52. Seifrid adds the point that the LXX's translation of the Hebrew reinforces the conclusion that the verse conveys purpose.

[217] Schreiner, Seifrid, and Weiser make a significant mistake at this point, confusing what the psalmist *does* with what he *says*. They first note David's confession and then explain the purpose clause by stating *an effect* of the sin, namely, that God's judgment is just. However, this makes no sense of the purpose clause. If the purpose clause connects to v. 4a, then it explains the content of what David said, i.e. "I sinned," not the act of confession itself. Seifrid simply overlooks the words of the psalm itself when he claims, "[T]he psalmist *confesses that his sin effected the hidden and strange purpose of God*" [my emphasis]. David confessed his sin, not God's purpose for the sin. Similarly, Schreiner explains the purpose clause in this way: "Since David sinned against God, any judgment imposed on him is just." Again, the effect of David's sin (that God would be right to judge) must not be confused for the purpose of the verb, which is David's sinning (if one links v. 4b to v. 4a). See Seifrid, *Christ*, 58; Schreiner, *Romans*, 152; Artur Weiser, *The Psalms: A Commentary* (Philadelphia, Pa.: Westminster Press, 1962), 404.

[218] This option is listed as a possibility but is not discussed in Frank-Lothar Hossfeld and Erich Zenger, *Psalms 2: A Commentary on Psalms 51–100* (trans. Linda M. Maloney; Minneapolis, Minn.: Fortress, 2005), 13. They also deny v. 4 indicates result (p. 13). Tate thinks reading v. 4 as a result has difficulties but "avoids the theologizing required by the purpose clause and still allows v. 6c [v. 4b in ESV] to reflect an element of the 'doxology of judgment'." See Marvin E. Tate, *Psalms 51–100* (WBC 20; Dallas, Tex.: Word Books, 1990), 18. However, Tate does not interact with the view offered in this chapter; therefore, he does not see that a purpose clause fits naturally from the context and grammar and does not require "theologizing." Other texts show ὅπως ἄν and/or לְמַעַן can be separated from the action that it modifies by another clause. See Num 15:39–40; Ps 9:13–14 (vv. 14–15 in LXX); Hos 2:2–3 (4–5 LXX).

[219] The flow of thought in vs. 1–4 is also evident elsewhere, including Ps 41:4; 106:4–8, 30–47; 143:1–2; Jer 3:22–4:2; 14:7. Indeed, this verbal movement from God's giving salvation "because" of sin parallels the move from Rom 1:16–17 to Rom 1:18ff. In addition, like the writer of Ps 51, after talking about sin, Paul (in Rom 3–4) shifts the focus to God's faithfulness and righteousness. Some may argue that the purpose should link directly with the preceding clause, however OT texts show both Hebrew and Greek grammar allow a "skip" between action and purpose, as noted in the previous footnote.

demonstrate his righteousness by being faithful to David *despite* his sin. Verse 14 confirms this reading. David reiterates the point made by vv. 1–2, 4b, but omits any mention of sin (as in vv. 3–4a). In Ps 51:14, he restates, "Deliver me from bloodguiltiness, O God, O God of my salvation, and *my tongue will sing aloud of your righteousness.*" God's saving David despite his sin leads to the proclamation of God's righteousness. After all, God made a covenant with Abraham and with David (2 Sam 7). David overtly disavows trust in works of the law (Ps 51:16–19), instead affirming the efficacy of a right heart (Ps 51:6, 10–12, 17). Thus, the broader context of Ps 51 is also comparable to that of Romans.

In Rom 3, God's righteousness is tied to promises to Israel. Their *ultimate* fulfillment is not conditioned on human faithfulness. God's *saving* righteousness (i.e. "faithfulness" in v. 3) is in view, not his retributive justice. For Paul to appeal to God's penal justice would not actually answer the objection posed by v. 3. God's "faithfulness" *with respect to Israel* is consistently positive in the OT, i.e. bringing salvation. With regard to Israel, God's "faithfulness" is even *contrasted* with his punishing Israel for her sins, as in Ps 89:28–38 (note the contrastive "but" [δὲ, ו] in vv. 33, 38). In short, according to the psalmist, it is not in punishing disobedience that God proves his faithfulness but rather in his salvation. Thus, God says, "I will not lie to David" (Ps 89:33; cf. Ps 89:14). This reading aptly fits the context of Rom 3:4. Despite human shame, "God's truth abounds to his glory" (Rom 3:7). If God will be faithful in the face of sin, the interlocutor interjects, "why not do evil that good may come?" (Rom 3:8).[220]

---

[220] Schreiner (responding to Piper) mistakenly assumes that interpreting righteousness as *saving* righteousness implies that Paul's opponents are antinomians who think they can sin since God gets glory by still saving them contrary to their sin. Thus, he claims the unlikelihood that these Jews were antinomian

Does v. 9 shift the focus away from Jews to all individuals? Paul says, "What then? Are we Jews any better off? No, not at all. For we have already charged that all, both Jews and Greeks, are under sin." Here, the point made earlier about *emphasis* is important to grasp. Given the Jewish focus in the immediate context, the string of OT citations that follows v. 9, and the blatant remarks in Rom 3:27–Rom 4, it is more likely that Paul has not left ethnicity behind.[221] While it is true that all have sinned, Paul's point is more acute. He simply highlights the *appropriate shift in thinking* that his Jewish readers should have of themselves.[222] They ("*we*" in v. 9a) are just like the Gentiles.

Romans 3:19–26 continue Paul's defense of God's righteousness against ethnocentrism. In tragic irony, the Jews' boasting in the law acts as self-condemning testimony. The righteousness of God of Rom 1:17 and 3:4–5 was first taught in the Law and Prophets. In Jesus' atoning death, God is now restoring the creation (Rom 8) by fulfilling his covenant with Abraham (Rom 4). The atonement system (appealed to in Rom 3:25) implies that God demands absolute perfection. Justification is no *mere* social

---

makes saving righteousness improbable. However, his inference is incorrect since 3:7–8 acts as a *reductio ad absurdum* where the absurdity is put into the mouth of Paul (hence their "slandering" of Paul in v. 8). See Schreiner, *Romans*, 153–57; He cites John Piper, *The Justification of God: An Exegetical and Theological Study of Romans 9:1–23* (Grand Rapids, Mich.: Baker, 1983), 108–13. Similarly, assuming the righteousness in v. 4 is also that of v. 5, Schreiner acknowledges that reading God's righteousness as punitive (in v. 5) "scarcely makes sense of the objection" (Schreiner, *Romans*, 155). Schreiner cites Piper's argument against Rom 3:5 being a punitive righteousness. See Piper, *The Justification of God*, 107. In the end, Schreiner affirms punitive righteousness in v. 4–5, speculating that the Jewish concern in Rom 3:5 is the implication that humans lack free will and thus God is unrighteous.

[221] It is suggestive to examine the context behind some of the verses that Paul cites in vv. 10–18. Paul may draw from Ps 5:9; 10:7 (9:28 LXX); 14:1–3; 36:1; 53:1–3; 140:3; Isa 59:7–8; perhaps also Prov 1:16; Eccl 7:20. The passages from Psalms and Isaiah all seem to appeal to God's righteousness and faithfulness to save his people. Also, a few places stress the idea these unrighteousness people deny the existence or authority of Israel's God. See Ps 10:4, 11; 14:1; 36:1; 53:1 (cf. Isa 59:13).

[222] If indeed that is the emphasis of the comment, and not *merely* a universal indictment, it would make sense of the ambiguous first-person plural προεχόμεθα in Rom 3:9, which literally translates, "Are *we* better off?" without specific reference to Jews. The ESV reads, "Are we Jews any better off?"

doctrine. Nevertheless, Paul speaks of atonement in thoroughly Jewish terms.[223] That

judgment accords with an absolute standard does not deny the point that Paul is

confronting ethnocentrism.[224] Finally, Jesus' death reveals God's righteousness via his

justifying those who have faith in Jesus (Rom 3:25–26).[225] The ESV translates v. 25b–

26a, "This was to show God's righteousness, because in his divine forbearance he had

passed over former sins."[226] Just as διὰ in Rom 4:25 conveys reason/purpose not cause,

so also it has that meaning in Rom 3:25. This conclusion is reinforced by the fact that

Rom 4:24–25 strongly echoes the themes of Rom 3:24–26.[227] The ἀνοχῇ recalls Rom 2:4,

where God's forbearance is *for the sake of* people's salvation.[228] People are not saved

---

[223] "Propitiation" (ESV) translates ἱλαστήριον and refers to the "mercy seat" in the Tabernacle (cf. Exod 25:17–22; Lev 16:13–15; Heb 9:5). Wright suggests "redemption" in Rom 3:24 points to Israel's exodus in Wright, *Romans*, 471. He lists Ps 71:19, 23–24, linking redemption and God's righteousness.

[224] Andrew Das makes this point in *Paul, the Law, and the Covenant* (Peabody, Mass.: Hendrickson Publishers, 2001), 43–44. Cited in Westerholm, "The 'New Perspective' at Twenty-Five," 22.

[225] The καὶ (v. 26) could mean "and" or possibly "that is" so as to specify what was just said. Here, God would be just *in that* he justifies believers (cf. Gal 3:8).

[226] In Greek: διὰ τὴν πάρεσιν τῶν προγεγονότων ἁμαρτημάτων ἐν τῇ ἀνοχῇ τοῦ θεοῦ. It is unclear what the exact time reference is for "προγεγονότων" (a *hapax legomenon* in Scripture), which refers what has happened beforehand. Perhaps, it refers to the sins committed before Christ's death or those prior to justification. Both are mentioned in vv. 24–25.

[227] See Michael Bird who argues the διὰ is "prospective" in his *Saving Righteousness*, 49–53. Also, see his work, "Raised for Our Justification," *Colloq* 35, no. 1 (2003): 31–46. For similar usages, see Rom 13:5 (x2); Col 1:5; 1 Tim 5:23; 2 Tim 2:10; Heb 1:14; 5:14. Having cited David in Rom 3:4, it is possible that the passing over of sin in Rom 3:26 anticipates Rom 4:6–8.

[228] Gathercole, in "Justified by Faith," affirms, "God's ἀνοχη in Romans 2 is primarily oriented to Israel" (p. 180 fn #125) but then inexplicably gives no reason for it not having that reference in 3:25. Instead, his argument that God's righteousness in v. 25 is God's judgment is nothing more that a subtle play on words. Speaking of ἀνοχη, he says, "the concept inevitably refers to a gracious delay, on God's part, of *judgment*: it is noteworthy that in Romans 2:4 that although the intended goal of ἀνοχη is repentance, its referent is God's delay of his judgment" (p. 181, emphasis original). One must recall that one is saved *from judgment*. Therefore, in effect, his argument hangs on nothing more than his simply flipping around the language of salvation into a "gracious delay" of God's judgment. This is no argument against interpreting v. 25 as saving righteousness but rather an argument for it but simply using terms about non-judgment. At best, Gathercole makes an argument-by-association since much of Rom 1:18–3:20 concerns sin (as one might expect when explaining God's salvation). In addition, he objects to "God's saving righteousness" on the grounds that the wording would be redundant in 3:25–26. However, the πρὸς in 3:26 may connote purpose, paralleling in εἰς v. 25; without contradiction, it may also mean "with reference to," recalling the prior mention of God's righteousness in v. 25. For this usage of πρὸς, see Bauer et al., "πρὸς," BDAG. BDAG suggests a possible translation: "in the time when God also showed forbearance." See Bauer et al., "προγίνομαι," BDAG. The ἐν τῷ νῦν καιρῷ ("as the present time") in v. 26b recalls the Νυνὶ in Rom 3:21 ("Now . . ."). Beale notes this inclusio in *A New Testament Biblical Theology*, 481. The saving

despite God's righteousness but rather *because* of his righteousness.[229] Therefore, the phrase "God's righteousness" here is consistent with its previous usage in Romans. In short, contra some Jewish expectations, it has always been God's plan that salvation would come through Christ, through whom God fulfills all his promises (cf. 2 Cor 1:20).[230]

Excursus: Exegeting Ethnocentrism Out of the Context?

Seifrid's analysis illustrates a problem that an HS perspective can correct. He says,

> Furthermore, the common assumption of the "new perspective," that Paul attacks a sort of Jewish ethnocentrism, does not match the charge which Paul lays at the feet of the moralist in Romans 2:1–16. . . . Yet he does not attack an obvious moral failure such as ethnocentrism, which the "new perspective" supposes, but the hidden failure of false–estimation.[231]

First of all, one must seriously question whether in Paul's cultural-historical context ethnocentrism would be seen as "an obvious moral failure," particularly by those whose scripture gave reason to believe they were God's chosen people. Second, the problem with ethnocentrism is precisely that of "false-estimation." Third, the ethnicity theme is a key aspect of Rom 2:9–16, climaxing in a theological conclusion in v. 11, grounded by the γὰρ in v. 12, where Paul begins giving extensive attention to ethnicity. Paul even adds the modifier "first" in Rom 2:9–10 (twice saying, "the Jew first and also the Greek"), making clear this is no generic formula for all humanity without respect to ethnic

---

"righteousness of God [which] has been manifested" (Rom 3:21) is explained in Rom 3:26c. Not surprisingly, Rom 3:27–30 elaborates on why righteousness manifests "apart from the law" (Rom 3:21).

[229] Demarest is representative in characterizing God's righteousness as that which justification overcomes. He says, "The biblical doctrine of justification deals with the fundamental issue of how guilty sinners can be acquitted and restored to favor with an infinitely righteous and just God." Therefore, one of the "obstacles" to acquitting sinners is the "holy and righteous character of God." See his work, *The Cross and Salvation*, 345, 362–63.

[230] One can easily see how Rom 3:21–4:23 essentially expands the message of Gal 3:6–18.

[231] Seifrid, "Unrighteousness," 124.

differences.[232] Seifrid himself says of Rom 2:1–16, "[Paul] has a Jewish problem in view. . . . In other words, Paul addresses a Jewish problem in Romans 2."[233] Seifrid qualifies himself, saying, "Paul is here treating a fault which is common among the Jews, *as a human problem*."[234] However, this is simply an argument from silence. Seifrid says, "[I]t is highly significant that Paul does not name his addressee in Romans 2:1–16 as a Jew."[235] He adds that Paul's shift from the plural in Rom 1:14 ("Greeks" and "barbarians") to the singular in Rom 2 "is itself an indication that his argument is oriented to individual persons, to mere human beings."[236] Seifrid's statement not only claims too much from Paul's rhetoric but it is itself incorrect. Paul refers to the "Gentiles" in v. 14 [ἔθνη] and v. 24 [ἔθνεσιν]. Also, the citation in v. 24 speaks collectively to Jews using the plural "you" [ὑμᾶς]. Verse 13 seems to refer to Jews as *hearers* of the law."[237]

More troubling is the apparent double standard Seifrid uses in Rom 1–2. He interprets Rom 1:14–15, "In addressing [Paul's] Roman audience as Ἕλληνες, he acknowledges their cultural identity and speaks to their sense of superiority over the barbarians, a social distinction which was fundamental to the world of his day."[238] One

---

[232] By analogy, if a teacher says, "Boys and girls, come here," the gender language is inconsequential. "Boys and girls" means "everyone." However, if a teacher said, "First, the boys will go, then the girls," there is a specific distinction being made on the basis of gender. Contra Seifrid (Ibid., 115.), it makes no difference to the present point that Paul uses "Greek" and not "Gentile," for Paul immediately grounds his comments in Rom 2:9–10 by talking about "Gentiles." Further, Rom 3:9 again uses "Greeks" even though he uses "Gentile" language in the surrounding context (Rom 2:14–29; 3:27–4:18). Once again, the reference to "Greeks" in Rom 10:12 comes right before the large Jew-Gentile discussion in Rom 11.

[233] Ibid., 121.

[234] Ibid. Emphasis in original. In addition, if Seifrid universalizes Rom 2:1–16 based on Rom 1:18–32, then should it not also bear weight that Rom 2:17 through Rom 4 deals directly with the Jew-Gentile divide? The δὲ in Rom 2:17 shows that what follows comes in response to what precedes.

[235] Ibid., 120. He speculates "ὦ ἄνθρωπε πᾶς ὁ κρίνων" in Rom 2:1 is "a mere human being."

[236] Ibid., 121.

[237] Greek: οἱ ἀκροαταὶ νόμου; Note contrast to Gentiles in 2:15.

[238] Seifrid, "Unrighteousness," 115. For support, he cites Martin Hengel, *Juden, Griechen und Barben: Aspekte der Hellenisierung des Judentums in vorchristlicher Zeit* (SBS 76; Stuttgart: Katholisches

raises the question, why does Seifrid allow Paul to address the problem of cultural-social distinctions at this crucial place in Romans,[239] even calling it "fundamental" to the context, yet *not* allow the same dynamic to be at work among the Jews who equally saw the Jew-Gentile divide as fundamental? Given that the latter division is rooted in a theological misunderstanding that brings God's own righteousness into question, wouldn't one *expect* that fact to provoke the sort of response seen in Romans? One has to ask the question, "If Paul *did* want to address ethnocentrism, what else would he have to say to prevent interpreters from exegeting it out of the text?"

Seifrid calls Ἕλλην an "honorific term," explaining at length the shift from "Greeks" in Rom 1:14 to the singular in Rom 1:16 signifies the Romans' self perception as cultured contra the barbarians.[240] If he is right, why can this not also explain the two singular usages of Ἕλλην in Rom 2:9–10? Instead of Paul individualizing his message, could he not intentionally use the "honorific" term in like manner with Rom 1:16? If anything, Paul subtly readies his Roman readers to apply to themselves the words he will speak against Jewish ethnocentrism. After all, they would be tempted to look down on the "barbarians" as the Jews did the Gentiles. This makes perfect sense in view of Paul's expressed desire in the letter to reach the Gentile barbarians (cf. Rom 1:5, 14; 15:9–12, 16–20). Paul's attack on Jewish ethnocentrism actually becomes key in gaining Roman support for his mission to Spain. Paul reverses their perceived status, first placing the Greek in honorable contrast to the barbarian in Rom 1:14. Afterwards, however, the

---

Biblewerk, 1976), 77–115.; Martin Hengel, *Judentum und Hellenismus* (2d. ed.; WUNT 10; Tübingen: Mohr [Siebeck], 1973), 120–43.

[239] Seifrid links vv. 14–15 with vv. 16–17 saying "Jew" and "Greek" "symbolize[d] the ideals which defined value and power in the world of Paul's addressees." See "Unrighteousness," 115.

[240] Ibid., 115 fn #27.

"Greek" becomes secondary to the Jew who is "first" (Rom 1:16; 2:9–10; cf. 3:9; 10:12). Paul is flipping the tables. What the Romans regarded as honorable ("Greek"), the Jews see as shameful, simply designating them "Gentiles." In fact, Paul's exegesis will further humble them, for they are sinners (Rom 3:9, 23), like Adam (Rom 5:12ff), and slaves (Rom 6:14–23). Moreover, they are dependent on the promise that comes via the *Jewish* king (Rom 1:1–4). A common interpretation of Rom 1–3 claims Paul is attempting to show the Jews are just like Gentiles; it may be that Paul is just as much helping the Roman "Greek" realize he is like the Jew who boasts in cultural identity. Ironically, from another perspective, the Greek finds he is nothing more than a "Gentile." Paul repeatedly appeals to their esteem for wisdom (cf. Rom 1:14) by warning of being wise in one's own eyes (Rom 1:22; 11:25; 12:16), admonishing them "to be wise as to what is good" (Rom 16:19), and exalting in the "only wise God" (Rom 16:27; cf. Rom 11:33).[241]

Consequently, a false dichotomy plagues Seifrid's understanding of identity. He begins correctly but then errs in his conclusion:

> A proper understanding of the individual involves a proper understanding of the community in which the individual has been placed by God (in judgment or mercy), and vice versa. . . . [God] shall replay *each one* according to his deeds (Rom 2:6). Paul does not speak of "Jews" and "Greeks" appearing before God as communities, but as individual persons who work evil or good, "Jew" and "Greek" (Rom 2:9–11).[242]

Seifrid severs personal identity from community. He forces a separation between the individual and his or her ethnicity as if people could have identities apart from their relationships. As seen in the discussion of HS and collectivistic thinking, a person's

---

[241] Romans applies "wisdom" language (σοφός, σοφία, φρόνιμος) 7 times, second only in Paul's writings to 1 Cor (24 times). Hence, this motif acts as a significant motif for contextualization within the letter. First Corinthians 1:12–31 deals heavily with division by speaking of "Jew and Greek," "wisdom," "shame," and "boasting."

[242] Seifrid, "Unrighteousness," 123. Emphasis in original

identity consists in how he or she is both different and alike compared to others. In essence, Seifrid simply illegitimates a person's having any sense of identity that uses an ethnic label. Furthermore, he seems to pose a strawman argument. He cites no one who actually says that Paul argues for salvation entirely based on ethnicity, as if all "Jews" and all "Greeks" are judged as two groups. A better explanation is this: Paul rebuts any collectivistic superiority, whether cultural or ethnic. The Jew does not necessarily believe he is saved *because* he is a Jew; rather, one must at least be a Jew in order to be saved.

Rom 3:27–5:11: Are We Justified in Boasting?

In Rom 3:28–30, Paul grounds his claim that no one can boast by a law of works, "For we hold that one is justified by faith apart from works of the law. Or is God the God of Jews only? Is he not the God of Gentiles also? Yes, of Gentiles also, since God is one—who will justify the circumcised by faith and the uncircumcised through faith." The disjunction set up between v. 28 and v. 29 is key: Either "one is justified by faith apart from works of the law" or else God is "God of the Jews only." By appealing to monotheism ("God is one," v. 30), Paul affirms the inclusion of Gentiles (v. 29b), which effectively negates the second half of Paul's disjunction. As a result, Paul upholds justification apart from works. Implicit to the argument is the fact that if justification is by works, then God shows himself to be God of the Jews only. Consequently, there is a definitive tie between "works of law" (3:28) and ethnicity. If "works of law" means simply good moral works (apart from Jewishness), then Rom 3:29 is a *non sequitur*. The unmistakable correlation is between "by works→God of Jews" or "apart-from-works→God of *both* Jews-and-Gentiles."[243] Dichotomizing ethnicity and acceptance

before God leads to mistaken conclusions like that of Hays, who says of this passage,

"The fundamental problem with which Paul is wrestling in Romans is *not* how a person

may find acceptance with God; the problem is to work out an understanding of the

relationship in Christ between Jews and Gentiles. This is the concern that surfaces clearly

in vv. 29–30." [244] Conceding that works primarily signify ethnicity does not remove the

vertical (God-person) orientation of justification since the problem is precisely that the

Jewish interlocutor absolutizes ethnicity with reference to God.

Gathercole argues in detail against an ethnic reading but ultimately fails to

account for the significance of the Jewish context *in particular* upon the meaning of

works.[245] Denying that Paul combats "Jewish exclusivism," Gathercole cites "very strong

evidence that the Jewish nation thought in terms of justification or vindication on the

basis of obedience to the Law."[246] His retort may work against certain forms of the NPP,

e.g., Sanders and Dunn. However, this reply does not undermine the present

interpretation that Jewish exclusivism remains a critical pre-condition for salvation since

---

[243] Without argument, Seifrid simply asserts, "Paul treats 'works' and 'circumcision' (with its obvious ethnic significance) as two distinct issues" in *Christ*, 68. On the other hand, Bird's suggestion is thorough and convincing: "A specific work in mind [in Rom 4:1–2] is probably circumcision since Paul appeals to Abraham's not-yet-circumcised-state in Gen. 15:6, the preceding reference in 3.27–31 pertains to boasting in Jewish identity which circumcision epitomized, circumcision was a sign of the Mosaic covenant (Gen 17.11; Acts 7.8; *Jub.* 12.26–28; *m. Ned.* 3.11), and reference to circumcision buttress the passage in 3:30 and 4.9–12. Furthermore, circumcision was regarded as the very means of entering Israel for Gentiles (Jdt. 14.10; Esth. 8:17; *m. Shab.* 19.3) and in several second-temple texts a necessary component for salvation (*Jub.* 15.25–34; CD 16.4–6; *T. Levi* 6.3; cf. Acts 15:11)." See Bird, *Saving Righteousness*, 73–74.

[244] My emphasis. Richard Hays, "'Have We Found Abraham to be our Forefather According to the Flesh': A Reconsideration of Rom 4:1," *NovT* 27, no. 1 (Jan 1985): 83–84. Quoted in Gathercole, *Boasting?*, 230.

[245] Simon Gathercole, "Justified by Faith, Justified by his Blood: The Evidence of Romans 3:21–4:5," in *The Paradoxes of Paul* (ed. D. A. Carson, Mark A. Seifrid, and Peter T. O'Brien; vol. 2 of *Justification and Variegated Nomism*; Grand Rapids, Mich.: Baker Academic, 2004), 152–61; Gathercole, *Where Is Boasting?*, 225–31.

[246] Gathercole, "Justified by Faith," 153–54.

the obedience under consideration is to a distinctly *Jewish* law given by the one true God. In that case, it is natural that some might absolutize the particular Jewish context. In addition, Gathercole says Rom 3:28–29 concerns works in general, adding "[Paul] does not criticize Israel for misunderstanding the Law as centered around specific works, or as centered around works misunderstanding in a nationalistic way."[247] However, Gathercole at best simply argues from silence. He seems to assume Paul's plea for "comprehensive, wholehearted obedience" does not address "boundary markers" like circumcision, which Paul in fact makes much of in the very next chapter.[248]

Gathercole suggests the ἤ in Rom 3:29 "does not necessarily form a logical progression" and that the verse "has the character of a *reductio ad absurdum.*"[249] However, he overlooks how the *reductio ad absurdum* argument works in this context, skipping from v. 28 to v. 30 by simply saying, "[T]he question in Rom 3:29 is not a serious point of inquiry."[250] In *reductio* arguments, one assumes an objector's point to demonstrate how it leads to an absurdity (e.g., a contradiction). In v. 29, Paul shows the absurdity of denying justification by faith. If affirming justification by works logically limits justification to the Jews, then God is "God of the Jews only." Works infer Jewishness (excluding Gentiles) because works signify that which separates Jews from Gentiles. Paul does not mean works in a general moral sense since that would not exclude the Gentiles, who could just as well presume upon their obedience. Gathercole's observation of a *reductio ad absurdum* actually confirms the point he wants to disprove. It is more precise to say Paul rebuts ethnocentrism, which entails obedience to God's

---

[247] Ibid., 154.
[248] Ibid., 155.
[249] Ibid.
[250] Ibid.

moral law. Gathercole's interpretation may be an overreaction when he says, "[T]he *content* of the doctrine of justification by faith should be distinguished from its *scope*."[251] In light of Rom 4:9–19 and Gal 3:7–14, where the focus is squarely on *who* can be Abraham's heir, it might be better to say the "scope" *is* the "content" of justification by faith. The doctrine of justification explains *who can be justified* by explaining how one is justified. "All nations" is the specific locus of the Abrahamic covenant. Faith simply explains how God undermines ethnic exclusivism and so keeps his promise.

The present interpretation is also supported by the observation that Gal 3:16 is functionally equivalent to Rom 3:28–30. Galatians 3 uses two premises to confirm that Gentiles are justified by faith not law. The first premise is that in Abraham, "all nations will be blessed [= justified]" (Gal 3:8; cf. Gal 3:14). Second, Gal 3:16 says, "the promises were made to Abraham to his offspring. It [is not] referring to many but referring to one." Somehow the appeal to "one" offspring shows how Gentles are justified/blessed yet without the Mosaic Law nullifying the Abrahamic promise.[252] In Rom 3:29–30, the Law does not limit the promise to one nation (i.e. Jews) since God is "one." This echoes the point that the promise is made to "one, who is Christ." Since God is one, making him God of both Jews and Gentiles, then justification is by faith not Jewish works. Likewise, since the offspring is one, making the offspring the only means of blessing for Jew and Gentile, justification must be by faith. This is because a justification via law would limit it to Jews, thus logically requiring both a Jewish and Gentile offspring. After all, a plurality of offspring is necessary to make possible "all nations" being blessed while still

---

[251] Ibid., 156. Emphasis in original

[252] The phrase "to give a human example" [κατὰ ἄνθρωπον λέγω] in v. 15 signals Paul's explaining the prior point (Gentiles justified/blessed, 3:8, 14). In v. 17, the phrase "this is what I mean" [τοῦτο δὲ λέγω] shows that v. 16 means to confirm the fact the Law did not void the promise, so restating v. 15.

claiming a justification by Law. Negatively, having one (Jewish) offspring makes it impossible for Gentiles to be blessed since there is no offspring for non-Jews (not having the Law). Hence, Rom 3:28–30 explains how, in Gal 3, the "one" offspring argument defends justification by faith. Further, the stress on singularity (i.e. the "one" offspring) confirms the Law does not nullify the promise.

More broadly, the arguments of Rom 3–4 and Gal 3 run parallel. Romans 4 stresses that the "promise" does not nullify the Law (Rom 3:31; 4:16) in order to defend Gentile inclusion via faith. On the other hand, Gal 3 asserts that the Law does not void the promise in order to affirm Gentile inclusion by faith. In both texts, Paul's appeal to singularity is decisive (i.e. one God and offspring). In Romans, justification by ethnicity is denied via an appeal to monotheism. In Galatians, it is denied via an Abrahamic Christology—the one offspring, who is Christ. In either text, Paul could have said, "For there is one God, and there is one mediator between God and men, the man Christ Jesus" (1 Tim 2:5). Paul's logic is the same in Rom 3:28–30 as in Gal 3:16. Paul, in both Gal 3:17 and Rom 3, has in mind works of the Mosaic Law.

The "one" God/offspring arguments in Rom 3/Gal 4 make evident that fact that Paul is concerned with the scope of justification. Because of "one," therefore "all nations" can be justified. The scope determines the means. Therefore, justification is by faith not by Law, since Law limits justification to Jews. This is Paul's logic: Justification is by faith because God's promise is for all nations. It is not by works because God's promise is not restricted to the Jews. Paul's argument fundamentally appeals to ethnicity.

What is implied by saying that Paul opposes ethnocentrism? Paul's opponents are not arguing, "If a Jew, therefore justified." Instead, they claim, "If justified, thus a Jew."

Paul is less focused on ethics than some suggest. This does not imply a purely social and non-soteriological doctrine. The Law assumed both sin and the need for atonement.

Romans 4 expands on the comments of Rom 3:27–30 and defends the claim that Paul is not "overthrow[ing] the law by this faith" (v. 30). A lengthier explanation as to how "we uphold the law" will wait until Rom 10:3–10. Romans 4:1–8 builds on Rom 3:27–28. Abraham and David (Rom 4:1–8) represent respectively the Gentile and the Jew, each in their own way "apart" from the law.[253] Not surprisingly, the strong ethnic emphasis of Rom 3:29–30a is clear in Rom 4:9–12 (cf. Rom 4:14, 16). Just as God is God of both Jews and Gentiles, likewise Abraham is father to the "circumcised" and "uncircumcised."[254] The question of Rom 4:9 is strikingly similar to Rom 3:29. Romans 4:9–12 (as with Rom 3:29) is supported on *theological* grounds in Rom 4:13ff [note γὰρ

---

[253] In the language of Rom 3:28, they represent those whom God justifies, "the uncircumcised through faith" and "the circumcised by faith."

[254] Hodge also notes that Gal 2:7–9 uses "circumcision" and "uncircumcision" language to refer to Jews and Gentiles respectively. See Hodge, *If Sons*, 59, 62.

in v. 13]. Romans 4:23–25 picks up on Rom 3:30b yet now with overtones from 3:23–26. Romans 4:1–8 and Rom 4:23–25 form an inclusio akin to Rom 3:27–28 and Rom 3:30b.

The wording in Rom 4 unmistakably confirms the interpretation that Paul speaks of ethnicity. The key verse is found in Rom 4:16, "That is why it depends on faith, in order that the promise may rest on grace and be guaranteed to all his offspring—*not only* to the adherent of the law but also to the one who shares the faith of Abraham, who is the father of us all." The "not only . . . but also" [μόνον ἀλλὰ καὶ] seems to suggest the "adherent of the law" can be righteous or saved in some sense distinguished from "to the one who shares the faith of Abraham." While the distinction is not absolute, since all must have faith, Paul plainly differentiates the Jew from the Gentile. In doing this, he uses law-language [οὐ τῷ ἐκ τοῦ νόμου μόνον]. To read "law" as simply or primarily a moral principle seems to create a way of salvation via works of law. The "Jewishness" implied by this descriptor (i.e. "law") seems blatantly in the foreground. Therefore, it does not work simply to put the relationship between law and Jewishness in the background, treating it as a secondary issue. Romans 4:16 clarifies Rom 4:14, which says, "For if it is the adherents of the law who are to be heirs, faith is null and the promise is void."[255] Paul's meaning in v. 14 is "if it is [*only*] the adherents."[256]

The argument of Rom 3:27–4:25 reiterates one of Paul's key points: in justification, God's own glory is as stake. So far, Paul has often spoken of God's glory in terms of righteousness (Rom 1:17; 3:3–7; 3:21–26). Even if one interprets God's righteousness elsewhere to mean his judgment, here Paul's sequence of thought makes

---

[255] In Greek: εἰ γὰρ οἱ ἐκ νόμου κληρονόμοι, κεκένωται ἡ πίστις καὶ κατήργηται ἡ ἐπαγγελία.
[256] Cf. similar constructions in related texts like Rom 10:4; Phil 3:9.

273

clear God's honor is wrapped up in the *salvation* of the world—Jews and Gentiles. The

God of creation of Rom 3:29–30 is the God of covenant in Rom 4:9–25. He "who gives

life from the dead and calls into existence the things that do not exist" fulfilled his

promise to Abraham, who "was as good as dead," by raising Jesus from the dead (Rom

4:17, 19, 24). Further, Abraham, in Rom 4, "*reverses* the Gentile folly, and God's

judgment upon it, as set out in 1.18–25."[257] Adams then concludes,

> In glorifying God, Abraham renders to God the very response which,
> according to 1.21, he is due as creator. Abrahamic faith it is implied, is, at
> its most basic, creaturely submission to the creator. To give glory to God
> is to fulfill the goal which God had in view in creating humanity (cf. Rom.
> 3.23). Abrahamic faith, justifying faith, realizes that goal.[258]

The chapter does more than defend justification by faith by way of a proof text of

Abraham's faith. Rather, *Paul poignantly shows that the Abrahamic covenant inherently*

nullifies boasting because Israel's God is the Creator who righteously keeps his covenant

promises as the means by which he will reign over the whole world. Justification depends

on faith *in order that* Gentiles can receive the promise by grace, not only Abraham's

descendents according to the flesh. Once again, Paul's theological point seeks to alleviate

distorted ethnic distinctions. In this particular passage, the reference to law demarcates

ethnicity. As Rom 4:14, 17 suggest, God's promise is at stake since he promised

Abraham "all nations," not simply one, namely Israel. At the heart of the Abrahamic

covenant is the justification of Gentiles (cf. Gal 3:8). Ethnicity plays a central role in

Paul's gospel. Paul particularly aims to nullify the *Jewish* boast, regardless of how one

---

[257] See Edward Adams, "Abraham's Faith and Gentile Disobedience: Textual Links Between Romans 1 and 4," *JSNT*, no. 65 (1997): 63. Emphasis in original.

[258] Ibid., 65. In a footnote, he rightly adds "That the Gentiles might glorify God for his mercy is stated in Romans 15.8–9 as the goal of Christ's mission (cf. 15.6)."

defines "works." The works-faith discussion serves the larger purpose of showing the righteousness of God manifest in the universal reign of Israel's resurrected king (cf. Rom 1:4; 4:25; 15:12).[259] Doing "works of law" drove Israel inward (ethnocentrism) instead of upward (to God) and outward (to Gentiles). This is bigger than mere moralism.

Genesis 15 is the explicit background of Rom 4. The verbal link between Gen 15:1 and Rom 4:4 reinforces the interpretation that Paul's bigger argument is how Abraham will gain an heir.[260] It is via God's promise (Rom 4:16; cf. Rom 9:6–13), which corresponds with human faith. It is important to distinguish main ideas from supporting ideas. Paul's main issue is theological—how God demonstrates his glorify by keeping his covenant promises to Abraham so as to reign over the world. The *corollary* is that human justification is by faith not by works, since at the heart of the Abrahamic covenant is "scope," that is, God's blessing "all nations." If God restricts justification to Israel, God is partial (Rom 2:11), only the God of Israel (Rom 3:30), and unfaithful to his promise (Rom 4:13–22). Historically, interpreters tend to miss or underemphasize the core of Paul's message as a corollary (albeit an important one). God justifies himself (cf. Rom 1:17; 3:25–26; 9:14ff). Pursuing righteousness by works rejects the Abrahamic covenant even if superficially upholding the Mosaic Covenant. Justification by works restricts God's blessing to one nation, not all (cf. Gal 3:14–18). Precisely because God's righteousness is at stake in Romans, Paul primarily focuses on nations, not individuals.

In exegeting Romans, one can unwittingly get pulled into the same sort of thinking as Paul's Jewish interlocutor. Emphasizing the individual may miss the big

---

[259] Wright points to echoes in Rom 15:12 to Rom 1:4 in Wright, *Romans*, 748.
[260] Wright, "Justification: Yesterday," 59.

picture (of which individual justification is just a part). The Jewish interlocutor's most basic categories are Jew and Gentile. One may similarly "stumble" (Rom 9:32–33) if the cornerstone of his or her theology is the individual rather than the group.

Faith in Christ should be understood as boasting to Christ. Hence, one's HS is inextricably wrapped up in Christ's own HS. Although people now share in his suffering and death (cf. Rom 6:3–4; 8:17), ultimately they will not be put to shame (Rom 9:33; 10:11, 13). The stress upon faith over works is simply another way of talking about the more fundamental issue of boasting. Rather than boasting in human distinctives (Rom 2:17, 23; 3:27; 4:2), the gospel commands one to "[boast] in God through our Lord Jesus Christ" (Rom 5:11).[261] In effect, Abraham's faith glorified God (Rom 4:20–21) because he "[boasted] in the hope of the glory of God . . . and hope does not put us to shame" (Rom 5:2–3). Boasting expresses one's HS perspective and thus sense of identity.[262]

Having Abraham's faith entails believing what he believed, namely, God will bless all nations through Abraham's offspring. The content of faith is not that God saves people by faith. Rather, the one true God will keep his promise to reign over the entire world and not simply one particular people or tract of land. Note the distinction between the promise (being heir to the world) and the response (faith) in Rom 4:13. The point is reinforced in Rom 4:17–18, citing Gen 17:5 and 15:5. The content is first of all a statement about who God is. Second, this gospel message (Gal 3:8) inherently

---

[261] In Rom 5.2, 3, and 11, the ESV uses "rejoice," however, the Greek is καυχάομαι, which is typically translated "boast" elsewhere, such as in Rom 2:17, 23. Also, for an in depth discussion on boasting in Romans 1–5, see Gathercole, *Boasting?*.

[262] Though I have serious concerns about Yeo's overall view of justification, he correctly points out that the Christian has "been set right by God from shame and curse so that now propriety, honor, and freedom characterizes the new and rightful relationship one has with God." See his work, *Musing*, 207. In almost identical terms, cf. Yeo, "Introduction: Navigating Romans," 14. However, here he says the δικαι-root emphasizes God's acting for a "group of people."

necessitates forsaking the primacy of ethnic identity. The gospel directly challenges ethnocentrism; it is no mere corollary or application.

Romans 5:12–6:23: Reconciling Righteousness and Human Shame

Although Rom 5–6 move away from Jew-Gentile language, instead speaking either of those "in Adam" or "in Christ," Rom 5:13–14 is a key exception. Paul says, ". . . sin indeed was in the world *before* the law was given, but sin is not counted where there is no law. Yet death reigned from Adam to Moses, even over those whose sinning was not like the transgression of Adam, who was a type of the one who was to come." These verses strongly confirm the previous interpretation that "law" refers to the Mosaic Law not a universalized ethical norm. Schreiner represents the latter view, "Paul's basic argument is this: (1) One must obey the law perfectly to be saved. (2) No one obeys the law perfectly. (3) Therefore, no one can be saved by works of the law."[263] However, Rom 5 makes that reading impossible since the law cannot make people perfect, *even in a theoretical sense*. A simple example demonstrates the incoherence of saying one could be saved by perfectly keeping the law (as Paul uses the word, i.e. *Law*). Suppose the Israelites, upon receiving the Law, perfectly obeyed it, never again sinning either in spirit or letter of the law. Yet, even then they could not be saved because they were *already* sinners. Sin is sin even when there was no Law. The word "law" in Rom 5:13 cannot take a more generalized meaning. Perfect obedience to the Law would not make any Israelite perfect since sin was in the world "from Adam to Moses." The problem here is at an analytical level. By analogy, consider the following sentence: A "woman" cannot become a "son."

---

[263] Thomas Schreiner, "Paul and Perfect Obedience to the Law: An Evaluation of the View of E. P. Sanders," *WTJ* 47, no. 2 (Fall 1985): 278.

Why? The impossibility lies in the very meaning of the words, not merely in whether one has the moral ability. In exegesis, one must distinguish between Paul's use of the specific word "law" and God's commands in a general sense, such as that given to Adam "*before the [Mosaic] law was given*" (Rom 5:13). In short, Paul conceives of the "law" within the context of Jewish collectivism not as universal moral decrees given to all humanity.

The major concern of Rom 5:12–6:23 is identity. Does one identify with Adam or Christ? This dictates whether one is a slave to sin or to righteousness (i.e. to God; cf. Rom 6:22). Paul's reminder is humbling: All people are slaves. The question is "a slave of *who*?"[264] Sin is a human problem, not a Jew-Gentiles issue. In Rom 3:27–5:11, Paul humbles the Jew by showing that honor is found surprisingly in being counted as one among many nations. It is therefore a bit ironic in Rom 5:12–6:21 that one should be ashamed for acting human (Rom 6:21). Paul's sermons in Acts (14:15–17; 17:22–31) exemplify a similar appeal to the one true God who unites humans without respect to ethnic membership. Paul's shift to royal language (Rom 5:14, 17, 21; 6:12) comes with his more direct discussion of Christ in Rom 5:12ff and builds on the gospel announcement that opens the letter (Rom 1:1–4). Identity derives from one's allegiance (i.e. faith), the king with whom one identifies. Christ is more than a mere judge in a juridical sense; he is a king that executes righteousness. He reclaims his kingdom from Adam's followers, setting slaves free from their shameful state.

Honor-Shame as both Problem and Solution in Romans

The book of Romans addresses three main HS problems. Missiologically, Paul

---

[264] Note Wright's reading on Rom 6:1–4 in Wright, *Romans*, 533–41.

undermines any sense of cultural superiority within the Roman church whose contrast between Greek and barbarian hinders their willingness both to be reconciled with Jews and to assist Paul in his mission to Spain. Anthropologically, Paul redefines HS in terms of Christ, relativizing every human distinctive and reversing soteriological expectations. Theologically, God is vindicated from any charge of unrighteousness to the end that all nations marvel at his grace and wisdom.

Practical implications extend to every part of human society. Competiveness and exclusion become normal means of face grabbing. In such disorder, God is disregarded and so dishonored. God alone is the measure of HS. By dividing the world into "us" or "them," one loses perspective of the one true God. Politically, people become disoriented for failure of recognizing the kingship of Christ (cf. Rom 1:2–4; 13:1–8). Socially, confusing HS leads to idolatry and exploiting one another for selfish gain (Rom 1:22–31). Ecclesiologically, factions cut across ethnic lines (cf. Rom 11). Churches split over preferred traditions and convictions about secondary issues (cf. Rom 14). The Jew-Gentile problem can take new forms in churches, such as when one particular spiritual gift, ministry, or position is prioritized over all others (Rom 12:3–8). Christians compete but not to order to "outdo one another in showing honour" (Rom 12:10). Missiologically, people may become "ashamed of the gospel" (Rom 1:16) and be less than eager to share spiritual and material blessings (cf. Rom 15:27).

A parallel idea to "justified by faith" is "honored through shame." Jesus' shameful death demonstrates God's righteous glory (Rom 3:24–26; cf. Heb 2:10–13; 11:1–2). Though Paul often suffered dishonor (cf. Rom 3:8; 2 Cor 6:8), he was not ashamed of the gospel because he knew all who believe the gospel are not put to shame

(Rom 1:16; 10:11). God overturns human boasting. Conversion moves one from the shame of sin through the shame of death by the glory of God unto glorification. The believer is likened to Jesus, "[who] was raised from the dead by the glory of the Father." The believer is ashamed of his old way (Rom 6:21). God's children are ". . . heirs of God and fellow heirs with Christ, provided we suffer with him in order that we may also be glorified with him. For I consider that the sufferings of this present time are not worth comparing with the glory that is to be revealed to us" (Rom 8:17–18). Yet, God freely uses his creation for "honorable [or] dishonorable use . . . in order to make known the riches of his glory for vessels of mercy, which he has prepared beforehand for glory" (Rom 9:21–23). In short, Paul constantly works towards the upheaval of conventional ways of thinking of HS. This is gospel ministry.

A Systematic Approach: What is the Relationship between Righteousness and Honor? Theologically, what is the relationship between righteousness and HS? The conclusions of this section arise from three premises. First, God's righteousness consists in his glorifying himself. If he did not uphold his own glory, then he would not be righteous. God's glory is the measure of righteousness. Second, because God is righteous, he justifies people. Third, inasmuch as humans are justified and found righteous, people have true honor before God. Therefore, human honor consists in and thus depends on God's own glory. This has many implications. First, people have honor only inasmuch as glorify God. Second, there is no human honor except that which derives from and is thus shared with God. Third, if God is not glorified, then neither is humanity.

"Righteousness" Consists in the Glory of God

"Righteousness," theologically speaking, is defined in relationship to God. It is foremost about God's glory-honor. The essence of rightness is glorifying God. Piper extensively shows this relationship.[265] Even if Piper's explanation is incomplete, the parallels remain clear because "God's glory, like his righteousness," manifests both in his vindication over the world and in salvation.[266] Regardless of particular details, one can still agree that Paul defends God's righteousness in terms of God's desire "to make known the riches of his glory" (Rom 9:14–23). In Rom 3:4–7, the succession of "justified," "righteous," and "glory" indicate semantic equivalence. Some pray for God to act in righteousness "for your own sake," overcoming shame (Dan 9:7–19; cf. Ps 31:1–3). Psalm 143:11 pleads, *"For your name's sake*, O LORD, preserve my life! *In your righteousness* bring my soul out of trouble!" Piper concludes that most fundamental to God's righteousness is "[his] unwavering commitment to preserve the honor of his name and display his glory."[267] In any circumstance or relationship, God's own righteousness is understood only in relation to his own glory. Even while emphasizing the forensic metaphors in Romans, du Toit locates the crux of sin and guilt in terms of God's own honor.[268] Specifically, humans are "unrighteousness" because "they did not honor him as God" (Rom 1:21).

God avenges sin by shaming humans thus vindicating his honor. God always defends his name. Someone may think that God sounds egotistical. If a man exalts himself, he is proud and sins because people do not have infinite value. However, God is

---

[265] Piper, *The Justification of God*.
[266] Seifrid, *Christ*, 45.
[267] Piper, *The Justification of God*, 119.
[268] du Toit, "Forensic Metaphors in Romans and Their Soteriological Significance," 70, 73.

perfectly magnificent. The Creator has perfect love, justice, patience, and power. If he does not honor himself above all else, he would give such honor to creation. This is wrong. Created things lack God's inherent worth (cf. Heb 3:3). If he most honors people, he lies. This is idolatry.[269] Other passages illustrate the point.[270] In Isa 59:18–19, God says, "According to their deeds, so will he repay, wrath to his adversaries, repayment to his enemies; to the coastlands he will render repayment. So they shall fear the name of the LORD from the west, and his glory from the rising of the sun; for he will come like a rushing stream, which the wind of the LORD drives." Likewise, Ps 149:5–9 warns,

> Let the godly exult in glory; let them sing for joy on their beds. Let the high praises of God be in their throats and two-edged swords in their hands, to execute vengeance on the nations and punishments on the peoples, to bind their kings with chains and their nobles with fetters of iron, to execute on them the judgment written! This is honor for all his godly ones. Praise the LORD!

The saints in fact rejoice in God's self-vindication.

Likewise, human righteousness necessarily gives glory to God. Abraham is justified by his justifying God, which consists in his believing God's promises.[271] The righteous are those who love and magnify God's name (Ps 5:11). God "leads [us] in paths of righteousness for his name's sake" (Ps 23:3). Pursing righteousness is equivalent to

---

[269] A fuller defense of this thinking is given by John Piper, "Why God Is Not a Megalomaniac in Demanding to Be Worshiped" (presented at the Evangelical Theological Society (ETS) Annual Meeting, Providence, Rhode Island, 20 Nov 2008), n.p. [cited 3 Jan 2012]. Online: http://www.desiringgod. org/resource-library/conference-messages/why-god-is-not-a-megalomaniac-in-demanding-to-be-worshiped; John Piper, "Is God for Us or for Himself?," *Desiring God*, 10 Aug 1980, n.p. [cited 3 Jan 2012]. Online: http://www.desiringgod.org/resource-library/sermons/is-god-for-us-or-for-himself; John Piper, "How Is God's Passion for His Own Glory Not Selfishness?," *Desiring God*, 24 Nov 2007, n.p. [cited 3 Jan 2012]. Online: http://www.desiringgod.org/resource-library/articles/how-is-gods-passion-for-his-own-glory-not-selfishness.

[270] Deuteronomy 32:35–36; Job 40:10–11; Ps 149:5–9; Isa 59:9–19 (esp. v. 18–19); 66:5–6; Jer 5:9, 29; 9:9; Ezek 38:16–18; Rom 9:22–23; Rev 15:1–8; 19:1–2. Also, compare Rom 12:19, 1 Thess 4:6. In Exod 34:5–7, God's glory or name is found in his punishing iniquity (v. 7b).

[271] Seifrid, *Christ*, 68–69. Elsewhere, he cites Rom 4:22 in his "Paul's Use of Righteousness," 60.

seeking the Lord (Isa 51:1). In Malachi, the righteous one honors God by serving him (Mal 1:6; 2:2; 3:16–18). Negatively, unrighteousness amounts to not honoring God (Rom 1:18, 21–28). According to 1 Pet 4:11–19, the righteous person is not to be ashamed for suffering as a Christian, but "in order that in everything God may be glorified through Jesus Christ." All that is truly righteous brings honor to God.

That justification centers on God's glory is confirmed by the way righteousness reorients boasting. Boasting has an important role within early Judaism and more broadly HS communities.[272] Watson notes, "Paul's boasting reorients the value system of his congregations."[273] John 7:18 clearly defines (un)righteousness in terms of glory: "The one who speaks on his own authority seeks his own glory [δόξαν]; but the one who seeks the glory [δόξαν] of him who sent him is true, and in him there is no falsehood [ἀδικία]."[274] The Gospels describe some Pharisees as "those who justify [οἱ δικαιοῦντες] yourselves before men" (Luke 16:15), contra to fact.[275] "Overthrowing social claims to honor, status, and wealth is key to" a disciple's righteousness.[276] Luther sees a relationship between righteousness, glory, and boasting in Rom 3:23,

> So the meaning is: They do not have a righteousness of which they can glory before God, as we read in 1 Cor. 1:29: "So that no human being might boast in the presence of God." And earlier we read (Rom. 2:17): "You boast of your relationship of God." Later, in chapter 5:11: "We rejoice in God through Jesus Christ." Therefore "They fall short of the glory of God," that is, they do not have anything of which they can glory in God and about God, as Ps. 3:3 says: "But Thou, O Lord, art a shield

---

[272] Again, see Gathercole, *Boasting?*. No matter whether boasting expresses superiority or confidence, boasting is public and HS oriented. On Romans' frequent use of "καύχησις ('boasting,' that is, 'claiming honor') (2.17, 23; 3.27; 4.2; 5.2, 3, 11; 15.17)," see Bryan, *A Preface to Romans*, 74.

[273] Bryan, *A Preface to Romans*, 74.

[274] The ESV obscures the meaning by translating "falsehood," not "unrighteousness." Other versions (NASB, HCSB) take the interpretive liberty of capitalizing the final pronoun "Him" despite the fact it follows the ascription "ἀληθής," speaking of "the one who seeks the glory of him who sent him."

[275] Note the use of δεδικαιωμένος in Luke 18:14. Cf. Mark 12:38–40; Luke 20:46–47.

[276] Pheme Perkins, "Justice, NT [δικαιοσύνη]," *NIDB* 3:475.

283

about me, my glory," that is, my glorying. So also below (Rom. 4:2): "If Abraham was justified by works, he has something to boast about, but not before God." Thus also they have a glory before men because of their works of righteousness. "Glory of God" is used in the same way as righteousness, wisdom, and virtue, that is, something which is given to us by God and because of which we can before Him glory in Him and about Him.[277]

In Rom 3:26–27, Paul immediately applies the doctrine of justification, "Then what becomes of our boasting? It is excluded." As previously observed, HS is at the root of the Galatians' errant view of justification (cf. Gal 4:17–18).[278]

Christian righteousness stems from boasting in Jesus. Paul's righteousness stems from his being among those who "glory [καυχώμενοι] in Christ Jesus and put no confidence in the flesh" (Phil 3:3). The justified are those who boast only in the cross (Gal 6:12–14). In fact, God's whole scheme of salvation is "so that no one may boast" (Eph 2:9; cf. 1 Cor 1:26–31). Paul defends his ministry of "righteousness" by boasting in his weaknesses (2 Cor 3:9; 11:15; 12:5–10). One reason boasting is so important is because the Father honors those who honor the Son (John 5:22–24; 12:23–28). Seifrid adds, "By virtue of Christ, its object, this faith is nothing other than the 'boasting' in the 'hope of the glory of God' (5:1–2), a glory which entails the resurrection from the dead (cf. 6:4; 8:17, 21, 30)."[279] Faith then is essentially boasting in Christ.[280]

The OT likewise conceives of faith. In Ps 44:6–8, trust is confirmed in continual boasting in God [ἐν τῷ θεῷ ἐπαινεσθησόμεθα], resulting in salvation, not being put to

---

[277] Luther, *Works*, 25:218.

[278] Numerous texts illustrate the connect righteousness with what one honors. See 1 Sam 2:29–30; Dan 5:18–23; Rom 4:2–3 (via contrast); Heb 1:9 (cf. 1:3, 13); Jas 3:5–6; 1 Pet 3:12–15.

[279] Seifrid, *Christ*, 69–70.

[280] Piper observes in 2 Cor 1:24 and Phil 1:25, "joy and faith are almost interchangeable." See John Piper, "Savoring, Instilling, and Spreading the Vision at Bethlehem Baptist Church," *Desiring God*, 20 Sept 1987, n.p. [cited 9 Jun 2012]. Online: http://www.desiringgod.org/ resource-library/sermons /savoring-instilling-and-spreading-the-vision-at-bethlehem-baptist-church. Luther, *Works*, 25:248.

shame. Israel was reminded, "He is your praise [καύχημά, i.e. boast]. He is your God,"
(Deut 10:21). What does God rejoice in? The Lord says in Jer 9:23–24, "[L]et him who
boasts boast in this, that he understands and knows me, that I am the LORD who
practices steadfast love, justice, and righteousness in the earth. For in these things I
delight, declares the LORD." God rejoices in those he makes righteous, taking away their
shame and dishonor (Isa 61:3–62:5).[281] Conversely, "Then they shall be dismayed and
ashamed because of Cush their hope and of Egypt their boast [δόξα]" (Isa 20:5).

Because God is Righteous, People Are Regarded as Righteous

Second, human righteousness is based on God's being righteous. Galatians 3:8 is a case-
in-point: "And the Scripture, foreseeing that God would justify the Gentiles by faith,
preached the gospel beforehand to Abraham, saying, 'In you shall all the nations be
blessed.'" If God does not keep his promise, he is not righteous. If God is not righteous,
no one is righteous. God's δικαιοσύνη is seen in his faithfulness to Israel,

> . . . vindicating her cause . . . acting, in other words, as Israel's faithful
> benefactor. In an honor-shame society such faithfulness is, needless to say,
> bound up also with honor, and the distinction between *iustitia salutifera*
> and action for the vindication of one's name would not, perhaps, be
> readily apparent.[282]

Referencing Isaiah, Oswalt summarizes, "In 40–55, the term [righteousness] is almost as
[*sic*] exclusively used to describe God's character as deliverer (46:13, 51:5). It is an
expression of God's rightness that he will not leave his covenant partner to suffer shame
and disgrace."[283] Therefore, one can understand the prayer in Ps 143. Precisely because

---

[281] For divine rejoicing in the NT, see Matt 11:25–27; Luke 10:17–22.
[282] Bryan, *A Preface to Romans*, 69–70.
[283] J. Oswalt, "Isaiah 60–62: The Glory of the Lord," *CTJ* 40 (2005): 97.

"no one living is righteous before you" (Ps 143:2), the psalmist actually appeals to God's own righteousness (Ps 143:1, 11). If people are to glorify God, then he must save them for his name's sake (Ps 143:11). The psalmist prays for God's righteousness (Ps 35:24) unto "salvation" (יְשׁוּעָה; Ps 35:3, 9; cf. v. 10, 17).

In the NT, justification results from God's righteousness in Christ. In Rom 5:18–19, Paul says, "one act of righteousness leads to justification and life for all men"; through Christ, "the many will be made righteous." The logic of Rom 3:23–26 is subtle. Piper calls Rom 3:25–26 the "ground of justification."[284] Romans 3:26 explains Christ's death, "It was to show his righteousness at the present time, so that he might be just and the justifier of the one who has faith in Jesus." Two points are noteworthy. First, the phrase "so that he might be just" [εἰς τὸ εἶναι αὐτὸν δίκαιον] speaks to more than demonstrating or doing righteousness. One cannot separate who God is from what he does. Second, the word ἔνδειξιν ["to show" in vv. 25, 26] and its related words all have a public connotation, vindicating, or proving something to be true.[285] Tying these two points together, the public *demonstration* of God's righteousness constitutes his claim to *being* righteous. Therefore, God is honored in believers' justification.

Human Righteousness Results in Honor not Shame before God

The righteous are exalted in honor (Ps 112:9). His "soul makes its boast in the LORD," therefore "their faces shall never be ashamed." (Ps 34:2, 5; cf. Ps 34:15, 17, 19, 21). Righteousness, salvation, and shame converge in Ps 132:9, 16, 18: "Let your priests be

---

[284] Piper, *The Justification of God*, 140.
[285] Louw and Nida, "ἔνδειξις," *L&N*.

clothed with righteousness, and let your saints shout for joy. . . . Her priests I will clothe with salvation, and her saints will shout for joy. . . . His enemies I will clothe with shame, but on him his crown will shine." Habakkuk 2:4, a critical text for the doctrine of justification, is situated in a HS context. In Hab 1:4, one sees the problem: "So the law is paralyzed, and justice never goes forth. For the wicked surround the righteous [הצדיק־את]; so justice goes forth perverted." Thus, what does it mean the righteous will live by faith in Hab 2:4? First, the righteous man in v. 4b is contrasted with the one whose "soul is puffed up; it is not upright within him" (v. 4a). The unrighteous man claims too much honor for himself. Second, God's eradication of unrighteousness is explained, "For the earth will be filled with the knowledge of the glory of the LORD as the waters cover the sea" (Hab 2:14). Third, judgment is given, "You will have your fill of shame instead of glory. Drink, yourself, and show your uncircumcision! The cup in the LORD's right hand will come around to you, and utter shame will come upon your glory!" (Hab 2:16).[286] At the cross, Jesus is honored and God is glorified [ἐδόξαζεν] when the centurion confesses, "Certainly this man was innocent [δίκαιος]!" (Luke 23:47). More significant is 1 Tim 3:16 where Jesus himself is "justified in the Spirit" (CHSB).[287] The verse situates Jesus' vindication between his life and ascension, pointing to his resurrection.[288] In Rom 1:4, by the Spirit, Jesus "was declared to be the Son of God in power." The resurrection publicly authenticates Jesus' identity. God himself glorified Jesus though Jesus suffered disgrace by shameful men. Jesus was "raised for our justification" (Rom 4:25). Using 1 Cor

---

[286] Cf. Ps 69:6–7, 19, 27; 84:11; Ezek 6–7, 15–38.

[287] In Greek: ἐδικαιώθη ἐν πνεύματι. ESV uses "vindicated."

[288] Notice the stress in Acts upon God's raising Jesus in the face of Jewish/Roman rejection, i.e. God's vindication of Jesus. Cf. Acts 2:23–24, 31–32; 3:15; 4:10; 10:39–40.

15:17–18, one interprets Rom 4:25 to mean God justifies people because he has justified Christ.[289] Jesus' own justification leads not only to his own royal honor (Rom 1:4), but also human honor for all who identify with him.[290]

Shame is a consequence of unrighteousness. Proverbs is succinct, "Whoever pursues righteousness and kindness will find life, righteousness, and honor" (Prov 21:21); similarly, "The righteous hates falsehood, but the wicked brings shame and disgrace" (Prov 13:5). The principle applies to God's own actions, as in Isa 41:10–11, ". . . I will uphold you with my righteous right hand. Behold, all who are incensed against you shall be put to shame and confounded." By inference, God condemns unrighteousness, which is (explicitly) due to idolatry (Isa 41:7). After all, "how should my name be profaned? My glory I will not give to another" (Isa 48:11). Regarding those who do not delight in God's righteousness, the psalmist pleads, "Let them be put to shame and disappointed altogether who rejoice at my calamity! Let them be clothed with shame and dishonor who magnify themselves against me!"(Ps 35:26; cf. Ps 35:27). Jeremiah customarily equates judgment and shame.[291] Jeremiah castigates the unrighteous:

> But the LORD is with me as a dread warrior; therefore my persecutors will stumble; they will not overcome me. They will be greatly shamed, for they will not succeed. Their eternal dishonor will never be forgotten. O LORD of hosts, who tests the righteous, who sees the heart and the mind, let me see your vengeance upon them, for to you have I committed my cause (Jer 20:11–12).

---

[289] Wright, *Romans*, 503–4.

[290] There might be a similar connection in Rom 8:30, where scholars have constantly struggled to explain the aorist tense of "gloried" [ἐδόξασεν], typically denoting past action. In keeping with John 17:22, for example, it may be possible that Rom 8:30 does indeed speak to some sense in which the Christian has already been glorified, though not in whole (even as one is already sanctified, 1 Cor 1:2; 6:11; Heb 10:10).

[291] For example, Jer 2:35–36, 3:25; 20:11–12, 18; 48:20–21.

Ezekiel 16 also deals with Israel's unrighteousness (Ezek 16:51–52) in light of her "shame," "disgrace," and "reproach" (Ezek 16:52, 54, 57, 63). Yet, God will "atone for" [בכפרי־לך] her shame (Ezek 16:63).[292]

God's justification of his people means they will not be put to shame. In Rom 9:30–10:13, Paul explicitly and implicitly uses HS to describe justification. Paul quotes Isa 49:23 in Rom 9:33 and 10:11, "Everyone who believes in him will not be put to shame." Often unnoticed is Rom 10:13, "everyone who calls on the name of the Lord will be saved," citing Joel 2:32. In context, what are they saved from? Joel 2:26–27 says they are saved from shame: "And my people shall never again be put to shame."[293] Romans 8:33 and maybe Rom 1:16–17 draw from Isa 50:7–8.[294] Isaiah brings together a nexus of themes in Isa 50:6–7, "I hid not my face from disgrace and spitting. But the Lord GOD helps me; therefore I have not been disgraced; therefore I have set my face like a flint, and I know that I shall not be put to shame." Why this confidence? Because "He who vindicates me [ὁ δικαιώσας με] is near," one has faith (Isa 50:8, 10). The flow of logic in Rom 3:23–26 indicates justification solves the problem of people's lacking God's glory.[295] When comparing Adam and Christ, Paul uses HS language in 1 Cor 15:40–49 comparable to Rom 5's use of "righteousness." His reasoning is similar and grounded on

---

[292] Margaret Odell's exegesis shows the interplay of HS within the passage. The expected order of forgiveness and shame in Ezek 16:63 are inversed. The reason is that Israel was put to shame precisely by God's forgiveness since Israel had questioned God's faithfulness. Thus, in questioning God's honor, they are ashamed before him, while also restored (honored) before the nations. See Hamilton Jr., *God's Glory*.

[293] Peter's use of Joel 2:28–31 at Pentecost further reinforces the importance of the passage.

[294] For Rom 8:33, see Schreiner, *Romans*, 462. For Rom 1:16, see his work, *Romans*, 462.

[295] Mark Seifrid, "Romans," in *Commentary on the New Testament Use of the Old Testament* (ed. G. K. Beale and D. A. Carson; Grand Rapids, Mich.: Baker, 2007), 635–6.

the resurrection. "In Adam" one inherits unrighteousness, death and dishonor; "in Christ,"

righteousness, life, and honor (cf. 1 Cor 15:22).

"God's righteous judgment" depends on whether or not people "in well-doing

seek for glory and honor and immortality" (Rom 2:5–7). Otherwise, they are

"unrighteous" (Rom 2:8). Romans 2:9–10 lists two possible results, "tribulation and

distress" or "glory and honor and peace for everyone who does good." However, the

person in v. 10 is then justified in v. 13. He gains glory, honor and peace. Verse 7 also

helps one understand the law. Why? In Rom 3:10, Paul says no one is righteous. Yet,

Rom 2:13 claims, "[T]he doers of the law who will be justified." Romans 2:7 offers

clarification.[296] The lone Greek verb in v. 7 is "seek" [ζητοῦσιν], not "well-doing" [ἔργου

ἀγαθοῦ, or "good works"]. Works are seen as a *means* to honor and glory. Paul says in

Rom 2:29, "But a Jew is one inwardly, and circumcision is a matter of the heart, by the

Spirit, not by the letter. His praise [ἔπαινος] is not from man but from God."[297] The

justified pursue glory although not the sort typically desired by people.

Wright observes that salvation and "not be put to shame" are "functional

equivalents."[298] This pattern is seen in the OT,[299] the NT, and extra biblical writings.[300]

---

[296] The Greek for Rom 2:7: "τοῖς μὲν καθ᾽ ὑπομονὴν ἔργου ἀγαθοῦ δόξαν καὶ τιμὴν καὶ ἀφθαρσίαν ζητοῦσιν ζωὴν αἰώνιον."

[297] Though I have serious concerns about Yeo's overall view of justification, he correctly points out that the Christian has "been set right by God from shame and curse so that now propriety, honor, and freedom characterizes the new and rightful relationship one has with God." See his work, *Musing*, 207. In almost identical terms, cf. Yeo, "Introduction: Navigating Romans," 14. However, here he says the δικαι-root emphasizes God's acting for a "group of people."

[298] Wright, *Romans,* 517, 665.

[299] See Ps 22:5; 31:1–2, 17–18; 34:5–6; 40:11, 15–18 (implicit); 44:4–8; 53:5–6 (via contrast); 70:1–2; 71:1–3; 72:1–3, 15, 24; 86:16–17 (via contrast); 109:26–31; 119:116–117; 132:16–18 (via contrast); Isa 1:27–29 (via contrast); 45:16–17 (via contrast); 48:19–20 (via contrast); 49:24–25; Jer 2:26–27 (via contrast); 17:13–14 (via contrast); 46:24, 27 (distant contrast); Zeph 3:17–20; Zech 10:5–6; Joel 2:27, 32; Dan 12:1–2.

[300] Mark 8:35–38; Luke 9:24–26; Rom 1:16 (implicit via contrast); 5:5, 9–10; 10:9–13; Phil 1:19–20. Also, see Sir 2:10–11.

Zephaniah 3:9–20 captures the various elements discussed here and are summarized by v. 19, "Behold, at that time I will deal with all your oppressors. And I will save the lame and gather the outcast, and I will change their shame into praise and renown in all the earth." Naturally then, salvation is found in honor. In Ps 91:15–16, God says, "When he calls to me, I will answer him; I will be with him in trouble; I will rescue him and honor him. With long life I will satisfy him and show him my salvation." Likewise, "On God rests my salvation and my glory" (Ps 62:7). In Rom 5:10, salvation is eschatological and refers to one's "hope in the glory of God" and that "hope does not put us to shame" (Rom 5:2, 5). In Rom 10, Paul says all who believe and confess Jesus as the risen Lord will be saved. The γὰρ in Rom 10:11 and the original context of the Joel citation in Rom 10:13 show Paul specifically means people will be saved *from shame*.[301]

Finally, HS language is employed to explain eschatological righteousness. John offers pastoral counsel, "And now, little children, abide in him, so that when he appears we may have confidence and not shrink from him in shame at his coming. If you know that he is righteous, you may be sure that everyone who practices righteousness has been born of him" (1 John 2:28–29). Romans 2:5–13 has been mentioned. Paul adds in Rom 6:20–21, "For when you were slaves of sin, you were free in regard to righteousness. But what fruit were you getting at that time from the things of which you are now ashamed? *For the end of those things is death*" (cf. 1 Cor 10:34). On the one hand, "For whoever is ashamed of me and of my words, of him will the Son of Man be ashamed when he comes in his glory and the glory of the Father and of the holy angels" (Luke 9:26). On the other hand, Isaiah foretells of God making his people righteous. Isaiah 60:21 says, "Your

---

[301] Cf. Joel 2:26–27, 32. Also, worth of attention is 2:17–23 where Israel awaits "vindication" (v. 23) and is called "a reproach of the nations" in v. 19. Also, God's honor is at stake in Joel 2:17.

people shall all be righteous . . . that I might be gloried" (cf. Isa 61:3). Eschatological judgment is emphatically public (cf. Rev 20:11–13).[302] A number of extra-biblical sources speak of "eschatological glory" for the righteous.[303] Edwards summarizes, "The saints shall be judged again, not because their state is not already determined, but to make God's righteousness in their justification manifest before the whole universe convened, and for their more public honor."[304] The righteous await eschatological honor.

Summary

In justification, the Creator, the one true God, vindicates his own glory. By countering ethnocentrism, he reorients collectivistic and individual honor claims. What the world regards as shameful, God honors. Likewise, God puts to shame those who boast in anything else but Christ. As a result, justification signifies one's group identity. The Christian is a member of God's family, which consists of those from among all nations who give their allegiance to Jesus the King. For all who are in Christ, God restores honor and removes our shame.

---

[302] Drawing from Rev 14:9–11, deSilva also observes, "The public nature of the torment reveals that dishonor is a key factor in motivating the hearers to shun the course of action that leads to such eternal shame." See deSilva, *The Hope of Glory*, 19.

[303] Blackwell, "Immortal Glory," 290–91. He mentions 4 Ezra 7:116–31; 2 Bar 15:1–19:8; 54:13–21. At Qumran, 1QS 4:22–23 (cf. 1QS 4:6–8); 19 CD 3:19–20; 1QH 4:14–15 [17:14–15]. *1 En.* 50.1; 62.13–16; 104:1–6; 108:11–15; 1QH 15:22–25; 1QS 4:6–8; *T. Benj.* 10:6–8; *4 Ezra* 7:38–42, 75–101 (esp. 95–98); 8:51–54; 9:31–37; *2 Bar* 48:49–51:12; 54:14–22; He adds, "and possibly" Wis 3:4–8 and *T. Mos* 10:9."

[304] Jonathan Edwards, *"The 'Miscellanies,' Entry Nos. 501–832."* (ed. Ava Chamberlain; vol. 18 of *Works of Jonathan Edwards Online*; New Haven, Conn.: Yale University Press, 2000), 209. Cited 2 Jan 2012]. Online: http://edwards.yale.edu/.

CHAPTER 6: CONCLUSION

Theological Contextualization: How Chinese Culture Shapes a Biblical Soteriology

This book uses a dialogical approach to contextualization. It examines key features of

Chinese culture and then compares various methods of contextualizing theology in China.

The honor-shame (HS) concept helpfully connects Chinese context, ancient biblical

cultures, and the biblical world. The study culminated by developing a doctrine of

salvation from an HS perspective. Overall, the argument of the book shows the difficulty

of distinguishing missiology and theology. In many respects, one even finds that these

two fields of study are mutually dependent on one another.

Missionaries and theologians have largely assumed a particular understanding of

the gospel and consequently reduce contextualization to a kind of application or

communication. Those most influenced by Western theology typically give a gospel

presentation that presumes law as its primary metaphor. As a result, many people who

hear this gospel will first need to think like westerners in order receive the message and

become Christians. The one Creator God, however, is not partial to any particular culture.

He reveals himself in Scripture so that people from any culture can understand his

message. Therefore, one needs to reconsider the meaning of contextualization.

Fundamentally, contextualization begins by interpreting the Bible from the perspective of

others who live in a particular cultural context. A person's culture provides the lens

through which one understands biblical truth. Even though culture directs the

293

contextualization process, Scripture ultimately determines theological truth. General revelation acts as a framework for special revelation. Different cultures highlight different themes, many of which are also found in the Bible. Those who want to contextualize theology can compensate for their own cultural limitations by using an interdisciplinary approach that emphasizes dialogue between people of different cultures.

A study of Chinese culture focused attention on a number of themes commonly underemphasized within Western theology. In general, Chinese people typically lay stress on their collective identity, hierarchy, tradition, and "face." Social life requires people to constantly negotiate their relationships in order to strategically pursue honor and avoid shame. A person's identity consists in how others regard him or her. Face and identity arise both from one's network of relationships (ascribed HS) and from individual actions (achieved HS). Although this book offers a mere composite sketch of a complex and integrated worldview, it is evident that a Chinese perspective can broaden the lens through which one reads the Bible and formulates theology.

Accordingly, scholars have discussed potential ways to forge ahead in the task of contextualization. At the level of abstraction, one finds a great deal of consensus. For example, many people concur as to what are key themes in Chinese culture. The Western church has much to learn from non-Western Christians; thus, contextualized theologies are important. One gains many insights by reading the plethora of articles and books on contextualization, Chinese Christianity, and HS. The concept of HS is pervasive in the Bible and throughout the world, especially in a Chinese context. However, in practical terms, few thinkers can agree on how to relate the Bible and culture in contextualization. The possible reasons for this could be many, including cultural naivety, theological reductionism, prejudice, the oversimplification of methods, and perhaps a lack of training and awareness.

Theologian-missionaries can utilize an HS perspective to develop a soteriology that is faithful to the biblical narrative. Although this contextualized soteriology does not primarily emphasize law-categories, they are not contrary to HS and should not be categorically excluded from one's theology. People must pay careful attention to how they understand and use metaphors that are common to a culture and Scripture. The doctrine of salvation must be oriented to the gospel. The Bible explicitly and frequently articulates a gospel that carries definite royal overtones and that is deeply rooted in the OT narrative. Thus, the gospel tells how God keeps his promises in Christ, who defeated God's enemies and saves people from among all nations. A biblical view of the atonement underscores how Jesus glorifies his Father, "saving God's face" from the shame of his image bearers. Jesus restores honor to God's people, whose collective identity is in Christ.

HS also shapes a biblical view of justification and righteousness. Since justification identifies one with Christ, it is a thoroughly public demonstration of honor. Christian identity derives from the head of the collective Church, Jesus the Christ, in whom none will be put to shame. Hence, this book proposes a reading of Romans that integrates soteriology and ecclesiology. Whether Greeks or Jews, people should not boast in their cultural or ethnic identity. True faith entails a conversion of one's HS standards. There is an unmistakable social dimension of the justification and the gospel. Like Paul, missionaries can use HS to overcome cultural pride, build church unity, and mobilize missionaries to be a blessing to all nations, including China.

Implications for Contextualization and Chinese Theology

If contextualization begins with interpretation, the church must reevaluate how it trains missionaries. Such training will use an interdisciplinary approach. Missionaries should receive high-level training across academic disciplines, with a special focus on hermeneutics, theology, and culture. In addition to learning a grammatical-historical method of interpretation, missionaries would benefit from studying cross-cultural hermeneutics, global theologies, as well as basic categories of philosophy. Given the complexities of culture, missionaries need extensive, on-going training while on the field, comparable to the continuing education provided to those in other professionals (for example, doctors, lawyers, teachers). Additionally, equal or greater stress will be given to biblical theology as to systematic theology. Naturally, one should become familiar with contextualization theories. The church should become more open to the value of contextual theologies from around the world.

Missionary strategy should reflect the dialogical and integrated nature of the contextualization. By prioritizing theological education within a spectrum of approaches, missionaries equip national partners to better contribute to and lead the contextualization process. Comprehensive missiological thinking seeks to affect the "DNA" of a local church, even if this means sacrificing rapid growth. Strategies cannot focus only on one kind of ministry (e.g., evangelism) or utilize a narrow range of tools and theological categories. In order to lay a proper foundation, missionaries will exercise patience in language and cultural acquisition. Of course, the sort of contextualization proposed in this book will place a premium on recruiting and retaining long-term workers.

The present study has highlighted the sometimes subtle but pervasive influence of culture on one's own missiological and theological views. Positively, general revelation can provide common ground on which to explore answers raised by special revelation. On the other hand, cross-cultural workers also need the humility to question their own theology and worldview assumptions. Missionaries and theologians cannot assume that others around the world share their cultural values and categories of thought. In fact, people should not be surprised to find some parts of their theology are more shaped by culture than by careful biblical exegesis. Besides critical thinking skills, it is important that missionaries learn to listen to others. Our study of Romans also reminds us of the detrimental effects of prejudice. Feelings of cultural superiority and ethnic pride create a false basis for group unity. Whether in evangelism or personal reflection, people must consider what it is they boast in. Where do they find their identity? Who do they want to please? This warning is not merely for those who are evangelized. It challenges missionaries to examine how their ministries may be hindered by cultural pride and stereotypes that perpetuate perceptions of imperialism.

Furthermore, people should reconsider the role of ethnic identity within Paul's gospel. His main distinction is not between faith and mere rule keeping as such. Rather, Paul counters the presumption that ethnic identification was a pre-condition to becoming part of God's people. In the mind of Paul's Jewish opponents, group membership is necessary for salvation. This is not the same thing as saying that group identification is *sufficient* for salvation. In other words, we should not suppose that people are trusting merely in their ethnic identity. One could grant the point that some Jews believed in works-righteousness (i.e. somehow contributing synergistically to their salvation).

However, it is important to note that such Jews would only regard such works as having moral worth within the context of Israel. Therefore, Paul's objection is subtler than some might suppose. He is not primarily opposing works-righteousness *qua* works-righteousness. Instead, he is addressing the more basic assumption that the scope of salvation was limited to the Jewish people. To say this does not negate that possibility that some pursued justification via doing good works. Rather, the present point simply gives a proper context in which to understand the significance of those works. In short, works-righteousness would only have made sense within an Israel-centric worldview.

What are some implications for the Chinese church? First, Chinese Christians must reckon with their own sense of identity and loyalty. Doing so will require people to reject typical ways of dividing the world, whereby ethnicity, gender, and social status categorize those who are "insiders" and "outsiders." This leads to a second implication. Paul challenges not only Jews and Greeks, but also the Chinese church as it considers its own calling to send missionaries cross-culturally among fellow Gentiles. Third, the Bible spurs Chinese Christians to see the church as family, not laying excessive stress on bloodline.[1] No doubt, there are many practical applications for family life and for addressing social problems like orphan care and abortion. Similarly, a gospel-oriented view of HS cultivates unity by undermining the ambition to create a "brand church."[2]

HS provides the framework for understanding and communicating the gospel of salvation. Since HS touches on so many aspects of human life, understanding the

---

[1] Note Joseph H. Hellerman, *When the Church Was a Family: Recapturing Jesus' Vision for Authentic Christian Community* (Nashville, Tenn.: B & H Academic, 2009).
[2] Cao, *China's Jerusalem*, 77. The phrase (*pinpai jiaohui*) comes a Wenzhou church leader who says, "'Building churches is more influential than evangelization' and 'using the name of the Wenzhou people and of the Wenzhou church to cultivate a positive image is more powerful'" (p. 77).

dynamics of HS can help people examine their own hearts. Furthermore, one sees the importance of metaphors for interpreting the Bible and sharing the gospel. Practitioners can reassess common evangelistic paradigms to ensure the message preached draws from the entire canon. Naturally, new methods can be developed.

The Western church can better grasp a biblical view of HS. Regardless of one's culture, HS has practical importance for daily life, even if one does not use the specific terms "honor," "shame, and "face." HS is a human category, not merely an "Eastern" way of thinking. Faith involves one's boasting, loyalty, and sense of identity. HS shows how conversion and discipleship cohere together. By understanding the dynamics of HS, Christians can become more fully "human" and holistic in their ministry; that is, the concept of HS helps people to reflect more fully the image of the one true God and not simply express the distinctives of their local culture.

A number of questions spawn from this study. For example, what other doctrines might be amended if we change our fundamental point of reference from the individual to a collective? How might HS affect ecclesiology and church leadership? How do socio-rhetorical studies integrate with a grammatical-historical method of exegesis? Aside from HS and China, how might other themes and cultures add to our biblical understanding? How might the insights of missiologists contribute to ongoing debates within the field of theology? Also, how does HS subtly shape the Western church and its theology?

BIBLIOGRAPHY

Achtemeier, P. J. "Righteousness." Pages 80–99 in vol. 4 of *The Interpreter's Dictionary of the Bible*. Edited by George Arthur Buttrick. 5 vols. New York, N.Y.: Abingdon, 1962.

Adams, Edward. "Abraham's Faith and Gentile Disobedience: Textual Links Between Romans 1 and 4." *Journal for the Study of the New Testament*, no. 65 (1997): 47–66.

Adeney, Frances S. "Contextualizing Universal Values: A Method for Christian Mission." *International Bulletin of Missionary Research* 31, no. 1 (January 2007): 33–37.

Ai, Jiawen. "The Refunctioning of Confucianism: The Mainland Chinese Intellectual Response to Confucianism since the 1980s." *Issues & Studies* 44, no. 2 (June 2008): 29–78.

Aikman, David. *Jesus in Beijing: How Christianity is Transforming China and Changing the Global Balance of Power*. Lanham, Md.: Regnery, 2003.

Akin, Daniel L., David P. Nelson, and Peter R. Schemm Jr., eds. *A Theology for the Church*. Nashville, Tenn.: B & H, 2007.

Alexander, T. Desmond, and Brian S. Rosner, eds. "Honour." Page 559 in *New Dictionary of Biblical Theology*. Downers Grove, Ill.: IVP, 2000.

Alloway, Wayne L., Jr., John G. Lacey, and Robert Jewett, eds. *The Shame Factor: How Shame Shapes Society*. Eugene, Ore.: Cascade, 2010.

An Introduction to the Mainland Chinese Soul. Raleigh, N.C.: LEAD Consulting, 2001.

Anderson, Charles A., and Michael J. Sleasman. "Putting into Practice: Weddings for Everyday Theologians." *Everyday Theology: How to Read Cultural Texts and Interpret Trends*. Edited by Kevin Vanhoozer. Grand Rapids, Mich.: Baker Academic, 2007.

Anderson, Gary A. *Sin: A History*. New Haven, Conn.: Yale, 2009.

Anderson, Gary A., trans. *Apocalypse of Moses*. No Date. Online: http://www2.iath. virginia.edu/anderson/vita/english/vita.gre.html#per20.

Anderson, Gerald. "A Response to Professor Li Deng Fucun." Pages 312–18 in *Christianity and Chinese Culture*. Edited by Mikka Ruokanen and Paulos Huang. Grand Rapids, Mich.: Eerdmans, 2010.

Anderson, Justice, and Don Jones, eds. *Contextualizing the Gospel*. Richmond, Va.: International Centre for Excellence in Leadership, International Mission Board, 2000.

Andreasen, Niels-Eriek A. "Atonement/Expiation in the OT." Pages 76–77 in *Mercer Dictionary of the Bible*. Edited by Watson E. Mills and Roger Aubrey Bullard. Macon, Ga.: Mercer University Press, 1990.

Armstrong, James F. "A New Look at Some Old Problems." *Theology Today* 21, no. 1 (April 1964): 9–12.

Arnold, Bill T., and Bryan E. Beyer, eds. *Readings from the Ancient Near East*. Grand Rapids, Mich.: Baker, 2002.

Atkins, R. "Pauline Theology and Shame Affect: Reading a Social Location." *Listening* 31, no. 2 (1996): 137–51.

Baker, Mark D., and Joel B. Green. *Recovering the Scandal of the Cross: Atonement in New Testament and Contemporary Contexts*. Downers Grove, Ill.: IVP Academic, 2000.

Baker, Susan S. "The Social Sciences for Urban Ministry." Pages 60–82 in *The Urban Face of Mission: Ministering the Gospel in a Diverse and Changing World*. Edited by Manuel Ortiz and Susan S. Baker. Phillipsburg, N.J.: P & R Publishing, 2002.

Bauer, Walter, F. W. Danker, W. F. Arndt, and F. W. Gingrich, eds. *Greek-English Lexicon of the New Testament and Other Early Christian Literature*. Chicago, Ill.: University of Chicago Press, 2000.

Bavinck, John H. *An Introduction to the Science of Missions*. Phillipsburg, N.J.: P & R Publishing, 1992.

Baxter, Richard, and William Orme. Page 616 in vol. 12 of *The Practical Works of Richard Baxter: With a Life of the Author and a Critical Examination of His Writings by William Orme*. 23 vols. London: J. Duncan, 1830.

Beale, G. K. *A New Testament Biblical Theology: The Unfolding of the Old Testament in the New*. Grand Rapids, Mich.: Baker, 2011.

Bechtel, Lyn M. "Shame as a Sanction of Social Control in Biblical Israel: Judicial, Political, and Social Shaming." *Journal for the Study of the Old Testament* 49 (1991): 47–76.

Bedford, Olwen. "Guilt and Shame in American and Chinese Culture." PhD diss., Boulder, Colo: University of Colorado, 1994.

Bedford, Olwen, and Kwang-Kuo Hwang. "Guilt and Shame in Chinese Culture: A Cross-Cultural Framework from the Perspective of Morality and Identity." *Journal for the Theory of Social Behaviour* 33, no. 2 (June 1, 2003): 127–44.

Berkhof, Louis. *Systematic Theology*. Grand Rapids, Mich.: Eerdmans, 1996.

Berring, Jr., Robert C. "Rule of Law: The Chinese Perspective." *Journal of Social Philosophy* 35, no. 4 (Winter 2004): 449–456.

Bevans, Stephen. *Models of Contextual Theology*. Rev. and expanded ed. Maryknoll, N.Y.: Orbis Books, 2002.

Biehl, Craig. *The Infinite Merit of Christ: The Glory of Christ's Obedience in the Theology of Jonathan Edwards*. Jackson, Miss.: Reformed Academic Press, 2009.

Binau, Brad A. "When Shame is The Question, How Does The Atonement Answer?" *Journal for Pastoral Theology* 12, no. 1 (January 2002): 89–113.

Bird, Michael. "Justification as Forensic Declaration and Covenant Membership: A *Via Media* between Reformed and Revisionist Readings of Paul." *Tyndale Bulletin* 57, no. 1 (2006): 109–30.

———. "Raised for Our Justification." *Colloquium* 35, no. 1 (2003): 31–46.

———. *The Saving Righteousness of God: Studies on Paul, Justification and the New Perspective*. New York, N.Y.: Wipf & Stock, 2007.

———. "What Is There Between Minneapolis and St. Andrews? A Third Way in the Piper-Wright Debate." *Journal of the Evangelical Theological Society.* 54, no. 2 (2011): 299–310.

Blackman, E. C. "Justification, Justify." Pages 1028–30 in *The Interpreter's Dictionary of the Bible*. Edited by George Arthur Buttrick. New York, N.Y.: Abingdon, 1962.

Blackwell, Ben C. "Immortal Glory and the Problem of Death in Romans 3.23." *Journal for the Study of the New Testament* 32, no. 3 (March 2010): 285–308.

Blocher, Henri A. "The Luther-Catholic Declaration on Justification." *Justification in Perspective: Historical Developments And Contemporary Challenges*. Edited by Bruce L. McCormack. Grand Rapids, Mich.: Baker, 2006.

Bo, Zhu. "Chinese Cultural Values and Chinese Language Pedagogy." Master's Thesis, Columbus, Ohio: The Ohio State University, 2008.

Bonhoeffer, Dietrich. *Nachfolge*. Edited by Hg. Martin Kuske and Ilse Tödt. München: Kaiser, 1989.

Bosch, David. *Transforming Mission: Paradigm Shifts in Theology of Mission.* Maryknoll, N.Y.: Orbis Books, 1991.

Bowen, Nancy R. "Damage and Healing: Shame and Honor in the Old Testament." *Koinonia* 3, no. 1 (Spring 1991): 29–36.

Boyd, Gregory A. "'Christus Victor Response' to Penal Substitution View." Pages 99–105 in *The Nature of the Atonement: Four Views.* Edited by James Beilby and Paul R. Eddy. Downers Grove, Ill.: IVP Academic, 2006.

Boyle, Timothy D. "Communicating the Gospel in Terms of Shame." *Japan Christian Quarterly* 50, no. 1 (Winter 1984): 41–46.

Brondos, David A. *Fortress Introduction to Salvation and the Cross.* Minneapolis, Minn.: Fortress, 2007.

———. *Redeeming the Gospel: The Christian Faith Reconsidered.* Philadelphia, Pa.: Fortress, 2010.

Bryan, Christopher. *A Preface to Romans: Notes on the Epistle in Its Literary and Cultural Setting.* New York, N.Y.: Oxford University Press, 2000.

Bultmann, Rudolf. "Christ and the End of the Law." *Essays Philosophical and Theological.* English trans. London: SCM Press, 1995.

Bultmann, Rudolph. "*Aidos.*" Page 170 in vol. 1 of *Theological Dictionary of the New Testament.* Edited by Gerhard Kittel, Gerhard Friedrich, Geoffrey William Bromily. 10 vols. Grand Rapids, Mich.: Eerdmans, 1964.

Burke, Trevor J. *Adopted into God's Family: Exploring a Pauline Metaphor.* Downers Grove, Ill.: IVP Academic, 2006.

Burks, Robert E. "Atonement/Expiation in the NT." Pages 75–76 in *Mercer Dictionary of the Bible.* Edited by Watson E. Mills and Roger Aubrey Bullard. Macon, Ga.: Mercer University Press, 1990.

Burton, Laurel Arthur. "Original Sin or Original Shame." *Quarterly Review* 8, no. 4 (Winter 1988): 31–41.

Byrne, Brendan. "Living Out the Righteousness of God: The Contribution of Rom 6:1–8:13 to an Understanding of Paul's Ethical Presuppositions." *Catholic Biblical Quarterly* 43, no. 4 (October 1981): 557–81.

Callahan, William C. "History, Identity, and Security: Producing and Consuming Nationalism in China." *Critical Asian Studies* 38, no. 2 (2006): 179–208.

———. "National Insecurities: Humiliation, Salvation, and Chinese Nationalism." *Alternatives: Global, Local, Political* 29, no. 2 (Mar-May 2004): 199–218.

Campbell, Douglas. *The Deliverance of God: An Apocalyptic Rereading of Justification in Paul*. Grand Rapids, Mich.: Eerdmans, 2009.

—. "The Interpretation of Paul's *dikaio* Language." London, 2011. Online: http://gcitv.net/dl/MiscVid/2011CampbellConf/Day2PMSession1.mp3.

—. "The Meaning of *Pistis* and *Nomos* in Paul: A Linguistic and Structural Perspective." *Journal of Biblical Literature* 111, no. 1 (1992): 91–103.

Campbell, Jonathan. "Releasing the Gospel from Western Bondage." *International Journal of Frontier Missions* 16, no. 4 (Winter 2000): 167–71.

Cao, Deborah. *Chinese Law: A Language Perspective*. Burlington, Vt.: Ashgate, 2004.

Cao, Nanlai. *Constructing China's Jerusalem: Christians, Power, and Place in Contemporary Wenzhou*. Palo Alto, Calif.: Stanford University Press, 2010.

Carson, D. A., Mark A. Seifrid, and Peter T. O'Brien, eds. *The Complexities of Second Temple Judaism*. Vol. 1 of *Justification and Variegated Nomism*. Grand Rapids, Mich.: Baker Academic, 2001.

—. *The Paradoxes of Paul*. Vol. 2 of *Justification and Variegated Nomism*. Grand Rapids, Mich.: Baker Academic, 2004.

Carson, D. A. and Timothy J. Keller, eds. *The Gospel as Center: Renewing our Faith and Reforming our Ministry Practices*. Wheaton, Ill.: Crossway, 2012.

Carson, D. A. "Reflections on Contextualization: A Critical Appraisal of Daniel Von Allmen's 'Birth of Theology'." *East Africa Journal of Evangelical Theology* 4, no. 1 (1984): 16–59.

—. "The Vindication of Imputation: On Fields of Discourse and Semantic Fields." Pages 46–78 in *Justification: What's at Stake in the Current Debates*. Edited by Mark Husbands and Daniel J. Treier. Downers Grove, Ill.: IVP, 2004.

Chan, Carol K. K, and Nirmala Rao. "Moving Beyond Paradoxes: Understanding Chinese Learners and Their Teachers." Pages 3–32 in *Revisiting the Chinese Learner: Changing Contexts, Changing Education*. Edited by Carol K. K. Chan and Nirmala Rao. Seattle, Wash.: University of Washington Press, 2010.

Chan, Carol K. K., and Nirmala Rao, eds. *Revisiting the Chinese Learner: Changing Contexts, Changing Education*. Seattle, Wash.: University of Washington Press, 2010.

Chan, Che-po, and Brian Bridges. "China, Japan, and the Clash of Nationalisms." *Asian Perspective* 30, no. 1 (2006): 127–56.

Chan, Wing Tsit. "The Individual in Chinese Religions." *The Chinese Mind*. Honolulu, Hawaii: East-West Center Press, 1967.

Chang, Hui Ching, and G. Richard Holt. "A Chinese Perspective on Face: A Inter-Relational Concern." Pages 95–131 in *The Challenge of Facework: Cross-Cultural and Interpersonal Issues*. Edited by Stella Ting-Toomey. Suny Series in Human Communication Processes. Albany, N.Y.: State University of New York Press, 1994.

Chang, Hui-Ching, and G. Richard Holt. "More Than Relationship: Chinese Interaction and the Principle of Kuan-Hsi." *Communication Quarterly* 39, no. 3 (Summer 1991): 251–71.

Chang, Lit-Sen. *Asia's Religions: Christianity's Momentous Encounter with Paganism*. Phillipsburg, N.J.: P & R Publishing, 2000.

Chao, Jonathan. "The Gospel and Culture in Chinese History." Pages 9–23 in *Chinese Intellectuals and the Gospel*. Edited by Samuel D. Ling and Stacey Bieler. San Gabriel, Calif.: China Horizon, 1999.

Chapell, Bryan. "What is the Gospel?" Pages 115–34 in *The Gospel as Center: Renewing our Faith and Reforming our Ministry Practices*. Edited by D. A. Carson and Timothy J. Keller; Wheaton, Ill.: Crossway, 2012.

Chen, Yongtao. "Christ and Culture: A Reflection by a Chinese Christian." Pages 339–54 in *Christianity and Chinese Culture*. Edited by Mikka Ruokanen and Paulos Huang. Grand Rapids, Mich.: Eerdmans, 2010.

Cheng, Chung-Ying. "Justice and Peace in Kant and Confucius." *Journal of Chinese Philosophy* 34, no. 3 (September 2007): 345–57.

———. "The Concept of Face and Its Confucian Roots." *Journal of Chinese Philosophy* 13 (1986): 329–48.

Chester Chun-Seng Kam, and Michael Harris Bond. "Emotional Reactions of Anger and Shame to the Norm Violation Characterizing Episodes of Interpersonal Harm." *British Journal of Social Psychology* 48, no. 2 (June 2009): 203–19.

Cheung, Kat, and Ling Chen. "When a Confucian Manages Individualists: A Study of Intercultural Conflict Between Chinese Managers and Western Subordinates." Paper presented at the Annual Meeting of the International Communication Association,, New York, N.Y., May 5, 2009. Online: http://www. allacademic.com/meta/p13416_index.html.

Chin, Ken-Pa. "The Paradigm Shift: From Chinese Theology to Sino-Christian Theology–A Case Study on Liu Xiaofeng." Pages 139–57 in *Sino-Christian Theology*. Edited by Pan-chiu Lai and Jason Lam. New York, N.Y.: Peter Lang, 2010.

Chuang Tzu. "The Writings of Chuang Tzu, Book 29: The Robber Kih," December 1, 2011. Online: http://nothingistic.org/library/chuangtzu/chuang87.html.

Chuang, Yao-Chia. "Effects of Interaction Pattern on Family Harmony and Well-Being: Test of Interpersonal Theory, Relational-Models Theory, and Confucian Ethics." *Asian Journal of Social Psychology* 8 (2005): 272–91.

Clapp, Rodney. *A Peculiar People: The Church as Culture in a Post-Christian Society.* Downers Grove, Ill.: IVP, 1996.

Clark, David K. *To Know and Love God: Method for Theology.* Wheaton, Ill.: Crossway, 2003.

Clark, Gordon H. "Classical Apologetics." *The Trinity Review* 45 (October 1998): 1–5.

Confucius. "The Doctrine of the Mean, Chapters 18 to 20," December 1, 2011. Online: http://nothingistic.org/library/confucius/mean/mean03.html.

Cook, Richard. "Overcoming Missions Guilt." Pages 35–45 in *After Imperialism: Christian Identity in China and the Global Evangelical Movement.* Edited by Richard R. Cook and David W. Pao. Eugene, Ore.: Pickwick, 2011.

Cook, Richard R., and David W. Pao, eds. *After Imperialism: Christian Identity in China and the Global Evangelical Movement.* Eugene, Ore.: Pickwick, 2011.

Cook, W. Robert. "The 'Glory' Motif in the Johannine Corpus." *Journal of the Evangelical Theological Society* 27, no. 3 (September 1984): 291–97.

Coppedge, Allan. *The God Who Is Triune: Revisioning the Christian Doctrine of God.* Downers Grove, Ill.: IVP, 2007.

Corduan, Winfried. *Neighboring Faiths: A Christian Introduction to World Religions.* Downers Grove, Ill.: IVP Academic, 1998.

Corwin, Charles. "Communicating the Concept of Sin in the Chinese Context." *The Network for Strategic Missions.* No Date. Cited 28 Dec 2011. Online: http://www.strategicnetwork.org/index.php?loc=kb&view=v&id=4588.

Covell, Ralph. *Confucius, the Buddha, and Christ: A History of the Gospel in Chinese.* Maryknoll, N.Y.: Orbis Books, 1986.

Crawley, Winston. "Interpreting the Bible in Chinese Context." *Taiwan Baptist Theological Seminary Annual Bulletin* (September 2005): 29–39.

Crook, Zeba. "Reconceptualizing Conversion: Patronage Loyalty, and Conversion in the Religions of the Ancient Mediterranean." PhD diss., Toronto: University of St. Michael's College, 2003.

Cru. "Four Spiritual Laws." No Date. Online: http://www.campuscrusade.com/fourlawseng.htm.

—————. "The Theological Background of the Four Spiritual Laws." *There is Hope Ministries*, November 2005. Online: http://www.hope365.co.za/sites/hope365.co.za/files/i%20FN%201S01B%20$%20Theology%20of%20the%20Four%20Spiritual%20Laws.pdf.

Dao, John. "Toward a Contextual Theology for the Chinese–A Case Study from Translation and Interpretation of the Greek Logos and Chinese Dao." *Global Missiology* 2, no. 3 (January 2006). Online: http://ojs.globalmissiology.org/index.php/english/article/view/420/1071.

Das, A. Andrew. *Paul, the Law, and the Covenant*. Peabody, Mass.: Hendrickson Publishers, 2001.

David Yau-Fai Ho, Wai Fu, and S. M. Ng. "Guilt, Shame and Embarrassment: Revelations of Face and Self." *Culture & Psychology* 10, no. 1 (March 2004): 64–84.

Dean Flemming. "Paul the Contextualizer." Pages 1–19 in *Local Theology for the Global Church: Principles for an Evangelical Approach to Contextualization*. Edited by Matthew Cook, Rob Haskell, Ruth Julian, and Natee Tanchanpongs. Pasadena, Calif.: William Carey Library, 2010.

Demarest, Bruce. *The Cross and Salvation: The Doctrine of God*. Wheaton, Ill.: Crossway, 2006.

Deng, Fucun. "The Basis for the Reconstruction of Chinese Theological Thinking." Pages 297–308 in *Christianity and Chinese Culture*. Edited by Mikka Ruokanen and Paulos Huang. Grand Rapids, Mich.: Eerdmans, 2010.

deSilva, David A. *An Introduction to the New Testament: Contexts, Methods, and Ministry*. Downers Grove, Ill.: IVP, 2004.

—————. "Despising Shame: A Cultural-Anthropological Investigation of the Epistle to the Hebrews." *Journal of Biblical Literature* 113 (1994): 439–61.

—————. *Despising Shame: Honor Discourse and Community Maintenance in the Epistle to the Hebrews*. Revised ed. Atlanta, Ga.: Society of Biblical Literature, 2008.

—————. "Honor and Shame." Pages 287–300 in *Dictionary of the Old Testament: Wisdom, Poetry and Writings*. The IVP Bible Dictionary Series. Edited by Tremper Longman and Peter Enns. Downers Grove, Ill.: IVP Academic, 2008.

—————. "Honor and Shame." Pages 431–36 in *Dictionary of the Old Testament: Pentateuch*. The IVP Bible Dictionary Series. Edited by T. Desmond Alexander and David Baker. Downers Grove, Ill.: IVP Academic, 2002.

————. *Honor, Patronage, Kinship & Purity: Unlocking New Testament Culture*. Downers Grove, Ill.: IVP, 2000.

————. *The Hope of Glory: Honor Discourse and New Testament Interpretation*. Collegeville, Minn.: Liturgical Press, 1999.

Dever, Mark. *The Gospel and Personal Evangelism*. Wheaton, Ill.: Crossway, 2007.

————. *What is a Healthy Church?* Wheaton, Ill.: Crossway, 2007.

————. "The Whiteboard Sessions—Mark Dever." Interview with Ed Stetzer at The Whiteboard Conference, Reston, Va., 23 May 2008. Cited 29 Aug 2012. Online: http://www.ustream.tv/recorded/431730.

DeVries, Grant. "Explaining the Atonement to the Arabic Muslim in terms of Honour and Shame: Potentials and Pitfalls." *St. Francis Magazine* 2, no. 4 (March 2007): 1–68.

DeVries, S. J. "Shame." Pages 305–6 in vol. 4 of *The Interpreter's Dictionary of the Bible*. Edited by George Arthur Buttrick. 5 vols. New York, N.Y.: Abingdon, 1962.

DeYoung, Kevin, and Greg Gilbert. *What Is the Mission of the Church?: Making Sense of Social Justice, Shalom, and the Great Commission*. Wheaton, Ill.: Crossway, 2011.

Dickson, John. "Gospel as News: ευαγγελ- from Aristophanes to the Apostle Paul." *New Testament Studies* 51 (2005): 212–30.

Dien, Dora ShuFang. *The Chinese Worldview Regarding Justice and the Supernatural: The Cultural and Historical Roots of Rule by Law*. New York, N.Y.: Nova Science Publishers, 2007.

Dille, Sarah J. *Mixing Metaphors: God as Mother and Father in Deutero-Isaiah*. New York, N.Y.: T&T Clark, 2004.

Dillon, Michael. "Feudalism." Pages 61–62 in *Dictionary of Chinese History*. New York, N.Y.: Routledge, 1979.

Ding, Guangxun. "Religious Policy and Theological Reorientation in China." *China Notes* 18, no. 3 (Summer 1980): 121–24.

Discovering God in Chinese Characters. Langley, BC, Canada: Intercultural Network Canada, 2007. Online: http://interculturalnetwork.com/resources/discovering-god/.

Dixon, S. *The Roman Family*. Baltimore: Johns Hopkins, 1992.

Dougherty, Jude P. *Western Creed, Western Identity: Essays in Legal and Social Philosophy*. Washington, D.C.: Catholic University of America, 2000.

Downing, F. Gerald. "Honor." Pages 884–85 in *The New Interpreter's Dictionary of the Bible*. Edited by Katharine Sakenfeld. Nashville: Abingdon, 2006.

———. "'Honor' and Exegetes." *Catholic Biblical Quarterly* 61 (1999): 53–73.

Doyle, G. Wright. "A Review of Reading Christian Scriptures in China." *Global China Center*, September 4, 2008. Online: http://www.globalchinacenter.org/analysis/christianity-in-china/reading-christian-scriptures-in-china.php.

———. "Review of Faith of Our Fathers: God in Ancient China." *Global Chinese Center: Christianity in China*, March 20, 2007. Online: http://www.globalchina center.org/analysis/christianity-in-china/faith-of-our-fathers-god-in-ancient-china.php.

Driscoll, Mark and Gerry Breshears. *Doctrine: What Christians Should Believe*. Wheaton, Ill: Crossway, 2011.

Dunn, James D. G. *The New Perspective on Paul*. Grand Rapids, Mich.: Eerdmans, 2008.

Dyrness, William A. *Invitation to Cross-Cultural Theology: Case Studies in Vernacular Theologies*. Grand Rapids, Mich.: Zondervan, 1992.

Edin, Mary Hinkle. "Learning What Righteousness Means: Hosea 6:6 and the Ethic of Mercy in Matthew's Gospel." *Word & World* 18, no. 4 (Fall 1998): 355–63.

Edwards, Jonathan. "The End for Which God Created the World." Pages 117–252 in *God's Passion for His Glory*. Edited by John Piper. Wheaton, Ill.: 1998.

———. *"The Miscellanies," Entry Nos. 501–832*. Vol. 18 of *Works of Jonathan Edwards Online*. Edited by Ava Chamberlain. New Haven, Conn.: Yale University Press, 2000. Cited 2 January 2012. Online: http://edwards.yale.edu/.

———. *Sermons and Discourse, 1734–1738*. Vol. 19 of *Works of Jonathan Edwards Online*. Edited by M. X. Lesser. New Haven, Conn.: Yale University Press, 2000. No Pages. Cited 19 July 2012. Online: http://edwards.yale.edu/.

Elman, Benjamin A. *A Cultural History of Civil Examinations in Late Imperial China*. Berkeley, Calif.: University of California Press, 2000.

Elmer, Duane. *Cross-Cultural Conflict: Building Relationships for Effective Ministry*. Downers Grove, Ill.: IVP, 1993.

Erickson, Millard. *Christian Theology*. 2nd ed. Grand Rapids, Mich.: Baker, 2002.

Esler, Philip Francis. *Conflict and Identity in Romans*. Minneapolis, Minn.: Fortress Press, 2003.

Evangelism Explosion. "Steps to Life." No Date. Online: http://www.eeinternational.org/pages/page.asp?page_id=31469.

Fällman, Fredrik. "A Response to Professor Li QiuLing." Pages 287–90 in *Christianity and Chinese Culture*. Edited by Mikka Ruokanen and Paulos Huang. Grand Rapids, Mich.: Eerdmans, 2010.

Fan, Lizhu, and James D. Whitehead. "Spirituality in a Modern Chinese Metropolis." Pages 12–29 in *Chinese Religious Life*. Edited by David A. Palmer, Glenn Landes Shive, and Philip L. Wickeri. New York, N.Y.: Oxford University Press, 2011.

Farrar, Lara. "Chinese Companies 'Rent' White Foreigners." *CNN.com*, June 29, 2010, U.S. edition, sec. Business.

Feinberg, Joel. "Collective Responsibility." *The Journal of Philosophy* 65, no. 21 (November 7, 1968): 674–88.

Ferguson, Sinclair. "Preaching the Atonement." Pages 426–43 in *The Glory of the Atonement: Biblical, Theological & Practical Perspectives*. Edited by Charles E. Hill and Frank A. James III. Downers Grove, Ill.: IVP Academic, 2004.

Fingarette, Herbert. "Human Community as Holy Rite: An Interpretation of Confucius' Analects." *Harvard Theological Review* 59, no. 1 (January 1966): 53–67.

Fischer, Agneta H., Antony S.R. Manstead, and Patricia M. Rodriguez Mosquera. "The Role of Honour-related vs. Individualistic Values in Conceptualising Pride, Shame, and Anger: Spanish and Dutch Cultural Prototypes." *Cognition & Emotion* 13, no. 2 (March 1999): 149–79.

Flanders, Christopher L. "About Face: Reorienting Thai Face For Soteriology and Mission." PhD diss., Pasadena, Calif.: Fuller Theological Seminary, 2005.

—————. "Fixing the Problem of Face." *Evangelical Missions Quarterly* 45, no. 1 (January 2009): 12–19.

—————. "Shame." Pages 813–17 in *Global Dictionary of Theology*. Edited by William A. Dyrness, Veli-Matti Karkkainen, Juan Francisco Martinez, and Simon Chan. Downers Grove, Ill.: IVP Academic, 2010.

Flemming, Dean. *Contextualization in the New Testament: Patterns for Theology and Mission*. Downers Grove, Ill.: IVP Academic, 2005.

Forrest, Peter. "Collective Guilt: Individual Shame." *Midwest Studies in Philosophy* 30 (2006): 145–53.

Francis, Glen R. "The Gospel in a Sin/Shame Based Society." *Taiwan Mission Quarterly* 2, no. 2 (October 1992): 5–16.

Fuller, Daniel. *The Unity of the Bible: Unfolding God's Plan for Humanity.* Grand Rapids, Mich.: Zondervan, 1992.

Funderburke, G. B. "Shame." Pages 372–73 in vol. 5 of *The Zondervan Pictorial Encyclopedia of the Bible.* 5 vols. Edited by Merrill C. Tenney. Grand Rapids, Mich.: Zondervan, 1975.

Gaffin, Richard B. "The Glory of God in Paul's Epistles." Pages 127–52 in *The Glory of God.* Edited by Christopher Morgan and Robert A. Peterson. Wheaton, Ill.: Crossway, 2010.

Gan, Chun Song. "Decline of the Imperial Examination System and the Disintegration of Institutional Confucianism [Abstract]." *Social Sciences in China* 23 (February 2002). Online: http://en.cnki.com.cn/Article_en/CJFDTOTAL-ZSHK200202009.htm.

Gao, Jun, Aimin Wang, and Mingyi Qian. "Differentiating Shame and Guilt from a Relational Perspective: A Cross-Cultural Study." *Social Behavior and Personality* 38, no. 10 (2010): 1401–7.

Gao, Shining. "The Impact of Contemporary Chinese Folk Religions on Christianity." Pages 170–71 in *Christianity and Chinese Culture.* Edited by Mikka Ruokanen and Paulos Huang. Grand Rapids, Mich.: Eerdmans, 2010.

Garcia, Mark A. "Imputation as Attribution: Union with Christ, Reification and Justification as Declarative Word." *International Journal of Systematic Theology* 11, no. 4 (October 2009): 415–27.

Garlington, Don B. "Imputation or Union with Christ? A Response to John Piper." *Reformation & Revival* 12, no. 4 (Fall 2003): 45–113.

Garrison, David and Richard Beckham. "Lesson 1–God's Plan of Salvation." *T4T Online Trainer's Manual* (Feb 2011): 55. Cited 31 Aug 2012. Online: http://t4t online.org/wp-content/uploads/2011/02/T4TOnline-Trainers-Manual.pdf

Gathercole, Simon J. *Where Is Boasting?: Early Jewish Soteriology and Paul's Response in Romans 1–5.* Grand Rapids, Mich.: Eerdmans, 2002.

———. "Justified by Faith, Justified by his Blood: The Evidence of Romans 3:21–4:5." Pages 147–84 in *The Paradoxes of Paul.* Edited by D. A. Carson, Peter T. O'Brien, and Mark Seifrid. Vol. 2 of *Justification and Variegated Nomism.* Grand Rapids, Mich.: Baker Academic, 2004.

Geertz, Clifford. *Local Knowledge.* New York, N.Y.: Harper Collins, 1983.

Georges, Jayson. "From Shame to Honor: A Theological Reading of Romans for Honor-Shame Contexts." *Missiology* 38, no. 3 (July 2010): 295–307.

Gilbert, Greg. *What Is the Gospel?* Wheaton, Ill.: Crossway, 2010.

————. "What is the Gospel?" Breakout Session presented at the Together for the Gospel, Louisville, Ky., April 2010. Online: http://t4g.org/media/2010/04/what-is-the-gospel/.

Gitay, Yehoshua. "Review of Katharine Doob Sakenfeld, 'The Meaning of Hesed in the Hebrew Bible: A New Inquiry'." *Journal of Biblical Literature* 98, no. 4 (December 1979): 583–84.

Glatt-Gilad, David A. "Yahweh's Honor at Stake: A Divine Conundrum." *Journal for the Study of the Old Testament* 26, no. 4 (June 2002): 63–74.

Goheen, Michael W. *A Light to the Nations: The Missional Church and the Biblical Story.* Grand Rapids, Mich.: Baker Academic, 2011.

Gold, Thomas, Doug Guthrie, and David L. Wank, eds. *Social Connections in China: Institutions, Culture, and the Changing Nature of Guanxi.* Cambridge: Cambridge University, 2002.

Gombis, Tim. Blog Comment. *The Gospel and Double Imputation*, October 25, 2011. Cited 25 October 2011. Online: http://www.patheos.com/community/jesuscreed/2011/10/25/the-gospel-and-double-imputation/?utm_source=feedburner&utm_medium=feed&utm_campaign=Feed%3A+PatheosJesusCreed+%28Blog+-+Jesus+Creed%29.

Gordon, M. R. "Glory." Pages 730–35 in vol. 2 of *The Zondervan Pictorial Encyclopedia of the Bible.* 5 vols. Edited by Merrill C. Tenney. Grand Rapids, Mich.: Zondervan, 1975.

Gorman, Michael J. "Effecting the New Covenant: A (Not So) New, New Testament Model for the Atonement." *Ex Auditu* 26 (2010): 26–59.

Gosnell, Peter W. "Honor and Shame Rhetoric as a Unifying Motif in Ephesians." *Bulletin for Biblical Research* 16, no. 1 (2006): 105–28.

Gospel Bridge [福音侨]. Singapore: Bible Society of Singapore, 2000.

Goulder, Alvin. "The Norm of Reciprocity: A Preliminary Statement." *American Sociological Review* 25 (1960): 161–79.

Graesser, Carl. "Righteousness, Human and Divine." *Currents in Theology and Mission* 10, no. 3 (1983): 134–41.

Graham, Keith. *Practical Reasoning in a Social World: How We Act Together.* Cambridge, UK: Cambridge University Press,, 2002.

Greeson, Kevin. *The Camel: How Muslims Are Coming to Faith in Christ!* Revised ed. Monument, Colo: WIGTake Resources, 2010.

Gries, Peter Hays. *China's New Nationalism: Pride, Politics, and Diplomacy.* Berkeley: University of California Press, 2004.

Gundry, Robert H. "The Nonimputation of Christ's Righteousness." Pages 17–45 in *Justification: What's at Stake in the Current Debates.* Edited by Mark Husbands and Daniel J. Treier. Downers Grove, Ill.: IVP, 2004.

Guo, Peilan. *Shangdi zai Yazhou renmin zhi zhong [God in the Midst of the Asian People].* Hong Kong: Jidujiao wenyi chubanshe, 1993.

Guthrie, Donald. *New Testament Theology.* Leicester: IVP, 1981.

Hafemann, Scott J. *The God of Promise and the Life of Faith: Understanding the Heart of the Bible.* Wheaton, Ill.: Crossway, 2001.

Hagedorn, Anselm C. "Honor and Shame." Pages 497–501 in *Dictionary of the Old Testament: Historical Books.* Edited by Bill T. Arnold and H. G. M. Williamson. The IVP Bible Dictionary Series. Downers Grove, Ill.: IVP Academic, 2005.

————. "Guarding the Parents' Honour—Deuteronomy 21.18–21." *Journal for the Study of the Old Testament* 88 (June 2000): 101–21.

Hagner, D. A. "Law, Righteousness, and Discipleship in Matthew." *Word & World* 18, no. 4 (1998): 364–71.

Halsall, Paul. "Chinese Cultural Studies: Concise Political History of China." Edited by Alan Zisman. *Compton's Living Encyclopedia.* Carlsbad, Calif.: Compton's NewMedia, August 1995. No Pages. Cited 5 March 2012. Online: http://academic.brooklyn.cuny.edu/core9/phalsall/ texts/chinhist.html.

Hamilton Jr., James. *God's Glory in Salvation through Judgment: A Biblical Theology.* Wheaton, Ill.: Crossway, 2010.

————. "The Glory of God in Salvation through Judgment: The Centre of Biblical Theology?" *Tyndale Bulletin* 57, no. 1 (2006): 57–84.

Hamilton, Victor P. *Handbook on the Pentateuch.* Grand Rapids, Mich.: Baker, 1982.

Harling, Mark. "De-westernizing Doctrine and Developing Appropriate Theology in Missions." *International Journal of Frontier Missions* 22, no. 4 (WInter 2005): 159–66.

313

Harrelson, W. "Honor." Pages 639–40 in vol. 2 of *The Interpreter's Dictionary of the Bible*. Edited by George Arthur Buttrick. 5 vols. New York, N.Y.: Abingdon, 1962.

Hays, Richard. "'Have We Found Abraham to be our Forefather According to the Flesh': A Reconsideration of Rom 4:1." *Novum Testamentum* 27, no. 1 (January 1985): 76–98.

He, Guanghu. "A Methodology of and Approaches to Sino-Christian Theology." Pages 106–119 in *Sino-Christian Studies in China*. Edited by Yang Huilin and Daniel H. N. Yeung. Newcastle, UK: Cambridge Scholars Publishing, 2006.

———. "The Basis and Significance of Sino-Christian Theology." Pages 120–132 in *Sino-Christian Studies in China*. Edited by Yang Huilin and Daniel H. N. Yeung. Newcastle, UK: Cambridge Scholars Publishing, 2006.

Hegermann, H. "δοξα." Pages 344–48 in vol. 1 of *Exegetical Dictionary of the New Testament*. 3 vols. Edited by Horst Balz and Gerhard Schneider. Grand Rapids, Mich.: Eerdmans, 1990.

Hellerman, Joseph H. *When the Church Was a Family: Recapturing Jesus' Vision for Authentic Christian Community*. Nashville, Tenn.: B & H Academic, 2009.

Hengel, Martin. *Juden, Griechen und Barben: Aspekte der Hellenisierung des Judentums in vorchristlicher Zeit*. SBS 76. Stuttgart: Katholisches Biblewerk, 1976.

———. *Judentum und Hellenismus*. 2d. ed. WUNT 10. Tübingen: Mohr [Siebeck], 1973.

Hesselgrave, David J. "Missionary Elenctics and Guilt and Shame." *Missiology* 11, no. 4 (October 1983): 461–83.

Hesselgrave, David J., and Edward Rommen. *Contextualization: Meanings, Methods, and Models*. Grand Rapids, Mich.: Baker, 1989.

Hiebert, Dennis, and Edmund Neufeld. "Me and Jesus? Countering Individualism with a More Collectivist Reading of Scripture." Paper presented at the Annual Meeting of the Evangelical Theological Society, Chicago, Ill., November 1994.

Hiebert, Paul. *Anthropological Insights for Missionaries*. Grand Rapids, Mich.: Baker, 1985.

———. *Anthropological Reflections on Missiological Issues*. Grand Rapids, Mich.: Baker, 1994.

———. "Cultural Difference and the Communication of the Gospel." Pages 373–83 in *Perspectives on the World Christian Movement: A Reader*. Edited by Ralph Winter, Steven C. Hawthorne, Darrell R. Dorr, D. Bruce Graham, and Bruce A. Koch. 3rd ed. Pasadena, Calif.: William Carey Library, 1999.

―――. "The Social Sciences and Missions: Applying the Message." Pages 184–216 in *Missiology and the Social Sciences: Contributions, Cautions, and Conclusions*. Edited by Gary Corwin and Edward Rommen. Pasadena, Calif.: William Carey Library, 1996.

―――. *Transforming Worldviews: An Anthropological Understanding of How People Change*. Grand Rapids, Mich.: Baker, 2008.

Hill, Charles. "Atonement in the Old and New Testaments." Pages 23–34 in *The Glory of the Atonement: Biblical, Theological & Practical Perspectives*. Edited by Charles E. Hill and Frank A. James III. Downers Grove, Ill.: IVP Academic, 2004.

Hill, Charles E., and Frank A. James III, eds. *The Glory of the Atonement: Biblical, Theological & Practical Perspectives*. Downers Grove, Ill.: IVP Academic, 2004.

Hill, David. *Greek Words and Hebrew Meanings: Studies in the Semantics of Soteriological Terms*. London: Cambridge University Press, 1967.

Hirsch, E. D. *Validity in Interpretation*. New Haven, Conn.: Yale, 1967.

Ho, D. Y. F. "Relational Orientation and Methodological Individualism." *Bulletin of the Hong Kong Psychological Society*, no. 26/27 (1991): 81–95.

Ho, David Yau-fai. "On the Concept of Face." *American Journal of Sociology* 81, no. 4 (1976): 866–84.

Hobbs, T. R. "Critical Notes: Reflections on Honor, Shame, and Covenantal Relations." *Journal of Biblical Literature* 116, no. 3 (1997): 501–3.

Hodge, Caroline Johnson. *If Sons, Then Heirs: A Study of Kinship and Ethnicity in the Letters of Paul* (Oxford: Oxford University Press, 2007).

Hoekema, Anthony. *Created in God's Image*. Grand Rapids, Mich.: Eerdmans, 1986.

―――. *Created in God's Image*. Grand Rapids, Mich.: Eerdmans, 1986.

Hofstede, Geert H. *Culture's Consequences: Comparing Values, Behaviors, Institutions, and Organizations Across Nations*. 2nd ed. Thousand Oaks: Sage, 2001.

Hong, Fu, David Watkins, and Eadaoin K. P. Hui. "Forgiveness and Personality in a Chinese Cultural Context." *IFE PsychologIA* 16, no. 1 (2008): 1–15.

―――. "Personality Correlates of the Disposition towards Interpersonal Forgiveness: A Chinese Perspective." *International Journal of Psychology* 39, no. 4 (2004): 305–16.

Hossfeld, Frank-Lothar, and Erich Zenger. *Psalms 2: A Commentary on Psalms 51–100*. Translated by Linda M. Maloney. Minneapolis, Minn.: Fortress, 2005.

Hou, Xiang-lang, and Liu He. "Comparative Study of Chinese Family and American Family." *US-China Foreign Language* 6, no. 7 (July 2008): 66–68.

How, Chuang Chua. "Revelation in the Chinese Characters: Divine or Divined?" Pages 229–39 in *Contextualization and Syncretism: Navigating Cultural Currents*. Edited by Gailyn Van Rheenen. Pasadena, Calif.: William Carey Library, 2006.

Howard, George, "Romans 3:21–31 and the Inclusion of the Gentiles." *Harvard Theological Review* 63 (1970): 223–233.

Hsiang, T. C. *Research on Chinese Charactoristics*. Taipei: Shang-wu Publishing, 1974.

Hsu, Evan Chen-Yih. "Yuan Zhiming's Treatment of Dao and Christian Theism: A Study of the Perceptions of Yuan's Approach to Contextualization Among Contemporary Chinese Intellectuals and Church Leaders." PhD diss., Deerfield, Ill.: Trinity International University, 2006.

Hu, Hsien Chin. "The Chinese Concepts of 'Face'." *American Anthropologist* 46, no. 1 (March 1944): 45–64.

Hu, Wenzhong, and Cornelius Lee Grove. *Encountering the Chinese: A Guide for Americans*. Yarmouth, Maine: Intercultural Press, 1991.

Huang, Paulos. "A Response to He Guanghu." Pages 70–84 in *Christianity and Chinese Culture*. Edited by Mikka Ruokanen and Paulos Huang. Grand Rapids, Mich.: Eerdmans, 2010.

Hüber, H. "τιμη." Pages 357–59 in vol. 3 of *Exegetical Dictionary of the New Testament*. 3 vols. Edited by Horst Balz and Gerhard Schneider. Grand Rapids, Mich.: Eerdmans, 1990.

Huber, Lyn Bechtel. "The Biblical Experience of Shame/Shaming in Biblical Israel in Relation to Its Use as Religious Metaphor." PhD diss., Madison, N.J.: Drew University, 1983.

Huilin, Yang, and Daniel H. N. Yeung, eds. *Sino-Christian Studies in China*. Newcastle: Cambridge Scholars Publishing, 2006.

Hundley, Raymond. "Towards An Evangelical Theology of Contextualization." PhD diss., Deerfield, Ill.: Trinity Evangelical Divinity School, 1993.

Hung, Daniel M. "Mission Blockade: Ancestor Worship." *Evangelical Missions Quarterly* 19, no. 1 (January 1983): 32–40.

Hwang, Kwang-Kuo. "Filial Piety and Loyalty: Two Types of Social Identification in Confucianism." *Asian Journal of Social Psychology* 2 (1999): 163–83.

———. *Foundations of Chinese Psychology: Confucian Social Relations*. New York, N.Y.: Springer, 2012.

———. "Moral Face and Social Face: Contingent Self-Esteem in Confucian Society." *International Journal of Psychology* 41, no. 4 (2006): 276–81.

———. "Two Moralities: Reinterpreting the Findings of Empirical Research on Moral Reasoning in Taiwan." *Asian Journal of Social Psychology* 1 (1998): 211–38.

Jackson, Bernard S. "Justice and Righteousness in the Bible: Rule of Law or Royal Paternalism?" *Zeitschrift für altorientalische und biblische Rechtsgeschichte* 4 (1998): 218–62.

Jacobs, Andrew. "Chinese Christians Defend Persecuted Underground Church." *The New York Times*, May 12, 2011, Online edition, sec. World/Asia Pacific. Online: http://www.nytimes.com/2011/05/13/world/asia/13china.html.

Jenkins, Philip. *The New Faces of Christianity: Believing the Bible in the Global South*. Oxford: Oxford University Press, 2006.

Jennings, J. Nelson. "A Missional Theology of the Glory of God." *The Glory of God*. Edited by Christopher Morgan and Robert A. Peterson. Wheaton, Ill.: Crossway, 2010.

Jervell, Jacob. *Imago Dei. Gen 1, 26 f. im Spätjudentum, in der Gnosis und in den paulinischen Briefen*. Göttingen: Vandenhoeck & Ruprecht, 1960.

Jewett, Robert. "Aimed at Overcoming Shameful Status-Romans as a Missionary Letter." *Hong Kong Theological Seminary Newsletter*. August 2008 edition.

———. "Honor and Shame in the Argument of Romans." Pages 258–76 in *Putting Body and Soul Together: Essays in Honor of Robin Scroggs*. Edited by Virginia Wiles, Alexandra R. Brown, and Graydon F. Snyder. Valley Forge, Pa.: Trinity Press, 1997.

———. *Romans: A Commentary*. Edited by Eldon Jay Epp. Minneapolis, Minn.: Fortress Press, 2006.

———. *Saint Paul Returns to the Movies: Triumph over Shame*. Grand Rapids, Mich.: Eerdmans, 1998.

———. "Shame and Atonement in Romans: A Potential Resources for Theology in Korea," Yonsei University, Seoul, Korea, November 1, 2007. Online:http://café 321.daum.net/_c21_/bbs_search_read?grpid=DzmC&fldid=TMZ2&contentval =00001zzzzzzzzzzzzzzzzzzzzzzzzz&nenc=&fenc=&from=&q=%B0%A5%B6%

F3%B5%F0%BE%C6%BC%AD%BF%E4%BE%E0&nil_profile=cafetop&nil_
menu=sch_updw&listnum=.

Jochim, Christian. *Chinese Religions*. Upper Saddle River, N.J.: Prentice-Hall, 1986.

Johnson, Dennis E. *Him We Proclaim: Preaching Christ From All the Scriptures*.
Phillipsburg, N.J.: P & R Publishing, 2007.

Johnson, Gary L. W., and Guy Prentiss Waters. *By Faith Alone: Answering the
Challenges to the Doctrine of Justification*. Wheaton, Ill.: Crossway Books, 2006.

Kang, C.H., and Ethel R. Nelson. *The Discovery of Genesis: How the Truths of Genesis
Were Found Hidden in the Chinese Language*. St. Louis, Mo.: Concordia, 1979.

Kasemann, Ernst. *Commentary on Romans*. Edited by Geoffrey W. Bromiley. Translated
by Geoffrey W. Bromiley. Grand Rapids, Mich.: Eerdmans, 1980.

Kato, Byang H. "The Gospel, Cultural Context, and Religious Syncretism." Pages 1216–
23 in *Let the Earth Hear His Voice*. Edited by J. D. Douglas. Minneapolis, Minn.:
World Wide, 1975.

Kaufman, Whitley. "Understanding Honor: Beyond the Shame/Guilt Dichotomy." *Social
Theory & Practice* 37, no. 4 (October 2011): 557–73.

Kekes, John. "Shame and Moral Progress." *Midwest Studies in Philosophy* 13, no. 1
(1988): 282–96.

Kennett, R. H., Adela Marion Adam, and H. M. Gwatkin. *Early Ideals of Righteousness:
Hebrew, Greek and Roman*. Edinburgh: T&T Clark, 1910.

Keown, Gerald L., Pamela J. Scalise, and Thomas G. Smothers. *Jeremiah 26–52*. WBC.
Dallas, Tex.: Word Books, 1995.

Kipnis, Andrew. *Producing Guanxi: Sentiment, Self, and Subculture in a North China
Village*. Durham, N.C.: Duke University Press, 1997.

Kittel, Gerhard. "δόξα." Pages 232–55 in vol. 2 of *Theological Dictionary of the New
Testament*. Edited by Gerhard Kittel, Gerhard Friedrich, Geoffrey William
Bromily. 10 vols. Grand Rapids, Mich.: Eerdmans, 1964.

Kline, Meredith. *Kingdom Prologue*. Overland Park, Kans.: Two Age Press, 2000.

Ko, N. H. "Familism in Confucianism" presented at the International Conference of
Women's Global Connection, San Antonio, 2004. Online:
http://wgc.womensglobalconnection.org/pdf/11naihuako.pdf.

Koch, Pamela. "Conflict, Collectivism and Confucianism: A Study of Interpersonal
Relationships in Hong Kong Organizations." Paper presented at the Annual

Meeting of the International Communication Association, New York, N.Y., May 5, 2009. Online: http://www.allacademic.com/meta/p14066_index.html.

Kraft, Charles H. "Culture, Worldview, and Contextualization." Pages 384–91 in *Perspectives on the World Christian Movement: A Reader*. Edited by Ralph Winter, Steven C. Hawthorne, Darrell R. Dorr, D. Bruce Graham, and Bruce A. Koch. 3rd ed. Pasadena, Calif.: William Carey Library, 1999.

Kraus, C. Norman. *Jesus Christ Our Lord: Christology from a Disciple's Perspective*. New York, N.Y.: Wipf & Stock, 2004.

———. "The Cross of Christ: Dealing with Shame and Guilt." *Japan Christian Quarterly* 53, no. 4 (Fall 1987): 221–27.

Kuyper, Abraham. *The Work of the Holy Spirit*. Translated by Henri De Vries. New York, N.Y.: Funk and Wagnalls, 1900.

Kuyper, Lester Jacob. "Righteousness and Salvation." *Scottish Journal of Theology* 30, no. 3 (1977): 233–52.

Lai, Pan-chiu. "Chinese Culture and the Development of Chinese Christian Theology." *Studies in World Christianity* 7, no. 2 (2001): 219–40.

———. "Chinese Religions and the History of Salvation: A Theological Perspective." *Ching Feng* 40, no. 1 (March 1997): 15–40.

Lai, Pan-chiu, and Jason T. S. Lam. "Retrospect and Prospect of Sino-Christian Theology: An Introduction." Pages 1–20 in *Sino-Christian Theology*. Edited by Pan-chiu Lai and Jason T. S. Lam. New York, N.Y.: Peter Lang, 2010.

Lai, Pan-chiu, and Jason Lam, eds. *Sino-Christian Theology*. New York, N.Y.: Peter Lang, 2010.

Lai, Pan-chiu. "Sino-Christian Theology, Bible, and Christian Tradition." Pages 161–78 in *Sino-Christian Theology*. Edited by Jason Lam and Pan-chiu Lai. New York, N.Y.: Peter Lang, 2010.

Lam, Wing-Hung. *Chinese Theology in Construction*. Pasadena, Calif.: William Carey Library, 1983.

Lawrence, Michael. *Biblical Theology in the Life of the Church: A Guide for Ministry*. Wheaton, Ill.: Crossway, 2010.

Lebra, Takie Sugiyama. "Compensative Justice and Moral Investment among Japanese, Chinese, and Koreans." Pages 43–60 in *Japanese Culture and Behavior: Selected Readings*. Edited by Takie Sugiyama Lebra and William P. Lebra. 2d. ed. Hawaii: University of Hawaii, 1986.

Lee, David Y. T. "Chinese Contextual Theology: A Possible Reconstruction." Pages 193–219 in *After Imperialism: Christian Identity in China and the Global Evangelical Movement*. Edited by Richard R. Cook and David W. Pao. Eugene, Ore.: Pickwick, 2011.

Lee, Sunny. "Beijing Suspicious of Japan's War Crime Apology." *The National*. Beijing, April 13, 2010, sec. Asia Pacific. Online: http://www.thenational.ae/news/world/asia-pacific/beijing-suspicious-of-japans-war-crime-apology.

Legge, James, trans. "The Great Learning and the Doctrine of the Mean." Pages 357–58 in vol. 1 of *The Chinese Classics*. 40 vols. Oxford: Clarendon Press, 1893. Online: http://ctext.org/liji/da-xue.

Lei, Duo. "Guanxi and Its Influence on Chinese Business Practices." *Harvard China Review* (Spring 2005): 81–84.

Leigh, Jackie D. "Honor, Shame, Resurrection." *Proceedings–Eastern Great Lakes and Midwest Biblical Societies* 23 (2003): 101–108.

Leland, Ryken, Jim Wilhoit, and Tremper Longman, eds. "Honor." Downers Grove, Ill.: IVP, 1998.

Lemche, Niels Peter. "Kings and Clients: On Loyalty Between the Rule and the Ruled in Ancient 'Israel'." *Semia* 66 (1994): 119–32.

Léon-Dufour, Xavier. "Glory." Pages 204–5 in *Dictionary of Biblical Theology*. 2d ed. Edited by Xavier Léon-Dufour. New York, N.Y.: Seabury Press, 1973.

Leske, Adrian M. "Righteousness as Relationship." Pages 125–37 in *Festschrift: A Tribute to Dr. William Hordern*. Edited by Walter Freitag. Saskatoon, Canada: University of Saskatchewan, 1985.

Li, Jin, Lianqin Wang, and Kurt W. Fischer. "The Organisation of Chinese Shame Concepts?" *Cognition & Emotion* 18, no. 6 (October 2004): 767–97.

Li, L., C. Lin, Z. Wu, S. Wu, M. J. Rotheram-Borus, R. Detels, et al. "Stigmatization and Shame: Consequences of Caring for HIV/AIDS Patients in China." *AIDS Care* 19, no. 2 (February 2007): 258–63.

Li, Pengye. "The Characteristics of Chinese Religion and the Development of Christianity in China." Pages 325–32 in *Sino-Christian Studies in China*. Edited by Yang Huilin and Daniel H. N. Yeung. Newcastle, UK: Cambridge Scholars Publishing, 2006.

———. "How Do Social and Psychological Needs Impact the Existence and Growth of Christianity in Moden China?" Pages 211–27 in *Christianity and Chinese Culture*. Edited by Mikka Ruokanen and Paulos Huang. Grand Rapids, Mich.: Eerdmans, 2010.

Li, Qiuling. "The Position of Religion in Chinese Society." Pages 276–86 in *Christianity and Chinese Culture*. Edited by Mikka Ruokanen and Paulos Huang. Grand Rapids, Mich.: Eerdmans, 2010.

Liang, Zhiping. "Explicating 'Law': A Comparative Perspective of Chinese and Western Legal Culture." *Journal of Chinese Law* 3, no. 1 (1989): 55–92.

Lienhard, Ruth. "Restoring Relationships: Theological Reflections on Shame and Honor Among the Daba and Ban of Cameroon." Dissertation, Pasadena, Calif.: Fuller Theological Seminary, 2000.

Lin, Canchu. "Western Research on Chinese Culture and Leadership" presented at the Annual Meeting of the International Communication Association, New Orleans Sheraton, New Orleans, La., May 27, 2004. Online: http://www.allacademic. com/meta/p113422_index.html.

Lin, Yutang. *My Country and My People*. New York, N.Y.: Reynal & Hitchcock, 1935.

Ling, Wenquan, Rosina Chia, and LiLuo Fang. "Chinese Implicit Leadership Theory." *The Journal of Social Psychology* 140, no. 6 (2000): 729–39.

Littlejohn, Ronnie. *Confucianism: An Introduction*. New York, N.Y.: I. B. Tauris, 2010.

Liu, Dilin. *Metaphor, Culture, and Worldview: The Case of American English and the Chinese Language*. Lanham, Md.: University Press of America, 2002.

Liu, Hai-feng. "On the Development and Multiplication of the Imperial Examination System and Confucianism [Abstract]." *Journal of China University of Geosciences (Social Sciences Edition)* 45, no. 9 (January 2009). Online: http://en.cnki.com.cn/Article_en/CJFDTOTAL-DDXS200901002.htm.

Liu, Li. "Filial Piety, Guanxi, Loyalty, and Money: Trust in China." Pages 51–73 in *Trust and Distrust: Sociocultural Perspectives*. Edited by Ivana Marková and Alex Gillespie. Charlotte, N.C.: Information Age Publishing, 2008.

Liu, Qiuling. "Historical Reflections on 'Sino-Christian Theology'." Pages 35–52 in *Sino-Christian Studies in China*. Edited by Huilin Yang and Daniel H. N. Yeung, Translated by Alison Hardie. Newcastle: Cambridge Scholars, 2006.

Liu, Xiaofeng. *Hanyu Shenxue yu Lishi Zhexue [The Sino-Christian Theology and Philosophy of History]*. Hong Kong: Institute of Sino-Christian Studies, 2000.

Longenecker, Richard N. *Introducing Romans: Critical Issues in Paul's Most Famous Letter*. Grand Rapids, Mich.: Eerdmans, 2011.

Louw, Johannes, and Eugene Nida, eds. "ἔνδειξις." *Greek-English Lexicon of the New Testament Based on Semantic Domains*. New York, N.Y.: United Bible Societies, 1988.

Luo, Guanzong. "'Foreword'." Pages 1–18 in *Remembering the Past as a Lesson for the Future*. Edited by Guanzong Luo. Beijing: Religious Culture Publishers, 2003.

Luther, Martin. *Lectures on Romans: Glosses and Scholia*. Vol. 25 of *Luther's Works*. Edited by Hilton C. Oswald. Translated by Walter G. Tillmans and Jacob Preus. St. Louis, Mo.: Concordia, 1972.

———. *Table Talk*. Edited by William Hazlitt. Gainesville, Fla.: Bridge-Logos, 2004.

Luzbetak, Louis J. *The Church and Cultures: New Perspectives in Missiological Anthropology*. Maryknoll, N.Y.: Orbis Books, 1988.

Malina, Bruce. "Collectivism in Mediterranean Culture." Pages 17–28 in *Understanding the Social World of the New Testament*. Edited by Dietmar Neufeld and R. E. DeMaris. New York, N.Y.: Routledge, 2010.

Malina, Bruce, and Jerome H. Neyrey. *Portraits of Paul: An Archaeology of Ancient Personality*. Louisville, Ky.: Westminster John Knox Press, 1996.

Malina, Bruce. *The New Testament World: Insights from Cultural Anthropology*. 3rd ed. Atlanta, Ga.: John Knox, 2001.

Marquand, Robert. "US 'Sorry' Heard in Beijing as an Apology." *Christian Science Moniter*, April 12, 2001. Online: http://www.csmonitor.com/2001/0412/p1s2.html.

May, David M. "'Drawn from Nature or Common Life': Social and Cultural Reading Strategies for the Parables." *Review and Expositor* (1997): 199–214.

Mbuvi, Andrew M. "African Theology from the Perspective of Honor and Shame." Pages 279–95 in *The Urban Face of Mission: Ministering the Gospel in a Diverse and Changing World*. Edited by Manuel Ortiz and Susan S. Baker. Phillipsburg, N.J.: P & R Publishing, 2002.

McCarthy, Dennis J. "Notes on the Love of God in Deuteronomy and the Father-Son Relationship Between Yahweh and Israel." *Catholic Biblical Quarterly* (April 1, 1965): 144–47.

McDowell, Josh. *Deception or Reality*. Ephrata, Pa.: Multilanguage Media, No Date. Online: http://www.multilanguage.com/css/Default.htm.

McCartney, Dan. "Atonement in James, Peter, and Jude." Pages 180–89 in *The Glory of the Atonement: Biblical, Theological & Practical Perspectives*. Edited by Charles E. Hill and Frank A. James III. Downers Grove, Ill.: IVP Academic, 2004.

McKay, J. W. "Man's Love for God in Deuteronomy and the Father/Teacher-Son/Pupil Relationship." *Vetus Testamentum* (October 1, 1972): 426–35.

McKnight, Scot. *A Community Called Atonement: Living Theology.* Nashville, Tenn.: Abingdon, 2007.

———. *The King Jesus Gospel: The Original Good News Revisited.* Grand Rapids, Mich.: Zondervan, 2011.

McQuilkin, Robert. "Use and Misuse of the Social Sciences: Interpreting the Biblical Text." Pages 165–83 in *Missiology and the Social Sciences: Contributions, Cautions, and Conclusions.* Edited by Edward Rommen and Gary Corwin. Pasadena, Calif.: William Carey Library, 1996.

Mencius. "The Works of Mencius, Book 2, Part 1: Kung-sun Ch'au," December 1, 2011. Online: http://nothingistic.org/library/mencius/mencius12.html.

———. "The Works of Mencius, Book 6, Part 1: Kai Tsze," December 1, 2011. Online: http://nothingistic.org/library/mencius/mencius42.html.

———. "The Works of Mencius, Book 7, Part 1: Tsin Sin," December 1, 2011. Online: http://nothingistic.org/library/mencius/mencius49.html.

Moo, Douglas J. "Israel and the Law in Romans 5–11: Interaction with the New Perspective." Pages 39–74 in *The Paradoxes of Paul.* Edited by D. A. Carson, Peter T. O'Brien, and Mark Seifrid. Vol. 2 of *Justification and Variegated Nomism.* Grand Rapids, Mich.: Baker Academic, 2004.

Moran, William L. "The Ancient Near Eastern Background of the Love of God in Deuteronomy." *Catholic Biblical Quarterly* 25 (January 1, 1963): 77–87.

Moreau, Scott. "Contextualization That Is Comprehensive." *Missiology: An International Review* 34, no. 3 (July 2006): 325–35.

———. "Evangelical Models of Contextualization." Pages 165–93 in *Local Theology for the Global Church: Principles for an Evangelical Approach to Contextualization.* Edited by Matthew Cook, Rob Haskell, Ruth Julian, and Natee Tanchanpongs. Pasadena, Calif.: William Carey Library, 2010.

Morgan, Christopher, and Robert A. Peterson, eds. *The Glory of God.* Wheaton, Ill.: Crossway, 2010.

Morris, Leon. *The Apostolic Preaching of the Cross.* 3d. ed. Grand Rapids, Mich.: Eerdmans, 1965.

———. *The Epistle to the Romans.* Grand Rapids, Mich.: Eerdmans, 1988.

Mounce, Robert H. *Romans.* The New American Commentary 27. Nashville, Tenn.: B & H, 1995.

Moxnes, Halvor. "Honor and Shame." *Biblical Theology Bulletin* 23, no. 4 (1993): 167–76.

———. "Honor, Shame, and the Outside World in Paul's Letter to the Romans." Pages 207–18 in *Social World of Formative Christianity and Judaism*. Philadelphia, Pa.: Fortress Press, 1988.

———. "Honour and Righteousness in Romans." *Journal for the Study of the New Testament* 32 (1988): 61–77.

———. "Paulus og den norske vaerematen': Skam' og 'aere' i Romerbrevet." *Norsk Teologisk Tidsskrift* 86, no. 3 (1985): 129–40.

———. "The Quest for Honor and the Unity of the Community in Romans 12 and in the Orations of Dio Chrysostom." Pages 203–30 in *Paul in His Hellenistic Context*. Edited by Engberg-Pedersen, T. Minneapolis, Minn.: Fortress Press, 1995.

———. *Theology in Conflict: Studies in Paul's Understanding of God in Romans*. Leiden: Brill, 1980.

Müller, Roland. *Honor and Shame: Unlocking the Door*. Bloomington, Ind.: Xlibris, 2001.

———. "Shame Tract." *rmuller.com*. No Date. Online: http://www.rmuller.com/ShameTract.pdf.

Müller, Roland. *The Messenger, the Message and the Community: Three Critical Issues for the Cross-Cultural Church Planter*. 2nd ed. Osler, Canada: CanBooks, 2010.

Murray, John. *Redemption: Accomplished and Applied*. Grand Rapids, Mich.: Eerdmans, 1980.

———. *The Epistle to the Romans*. Grand Rapids, Mich.: Eerdmans, 1997.

Musk, Bill A. "Honour and Shame." *Evangelical Review of Theology* 20, no. 2 (April 1996): 155–67.

Neumann, Mikel. "Contextualization: Application or Interpretation." Evangelical Theological Society papers; ETS-5017. Orlando, Fla., 1998.

Newbigin, Lesslie. *The Gospel in a Pluralist Society*. Grand Rapids, Mich.: Eerdmans, 1989.

Neyrey, Jerome H. *Honor and Shame in the Gospel of Matthew*. Louisville, Ky.: Westminster John Knox Press, 1998.

Ng, Margaret N. "Internal Shame as a Moral Sanction." *Journal of Chinese Philosophy* 8 (March 1981): 75–86.

Ni, Huiliang. "Sinicizing Jesus in the First Half of the Twentieth Century: How Chinese Christians Understood Jesus." PhD diss., Claremont, Calif.: Claremont Graduate University, 2008.

Nicholls, Bruce J. "Contextualisation in Chinese Culture." *Evangelical Review of Theology* 19, no. 4 (October 1995): 368–80.

———. *Contextualization: A Theology of Gospel and Culture*. Vancouver, BC: Regent College, 2003.

———. "The Role of Shame and Guilt in a Theology of Cross-Cultural Mission." *Evangelical Review of Theology* 25, no. 3 (July 2001): 231–41.

———. "The Servant Songs of Isaiah in Dialogue with Muslims." *Evangelical Review of Theology* 20 (1996): 168–77.

———. "Theological Education and Evangelization." Pages 634–48 in *Let the Earth Hear His Voice*. Edited by J. D. Douglas. Minneapolis, Minn.: World Wide, 1975.

Nicole, Emile. "Atonement in the Pentateuch." Pages 35–50 in *The Glory of the Atonement: Biblical, Theological & Practical Perspectives*. Edited by Charles E. Hill and Frank A. James III. Downers Grove, Ill.: IVP Academic, 2004.

Nicole, Roger. "Postscript on Penal Substitution." Pages 445–52 in *The Glory of the Atonement: Biblical, Theological & Practical Perspectives*. Edited by Charles E. Hill and Frank A. James III. Downers Grove, Ill.: IVP Academic, 2004.

Nisbett, Richard E. *The Geography of Thought: How Asians and Westerners Think Differently . . . and Why*. New York, N.Y.: Free Press, 2003.

Van Norden, Bryan W. "The Emotion of Shame and the Virtue of Righteousness in Mencius." *Dao: A Journal of Comparative Philosophy* 2, no. 1 (Winter 2002): 45–77.

Nwachukwu, M. S. C. *Creation-Covenant Scheme and Justification by Faith: A Canonical Study of the God-Human Drama in the Pentateuch and the Letter to the Romans*. Tesi Gregoriana, Serie Teologia 89. Rome: Editrice Pontificia Università Gregoriana, 2002.

O'Neill, Barry. *Honor, Symbols, and War*. Ann Arbor, Mich.: University of Michigan Press, 2001.

O'Reilly, Matt. "Robert Jewett, Romans: a Commentary." *Princeton Theological Review* 14, no. 39 (Fall 2008): 117–19.

Oden, Thomas C. *The Justification Reader*. Grand Rapids, Mich.: Eerdmans, 2002.

Olyan, Saul M. "Honor, Shame, and Covenant Relations in Ancient Israel and Its Environment." *Journal of Biblical Literature* 115, no. 2 (Sum 1996): 201–18.

Osborne, Grant. *The Hermeneutical Spiral: A Comprehensive Introduction to Biblical Interpretation.* 2nd ed. Downers Grove, Ill.: IVP, 2006.

Oswalt, J. "Isaiah 60–62: The Glory of the Lord." *Calvin Theological Journal* 40 (2005): 95–103.

Oswalt, J. N. "Justice and Righteousness." Pages 606–9 in *Dictionary of the Old Testament: Historical Books.* The IVP Bible Dictionary Series. Edited by Bill T. Arnold and H. G. M. Williamson. Downers Grove, Ill.: IVP Academic, 2005.

Oyserman, Daphna, Heather M. Coon, and Markus Kemmelmeier. "Rethinking Individualism and Collectivism: Evaluation of Theoretical Assumptions and Meta-Analyses." *Psychological Bulletin* 128, no. 1 (2002): 3–72.

Packer, J. I. *Evangelism and the Sovereignty of God.* Downers Grove, Ill.: IVP, 2008.

———. *Knowing God.* 20th Anniversary ed. Downers Grove, Ill.: IVP, 1993.

———. "The Atonement in the Life of the Christian." Pages 409–25 in *The Glory of the Atonement: Biblical, Theological & Practical Perspectives.* Edited by Charles E. Hill and Frank A. James III. Downers Grove, Ill.: IVP Academic, 2004.

Pan, James. "Contextualization: A Methodological Enquiry with Examples from the History of Theology." *South East Asia Journal of Theology* 21, no. 2–1 (1981): 47–64.

Parsons, Martin. *Unveiling God: Contextualizing Christology for Islamic Culture.* Pasadena, Calif.: William Carey Library, 2006.

Patterson, Richard. "Parental Love as a Metaphor for Divine-Human Love." *Journal of the Evangelical Theological Society* 46, no. 2 (January 2003): 205–16.

Paz, Regina, Felix Neto, and Etienne Mullet. "Forgiveness: A Chinese-Western Europe Comparison." *The Journal of Psychology* 142, no. 2 (2008): 147–57.

Peristiany, J. G., and Julian Pitt-Rivers. *Honor and Grace in Anthropology.* Cambridge, UK: Cambridge University Press, 2005.

Perkins, Pheme. "Justice, NT [δικαιοσυνη]." Pages 475–76 in vol. 3 of *The New Interpreter's Dictionary of the Bible.* 5 vols. Edited by Katharine Sakenfeld. Nashville: Abingdon, 2006.

Peters, George W. "Issues Confronting Evangelical Missions." Pages 156–71 in *Evangelical Missions Tomorrow.* Edited by E. L. Frizen and Wade Coggins. Pasadena, Calif.: William Carey Library, 1977.

Pilch, John. *Handbook of Biblical Social Values*. Updated ed. Peabody, Mass.: Hendrickson, 2000.

Piper, John. *Counted Righteous in Christ: Should We Abandon the Imputation of Christ's Righteousness?* Wheaton, Ill.: Crossway, 2002.

———. *Desiring God: Meditations of a Christian Hedonist*. Sisters, Ore.: Multnomah Books, 1996.

———. *Future Grace*. Sisters, Ore.: Multnomah Press, 1995.

———. *God Is the Gospel: Meditations on God's Love as the Gift of Himself*. Reprint. Wheaton, Ill.: Crossway, 2011.

———. "How Is God's Passion for His Own Glory Not Selfishness?" *Desiring God*, November 24, 2007. Online: http://www.desiringgod.org/resource-library/articles/how-is-gods-passion-for-his-own-glory-not-selfishness.

———. "Is God for Us or for Himself?" *Desiring God*, August 10, 1980. Online: http://www.desiringgod.org/resource-library/sermons/is-god-for-us-or-for-himself.

———. *Let the Nations Be Glad!: The Supremacy of God in Missions*. Grand Rapids, Mich.: Baker, 1993.

———. "Savoring, Instilling, and Spreading the Vision at Bethlehem Baptist Church." *Desiring God*, September 20, 1987. Online: http://www.desiringgod.org/resource-library/sermons/savoring-instilling-and-spreading-the-vision-at-bethlehem-baptist-church.

———. "The Demonstration of God's Righteousness, Part 3." *Desiring God*, May 23, 1999. Online: http://www.desiringgod.org/resource-library/sermons/the-demonstration-of-gods-righteousness-part-3.

———. *The Justification of God: An Exegetical and Theological Study of Romans 9:1–23*. 2nd ed. Grand Rapids, Mich.: Baker Academic, 1993.

———. *The Justification of God: An Exegetical and Theological Study of Romans 9:1–23*. Grand Rapids, Mich.: Baker, 1983.

———. *The Passion of Jesus Christ: Fifty Reasons Why He Came to Die*. Wheaton, Ill.: Crossway, 2004.

———. *The Pleasures of God*. Colorado Springs, Colo.: Multnomah Books, 2000.

———. "The Revelation of God's Righteousness Where There Is No Church." *Desiring God*, November 7, 1999. Online: http://www.desiringgod.org/resource-library/sermons/the-revelation-of-gods-righteousness-where-there-is-no-church.

————. "Why God Is Not a Megalomaniac in Demanding to Be Worshiped." Presented at the Evangelical Theological Society (ETS) Annual Meeting, Providence, Rhode Island, November 20, 2008. Online: http://www.desiringgod.org/resource-library/conference-messages/why-god-is-not-a-megalomaniac-in-demanding-to-be-worshiped.

————. "Why God Tells Us He Delights in His Children." *Desiringgod.org*, August 23, 2006. Online: http://desiringgod.org/resource-library/taste-see-articles/why-god-tells-us-he-delights-in-his-children.htm.

Pitt-Rivers, Julian. "Honour and Social Status." Pages 19–77 in *Honour and Shame: The Values of Mediterranean Society.* Edited by Jean G. Peristiany. Chicago, Ill.: University of Chicago Press,, 1966.

Poceski, Mario. *Chinese Religions: The eBook.* State College, Pa.: JBE Online Books, 2009.

Porras, Nancy. "Doing Theology in a Chinese Context." *International Journal of Frontier Missions* 4 (January 1987): 53–67.

Porter, Calvin. "God's Justice and the Culture of the Law: Conflicting Traditions in Paul's Letter to the Romans." *Encounter* 59, no. 1–2 (1998): 135–55.

Pratt, Zane. "Biblical Foundations and Guidelines for Contextualization." No Date. This was an internal document passed around to PhD seminar students at Southeastern Baptist Theological Seminary, Wake Forest, N.C. in 2010.

Priest, Robert J. "Shame." Pages 870–71 in *Evangelical Dictionary of World Missions.* Edited by Scott Moreau. Grand Rapids, Mich.: Baker, 2000.

Promfret, John. *Chinese Lessons: Five Classmates and the Story of the New China.* New York, N.Y.: Henry Holt & Co, 2006.

Pruyser, Paul W. "Anxiety, Guilt, and Shame in the Atonement." *Theology Today* 21, no. 1 (April 1964): 15–33.

Przybylski, Benno. *Righteousness in Matthew and His World of Thought.* Cambridge: Cambridge University Press, 1980.

Pye, Lucian W. "How China's Nationalism was Shanghaied." *Australian Journal of Chinese Affairs*, no. 29 (January 1993): 107–33.

Rappa, Antonio L., and Sor-Hoon Tan. "Political Implications of Confucian Familism." *Asian Philosophy* 13, no. 2/3 (2003): 87–102.

Reiff, Mark R. "Terrorism, Retribution, and Collective Responsibility." *Social Theory and Practice* 34, no. 2 (April 2008): 209–42.

Reumann, John. "Righteousness." Pages 724–73 in vol. 5 of *The Anchor Bible Dictionary*. 6 vols. Edited by David Noel Freedman. New York, N.Y.: Doubleday, 1992.

Rheenen, Gailyn Van, ed. *Contextualization and Syncretism*. Pasadena, Calif.: William Carey Library, 2006.

Richardson, Don. *Peace Child*. Glendale, Calif.: Regal Books, 1974.

————. "Redemptive Analogy." Pages 397–403 in *Perspectives on the World Christian Movement: A Reader*. Edited by Ralph Winter, Steven C. Hawthorne, Darrell R. Dorr, D. Bruce Graham, and Bruce A. Koch. 3rd ed. Pasadena, Calif.: William Carey Library, 1999.

Richter, Sandra L. *The Epic of Eden: A Christian Entry into the Old Testament*. Downers Grove, Ill.: IVP, 2008.

Robinson, Edward. "δικαιοω." *A Greek and English Lexicon of the New Testament*. Boston, Mass.: Crocker and Brewster, 1836.

Rommen, Edward and Gary Corwin, eds. *Missiology and the Social Sciences: Contributions, Cautions and Conclusions*. Pasadena, Calif.: William Carey Library, 1996.

Rosenthal, Elisabeth. "Chinese Distaste For Apologies Means Business: Companies Ask Forgiveness, Lose Face, for San Francisco Chronicle." *www.SFGate.com*. San Francisco, Calif., January 7, 2001, sec. Business.

Routledge, Robin. "*Hesed* as Obligation: A Re-Examination." *Tyndale Bulletin* 46, no. 1 (May 1995): 179–96.

Ryken, Leland, Jim Wilhoit, and Tremper Longman, eds. "Shame." Page 780 of *Dictionary of Biblical Imagery*. Downers Grove, Ill.: IVP, 1998.

Ryken, Philip Graham. *Justification*. Wheaton, Ill.: Crossway, 2011.

Sakenfeld, Katharine Doob. *The Word Hesed in the Hebrew Bible: A New Inquiry*. Missoula, Mont.: Scholars Press, 1978.

Sanders, E. P. *Paul and Palestinian Judaism: A Comparison of Patterns of Religion*. Philadelphia, Pa.: Fortress Press, 1977.

Sawatzky, Sheldon. "Body as Metaphor in Chinese Religious Cultures: Implications for Chinese Ecclesiology." *Taiwan Journal of Theology* 16 (1994): 93–121.

————. "Chinese Ecclesiology in Context." *Taiwan Journal of Theology*, no. 5 (1983): 149–64.

Schreiner, Thomas, Gregory A. Boyd, Joel B. Green, and Bruce R. Reichenbach. *The Nature of the Atonement: Four Views*. Edited by James Beilby and Paul R. Eddy. Downers Grove, Ill.: IVP Academic, 2006.

Schreiner, Thomas. "Did Paul Believe in Justification by Works? Another Look at Romans 2." *Bulletin for Biblical Research* 3 (1993): 131–55.

———. "Is Perfect Obedience to the Law Possible? A Re-examination of Galatians 3:10." *Journal of the Evangelical Theological Society* 27, no. 2 (1984): 151–60.

———. *New Testament Theology: Magnifying God in Christ*. Grand Rapids, Mich.: Baker Academic, 2008.

———. "Paul and Perfect Obedience to the Law: An Evaluation of the View of E. P. Sanders." *Westminster Theological Journal* 47, no. 2 (Fall 1985): 245–78.

———. *Paul, Apostle of God's Glory in Christ: A Pauline Theology*. Downers Grove, Ill.: IVP, 2001.

———. "Review of Romans: A Commentary. Robert Jewett." *Bulletin for Biblical Research* 19 (2009): 446–48.

———. *Romans*. Grand Rapids, Mich.: Baker Academic, 1998.

———. "'Works of Law' in Paul." *Novum Testamentum* 33, no. 3 (1991): 217–44.

———. "Penal Substitution View." Pages 67–98 in *The Nature of the Atonement: Four Views*. Edited by James Beilby and Paul R. Eddy. Downers Grove, Ill.: IVP Academic, 2006.

———. "Review of Scott Hafemann, 'Paul, Moses, and the History of Israel: The Letter/Spirit Contrast and the Argument from Scripture in 2 Corinthians 3'." No Date. Online: http://www.sbts.edu/documents/tschreiner/review_Hafemann2Cor3.pdf.htm.

Seifrid, Mark. *Christ, Our Righteousness: Paul's Theology of Justification*. New Studies in Biblical Theology 9. Downers Grove, Ill.: IVP, 2000.

———. *Justification by Faith: The Origin and Development of a Central Pauline Theme*. NovTSup 68. Leiden: Brill, 1992.

———. "Paul's Use of Righteousness Language Against Its Hellenistic Background." Pages 39–74 in *The Paradoxes of Paul*. Edited by D. A. Carson, Peter T. O'Brien, and Mark Seifrid. Vol. 2 of *Justification and Variegated Nomism*. Grand Rapids, Mich.: Baker Academic, 2004.

———. "Righteousness Language in the Hebrew Scriptures and Early Judaism." Pages 415–42 in *The Complexities of Second Temple Judaism*. Edited by D. A. Carson,

Peter T. O'Brien, and Mark Seifrid. Vol. 1 of Justification and Variegated Nomism. Grand Rapids, Mich.: Baker Academic, 2001.

———. "Righteousness, Justice, and Justification." Pages 740–45 in *New Dictionary of Biblical Theology*. Edited by T. Desmond Alexander and Brian S. Rosner. Downers Grove, Ill.: IVP, 2000.

———. "Romans." Pages 607–94 in *Commentary on the New Testament Use of the Old Testament*. Edited by G. K. Beale and D. A. Carson. Grand Rapids, Mich.: Baker, 2007.

———. "Unrighteousness by Faith: Apostolic Proclamation in Romans 1:18–3:20." Pages 105–46 in *The Paradoxes of Paul*. Edited by D. A. Carson, Mark A. Seifrid, and Peter T. O'Brien. Vol. 2 of *Justification and Variegated Nomism*. Grand Rapids, Mich.: Baker Academic, 2004.

Sessions, William Lad. "Honor and God." *The Journal of Religion* 87, no. 2 (April 2007): 206–24.

Shan, Mark C. H. *Beware of Patriotic Heresy in the Church in China: Drawing on the Historical Lessons of the Nazis' Volk Church to Analyze the Zhao Xiao Phenomenon*. Boston, Mass.: Chinese Christian Theological Association, 2012.

Shen, Deyong. "Chinese Judicial Culture: From Tradition to Modernity." *BYU Journal of Public Law* 25 (October 21, 2009): 131–41.

Shive, Glenn. "Conclusion: The Future of Chinese Religious Life." Pages 241–54 in *Chinese Religious Life*. Edited by David A. Palmer, Glenn Landes Shive, and Philip L. Wickeri. New York, N.Y.: Oxford University Press, 2011.

Shun, Kwong-loi. *Mencius and Early Chinese Thought*. Palo Alto, Calif.: Stanford University Press, 1997.

Sills, M. David. *Reaching and Teaching: A Call to Great Commission Obedience*. Chicago, Ill.: Moody Publishers, 2010.

Smith, Huston. "Chinese Religion in World Perspective." *Dialogue and Alliance* 4, no. 2 (Summer 1990): 4–14.

Smith, Steve. "Gospel Presentations Used in T4T Packages." www.t4tonline.org, 2011. No Pages. Cited 21 Feb 2012. Online: http://t4tonline.org/wpcontent/uploads/2011/02/3d-Gospel-Presentations-Used-in-T4T-Packages.pdf.

Smith, Steve, and Ying Kai. *T4T: A Discipleship ReRevolution*. Monument, Colo: WIGTake, 2011.

Song, C. S. "Christian Theology: Towards An Asian Reconstruction." Paper presented at the Conference of World Mission and the Role of Korean Churches, Seoul, Korea,

November 1995. Online: http://www.religion-
online.org/showarticle.asp?title=128.

———. "In The Beginning Were Stories, Not Texts." *Madong* 14 (December 2010): 7–
16.

———. "The New China and Salvation History: A Methodological Enquiry." *South East
Asia Journal of Theology* 15, no. 2 (1974): 52–67.

———. *Third-Eye Theology: Theology in Formation in Asian Settings.* Eugene, Ore.:
Wipf & Stock, 2002.

"Sons of Heaven: Inside China's Fastest-Growing Non-Governmental Organization." *The
Economist*, October 2, 2008. No Pages. Cited 28 Oct 2010. Online:
http://www.economist.com/node/12342509?story_id=12342509.htm.

SpreadTruth. "View the Story." No Date. Online: http://viewthestory.com/.

Sprinkle, Preston. "The Afterlife in Romans: Understanding Paul's Glory Motif in Light
of the Apocalypse of Moses and 2 Baruch." Pages 201–33 in
*Lebendige Hoffnung–ewiger Tod?!: Jenseitsvorstellungen im Hellenismus,
Judentum und Christentum.* Edited by Manfred Lang and Michael Labhan.
Arbeiten zur Bibel und ihrer Geschichte 24; Leipzig: Evangelische Verlagsanstalt:
2007), 205–6.

Sproul, R. C., and Keith A. Mathison, eds. "Commentary on Ps 116:11." Page 841 in *The
Reformation Study Bible: English Standard Version.* Orlando, Fla.: Ligonier
Ministries, 2005.

Standaert, Nicolas. *Inculturation: On the Gospel and Culture.* Translated by Chen
Kuanwei. Taibei: Kuang Chi, 1993.

Standaert, Nicolas, ed. *Handbook of Christianity in China: 635–1800.* Vol. 1 of
Handbook of Oriental Studies. 8 vols. Leiden: Brill, 2001.

Stendahl, Krister. *Paul Among Jews and Gentiles, and Other Essays.* Philadelphia, Pa.:
Fortress Press, 1976.

Stewart, Edward C. *American Cultural Patterns: A Cross-Cultural Perspective.*
Yarmouth, Maine: Intercultural Press, 1972.

Stover, Leon. *The Cultural Ecology of Chinese Civilization: Peasants and Elites in the
Last of the Agrarian States.* New York, N.Y.: New American Library, 1974.

Strand, Mark. "Explaining Sin in a Chinese Context." *Missiology: An International
Review* 28, no. 4 (2000): 427–42.

Strauss, Steve. "The Role of Context in Shaping Theology." Pages 99–128 in *Contextualization and Syncretism: Navigating Cultural Currents*. Edited by Gailyn Van Rheenen. Pasadena, Calif.: William Carey Library, 2006.

Striblen, Cassie. "Guilt, Shame, and Shared Responsibility." *Journal of Social Philosophy* 38, no. 3 (Fall 2007): 469–85.

Stults, Donald Leroy. *Developing an Asian Evangelical Theology*. Manila: OMF, 1989.

Sun, Catherine Tien-Lun. *Themes in Chinese Psychology*. Cengage Learning: Singapore, 2008.

Tak, Sing Cheung, Man Chan Hoi, Man Chan Kin, Ambrose Y. C. King, Yue Chiu Chi, and Fang Yang Cheng. "How Confucian Are Contemporary Chinese? Construction of an Ideal Type and Its Application to Three Chinese Communities." *European Journal of East Asian Studies* 5, no. 2 (2006): 157–80.

Talman, Harley. "Islam, Once a Hopeless Frontier, Now? Comprehensive Contextualization." *International Journal of Frontier Missions* 21, no. 1 (Spring 2004): 6–12.

Tan, Betty O. S. "The Contextualization of the Chinese New Year Festival." *Asia Journal of Theology* 15, no. 1 (2001): 115–32.

Tang, Edmond. "Chinese Theologies." Pages 38–40 in *Dictionary of Third World Theologies*. Edited by Virginia Fabella and R. S Sugirtharajah. Maryknoll, N.Y.: Orbis Books, 2000.

———. "The Cosmic Christ: The Search for a Chinese Theology." *Studies in World Christianity* 1, no. 2 (1995): 131–42.

Tan, Hann-Tzuu (Joey). *The Chinese Way—Contextualizing the Gospel for the Chinese*. Kindle Edition. Self-Published, 2012.

Tate, Marvin E. *Psalms 51–100*. Word Biblical Commentary 20. Dallas, Tex.: Word Books, 1990.

Tennent, Timothy C. *Theology in the Context of World Christianity: How the Global Church Is Influencing the Way We Think about and Discuss Theology*. Grand Rapids, Mich.: Zondervan, 2007.

The Cambridge Declaration of the Alliance of Confessing Evangelicals, April 20, 1996. Online: http://www.reformed.org/documents/index.html? mainframe=http://www.reformed.org/documents/cambridge.html.

The NET Bible Version 1.0. 3rd; Electronic Version for BibleWorks 7.0. Bible Studies Foundation, Copyright © 2004, 2005. The Net Bible maps are Copyright © 2004 ROHR Productions. All Rights Reserved

"The Roman Road." No Date. Online: http://theromanroad.org/.

Thielman, Frank. "The Group and the Individual in Salvation: The Witness of Paul."
    Pages 136–53 in *After Imperialism: Christian Identity in China and the Global
    Evangelical Movement*. Edited by Richard R. Cook and David W. Pao. Eugene,
    Ore.: Pickwick, 2011.

Thomas, Bruce. "The Gospel for Shame Cultures: A Paradigm Shift." *Evangelical
    Missions Quarterly* (July 1994): 284–90.

Thompson, J. A. *The Book of Jeremiah*. NICOT. Grand Rapids, Mich.: Eerdmans, 1980.

Thong, Chan Kei, and Charlene L. Fu. *Faith of Our Fathers: God in Ancient China*.
    Shanghai: China Publishing Group Orient, 2005.

———. *Finding God in Ancient China: How the Ancient Chinese Worshiped the God of
    the Bible*. Grand Rapids, Mich.: Zondervan, 2009.

Tienou, Tite. "Biblical Foundations for African Theology." *Missiology* 10, no. 4 (October
    1982): 435–48.

Ting, K. H. *God is Love: Collected Writing of Bishop K. H. Ting*. Colorado Springs,
    Colo.: David C. Cook, 2004.

———. "Some Thoughts on the Subject of Theological Reconstruction." *Chinese
    Theological Review* 17 (2003): 110–17.

Ting-Toomey, Stella, ed. *The Challenge of Facework: Cross-Cultural and Interpersonal
    Issues*. Suny Series in Human Communication Processes. Albany, N.Y.: State
    University of New York Press, 1994.

du Toit, A. B. "Forensic Metaphors in Romans and Their Soteriological Significance."
    Verbum et Ecclesia 24, no. 1 (2003): 53–79.

Toon, Peter. "Righteousness." Pages 687–88 in *Baker Theological Dictionary of the
    Bible*. Edited by Walter Elwell. Grand Rapids, Mich.: Baker, 1996.

Toorman, Alex. "Selfless Love: The Missing Middle in Honor/Shame Cultures."
    Evangelical Missions Quarterly 47, no. 2 (April 2011): 160–67.

Torrance, Thomas F. *Atonement: The Person and Work of Christ*. Downers Grove, Ill.:
    IVP Academic, 2009.

Tracy, Karen. "The Many Faces of Facework." Pages 209–26 in *Handbook of Language
    and Social Psychology*. Edited by Howard Giles and W. P. Robinson. New York,
    N.Y.: John Wiley and Sons, 1990.

Vanhonacker, Wilfried. "Guanxi Networks in China." *The China Business Review* (June 2004): 48–53.

Vanhoozer, Kevin. "'One Rule to Rule Them All?' Theological Method in an Era of World Christianity." Pages 85–126 in *Globalizing Theology: Belief and Practice in an Era of World Christianity*. Edited by Craig Ott and Harold Netland. Grand Rapids, Mich.: Baker Academic & Brazos Press, 2006.

———. "The Atonement in Postmodernity: Guilt, Goats, and Gifts." Pages 367–404 in *The Glory of the Atonement: Biblical, Theological & Practical Perspectives*. Edited by Charles E. Hill and Frank A. James III. Downers Grove, Ill.: IVP Academic, 2004.

———. "Wrighting the Wrongs of the Reformation? The State of the Union with Christ in St. Paul and the Protestant Soteriology." Pages 235–59 in *Jesus, Paul and the People of God: A Theological Dialogue with N. T. Wright*. Edited by Nicholas Perrin and Richard B. Hays. Downers Grove, Ill.: IVP, 2011.

Vanhoozer, Kevin, ed. *Everyday Theology: How to Read Cultural Texts and Interpret Trends*. Grand Rapids, Mich.: Baker Academic, 2007.

Verhezen, Peter. "Guanxi: Networks or Nepotism?" Pages 89–106 in *Europe-Asia Dialogue on Business Spirituality*. Edited by Laszlo Zsolnai. Garant: Antwerpen-Apeldoorn, 2008.

Vermander, Benoît. "Jesus-Christ and the Chinese Religious World." *Studia Missionalia* 50 (2001): 391–405.

Vickers, Brian. *Jesus' Blood and Righteousness: Paul's Theology of Imputation*. Wheaton, Ill.: Crossway, 2006.

Wagner, Anne, and William Pencak. *Images in Law*. Burlington, Vt.: Ashgate Publishing, 2006.

Wah, Sheh Seow. *Chinese Leadership: Moving From Classical to Contemporary*. Tarrytown, N.Y.: Marshall Cavendish, 2009.

Walls, Andrew. *The Cross-Cultural Process in Christian History*. Maryknoll, N.Y.: Orbis, 2002.

———. "The Gospel as the Prisoner and Liberator of Culture." *Missionalia* 10, no. 3 (1982): 99.

Wan, Enoch. "Christianity In The Eye Of Traditional Chinese." *Global Missiology* 1, no. 1 (October 2003). No Pages. Cited 13 May 2011. Online: http://ojs.global missiology.org/index.php/english/ issue/view/27.

―――. "Critiquing the Method of Traditional Western Theology and Calling for Sino-Theology." *Global Missiology* 1, no. 1 (October 2003). No Pages. Cited 7 January 2011. Online: http://ojs.globalmissiology.org/index.php/english/article/view/438/1128#.

―――. "Exploring Sino-Spirituality." *Global Missiology* 1, no. 1 (October 2003). No Pages. Cited 8 May 2011. Online: http://ojs.globalmissiology.org/index.php/english/article/view/440/1135.

―――. "Jesus Christ for the Chinese." *Global Missiology* 1, no. 1 (October 2001). No Pages. Cited 27 July 2011. Online: http://www.globalmissiology.org.

―――. "Practical Contextualization: A Case Study of Evangelizing Contemporary Chinese." *Global Missiology* 1, no. 1 (October 2003). No Pages. Cited 27 Dec 2011. Online: http://ojs.globalmissiology.org/index.php/english/issue/view/27.

―――. "Tao—The Chinese Theology of God-Man." *His Dominion* 11, no. 3 (Spring 1985): 24–27.

―――. "Theological Contributions of Sino-Theology to the Global Christian Community (Part 1)." *Chinese Around the World* (July 2000). No Pages. Cited 27 Dec 2011. Online: http://www.missiology.org/new/wp-content/uploads/2011/01/Theo_contributions_of_sino_theo_to_the_global_chistian_comm_part_1_July_20001.pdf.

―――. "家的文北化传流：华人基督徒的信仰及实践." *地球华人宣教学期刊* 8 (April 2007). No Pages. Cited 29 November 2011. Online: http://www.enochwan.com/chinese/simplified/(1.5)%20articles.html.

Wan, Milton. "Chinese Religions." Pages 158–62 in *Global Dictionary of Theology*. Edited by William A. Dyrness, Veli-Matti Karkkainen, Juan Francisco Martinez, and Simon Chan. Downers Grove, Ill.: IVP Academic, 2010.

Wan, Sze-kar. "Chinese Theology." Pages 162–66 in *Global Dictionary of Theology*. Edited by William A. Dyrness, Veli-Matti Karkkainen, Juan Francisco Martinez, and Simon Chan. Downers Grove, Ill.: IVP Academic, 2010.

Wang, Aiming. "Understanding Theological Reconstruction in the Chinese Church: A Hermeneutical Approach." *Chinese Theological Review* 16 (2002): 145–46.

Wang, Chengmian. *Contextualization of Christianity in China: An Evaluation in Modern Perspective*. Collectanea serica. Sankt Augustin; Nettetal: Institut Monumenta Serica; Steyler Verlag, 2007.

Wang, Fengyan. "Confucian Thinking in Traditional Moral Education: Key Ideas and Fundamental Features." *Journal of Moral Education* 33, no. 4 (December 2004): 429–47.

Wasserstrom, Jeffrey N. *China in the 21st Century: What Everyone Needs to Know*. Oxford: Oxford Press, 2010.

Watson, David. *Honor Among Christians: The Cultural Key to the Messianic Secret*. Minneapolis, Minn.: Fortress Press, 2010.

Watson, Francis. *Paul, Judaism, and the Gentiles: Beyond the New Perspective*. Rev. and exp. ed. Grand Rapids, Mich.: Eerdmans, 2007.

Wedderburn, A. J. M. "Some Observations on Paul's Use of the Phrases 'in Christ' and 'with Christ'." *Journal for the Study of the New Testament* 25 (October 1985): 83–97.

Wee, Chow Hou, and Luh Luh Lan. *The 36 Strategies of the Chinese: Adapting Ancient Chinese Wisdom to the Business World*. Singapore: Addison-Wesley, 1998.

Weerstra, Hans M. "De-Westernizing the Gospel The Recovery of a Biblical Worldview." *International Journal of Frontier Missions* 16, no. 3 (Fall 1999): 129–34.

Weinfeld, Moshe. "'Justice and Righteousness': mshpt wtsdqh the Expression and Its Meaning." Pages 228–46 in *Justice and Righteousness*. Sheffield: JSOT Press, 1992.

———. *Social Justice in Ancient Israel and in the Ancient Near East*. Publications of the Perry Foundation for Biblical Research in the Hebrew University of Jerusalem. Minneapolis, Minn.: Magnes Press, 1995.

Weiser, Artur. *The Psalms: A Commentary*. Philadelphia, Pa.: Westminster Press, 1962.

Weldon, Brooklynn. "Restoring Lost 'Honor': Retrieving Face and Identity, Removing Shame, and Controlling the Familial Cultural Environment through 'Honor' Murder." *Journal of Alternative Perspectives in the Social Sciences* 2, no. 1 (2010): 380–98.

Welker, M. "Righteousness and God's Righteousness." *Princeton Seminary Bulletin* 1, no. suppl. (1990): 124–39.

Westerholm, Stephen. "The 'New Perspective' at Twenty-Five." Pages 1–38 in *The Paradoxes of Paul*. Edited by D. A. Carson, Peter T. O'Brien, and Mark Seifrid. Vol. 2 of *Justification and Variegated Nomism*. Grand Rapids, Mich.: Baker Academic, 2004.

———. "The 'New Perspective' at Twenty-Five." Pages 1–38 in *The Paradoxes of Paul*. Edited by D. A. Carson, Peter T. O'Brien, and Mark Seifrid. Vol. 2 of *Justification and Variegated Nomism*. Grand Rapids, Mich.: Baker, 2004.

Westphal, Merold. *Suspicion and Faith: The Religious Uses of Modern Atheism*. New York, N.Y.: Fordham, 1999.

White, Leland J. "Grid and Group in Matthew's Community-The Righteousness/Honor Code in the Sermon on the Mount." *Semeia* 35 (1986): 61–90.

Wiher, Hannes. "Understanding Shame and Guilt as a Key to Cross-Cultural Ministry: An Elenctical Study." PhD diss., Potchefstroom, South Africa: Potchefstroom University for Christian Higher Education, 2002.

Wikan, Unni. "Shame and Honour: A Contestable Pair." *Man* 19, no. 4 (December 1984): 635–52.

Witherington, Ben, and Darlene Hyatt. *Paul's Letter to the Romans: A Socio-Rhetorical Commentary*. Grand Rapids, Mich.: Eerdmans, 2004.

Witte, Jr., John. "Introduction." Pages 1–32 in *Christianity and Law: An Introduction*. Edited by John Witte, Jr. and Frank S. Alexander. Cambridge, UK: Cambridge University Press, 2008.

Wong, Joe. *Ancient of Days* [古人的上帝]. Singapore: Singapore Every Home Crusade Co., 2002.

Wong, Kam-Cheung. "Chinese Culture and Leadership." *International Journal of Leadership in Education* 4, no. 4 (2001): 309–19.

Wright, N. T. *Climax of the Covenant*. Minneapolis, Minn.: Fortress Press, 1993.

———. *How God Became King: The Forgotten Story of the Gospels*. New York, N.Y.: HarperOne, 2012.

———. *Jesus and the Victory of God*. Minneapolis, Minn.: Fortress Press, 1996.

———. *Justification: God's Plan & Paul's Vision*. Downers Grove, Ill.: IVP Academic, 2009.

———. "Justification: Yesterday, Today, and Forever." *Journal of the Evangelical Theological Society* 54, no. 1 (2011): 49–64.

———. *Paul: In Fresh Perspective*. Minneapolis, Minn.: Fortress Press, 2009.

———. "Righteousness." Pages 590–92 in *The New Dictionary of Theology*. Edited by Sinclair Ferguson, J. I. Packer, and David F. Wright. Downers Grove, Ill.: IVP, 1988.

———. *The Letter to the Romans*. The New Interpreter's Bible 10; Nashville, Tenn.: Abingdon, 2002.

———. *The New Testament and the People of God*. Atlanta, Ga.: Augsburg Fortress, 1992.

————. "The Paul of History and the Apostle of Faith." *Tyndale Bulletin* 29 (1978): 61–88.

Wu, Jackson. "Authority in a Collectivist Church: Identifying Crucial Concerns for a Chinese Ecclesiology." *Global Missiology* 1, no. 9 (October 2011). No Pages. Cited 21 Dec 2011. Online: http://www.globalmissiology.org.

Wu, James. "C. S. Song." Edited by Derek Michaud. *Boston Collaborative Encyclopedia of Western Theology*, 1994. No Pages. Cited 14 Feb 2012. Online: http://people.bu.edu/wwildman/bce/song.htm.

Wu, Xiaoxin. "The Dynamics of Chinese Face Mechanisms and Classroom Behaviour: A Case Study." *International Journal of Evaluation and Research in Education* 22, no. 2–4 (November 2009): 87–105.

Xie, Zhibin. "Religious Diversity and the Public Roles of Religion in Chinese Society." Pages 230–44 in *Sino-Christian Studies in China*. Edited by Huilin Yang and Xinan Yang. Newcastle, UK: Cambridge Scholars Press, 2006.

Yan, Yunxiang. *The Individualization of Chinese Society*. English ed. New York, N.Y.: Berg, 2009.

Yang, B. J. *Mengzi yizhu [Translated notes on Mencius]*. Beijing: Zhonghua Book Company, 1960.

Yang, C. K. *Religion in Chinese Society*. Berkeley, Calif.: University of California, 1961.

Yang, Dong Long. "Theological and Cultural Reflections on the Relationship between Church and Society in China." *Chinese Theological Review* (2003): 64–75.

Yang, Huilin. "Inculturation or Contextualization: Interpretation of Christianity in the Context of Chinese Christianity." Pages 150–72 in *Sino-Christian Studies in China*. Edited by Yang Huilin and Daniel H. N. Yeung. Newcastle, UK: Cambridge Scholars Publishing, 2006.

————. "The Value of Theology in Humanities: Possible Approaches to Sino-Christian Theology." Pages 101–23 in *Sino-Christian Theology*. Edited by Pan-chiu Lai and Jason Lam. New York, N.Y.: Peter Lang, 2010.

————. "Theological Translation and Transmission between China and West." Pages 83–99 in *Sino-Christian Theology*. Edited by Pan-chiu Lai and Jason Lam. New York, N.Y.: Peter Lang, 2010.

Yang, Lawrence Hsin, and Arthur Kleinman. "'Face' and the Embodiment of Stigma in China-The Cases of Schizophrenia and AIDS." *Social Science and Medicine* 30 (2008): 1–11.

Yang, Xiao. "Trying to Do Justice to the Concept of Justice in Confucian Ethics." *Journal of Chinese Philosophy* 24 (1997): 521–51.

Yao, Xinzhong. "Confucius, the Founder of Confucianism." *Dialogue and Alliance* 12, no. 2 (Fall/Winter 1998): 20–33.

————. "Success or Failure? Christianity in China." *History Today*, September 1, 1994. Online: http://www.historytoday.com/xinzhong-yao/success-or-failure-christianity-china.

Yeo, K. K. "Christian Chinese Theology: Theological Ethics of Becoming Human and Holy." Pages 102–115 in *Global Theology in Evangelical Perspective: Exploring the Contextual Nature of Theology and Mission*. Edited by Jeffrey P. Greenman and Gene Green. Downers Grove, Ill.: IVP, 2012.

————. "Introduction." Pages 1–28 in *Navigating Romans Through Cultures: Challenging Readings by Charting a New Course*. Edited by K. K. Yeo. New York, N.Y.: T&T Clark International, 2004.

————. "Li and Law in the Analects and Galatians: A Chinese Christian Understanding of Ritual and Propriety." *Asia Journal of Theology* 19 (October 2005): 309–32.

————. "Messianic Predestination in Romans 8 and Classical Confucianism." Pages 179–202 in *Sino-Christian Theology*. Edited by Pan-chiu Lai and Jason Lam. New York, N.Y.: Peter Lang, 2010.

————. *Musing with Confucius and Paul: Toward a Chinese Christian Theology*. Eugene, Ore.: Cascade, 2008.

————. "Paul's Ethic of Holiness and Chinese Morality of Renren." Pages 104–40 in *Cross-Cultural Paul: Journeys to Others, Journeys to Ourselves*. Edited by Charles H. Cosgrove, Herold Weiss, and K. K. Yeo. Grand Rapids, Mich.: Eerdmans, 2005.

————. *What Has Jerusalem to do with Beijing: Biblical Interpretation from a Chinese Perspective*. Harrisburg, Pa.: Trinity Press, 1998.

Yeung, Irene Y. M. "The Dynamism of Guanxi in Company Performance in China." MBA Thesis, Burnaby, Canada: Simon Fraser University, 1995.

Yeung, Maureen W. "Boundaries in 'In-Christ Identity': Paul's View on Table Fellowship and Its Implications for Ethnic Identities." Pages 154–74 in *After Imperialism: Christian Identity in China and the Global Evangelical Movement*. Edited by Richard R. Cook and David W. Pao. Eugene, Ore.: Pickwick, 2011.

Young, Katherine P. H., and Anita Y. L. Fok. *Marriage, Divorce, and Remarriage: Professional Practice in the Hong Kong Cultural Context*. Hong Kong: Hong Kong University Press, 2005.

Yu, Jiyuan. "Yi: Practical Wisdom in Confucius's Analects." *Journal of Chinese Philosophy* 33, no. 3 (2006): 335–48.

Yung, Hwa. *Mangoes or Bananas: The Quest for an Authentic Asian Christian Theology.* 2nd ed. Eugene, Ore.: Wipf & Stock, 2008.

Zaracho, Rafael. "Communicating the Gospel in a Shame Society." *Direction* 39, no. 2 (Fall 2010): 271–81.

Zetterholm, Magnus. *Approaches to Paul: A Student's Guide to Recent Scholarship.* Minneapolis, Minn.: Fortress Press, 2009.

Zhang, Haihua, and Geoffrey Baker. *Think Like Chinese.* Annandale, N.S.W.: Federation Press, 2008.

Zhang, Qingxiong. "Sino-Christian Theology: The Unfolding of 'Dao' in the Chinese Language Context." Pages 123–38 in *Sino-Christian Theology.* Edited by Pan-chiu Lai and Jason Lam. New York, N.Y.: Peter Lang, 2010.

Zhang, Richard X. Y. "Sino-Christian Theology and Nationalism." Pages 173–195 in *Sino-Christian Studies in China.* Edited by Huilin Yang and Daniel H. N. Yeung. Newcastle: Cambridge Scholars, 2006.

Zhang, Wenxi. "Christianity in the Chinese Cultural Context." Paper presented at the 22nd National Catholic China Conference, November 2006. www.holyredeemer.cc/pdf/Zhang.pdf.

Zhang, Xian. "Christianity, Marxism, and 'The End of History': An Analysis of History Strung Together with the Examples of Liberation Theology." Pages 204–21 in *Sino-Christian Studies in China.* Edited by Huilin Yang and Daniel H. N. Yeung. Newcastle: Cambridge Scholars, 2006.

Zhao, Zhien. "Fifty Years of Theological Transformation in Chinese Christianity." *Asia Journal of Theology* 15, no. 1 (April 2001): 133–39.

Zhong, Wu. "Beyond Confucius and Communism." *Asia Times*, October 3, 2007, Online Edition edition, sec. Greater China Section.

Zou, ZhiMin, and DengFeng Wang. "Guilt Versus Shame: Distinguishing the Two Emotions from a Chinese Perspective." *Social Behavior & Personality: An International Journal* 37, no. 5 (June 2009): 601–4.

郑明德. "关于信仰与科学关系的思考 (Reflections on the Relationship Between Religious Faith and Science)." *Social Sciences Journal of Colleges of Shanxi* 17, no. 11 (November 2005): 27–29.

351

Revelation

CPSIA information can be obtained at www.ICGtesting.com
Printed in the USA
LVOW03s1919090615

441778LV00031B/1137/P